1001 SNACKS

1001 SNACKS

FOR INSTANT GRATIFICATION

GREGG R. GILLESPIE

PHOTOGRAPHS BY ZEVA OELBAUM

BLACK DOG
& LEVENTHAL
PUBLISHERS
NEW YORK

Copyright © 1997 by Gregg R. Gillespie

Photographs copyright © 1997 by Black Dog & Leventhal, Inc.

All rights reserved. No part of this book may be reproduced in any form or by any electronic or mechanical means, including information storage and retrieval systems, without written permission from the publisher.

Published by

Black Dog & Leventhal Publishers, Inc.
151 West 19th Street
New York, NY 10011

Distributed by

Workman Publishing Company
708 Broadway
New York, NY 10003

Designed by Martin Lubin

Typesetting by Brad Walrod/High Text Graphics

Manufactured in Italy

ISBN: 1-884822-97-5

h g f e d c b a

Library of Congress Cataloging-in-Publication Data

Gillespie. Gregg R.,   1934
1001 snacks : for instant gratification / by Gregg R. Gillespie.
        p.   cm.
Includes index.
ISBN   1-884822-97-5
1.   Snack foods.   I. Title.
TX740. G468   1997
641 . 5'3—dc21 97-24312
CIP

ACKNOWLEDGMENTS

When one undertakes a project as enormous as this book, there are so many people who should be thanked that even with all the thanks I can give, inevitably I will leave out someone. I speak first to those I have forgotten—and you will know who you are. Thank you all, for without your help this book could never have come into being.

I have to give my special thanks to Gordon Allan, who as my right hand, always keeps track of what I must do, picks up after me and reminds me of what I have forgotten. Thanks Gordon, without your help and your patience (even when I stomp and swear) none of this would have been possible.

Before this book was written, there was J.P. Leventhal who, for the third time, believed my work worthy of publication. JP, your friendship has meant so much to me.

Oh yes! I mustn't forget a most important member of my team: Tess. She deserves a big pat—and a handful of those very special dog cookies.

Many thanks to my editor Pamela Horn; and to Mary Goodbody and Alice Thompson for their editorial contributions. Thanks to Zeva Oelbaum for her photographs and to food stylists Catherine Chatham, Fred Thompson, and Bettina Fisher.

CONTENTS

INTRODUCTION

Like all other projects of this size, writing this book was a daunting undertaking. It demanded the skills of more than a mere cook, yet it required kitchen skills that rarely are called upon, either. The challenge was to present 1,001 recipes for snack food. Many cookbooks contain fewer than 250 recipes and many contain far fewer. Many publishers consider a "big book" to hold between 300 and 400 recipes. But more than 1000?! Not an undertaking for the feint of heart.

Before I began, I had to define the term "snack" in a way agreeable to me and that could be applied to the recipes that eventually ended up on these pages. I'm convinced that a survey of the American public would reveal some surprising definitions of snacks. Some might mention a candy bar or sack of potato chips, others would talk about bowls of ice cream, while still others would mention crisp apples and juicy oranges. And all would be right on target. I propose that snacks also include moderately complicated cooked or prepared dishes.

A snack is not an appetizer, a salad, soup, main dish or dessert. It is all of them, and then some. A snack is something that is eaten between regular meals, though at times it takes the place of the more formal fare. A mid-morning cup of coffee and doughnut at your desk is a snack, but so is the hamburger and fries or bucket of chicken devoured after school or an afternoon of shopping or errand-running.

Party food is snack food, particularly if it is served as finger food or presented as a dazzling array on a buffet table. By my definition, food served at brunch and breakfast is snack food, too.

Not every recipe on the following pages will fall into every reader's definition of snack food, but each and every one is for food that is quickly cooked or easily prepared. Without question, some recipes can be served for light or casual meals, while others are ideal for brown bagging or picnicking. Still other recipes are great for easy snacking, filling the bill for those times when we are in the mood for "a little something" to hold hunger at bay.

Many of the recipes are for dips, spreads, flavored butters, dressings and fillings— those recipes that turn the mundane into the spectacular. I have used these creations as I like them best, but please feel free to devise your own flavor combinations by using these freely and extravagantly. A salad is only as good as its dressing, a canapé only as fancy as its flavorings, and a sandwich only as appetizing as its filling.

While I always put flavor above all else when developing a recipe, I also pay attention to presentation. This is not a book about how to make elegant hors d'oeuvres or pretty tea sandwiches, but a number of the recipes fall into these categories by default or definition. Take a little care with how the finished product looks because a well-prepared dish should appeal to all the senses, not just to taste.

With very few exceptions, I use easily available ingredients, even calling for name brands in many instances. This practice is deliberate so that you will not have any question about what I mean. Bisquick Baking Mix is called "Bisquick," not "commercial prepared baking mix," which could be confusing. Rice Krispies are called "Rice Krispies," not "puffed rice cereal," which might baffle some readers. However, you should not feel bound to these brands. Use another national or generic brand—or use a local brand that you especially like.

View this book as you would a sumptuous buffet. Pick and choose, take what you like. Fill your plate and your senses when and how it best suits and satisfies you.

Chapter 1

THE SNACK COOK'S KITCHEN

The snack cook celebrates food and cooking. He or she makes it part of everyday life, never over indulging but always enjoying light, delectable dishes and appreciating them for what they are: delicious and tempting, never overblown, always eaten with gusto and pleasure and in balance with regularly scheduled meals. To do so, the snack cook maintains a well-stocked kitchen and takes care when preparing food.

Finishing Touches

The recipes included here are straightforward and easy to prepare, but there are times when, with a little extra care and time, you can turn a simple preparation into something special. Many of these recipes serve as party fare, especially those in the chapters called Quick Snacks and Company's Coming Canapés. Arrange assortments on platters and then garnish them with one of the following. Almost instantly an ordinary plate of food becomes invitingly festive!

Buy good-looking, colorful, unblemished vegetables. Wash them carefully and, when appropriate, pat them dry with a kitchen or paper towel.

Celery Curls: Using a sharp knife, cut the celery stalks into four-inch pieces. Cut each length into narrow, lengthwise strips. Submerge the strips into ice water and the ends will curl. Keep them in the ice water until ready to use.

Carrot Curls: Using a sharp knife, trim the carrots. Using the same knife or vegetable slicer, slice the carrots lengthwise into paper-thin strips. Roll the strips into curls and fasten securely by threading wooden toothpicks through the coils. Submerge the curls in ice water until ready to use.

Radish Roses: Using a sharp knife, remove the root end of the radish, leaving a little bit of the green stem on top. Starting at the root end, cut slices into the radishes all the way around the globe, but do not cut through. Leave each slice attached at the stem end. After the first set of slices are made, make additional slices toward the center. Place the

radishes, root ends down, in ice water until the thin strips you have cut curl and the radishes resemble roses.

Fringed Cucumbers: Trim the cucumber and using the tines of a fork, scrape or score lines down the sides until the entire vegetable is scored. Using a sharp knife or vegetable slicer, slice the cucumber into paper-thin slices. Submerge the slices in ice water until ready to use. Add a tablespoon or so of vinegar to the ice water to keep the cucumbers crisp and white.

Pickle Fans: Use large kosher-style pickles or gerkins. Cut each pickle into three or four lengthwise slices without detaching them from the base of the pickle. Lay on a serving platter or tray and spread the slices to create a fan.

Minced Parsley: A bed of finely minced parsley is always impressive as a garnish. Thoroughly wash several parsley sprigs and shake to remove any moisture. Using scissors or kitchen shears, snip the herb into very fine pieces. Spread on a plate or serving platter and top with the food you are garnishing.

Grated Orange Peel: Peel the colorful part (zest) of several oranges, leaving the white pith behind, and transfer the zest to a food processor. Process until finely grated. If using the zest from only one orange, chop the peel with a sharp knife until fine. Any kind of orange works, but navel oranges have the thickest skin. This works with lemons and limes, too.

How to Cook Rice

Wash the rice several times under cold running water until the water runs clear. Transfer to a heavy aluminum saucepan and add enough cold water to cover by one to one and quarter inches. Cover and bring to a boil over medium heat. It's normal if the rice makes noise under the cover. Reduce the heat to a low simmer and cook for 30 minutes without disturbing—do not stir or remove the cover. When the rice is cooked, it will leave a crust on the bottom of the pan, which it should. The aluminum pan facilitates the crust forming. Many people like to eat the crust.

The Snack Pantry

I have assembled a list of those canned, packaged or frozen foods that you should have on hand for easy snack-making. While amounts are clearly stated in every recipe, the can, jar or package sizes listed here are typical of the sizes I keep in my own cupboard and which I find are the most useful.

Anchovy fillets—2 ounces

Applesauce—6 to 16 ounces

Baby corn ears—16 ounces

Balsamic vinegar—12¾ ounces

Blackberries, frozen—10 or 14 ounces

Blackberries, canned—14 or 16 ounces

Black currant spread—35 ounces

Blueberries, frozen—14 or 16 ounces

Blueberries, canned—14 ounces

Capers—3 ounces

Catsup—8 to 16 ounces

Cherry pie filling—21 ounces

Chili sauce—12 ounces

Chunk chicken—4½ to 6½ ounces

Chunk ham—5 ounces

Chunk light tuna—6 to 8 ounces

Clam juice—8 ounces

Coconut milk—14 ounces

Crabmeat—10 to 12 ounces

Deviled ham—4½ ounces to 6½ ounces

Dijon garlic mustard—4 ounces

Flavored yogurts—8 to 16 ounces

Honey Dijon mustard—7 ounces

Jumbo black pitted ripe olives—5¾ ounces

Jumbo green pitted olives—5¾ ounces

Liverwurst—4⅕ ounces

Luncheon meat—12 ounces

Mandarin orange segments—11 ounces

Mushrooms, stems and pieces—4 to 7 ounces

Oyster sauce—4 to 6 ounces

Peanut butter—6 to 28 ounces

Pimientos—2 to 4 ounces

Plain yogurt—8 to 16 ounces

Plum chutney—12¾ ounces

Plum preserves—16 ounces

Premade pastry crust—10 ounces (1 crust)

Premade pastry crust—14 ounces (2 crusts)

Raspberry spread—17 ounces

Ripe olive wedges—2¼ ounces

Ripe sliced olives—2⅓ ounces

Sandwich spread—16 ounces

Seafood cocktail sauce—12 ounces

Sliced mangos—15 ounces

Sockeye red salmon—3¾ ounces

Sour cream—8 to 16 ounces

Spiced and pimiento-stuffed olives—10 ounces

Strawberry glaze—14.5 ounces

Sweet pickle relish—10 ounces

Sweetened condensed milk—12 or 14 ounces

Water chestnuts, chopped—4 to 6.8 ounces

Water-packed artichoke hearts—6 to 13¾ ounces

White pearl onions—16 ounces

Whole new potatoes—15 ounces

A Look at Cheese

Cheese, on its own or combined with other ingredients, is one of the world's great foods and particularly well suited for snacks. Here I list some of my favorites and those that you should be able to find in a good supermarket or cheese shop almost anywhere in the country.

BLUE-VEINED CHEESES

Dana Blue
Dolcelatte
Gorgonzola
Roquefort
Saga Blue
Shropshire Blue
Stilton

FRESH CHEESE

Bucheron
Chenna
Cottage Cheese
Cream Cheese
Crema Dania
Creole Cream
Crescenze
Farmers
Neufchâtel
Panir
Petit Suisse
Pot Cheese
Ricotta Cheese
Queso Fresco
Stracchino

HARD CHEESE

Parmesan
Pecorino
Romano
Sapsago
Sbrinz
Schbzieger

PASTA FILATA

Caciocavallo
Manteca
Mozzarella
Provolone
Scamorze

SEMI-FIRM CHEESE

Appenzeller
Asiago
Brick
Caerphilly
Cantal
Chaource
Cheddar
Colby
Danbo
Derby
Edam
Fontina
Gjetost
Gloucester
Gruviera
Gruyère
Jarlsberg
Kasseri
Kuminost
Lancashire
Leicester
Longhorn
Manchego
Raclette
Tillamook

SEMI-SOFT CHEESE

Asadero
Banon
Bel Paese
Bellelay
Bonbel
Boursault
Cheshire
Chèvre
Chihuahua
Dunlop
Elbo
Emmental

Esrom
Explorateur
Gouda
Gourmandise
Handkase
Havarti
Herkimer
Herve
Hopfenkase
Leyden
Linderkranz
Monerey Jack
Mascarpone
Montrachet
Muenster
Nierkase
Oaxaca
Port-Salut
Processed Cheese
Pyramid
Samsoe
Swiss
Taleggio
Tilsit
Tybo
Vacherine Fribourgeois

SOFT RIPENED CHEESE

Brie
Camembert
Limburger
Liptauer
Pont-l'Evêque
Quark
Reblochon
Saint André
Teleme
Vacherin Mont d'Or
Vacherin d'Abondance
Vacherin des Dauges

WHEY CHEESE

Italian Ricotta

Chapter 2

QUICK SNACKS

The recipes in this chapter were purposely selected to meet the criteria of what most people classify as finger foods. The vast majority of recipes yield dishes appropriate for placing on a platter or serving tray. Others, however, are better suited to simpler snacking. This is not a book on entertaining, but by their nature, many of the recipes here fit nicely into that category. But, even when the party is over and the last guest has gone home, you can reach for the leftovers and indulge in a delicious midnight snack.

ANCHOVY AND BACON WRAPS

MAKES: *16 rolls*

8 strips bacon, cut in half
8 anchovy fillets
Drawn Butter Sauce (recipe follows)

1 Preheat the broiler.

2 Lay an anchovy fillet on each bacon piece and roll each tight. Fasten each with a toothpick and dip in butter sauce. Broil for several minutes, turning at least once, until the bacon is crisp. Serve immediately with the remaining butter.

DRAWN BUTTER SAUCE

MAKES: *1¾ cups*

3 tablespoons unsalted butter plus ¾ tablespoon butter
3 tablespoons all-purpose flour
1½ cups boiling water

In a small saucepan, over a medium-low heat, melt the 3 tablespoons of butter. Add the flour, stirring constantly until mixed and smooth. Add the water and cook for 5 minutes, stirring. Add the remaining butter, stir until incorporated and serve immediately.

ANCHOVY BALLS

MAKES: *8 servings*

2 tubes (1.6 ounces each) Reese® anchovy paste
2 large hard-cooked eggs, mashed with a fork
dash of Worcestershire sauce
dash of cayenne
¼ cup snipped fresh parsley

1 In a small bowl, combine all of the ingredients and mix well. Using a small baller, form the mixture into small balls. Lay in a single layer on a tray and chill for 1 hour until well chilled.

2 Serve cold on a bed of lettuce with toothpicks on the side.

4 large hard-cooked eggs, cut in half
and yolks removed
¼ cup Anchovy Butter (recipe
follows)
1 tablespoon minced parsley
paprika

1 In a small bowl, combine the
egg yolks, butter and parsley.
Using a pastry bag fitted with a
large fancy tip, press a liberal
amount of the filling into each
half egg white.

2 Sprinkle with paprika and
place on a plate, platter or tray.
Chill until ready to serve.

ANCHOVY-FLAVORED STUFFED EGGS
MAKES: *8 servings*

ANCHOVY BUTTER
MAKES: *About ¼ cup*

¼ cup unsalted butter
1 teaspoon anchovy paste
⅛ teaspoon lemon or lime juice

In a small bowl or cup, mash
the butter until soft and creamy
using a fork. Fold in the
anchovy paste and lemon juice,
blending thoroughly.

---

10 stalks celery, washed and leaves
removed
2 bunches green onions, washed and
roots removed
8 large lettuce leaves, washed and
dried
2 bunches radishes, washed, stems
and roots removed
1 can (6 ounces) black olives,
drained
1 can (6 ounces) green olives,
drained
1 jar (4 ounces) pimiento slices
2 cans (2 ounces each) anchovy
fillets
2 jars (7 ounces each) artichoke
hearts
4 ounces sliced Italian-style salami
4 ounces thin-sliced Provolone
cheese
4 ounces thin-sliced sharp Cheddar
cheese
4 ounces sliced prosciutto
6 small hard-cooked eggs
paprika
canola oil
red wine vinegar
garlic bread and Swedish-style rye
bread

1 Using a sharp knife, cut the
celery and onions into 4- to 5-
inch lengths. Lay the 8 lettuce
leaves on a large platter or tray.
Arrange all of the ingredients so
that there are 1 or 2 on a leaf. The
cheeses can be rolled into cones
and placed together; the slices of
salami and proscuitto can over-
lap each other. The eggs can be
cut in half and sprinkled with
paprika (or even a little finely
ground almond).

2 Sprinkle the ingredients with
oil and vinegar and arrange the
bread on the platter.

3 Have several small bowls of
sauces available for dipping. A
cheese or creamy sauce is good
for the vegetables and eggs; a
mustard sauce for the cheese and
meat. The idea behind this tray
is to make it as attractive as
possible.

ANTIPASTO TRAY
MAKES: *36 to 48 servings*

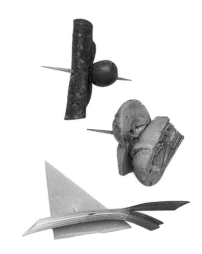

ASPARAGUS-IN-BREAD BITES

MAKES: *48 servings*

12 slices fresh white bread, crusts removed
½ cup Roquefort Cheese Butter (recipe follows)
12 asparagus spears, sautéed in butter
½ cup butter

1 Position the rack in the center of the oven and preheat to 375 degrees F.

2 On a flat surface, and using a rolling pin, roll the bread slices out to a thickness of ¼ inch. Using a spatula, spread the Roquefort butter evenly over the bread and lay 1 asparagus spear along an edge of the bread and roll up tight.

3 In a skillet over a low heat, melt the butter and roll the bread in the butter until completely coated. Place seam-side down on a baking sheet and bake for about 10 to 12 minutes, or until golden brown. Using a sharp knife, cut each roll into 4 equal pieces and serve on a bed of shredded lettuce.

ROQUEFORT CHEESE BUTTER

MAKES: *About ¾ cup*

½ cup unsalted butter
¼ cup Roquefort cheese
¼ teaspoon Worcestershire sauce

In a small bowl or cup, mash the butter with a fork until soft and creamy. Add the cheese and Worcestershire sauce and blend thoroughly.

ASPARAGUS-STUFFED HAM ROLLS

MAKES: *8 servings*

¼ cup Kraft® Dressing or mayonnaise
½ teaspoon prepared mustard
16 asparagus spears, trimmed
French dressing
16 slices thin-sliced smoked ham

1 In a cup, combine the dressing and mustard and chill.

2 Place the asparagus in a shallow bowl and spoon enough French dressing over to cover. Cover and chill for 4 hours.

3 Lay the smoked ham on a work surface and spread an even layer of the salad dressing-mustard mixture on each slice. Lay an asparagus spear on each slice of ham and roll into a tight roll. Chill for 1 hour before serving.

4 Serve the rolls with the mustard dressing on the side.

2 pounds jumbo shrimp, peeled and
   deveined
3 tablespoons red wine vinegar
3 tablespoons canola oil
1 clove garlic, mashed
1 teaspoon snipped fresh oregano
¼ teaspoon garlic powder
1 tablespoon chopped fresh parsley
1 red onion, sliced
salt and pepper
15 to 18 strips bacon, cut in half
   (depending on number of shrimp)

1 In a large bowl, combine all of
the ingredients except the bacon.
Cover and chill for 8 to 12 hours.
Remove the shrimp and set
aside. Pour the liquid into a small
saucepan.

2 Over medium-low heat, cook
the liquid until reduced to about
1 cup.

3 Position the broiler rack 6 inches from the heat and preheat the
broiler. Lightly grease a broiler
tray.

4 Wrap each shrimp with ½ a
strip of bacon and lay on the tray,
seasoning each with salt and
pepper before rolling up. Broil
for 3 to 4 minutes or until the
bacon is crisp. To serve, place the
liquid in a dipping cup in the
center of a plate or tray, arrange a
bed of lettuce leaves on the tray
and place the shrimp on the
leaves with toothpicks on the
side.

BACON-WRAPPED SHRIMP

MAKES: *6 servings*

8 ounces cooked scallops, chopped
2 cloves garlic, minced
2 tablespoons butter or margarine, at
   room temperature
½ cup grated Cheddar or Colby
   cheese
⅛ teaspoon Worcestershire sauce
salt and pepper
2 packages (11 ounces each) Betty
   Crocker® pie crust mix

1 Position the rack in the center
of the oven and preheat to 450
degrees F. Lightly grease 2 baking sheets.

2 In a skillet over medium heat,
sauté the garlic in the butter for 1
to 2 minutes, or until soft.
Remove from the heat and stir in
the remaining ingredients except
the pie crust mix.

3 Prepare the pie crust according
to the package directions and roll
out to ⅛- to ¼-inch thick. Using a
round or scalloped cookie cutter,
cut into 2-inches circles.

4 Using a pastry brush, moisten
the edges of the pastry circles
with water, place 1 teaspoon of
the scallop mix in the center, and
top with another circle, pressing
the edges together to seal securely. Prick the tops with a fork and
place on the prepared baking
sheets about 1 inch apart.

5 Bake for 8 to 10 minutes, or
until light golden brown. Transfer to a wire rack to cool slightly
before serving.

BAKED SCALLOPS

MAKES: *40 servings*

BEEF BALLS

MAKES: *8 servings*

1 package (3 ounces) cream cheese
1 teaspoon finely minced onions
salt and pepper
½ cup finely minced dried beef
Chili con Queso Dip (recipe
   follows)

1 In a small bowl, combine the cheese and onions. Adjust the seasoning. Cover and chill for 1 hour.

2 Using a small baller, form the mixture into small balls. Roll each ball in the dried beef and lay on a tray. Serve the dip on the side.

CHILI CON QUESO DIP

MAKES: *2 cups*

1 cup processed American cheese
   spread
½ cup grated Cheddar cheese
¼ cup evaporated milk
1 tomato, chopped
1 green chile, chopped
½ teaspoon garlic powder

In a double boiler over low heat, combine the cheese spread and grated cheese and stir until smooth. Add the milk, tomato, chile and garlic powder, cover, and cook for about 30 minutes until thick and smooth. Add more milk if a thinner dip is required. Serve warm.

BEEF-RICE CAKES

MAKES: *8 servings*

1 cup uncooked wild rice
3 eggs, slightly beaten
1 cup shredded Swiss cheese
1 package (3 ounces) sliced smoked
   beef, diced
Cheese Sauce (recipe follows)

1 Cook the rice according to the package directions.

2 Preheat a nonstick skillet or griddle until very hot or 400 degrees F.

3 In a medium bowl, blend all of the ingredients, including the rice, and drop by ½ cupfuls onto the hot skillet, cooking about 3 minutes, or only until the edges start to brown. Turn and cook 2 minutes on the reverse side. Serve with the sauce on the side.

BAKING NOTE: If necessary, spray the skillet or griddle with vegetable oil spray to prevent sticking.

CHEESE SAUCE

MAKES: *About 1 cup*

1 cup milk
1½ tablespoons flour, cornstarch or
   arrowroot
⅔ cup grated Gruyere or Swiss
   cheese
salt and pepper

1 In a small saucepan, stir together the milk and flour until smooth and free of lumps.

2 Bring to a boil over medium heat. Lower the heat and cook, stirring constantly, for 2 to 3 minutes, or until the mixture thickens. Remove from the heat.

3 Stir in the cheese and season with salt and pepper.

2 1-inch thick slices bologna, casing
  removed
9 small white cocktail onions
9 small cherry tomatoes
9 Ritz Crackers
Garden Variety Vegetable Dip
  (recipe follows)

1 Using a sharp knife, cut the
bologna slices into 9 bite-sized
pieces by making two cuts in one
direction and two cuts at a
ninety-degree angle. With a

toothpick, stab first the white
onion, then the tomato, and finally the cube of bologna.

2 Lay each set on a cracker, and
arrange on a bed of lettuce. Serve
at once, or chill in the refrigerator. Serve with the dip on the
side.

BOLOGNA, TOMATO AND ONION CUBES

MAKES: *9 appetizers*

GARDEN VARIETY VEGETABLE DIP

MAKES: *About 1¼ cup*

1 cup small-curd cottage cheese
2 tablespoons sour milk
1 tablespoon chopped green bell
  peppers
1 tablespoon chopped red bell
  peppers
1 tablespoon chopped green
  onions, green parts only
1 tablespoon chopped radish
pinch of celery salt

In a small bowl using an electric
mixer on medium speed, beat
the cheese and milk until
smooth. Using a spoon, stir in
the remaining ingredients until
well mixed. Cover with plastic
wrap and chill for at least 1
hour or overnight.

**BAKING NOTE: For a festive
occasion, hollow out the inside
of small squash and serve the
dip in the squash.**

1 unsliced loaf of bread
American processed cheese spread
1 bunch watercress
1 small tomato, sliced thin
additional watercress for garnish

1 Using a sharp knife, cut eight
¼-inch-thick slices of bread from
the middle of the loaf. Cut the
crust from the bread slices and
then cut the slices into 1½-inch
squares.

2 Spread each square with
cheese spread and lay 1 spray of
watercress from corner to corner.
Roll into the shape of a cone and
secure with a toothpick.

3 Cut the tomato slices into
wedges. Using the same toothpick, secure a tomato wedge to
the top of each cone. Chill for 1
hour before serving. The cheese
should have hardened and the
toothpick will be easy to remove.

BREAD CORNUCOPIAS

MAKES: *8 servings*

CABBAGE, TUNA AND PEPPER SANDWICHES

MAKES: 24 *open-faced sandwiches*

¾ cup mayonnaise
1 tablespoon fresh orange juice
½ small white onion, finely chopped
½ teaspoon salt
3 cups shredded cabbage (1 small head)
1 can (6 ounces) tuna
1 stalk celery, sliced
1 small green bell pepper, chopped
¼ cup chopped walnuts
butter or margarine, at room temperature
24 slices rye bread, toasted

1 In a small bowl, using a spoon, combine the mayonnaise, orange juice, onion and salt. Chill in the freezer while preparing the remainder of the recipe.

2 In a large bowl, combine the cabbage, tuna, celery, pepper and walnuts.

3 Spread the butter on the toast to the very edge. Place 1 to 1½ tablespoons of the tuna mixture on each slice of toast and serve.

CAVIAR-STUFFED EGGS

MAKES: *8 servings*

4 hard-cooked eggs, cut in half and yolks removed
¼ cup Caviar Spread (recipe follows)
2 drops fresh lemon juice
1 tablespoon minced parsley
paprika

In a small bowl, combine the egg yolks, spread, lemon juice and parsley. Using a pastry bag fitted with a large fancy tip, press a liberal amount of the filling into each half egg. Sprinkle with paprika and place on a plate, platter or tray. Chill until ready to serve.

CAVIAR SPREAD

MAKES: *About 1 cup*

3 ounces caviar
1 large hard-cooked egg, mashed
¾ cup Italian or vinaigrette salad dressing
1 tablespoon minced white onion
1 tablespoon minced pimiento

In a medium bowl, using a large spoon, blend the ingredients together until well incorporated. Cover and chill for at least 1 hour.

4 hard-cooked eggs, cut in half and
  yolks removed
3 tablespoons Limburger Cheese
  Spread (recipe follows)
¼ cup finely diced celery
finely chopped sweet pickle
paprika

In a small bowl, combine the egg
yolks, cheese spread and celery.
Using a pastry bag fitted with a
large fancy tip, press a liberal
amount of the filling into each
half egg. Sprinkle with pickle
and paprika and place on a plate,
platter or tray to serve. Chill until
ready to serve.

CELERY-AND-MAYONNAISE STUFFED EGGS

MAKES: *8 servings*

LIMBURGER CHEESE SPREAD

MAKES: *About ½ cup*

4 ounces ripe Limburger cheese
¼ cup unsalted butter, at room
  temperature
2 tablespoons freshly snipped
  chives
pinch of salt

In a medium bowl, using an
electric mixer on medium
speed, blend the ingredients
together until blended. Cover
and chill for at least 1 hour.

---

1 bunch celery
1¼ cups Spicy Chicken Sandwich
  Filling (recipe follows)

1 Using a sharp knife, cut the
leaves and tough white portion
from the celery stalks. Arrange
the smallest stalks in pairs. Fill
each stalk with the filling and
press together.

2 Stack on a plate or platter and
chill for at least 1 hour. Using a
sharp knife, cut the stalks into
slices and arrange in a circle of
overlapping pieces on a plate or
platter.

CELERY RINGS

MAKES: *16 servings*

SPICY CHICKEN SANDWICH FILLING

MAKES: *About 1 cup*

1 cup finely chopped cooked
  chicken
2 tablespoons finely diced crisp
  cooked bacon
2 drops Tabasco sauce
1 tablespoon lemon or lime juice
mayonnaise or softened cream
  cheese to bind

In a small bowl, combine the
chicken, bacon, Tabasco and
lemon juice. Add enough mayonnaise or cream cheese for a
creamy, spreadable consistency.
Cover and chill for at least 2
hours.

CELERY-SEED SNACKS

MAKES: *8 to 10 servings*

1 cup all-purpose flour
⅔ cup vegetable shortening
2 packages (3 ounces each) cream
   cheese
2 tablespoons celery seeds
celery salt for sprinkling
Curry Dip (recipe follows)

1 Position a rack in the center of
the oven and preheat to 375
degrees F. Lightly grease a baking sheet.

2 In a medium bowl, put the
flour, and using a pastry blender,
cut in the shortening and cream
cheese to make a soft dough. On
a floured work surface, roll the
dough to a thickness of ¼ inch.
Sprinkle with celery seeds and
celery salt. Cut into strips 4 to 6
inches long. Lay the strips on the
baking sheet and twist each one.

3 Bake for 4 to 6 minutes or until
light golden brown. Transfer to a
wire rack to cool slightly and
serve with the dip on the side.

CURRY DIP

MAKES: *1½ cups*

1 package (8 ounces) cream cheese
¼ cup sour cream
2 tablespoons chutney
1 tablespoon curry powder
1 tablespoon ginger-flavored
   brandy

In the container of a blender,
combine the ingredients on
medium speed for 12 to 15 seconds or until smooth. Chill for
at least 1 hour before serving.

LITTLE CHEESE AND BACON SANDWICHES

MAKES: *8 sandwiches*

8 slices cocktail-style bread
2 tablespoons melted butter or
   margarine
¼ cup Blue Cheese Mayonnaise
   (recipe follows)
2 tablespoons butter or margarine, at
   room temperature
2 cups grated Cheddar or Wisconsin
   cheese
2 teaspoons finely grated white
   onions
pinch of cayenne pepper
8 strips crisp cooked bacon,
   crumbled

1 Position the rack in the center
of the oven and preheat to 350
degrees F. Brush 1 side of the
bread slices with the melted butter and set on a baking sheet,
buttered side up.

2 In a medium bowl, and using a
spoon, combine the mayonnaise,
butter, cheese, onions and
cayenne pepper until well blended. Stir in the bacon. Spread the
mixture evenly over each slice of
bread and bake for 5 to 8 minutes
or until the cheese is melted.

BLUE CHEESE MAYONNAISE

MAKES: *About 1 cup*

1 package (3 ounces) cream cheese,
   at room temperature
½ cup mayonnaise
2 tablespoons crumbled blue
   cheese (about 1 ounce)
2 tablespoons frozen apple juice
   concentrate, thawed

In a small bowl, using an electric mixer on medium speed,
beat the cream cheese and mayonnaise together until smooth.
Using a fork, stir in the blue
cheese and apple juice concentrate, blending until smooth.
Chill for at least 30 minutes
before serving.

COOKING NOTE: **Finely chopped
apples can be added for texture and stronger apple flavor.**

1 jar (5 ounces) pasteurized processed cheese spread
1 cup finely crushed soda crackers
¼ cup butter or margarine
2 teaspoons chopped white onions
½ teaspoon Worcestershire sauce
½ cup snipped parsley

1 In a small bowl, using an electric mixer on medium speed, blend together the cheese, cracker crumbs, butter, onions, and Worcestershire sauce until smooth. Using your hands, shape into a large ball. Roll the ball in the parsley, cover with plastic wrap and chill for 8 to 12 hours, or overnight.

2 Serve in the center of a decorative dish or platter with cucumber slices and crackers on the side.

COOKING NOTE: **A different flavor can be achieved by using liquid flavorings, such as raspberry oil in place of the Worcestershire sauce. In that case, 3 drops of oil would be used to substitute for the sauce.**

CHEESE BALL

MAKES: *12 servings*

1 package (16 ounces) potato chips
¼ cup grated Parmesan or Romano cheese
Black Bean Dip (recipe follows)

1 Position the rack in the center of the oven and preheat to 400 degrees F. Lightly grease a baking sheet.

2 Spread the chips evenly on the baking sheet and sprinkle with the cheese. Bake for 3 to 5 minutes, or until the chips are hot. Remove from the oven, cool and serve with the dip.

CHEESE-FLAVORED POTATO CHIPS

MAKES: *6 to 8 servings*

BLACK BEAN DIP

MAKES: *About 2¾ cups*

2 packages (8 ounces) cream cheese, at room temperature
1 can (16 ounces) black beans, drained
1 small red onion, minced
2 tablespoons dry sherry or white port wine
1 small clove garlic, minced
¼ teaspoon hot red pepper sauce

In a small bowl, using an electric mixer on medium speed, beat the ingredients together until smooth. Cover and chill for at least 2 hours before serving.

CHEESE LOAF

MAKES: *8 servings*

1 package (8 ounces) cream cheese, at room temperature
½ cup pasteurized processed cheese spread
½ teaspoon dry mustard
2 packages (3 ounces each) chipped beef, chopped
¾ cup mayonnaise
½ cup chopped dill pickle
3 green onions, sliced
½ teaspoon prepared horseradish
5 slices whole-wheat bread
5 slices white bread

1 In a small bowl, using an electric mixer on medium speed, beat together the cream cheese, cheese spread and mustard until smooth. Cover and refrigerate for 30 minutes to 1 hour.

2 Meanwhile, in another small bowl, combine the chipped beef, mayonnaise, pickle, green onions and horseradish. Use ½ of the mixture to spread over each of the bread slices. Stack the bread slices to create 2 stacks of 4 slices each. Arrange the stacks end to end and top with the remaining slices of bread.

3 Spread the chilled cheese evenly over the top and sides of the bread stacks to create a loaf. The top can be decorated with olives, green onions, radishes, etc. Chill until ready to serve. Using a sharp knife, slice and serve.

COOKING NOTE: **Another interesting effect can be achieved by cutting the bread into decorative shapes before stacking, such as stars, clovers, etc. For stronger flavor, use a flavored mayonnaise.**

CHEESE MOUND

MAKES: *12 servings*

1 jar (5 ounces) pasteurized process cheese spread
1 cup finely crushed soda crackers
¼ cup butter or margarine
2 teaspoons chopped white onions
½ teaspoon Worcestershire sauce
½ cup snipped parsley
cucumber slices
snack crackers

1 In a small bowl, using an electric mixer on medium speed, blend together the cheese, cracker crumbs, butter, onions, and Worcestershire sauce until smooth. Using your hands, shape into a large ball.

2 Roll the ball in the parsley, cover with plastic wrap and chill for 8 to 12 hours, or overnight. Serve the ball in the center of a decorative dish or platter with cucumber slices and crackers on the side.

½ pound Swiss cheese
8 small cherry tomatoes
8 large pitted green or black olives
Clam Dip (recipe follows)

Using a sharp knife, cut the cheese into 1-inch cubes. Using toothpicks, spear a tomato, then a piece of cheese, and then an olive. Place on a tray and chill until ready to use. Serve with the dip on the side.

CHEESE ON PICKS
MAKES: *8 servings*

CLAM DIP
MAKES: *About 1¾ cup*

1 can (10½ ounces) minced clams
1 package (3 ounces) cream cheese
2 teaspoons Angostura bitters
1 tablespoon sour cream
¼ teaspoon Worcestershire sauce
¼ teaspoon prepared mustard

In the container of a blender, combine the ingredients and process on medium speed for 12 to 15 seconds or until smooth. Chill for at least 1 hour before using.

1½ cups all-purpose flour
¼ cup shelled hazelnuts, chopped fine
¼ cup pecan halves, chopped fine
⅔ cup butter or margarine
3 to 4 tablespoons ice water
2 packages (4½ ounces each) Brie cheese

1 Position the rack in the center of the oven and preheat to 425 degrees F. Lightly grease a baking sheet.

2 In a large bowl, combine the flour and chopped nuts. Using a pastry blender, cut in the butter to resemble a coarse meal. Using a large spoon, stir in the water and form the mixture into a soft dough. Divide the dough into quarters and roll each quarter into a 6-inch circle.

3 Place 2 circles on the baking sheet, one package of Brie in the center, and using a pastry brush, moisten the edges of the dough. Place a second dough circle on top of the first and crimp the edges to seal. Repeat with the second package of Brie and remaining dough circles.

4 Bake for 20 to 25 minutes, or until the pastry is a golden brown. Transfer to a wire rack to cool slightly before cutting and serving.

CHEESE POCKETS
MAKES: *6 to 8 servings*

CHEESE PUFFS

MAKES: *36 puffs*

2 cups shredded sharp Cheddar
cheese
½ cup butter or margarine, at room
temperature
1 cup all-purpose flour
1 teaspoon freeze-dried chives
¼ teaspoon salt
Hot Shrimp Dip (recipe follows)

1 Lightly grease a 14-by-12-inch baking sheet.

2 In a medium bowl, using an electric mixer on medium speed, blend together the cheese, butter, flour, chives and salt. Using your hands and a spoon, break off pieces of the dough and shape into small 1-inch balls, placing each ball on the prepared baking sheet. Cover with plastic wrap and chill in the refrigerator for 8 to 24 hours.

3 Position the rack in the center of the oven and preheat to 400 degrees F.

4 Bake for 15 to 20 minutes, or until they are light golden brown. Serve with the dip on the side.

COOKING NOTE: **To change the flavor, omit the salt and use ¾ teaspoon of garlic powder or onion powder. Freshly snipped chives may also be added. For something a little different, when forming the dough into balls, insert a small green pitted olive inside of the dough. Or, use a mild Cheddar cheese and insert a piece of apple into the dough.**

HOT SHRIMP DIP

MAKES: *About 3 cups*

2 packages (8 ounces each) cream
cheese, at room temperature
8 ounces cooked shrimp, chopped
1 red onion, diced
1 tomato, diced
3 small cloves garlic, minced
4 small hot chiles, diced

In the top of a double boiler, combine the ingredients and heat, stirring until smooth. Pour into a chafing dish and serve hot.

CHEESE-STUFFED PIMIENTOS

MAKES: *8 to 10 servings*

1 cup cooked green peas
1 cup small curd cottage cheese
½ teaspoon grated white onions
salt and white pepper
8 small whole pimientos, peeled and
cleaned
buttered bread crumbs for garnish
shredded lettuce for garnish

1 Position the rack in the center of the oven and preheat to 350 degrees F. Lightly grease a baking sheet.

2 In a small bowl, combine the peas, cottage cheese and onion and season with salt and pepper. Using a small spoon, stuff the mixture into the pimientos and place on the baking sheet. Sprinkle with the bread crumbs.

3 Bake for 4 to 5 minutes or until the crumbs start to brown. Remove from the oven, cool, slice into 1-inch pieces and place on a bed of shredded lettuce to serve.

COOKING NOTE: **Whole pimientos may be difficult to find. Canned pimientos can be used in place of fresh.**

½ cup butter or margarine, at room temperature
2 cups shredded Cheddar or Colby cheese, at room temperature
¼ teaspoon Worcestershire sauce
⅛ teaspoon cider vinegar
dash of hot pepper sauce
salt and pepper
1 cup all-purpose flour
paprika
Hot Mustard Sauce (recipe follows)

1 Position a rack in the center of the oven and preheat to 350 degrees F. Lightly grease a baking sheet.

2 In a large bowl, combine all of the ingredients except the flour and the mustard sauce and mix well with a large spoon. Add the flour a little at a time to make a dough. Knead lightly and form the dough into a log 1 inch in diameter. Using a sharp knife, slice the dough into ¼-inch slices. Lay the slices on the baking sheet leaving about ½ inch between them. Bake 12 to 15 minutes or until lightly browned around the edges. Sprinkle with paprika and transfer to a wire rack to cool completely. Serve with the sauce on the side.

CHEESE SLICES
MAKES: *20 servings*

HOT MUSTARD SAUCE
MAKES: *About ⅔ cup*

⅓ cup red wine vinegar
1 teaspoon ketchup
¼ teaspoon horseradish
⅓ cup canola oil
1 tablespoon hot dry mustard
2 cloves garlic, minced
salt and pepper

In a small bowl using a wire whip, beat the ingredients together. Cover and chill for at least 2 hours before serving.

2 cups water
8 frankfurters
8 slices white or wheat bread
2 tablespoons butter, at room temperature
1½ teaspoons prepared mustard
8 slices processed cheese
¼ cup butter or margarine, melted

1 Position the broiler rack to the lowest position and preheat the broiler. Have a baking sheet available.

2 In a saucepan over medium heat, bring the water to a boil. Add the frankfurters, cover, reduce the heat to a medium-low and simmer for 4 to 7 minutes.

3 In the meantime, lightly butter the bread and top with a thin layer of mustard. Place the bread on the baking sheet and lay a slice of cheese on each slice. Remove the frankfurters from the water and drain, discarding the water. Place 1 frankfurter on each slice of bread, laying it from corner to corner. Fold up each corner of the bread until they meet over the top of the frankfurter. Secure in place with toothpicks. Brush the outside of the bread with the melted butter and broil for 1 to 2 minutes, or until the edges of the bread start to turn brown. Serve immediately.

CHEESY DOGS
MAKES: *8 servings*

CHICKEN LIVER AND MUSHROOM CUPS

MAKES: *8 servings*

1 package (8 rolls) Brown N Serve®
  Butterflake or Dinner Rolls
2 tablespoons butter or margarine
½ pound chicken livers
½ cup sliced fresh mushrooms
¼ cup peach-flavored brandy

1 Separate the rolls and press two thin rounds of dough into each cup of a 2½-inch 8-cup muffin tin. Bake as directed on the package.

2 In a small skillet over medium heat, melt the butter. Sauté the livers and mushrooms. Remove from the heat, add the brandy, stir, and spoon into the baked pastry. Serve hot.

CHICKEN-STUFFED MUSHROOMS

MAKES: *24 stuffed mushrooms*

2 tablespoons canola oil
2 tablespoons white wine vinegar
1 ounce blue cheese, crumbled
pinch crumbled fresh oregano
  leaves
1 clove garlic, finely minced
salt and pepper
1 cup finely chopped cooked
  chicken
2 tablespoons finely chopped celery
2 tablespoons chopped chives
2 teaspoons chopped fresh cilantro
  (Chinese parsley)
24 large mushrooms
1 tablespoon butter or margarine
½ cup crushed potato chips

1 In a small bowl, combine the oil and vinegar, stirring until blended. Blend in the cheese, oregano, garlic, salt and pepper. Add the chicken, celery, chives and cilantro, stirring gently with a fork until blended. Cover with plastic wrap and chill for at least 30 minutes or overnight.

2 Remove the stems from the mushrooms (reserve for a later use) and wipe clean the mushrooms crowns. In a large skillet over a medium heat, melt the butter. Add the mushrooms, crown down. Cook for about 3 minutes or until the crown is just starting to turn brown. Remove from the heat and place on a baking sheet, browned side down.

3 Place approximately 2 teaspoons of the chilled chicken mixture into the hollow of the crown. Press lightly and sprinkle with the crushed potato chips.

4 Position the broiler rack in the lowest position and preheat the broiler.

5 Broil the mushrooms for 2 to 3 minutes until just hot. Serve immediately.

4 hard-cooked eggs, cut in half and
    yolks removed
¼ cup Bacon-Endive Sandwich
    Filling (recipe follows)
¼ cup chopped crisp fried bacon
paprika

In a small bowl, combine the egg
yolks, filling, and bacon. Using a
pastry bag fitted with a large
fancy tip, press a generous
amount of the filling into each
half egg to mound. Sprinkle with
paprika and place on a plate,
platter or tray. Chill until ready
to serve.

CHOPPED-BACON STUFFED EGGS

MAKES: *8 servings*

BACON-ENDIVE SANDWICH FILLING

MAKES: *About ½ cup*

5 tablespoons finely chopped crisp
    bacon
3 tablespoons chopped endive
dash of paprika
2 drops lemon juice

In a small bowl, combine the
ingredients and mix with a fork
until blended.

---

3 cups water
1 pound chicken livers, cleaned and
    trimmed
2 hard-cooked eggs, mashed with a
    fork
1 finely minced large onion
¼ teaspoon garlic powder
salt and pepper
2 tablespoons butter or margarine, at
    room temperature
sprigs of parsley for garnish
broccoli blossoms for garnish

1 In a medium saucepan over
medium heat, bring the water to
a boil. Add the livers and cook
for 5 to 8 minutes, or until no
longer pink. Drain.

2 Chop the livers and then mash
with a fork until smooth. In a
large bowl, combine the livers,
eggs, onions, garlic powder, and
season to taste with salt and
pepper.

3 Add the butter and mash until
mixed. Press the mixture into a
greased 3-inch diameter pan,
bowl or ring mold. Cover with
plastic wrap and chill for at least
4 hours before unmolding. Garnish with parsley and broccoli
blossoms and serve.

CHOPPED CHICKEN LIVER PÂTÉ

MAKES: *6 servings*

COCKTAIL KABOBS

MAKES: *24 servings*

12 6-inch strips of bacon
24 small raw oysters
24 small shrimp, shelled and
    deveined
24 small white cocktail onions
24 4-inch wooden skewers
mustard greens for garnish
Creamy Dip (recipe follows)

1 Position the broiler rack 6 inches from the heat and preheat the broiler.

2 Using a sharp knife, cut each strip of bacon into quarters. Thread 1 oyster, 1 shrimp and 1 onion on each skewer, separating each with a piece of bacon. All of the items on each skewer should be approximately the same size. Repeat with the remaining skewers and ingredients.

3 Lay the skewers on a broiler tray and broil for 3 to 4 minutes. Turn and cook for 2 to 4 minutes more or until the bacon is crisp. Transfer to a serving platter lined with mustard greens and serve the dip on the side.

CREAMY DIP

MAKES: *1¼ cup*

2 packages (3 ounces) cream
    cheese, at room temperature
¼ cup heavy cream
2 teaspoons snipped fresh chives
¼ teaspoon garlic powder
¼ teaspoon onion powder
dash of paprika

In a small bowl, combine the ingredients, whisking until smooth. Cover and chill for at least 2 hours before serving.

COLD-CUT PLATTER

MAKES: *16 to 20 servings*

½ cup Chili Dip (recipe follows)
½ cup Hot Mustard Sauce (see page
    29)
shredded lettuce
¼ pound sliced bologna
¼ pound sliced Swiss cheese
¼ pound sliced boiled ham
¼ pound sliced sharp Cheddar
    cheese
¼ pound sliced pressed ham
¼ pound sliced Colby cheese
¼ pound sliced roast beef
¼ pound sliced Havarti cheese
¼ pound sliced salami
¼ pound sliced chicken
¼ pound sliced turkey
cocktail breads or crackers for
    serving

1 Place the dip and sauce in small bowls and set in the center of a large square tray. Spread the shredded lettuce in a ring around the circumference of the tray.

2 Starting with the bologna, roll the remaining ingredients into tight rolls or cones and place on the tray to create a sunflower design emanating from the bowls. Cover and chill for at least 1 hour. Serve with the breads or crackers.

COOKING NOTE: **Dips can be hot or cold. Try not to put two meats alongside each other and use more shredded lettuce to divide where desired.**

CHILI DIP

MAKES: *1 to 1¼ cups*

1 cup salsa or chili sauce
1 teaspoon prepared horseradish
1 large radish, chopped
salt and pepper

In a small bowl, combine the ingredients, mixing until well blended. Cover and chill for at least 2 hours before serving.

1 package (8 ounces) cream cheese, at room temperature
1 teaspoon minced sweet pickle
1 teaspoon lemon juice
1 teaspoon mustard-flavored mayonnaise
red food coloring
1 cup very fine bread crumbs
yellow food coloring
small sprigs of parsley

1 In a bowl, use a spoon to mash together the cheese, pickle, lemon juice, and mayonnaise. Using a teaspoon, scoop out small amounts of the mixture and roll into balls. Set the balls on a plate or tray and chill for 1 hour.

2 Meanwhile, add enough red food coloring to ½ cup of the bread crumbs to color, tossing until evenly colored. (Do not over color and do not make the crumbs too moist.) Add enough yellow food coloring to the remaining ½ cup of bread crumbs, tossing until evenly colored. Roll ½ of the cheese balls in the red crumbs and ½ in the yellow crumbs. Insert a sprig of parsley in the top of each and chill until ready to serve. Serve on a bed of lettuce.

COLORED CREAM CHEESE BALLS

MAKES ABOUT: *16 balls*

---

vegetable oil for frying
2 cans (12 ounces each) whole-kernel corn, drained
2 large eggs
1 cup skim milk
1 tablespoon canola oil
3 cups all-purpose flour
2 tablespoons baking powder
salt and pepper
4 tablespoons minced green onions
2 teaspoons snipped fresh chives
Beef Dip (recipe follows)

1 Pour the vegetable oil into a large skillet to a depth of 2½ inches. Heat to 450 degrees F.

2 In a large bowl, using an electric mixer on medium speed, beat together the corn, eggs, milk and canola oil. Beat in the flour and baking powder and season with salt and pepper. Using a spoon, stir in the onions and chives.

3 Drop by teaspoonfuls into the hot oil and cook for 3 to 4 minutes, or until golden brown. Remove to a paper towel to drain and serve immediately with the dip on the side.

CORN FRITTERS

MAKES: *40 to 45 servings*

BEEF DIP

MAKES: *2½ cups*

1 cup sour cream or plain yogurt
2 packages (8 ounces) cream cheese, at room temperature
1 package (2½ ounces) chipped beef, chopped
½ teaspoon celery salt
½ teaspoon onion juice
½ cup chopped pecans

1 Position the rack to the center of the oven and preheat to 325 degrees F. Lightly grease an ovenproof casserole.

2 In a medium bowl, using an electric mixer on medium speed, blend the ingredients until smooth. Transfer to the casserole. Bake for about 30 minutes until heated through.

COTTAGE CHEESE-STUFFED EGGS

MAKES: *8 servings*

4 hard-cooked eggs, cut in half and yolks removed
¼ cup Cottage Cheese Filling (recipe follows)
2 tablespoons finely chopped kosher pickles
paprika

In a small bowl, combine the egg yolks, filling and pickles. Using a pastry bag fitted with a large fancy tip, press a generous amount of the filling into each half egg. Sprinkle with paprika and place on a plate, platter or tray. Chill until ready to serve.

COTTAGE CHEESE FILLING

MAKES: *About 2 cups*

1 carton (8 ounces) cottage cheese, at room temperature.
¼ cup finely chopped pitted black olives
½ cup chopped green bell pepper
½ cup chopped red bell pepper
½ teaspoon onion juice

In a medium bowl, using a electric mixer on medium speed, combine the ingredients and blend until smooth. Cover and chill for at least 2 hours.

CRAB-FILLED CUCUMBER CHIPS

MAKES: *8 servings*

2 large cucumbers, peeled and halved lengthwise
1 cup canned crabmeat or tuna, flaked
½ cup minced sweet pickles
1 tablespoon lemon juice
½ teaspoon onion juice
2 tablespoons cream cheese, at room temperature
2 large whole mushrooms, cleaned and sliced thin

1 Using a sharp knife, cut off the ends of the cucumbers and slice horizontally into 3-inch-long sections.

2 Using a melon baller, scoop out the insides of the cucumbers. In a small bowl, combine the remaining ingredients, except mushrooms, blending with a fork until smooth. Using a knife or spoon, pack the mixture into the center of the cucumbers, place on a plate, cover and chill for at least 2 hours.

3 When ready to serve, use a sharp knife to slice the cucumber section into ½-inch-wide slices. Lay the slices on a plate or tray and top with a mushroom slice.

COOKING NOTE: **Any creamy flavored butters or cheese spreads can be used in place of the seafood filling.**

1 cup chopped celery
1 tablespoon butter or margarine
1 can (10.75 ounces) condensed
   cream of shrimp soup
2 cans (7.5 ounces each) tiny
   deveined shrimp, drained
½ cup sour cream or plain yogurt
1 tablespoon grated lemon peel
dash of Angostura bitters
4 English muffins, split and toasted
dash of Hungarian paprika

1 In a large skillet over medium heat, combine the celery and butter and cook until the celery is tender, about 5 minutes.

2 Stir in soup, shrimp, sour cream, lemon peel and bitters. Heat just to boiling and spoon over the hot muffins. Sprinkle with paprika and serve immediately.

COOKING NOTE: Crabmeat or any flaked canned fish may be substituted for the shrimp.

CREAMED SHRIMP ON A MUFFIN

MAKES: *4 servings*

16 strips bacon
⅓ cup creamy peanut butter

1 Preheat the broiler.

2 Using a small spatula, spread the peanut butter over a strip of bacon, roll it up tight, and fasten with a toothpick. Repeat with remaining bacon and peanut butter. Place on a tray and broil until the bacon is crisp. Serve immediately.

CRISP BACON ROLLS WITH PEANUT BUTTER

MAKES: *16 Rolls*

CUCUMBER CRAB CAPS

MAKES: *36 caps*

4½ tablespoons mayonnaise
2½ tablespoons fresh lemon juice
5 teaspoons Dijon mustard
⅛ teaspoon Tabasco sauce
salt
1 cup shredded cooked crabmeat
¼ cup finely chopped celery
1 tablespoon chopped fresh chives
2 cucumbers (each about 6 inches long)

1 In a medium bowl, using a fork to blend, combine the mayonnaise, lemon juice, mustard and Tabasco sauce. Season to taste with salt. Stir in the crabmeat, celery and chives. Cover with plastic wrap and chill for 4 hours or overnight.

2 Under running water, thoroughly scrub the cucumbers. Using the tines of a fork, scratch lines on the cucumbers. Chill.

3 Using a sharp knife, slice the cucumber into thirty-six ⅓-inch-thick slices. Arrange the slices on a platter or serving tray and using a teaspoon, top each with crabmeat.

CUCUMBER STACKS

MAKES: *6 servings*

2 cucumbers
4 ounces sliced smoked salmon
3 or 4 white onions, sliced
⅛ teaspoon white pepper
⅛ teaspoon garlic powder
lemon wedges for garnish
snipped fresh parsley for garnish

1 Using a sharp knife, slice the cucumbers into ¼-inch-thick slices. Using a knife or a round cookie cutter, cut the salmon into circles about the same size as the cucumbers.

2 To assemble, place a slice of salmon on each cucumber slice and top with a slice of onion. Combine the pepper and garlic powder and sprinkle the salmon. Serve garnished with lemon wedges and parsley.

CURRY-FLAVORED MEATBALLS

MAKES: *20 to 32 balls*

1 pound lean ground beef
2 teaspoons curry powder
1 cup crushed saltine crackers
salt and pepper
½ cup butter or margarine, at room temperature
broccoli florets for garnish
Curry Dip (see page 24)

1 In a large bowl, combine the beef, curry powder and crackers. Season to taste with salt and pepper.

2 In a large skillet, melt the butter. Using a melon baller, form the beef mixture into small balls and cook, turning, for several minutes until browned. Drain on paper towels. Serve with toothpicks, garnish with broccoli and serve the dip on the side.

8 slices dried beef, each 2½ inches
  square
½ cup Chutney Butter (recipe
  follows)
8 pimiento-stuffed olives

Spread the butter evenly over
one side of each slice of beef. Roll
each into a tight roll and fasten
with a toothpick. Press an olive
on each toothpick and arrange on
a serving tray. Cover and chill
ready to serve.

**COOKING NOTE: This can be
made with any one of a number
of cold sliced meats and fillings
and butters.**

DRIED BEEF ROLLS

MAKES: *8 servings*

CHUTNEY BUTTER

MAKES: *About ¼ cup*

¼ cup unsalted butter
2 tablespoons mashed chutney

In a small bowl or cup, mash
the butter with a fork until soft
and creamy. Fold in the chutney, blending thoroughly.

---

8 large eggs
8 small whole pimientos, peeled and
  cleaned
buttered bread crumbs for garnish
shredded lettuce for garnish

1 Position the rack in the center
of the oven and preheat to 350
degrees F. Lightly grease a baking sheet.

2 In a small bowl or cup, beat the
eggs individually and pour 1
beaten egg into 1 pimiento. Using
a toothpick, secure the pimiento
closed and place on the baking
sheet. Bake for about 4 minutes.
Sprinkle with the bread crumbs
and bake until the crumbs begin
to brown. Cool and slice into 1-
inch pieces. Arrange on a bed of
shredded lettuce to serve.

**COOKING NOTE: Whole pimien-
tos may be difficult to find.
Canned pimientos can be used
in place of the fresh ones.**

EGG-STUFFED
PIMIENTOS

MAKES: *8 servings*

EVERYONE'S FAVORITE MELON PATCH

MAKES: *About 8 servings*

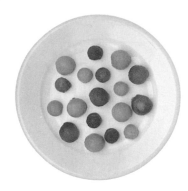

1 small watermelon
2 large cantaloupes
1 Persian melon
1 casaba melon
1 honeydew melon
1 crenshaw melon
1 Spanish melon
lettuce leaves for garnish

Using a sharp knife, cut the melons in half and remove any seeds and netting. Using a melon baller, cut as many balls as you can from each melon (see below). Transfer to a large bowl or arrange them in the scooped-out shells. Garnish with lettuce leaves and chill until ready to serve. Serve with small forks or toothpicks.

COOKING NOTE: **Although a wide range of melon varieties is represented in this recipe, it is not necessary to use all of them.**

FILLED BEETS

MAKES: *8 servings*

8 small cooked whole beets
2 hard-cooked eggs, chopped
¼ teaspoon dry mustard
1 teaspoon minced sweet pickles
1½ tablespoons mayonnaise
½ teaspoon salsa
salt and pepper
8 small pimiento-stuffed olives

1 Using a small melon baller, remove the center from the beets to make a cavity. Discard the beet flesh or save for another use.

2 In a small bowl, combine the eggs, mustard, pickles, mayonnaise, and salsa and season with salt and pepper and blend with a fork until smooth. Using a knife or spoon, pack the mixture into the beets and top with olives.

1 cup peeled, cored and mashed avocado
2 tablespoons prepared horseradish
½ teaspoon salsa or chili sauce
salt and pepper
16 stalks celery (each about 5 inches long)
paprika or finely chopped nuts

1 In a small bowl, combine the avocado, horseradish and chili sauce and season to taste with salt and pepper and blend with a fork until smooth.

2 Using a knife or spoon, spread the mixture into the celery and sprinkle with paprika or nuts. Cover with plastic wrap and chill for at least 2 hours before serving.

COOKING NOTE: Any creamy flavored butter or cheese spread can be used to fill the celery sticks.

FILLED CELERY STICKS

MAKES: *8 servings*

½- to 1-pound melon
16 orange slices, including rind
16 apricot halves
16 seedless grapes
Cheese Dip for Fruit (recipe follows)

Using a melon baller, cut 16 balls from the melon. Thread a wooden skewer with a grape, an apricot half and an orange slice, ending with the melon ball. Repeat until 16 skewers are filled. Serve with the dip on the side.

FRUIT PICKS

MAKES: *8 servings*

CHEESE DIP FOR FRUIT

MAKES: *About 2⅔ cups*

2 cups large-curd cottage cheese
⅔ cup skim milk
2 teaspoons freshly snipped chives
2 teaspoons balsamic vinegar
½ teaspoon salt

In the container of a blender, combine the ingredients and blend on medium speed for 1 minute or until smooth. Cover and chill for at least 2 hours or overnight.

FISH BALLS

MAKES: *8 to 10 servings*

1½ cups boned cooked white-fleshed fish
1 cup fresh white bread crumbs
2 tablespoons minced white onion
¼ cup grated carrots
½ teaspoon sugar
1 large egg, beaten
salt and pepper
1½ quarts Fish Stock (recipe follows)
2 tablespoons all-purpose flour
1 tablespoon cold water
¼ cup snipped chives
Onion Dip for Fish (recipe follows)

1 In a medium bowl, combine the fish, bread crumbs, onion, carrots, sugar and egg. Season with salt and pepper. Using a spoon or melon baller, form the mixture into small balls.

2 In a saucepan, bring the stock to a boil over medium heat. Drop in the fish balls and simmer for 40 minutes. Lift the fish balls from the stock with a slotted spoon and transfer to a bowl.

3 Blend the flour with the water to make a paste and stir into the hot stock. Bring to a boil again and stir until thickened and reduced by about half. Add the chives and pour over the balls. Serve with toothpicks and the dip on the side.

FISH STOCK

MAKES: *About 3 quarts*

2 quarts water
1 pound fish bones, heads and trimmings
2 teaspoons salt

1 Place all of the ingredients in a large saucepan or stockpot, cover and simmer over low heat for about 1 hour. Remove from the heat, strain through a sieve into a bowl. Discard the solids.

2 Let the stock cool slightly, cover and chill until ready to use. The stock can be frozen for up to 1 month.

ONION DIP FOR FISH

MAKES: *About 2⅓ cup*

1 cup canola oil
1 large egg yolk
2 tablespoons lemon juice
¼ cup drained, mashed capers
½ cup flaked tuna
6 anchovy fillets
2 tablespoons lime juice
1 tablespoon grated lemon zest
2 teaspoons minced white onion

1 In a small bowl, using an electric mixer on medium speed, beat together ¼ cup oil, the egg yolk and lemon juice. Beat in the remaining oil.

2 In a small bowl, combine the capers, tuna, anchovy, lime juice, zest, and onion and blend with a fork. Add to the egg mixture and beat well. Cover and chill for at least 2 hours.

1 package (15 ounces) prepared pie
  crust
20 cooked medium shrimp
¾ cup Dillweed Dip (recipe follows)

1 Position the rack in the center
of the oven and preheat to 450
degrees F. Lightly grease a baking sheet.

2 Unwrap the pie crust and cut
out as many 3-inch circles as possible. Roll out the scraps and continue to cut until all the pastry is
used. Dip each shrimp in the dip
and lay on a circle. Moisten the
edges with water and fold the
dough over, using a fork to crimp
and seal the edges together. Place
on the baking sheet and bake for
about 8 to 10 minutes or until
golden brown. Transfer to a plate
or platter lined with lettuce and
serve with the dip on the side.

FLAKY SHRIMP BITES

MAKES: *20 servings*

DILLWEED DIP

MAKES: *About 1½ cups*

¾ cup mayonnaise
¾ cup sour cream or plain yogurt
2 tablespoons minced white
  onions
2½ teaspoon snipped fresh
  dillweed
salt and pepper

In a small bowl, combine the
ingredients and stir until blended. Cover and chill for at least 2
hours before serving.

---

vegetable oil for frying
1 cup all-purpose flour
½ teaspoon garlic powder
pinch of salt
1 cup water
½ cup canola oil
4 large eggs
½ cup Parmesan or Romano cheese
1 tablespoon minced white onion
2 tablespoons Worcestershire sauce

1 Pour the oil into a deep skillet
to a depth of 2 to 3 inches, or use
a deep-fat fryer, and heat until
hot.

2 In a small bowl, combine the
flour, garlic powder and salt.
Add ¼ cup of water and stir to
make a paste.

3 In a saucepan over medium
heat, combine the remaining
water and the canola oil and
bring to a boil. Immediately add
the flour paste, stirring until the
mixture pulls away from the
sides of the pan. Remove from
the heat, and using a fork, vigorously stir in the eggs, one at a
time. Add the cheese, onion and
Worcestershire sauce and mix
well.

4 Using a spoon, drop the mixture into the hot oil and deep fry
for 2 to 3 minutes, or until golden
brown, turning to cook evenly.
Drain on paper towels and serve
hot.

FRIED CHEESE BALLS

MAKES: *20 servings*

FRIED CHEESE PUFFS

MAKES: *30 servings*

vegetable oil for frying
4 ounces Cheddar or Colby cheese
1 package (8 ounces) refrigerated biscuits
Seafood Cocktail Sauce (recipe follows)

1 Pour the oil into a deep skillet to a depth of 2 to 3 inches, or use a deep-fat fryer, and heat until hot.

2 Using a sharp knife, cut the cheese into 30 cubes. Separate the biscuits into slices. Using a sharp knife, cut each slice into thirds. Wrap each third around a cube and deep fry for 3 to 4 minutes or until brown. Drain on paper towels and serve with the dip on the side.

SEAFOOD COCKTAIL SAUCE

MAKES: *About ¼ cup*

¼ teaspoon garlic sauce
¾ teaspoon lime juice
3 tablespoons minced celery
3 to 4 drops Tabasco sauce
pinch of cayenne
¼ teaspoon prepared horseradish

In a small bowl, combine the ingredients and blend with a fork. Cover and chill for at least 2 hours.

FRIED SHRIMP

MAKES: *6 servings*

1 package (10 ounces) frozen cooked shrimp, thawed
1 cup all-purpose flour
vegetable oil for frying
1 cup Spicy Dip for Seafood (recipe follows)

1 Thoroughly wash and dry the shrimp between two paper towels and drop into a plastic bag. Add the flour and shake gently to coat. Spread the floured shrimp out on a paper towel, blotting any excess flour.

2 In a large skillet over medium heat, add oil to a depth of ⅛ inch and heat until hot. Arrange the shrimp in the oil so that they do not touch each other. (They may be cooked in batches if necessary.) Cook for 2 to 4 minutes, turning frequently, until golden brown. Drain on paper towels and serve on a lettuce-lined platter with toothpicks and the dip on the side.

SPICY DIP FOR SEAFOOD

MAKES: *About 1 cup*

1 cup mayonnaise
½ teaspoon curry powder
2 teaspoons store-bought salsa or chili sauce

In a small bowl, combine the mayonnaise, curry powder, and salsa and stir well. Cover and chill for at least 2 hours.

1 can (11 ounces) mandarin orange segments
4 cups strawberries
1 small watermelon
1 honeydew melon
1 cantaloupe melon
2 bananas, sliced
2 apples, cut into large bite-sized cubes
lime-flavored yogurt

1 Drain the oranges and discard the liquid. Wash the strawberries and remove the stems.

2 Using a sharp knife, cut the watermelon in half using a zigzag cut. Scoop out seeds and melon, leaving a ¾-inch shell. Cut the scooped out melon into pieces. Fill each watermelon half with the strawberries.

3 Cut the honeydew and cantaloupe melons in half, remove the seeds, and use a small melon baller to remove as much of the melon as possible. Add these pieces and the watermelon pieces to the watermelon halves. Top with bananas and apples. Serve with the yogurt on the side.

FRUIT ARRAY
MAKES: *6 servings*

¾ cup crushed pineapple, drained
¾ cup fresh raspberries
¾ cup sliced bananas
1 cup diced peaches
1 cup sour cream or berry-flavored yogurt
2 tablespoons brown sugar
pinch of ground cinnamon
bread or crackers for serving

1 In a large bowl, combine the pineapple, raspberries, bananas and peaches, tossing with a spoon. Cover and chill for 1 hour.

2 In a small bowl, combine the sour cream, sugar and cinnamon, beating well with a spoon or fork until the sugar is completely dissolved. Cover and chill for 1 hour.

3 Whisk the chilled sour cream mixture. Add the fruit and fold to incorporate. Transfer to a bowl and set the bowl in a larger one filled with ice chips. Serve with the bread or crackers.

FRUIT ECSTASY
MAKES: *6 servings*

2 envelopes unflavored gelatin
4 cups hot Chicken Stock (see page 295)
½ cup chopped cooked ham
1 cup chopped cooked chicken
1 pimiento, minced
½ cup chopped broccoli
pinch of garlic powder
lettuce, parsley and mayonnaise

1 In a cup, sprinkle the gelatin over ¼ cup of the Chicken Stock and set aside to soften.

2 In a large saucepan, combine the remaining stock and the gelatin, stirring to blend. Cook until the mixture is smooth. Using a large spoon, stir in the ham, chicken, pimiento, broccoli and garlic powder. Pour mixture into small decorative molds or into muffin tins. Chill for at least 8 hours until firm.

3 Unmold and serve on a bed of lettuce with mayonnaise and parsley for garnish.

HAM AND CHICKEN IN ASPIC
MAKES: *8 servings*

FRUIT KABOBS

MAKES: *24 appetizers*

1 can (8 ounces) pineapple rings
1 can (11 ounces) mandarin orange
   slices
1 can (8 ounces) apricot halves
1 bottle (8 ounces) maraschino
   cherries
1 can (7 ounces) pitted cooked
   prunes
¼ cup honey, warmed slightly
1¼ teaspoons lemon or lime juice
Orange Sauce (recipe follows)

1 Preheat the broiler and grease
a broiler pan.

2 Drain the cans of fruit except
the maraschino cherries. Cut the
pineapple rings into 4 wedges
each. Thread the fruit, alternating
the types, on long bamboo skewers. Lay on the broiler pan.

3 In a cup, combine the honey,
lemon juice and cherry juice and
blend thoroughly. Brush over the
fruit and broil about 5 inches
from the heat for 1½ to 2 minutes
or until edges of the fruit begin to
brown.

4 Turn once, brush again with
the honey mixture and broil for
about 1 minute longer. Serve on a
platter with the sauce on the side.

COOKING NOTE: **These may be
refrigerated after broiling and
served cold. Vary the fruit
depending on personal
preferences.**

ORANGE SAUCE

MAKES: *About 1¾ cups*

¼ cup sugar
1½ tablespoons cornstarch
¼ cup orange juice
1 tablespoon grated orange zest
1 tablespoon butter or margarine,
   at room temperature
1 cup water

In the container of a blender,
combine the ingredients and
blend on low for 3 to 4 seconds
until smooth. Pour into a
saucepan and bring to a boil
over a medium-high heat.
Reduce the heat and simmer for
3 to 4 minutes until thickened.
Transfer to a glass jar with a lid
and chill until ready to use.

COOKING NOTE: **The consistency can be adjusted by increasing or decreasing the amount
of water.**

FILLED PRUNES

MAKES: *8 servings*

¼ cup cream cheese
1 teaspoon unsweetened apple or
   pineapple juice
2 tablespoons chopped pecans
16 large pitted cooked prunes
Cheese Dip for Fruit (see page 39)

In a small bowl, combine the
cream cheese, apple juice and
pecans and mash with a fork
until smooth. Fill each prune
with the mixture and serve with
the dip on the side.

COOKING NOTE: **To make this
more decorative, lay a thin slice
of strawberry on each prune, or
set the prunes on kiwi slices.**

¼ cup cold water
1 packet unflavored gelatin
¼ cup boiling water
1 large avocado, peeled and pitted
1½ tablespoons fresh lemon juice
½ cup sour cream
¾ teaspoon chili powder
⅛ teaspoon hot pepper sauce
shredded lettuce leaves for garnish
tomato wedges for garnish
crackers or bread for serving

1 In the container of a blender, combine the cold water and gelatin and process on low speed until the gelatin is well moistened. Let stand for 3 minutes. Add the boiling water and process for 10 seconds on low speed. Add the avocado, lemon juice, sour cream, chili powder and pepper sauce and blend on medium speed until the mixture is smooth.

2 Brush a small ring mold lightly with vegetable oil and pour the mixture into it. Cover and chill for at least 8 hours or overnight.

3 Unmold by dipping the mold quickly in warm water and then sliding a knife in on one edge to release the vacuum. Invert onto a serving plate or platter and garnish with shredded lettuce leaves and tomato wedges. Serve with crackers or breads.

GUACAMOLE MOLD

MAKES: *8 appetizer servings*

½ cup mayonnaise
1 tablespoon evaporated milk or
  heavy cream
½ teaspoon prepared horseradish
1 large pear, coarsely chopped
1 stalk celery, sliced
1 can (11 ounces) mandarin orange
  segments, drained
2 fresh kiwi fruits, peeled, cut in
  half, and sliced
½ cup chopped pecans
½ cup flaked coconut
8 to 10 slices cold boiled ham
parsley
Horseradish Sauce (recipe follows)

1 In a medium bowl, blend together the mayonnaise, milk and horseradish. Add all of the remaining ingredients expect the ham and parsley. Cover and chill for 1 hour.

2 Spoon about ½ cup of the chilled mixture diagonally across each slice of ham and roll into a cone shape. Fasten with a wooden toothpick and arrange in a wheel fashion on top of a bed of fresh parsley. Serve the sauce on the side.

HAM CONES

MAKES: *8 to 10 servings*

HORSERADISH SAUCE

MAKES: *About 1¼ cups*

½ cup heavy cream
⅓ cup mayonnaise
¼ cup prepared horseradish
1 tablespoon sugar
1 teaspoon salt
dash hot pepper sauce

In a small bowl, using an electric mixer on high speed, beat the cream until foamy. Continue beating on high, adding the remaining ingredients as you do so. Mix until smooth and thick enough to spoon in dollops. Cover and chill until ready to serve.

HAM CORNUCOPIAS

MAKES: *About 8 servings*

1 package (3 ounces) cream cheese,
  at room temperature
3 tablespoon prepared horseradish
8 slices boiled ham, each about 2½
  inches square
Horseradish Sauce (see page 45)

In a small bowl, combine the cream cheese and horseradish. Spread the mixture evenly over one side of each slice of ham. Roll each slice into a horn or cornucopia and fasten with a toothpick. Arrange on a serving tray. Cover and chill in the refrigerator until ready to serve. Serve with the sauce on the side.

COOKING NOTE: **This can be made with other cold sliced meats.**

HAM-COVERED BREAD STICKS

MAKES: *8 servings*

4 slices white bread, crust removed
2 tablespoons butter or margarine,
  melted
grated Parmesan or Romano cheese
  for sprinkling
16 thin slices smoked ham
3 tablespoons prepared mustard or
  horseradish
Jalapeño Dip (recipe follows)

1 Preheat the broiler.

2 Using a sharp knife, cut each bread slice into 4 equal-sized strips, each as long as possible. Using a pastry brush, brush a very thin coating of the melted butter over the strips and sprinkle with the Parmesan cheese. Broil until they start to turn golden brown. Cool on a wire rack.

3 Lay the ham on a work surface and spread an even layer of the mustard on each slice. Lay a toasted bread stick down the center of the ham, allowing the ends of the bread to extend beyond the edge of the ham. Tightly wrap the ham around the bread sticks and chill for at least 1 hour before serving. Arrange the rolls on a platter with the dip on the side.

JALAPEÑO DIP

MAKES: *2 to 2¼ cups*

2 tablespoons butter or margarine
1 package (16 ounces) processed
  cheese spread
2 fresh jalapeño peppers,
  stemmed, seeded and chopped
1 tomato, peeled and chopped

1 In a saucepan over low heat, melt the butter. Add the cheese and cook, stirring constantly, until smooth.

2 Stir in the jalapeños and tomato until evenly incorporated. Serve warm.

COOKING NOTE: **To lessen the heat of the jalapeños, rinse them under cool running water and pat dry with paper towels before chopping.**

1 cup pickled herring
16 white cocktail onions
Pimiento Sauce (recipe follows)

Thoroughly drain the herring and using a sharp knife cut it into 1-inch squares. Thread a toothpick with an onion and then a piece of herring and another onion. Repeat to make 8 filled picks. Chill until ready to serve. Serve with the sauce on the side.

HERRING ON PICKS

MAKES: *8 servings*

PIMIENTO SAUCE

MAKES: *About 1 cup*

1 cup half-and-half
1½ tablespoons flour, cornstarch or arrowroot
2 tablespoons chopped pimientos
salt and pepper

1 In a small saucepan, combine the half-and-half and flour and whisk to remove lumps. Bring to a boil over medium heat, reduce the heat and cook, stirring constantly, for 2 to 3 minutes, or until the mixture thickens. Remove from the heat.

2 Stir in the pimientos and season to taste with salt and pepper. Serve hot.

---

8 cooked lean frankfurters, quartered
64 pimiento-stuffed olives
64 1-inch square cubes of Cheddar or Colby cheese
64 pickled white onions
64 ¼-inch slices dill pickles
Creole Sauce (recipe follows)

Skewer a piece of frankfurter into the center of a 4-inch skewer. Skewer 2 olives onto the pick, 1 on each side of the frankfurter. Skewer a cube of cheese next to each olive and then an onion next to each piece of cheese. Finish with a slice of pickle next to each onion. Repeat until the skewers and ingredients are used. Serve with the sauce on the side.

HOT DOG KEBOBS

MAKES: *8 to 10 servings*

CREOLE SAUCE

MAKES: *About 1¼ cups*

1 cup half-and-half
1½ tablespoons flour, cornstarch or arrowroot
1 tablespoon minced onion
¼ cup tomato paste
2 tablespoons chopped green bell pepper
salt and pepper

In a small saucepan, combine the half-and-half and flour and stir to remove lumps. Bring to a boil over medium heat. Reduce the heat and cook, stirring constantly, for 2 to 3 minutes, or until thickened. Add the onion, tomato paste, and bell pepper and season with salt and pepper. Serve hot.

HOT DOG BITES

MAKES: *16 servings*

4 lean frankfurters
2 slices white bread, crust removed
2 slices whole-wheat bread, crust removed
2 teaspoons Black Butter (recipe follows)
2 teaspoons butter or margarine, melted
Mustard Dip (recipe follows)

1 Position the rack in the center of the oven and preheat to 325 degrees F. Lightly grease a baking sheet.

2 Place a frankfurter on each slice of bread and brush with ½ teaspoon of Black Butter. Wrap the bread around the frankfurters and cut each into 4 equal lengths. Secure each with a toothpick and place on the baking sheet. Brush with the melted butter and bake for about 8 to 10 minutes, or until the bread is toasted. Serve warm with Mustard Dip on the side.

COOKING NOTE: **To vary the flavor, substitute another flavored butter for the Black Butter.**

BLACK BUTTER

MAKES: *About 1⅓ cups*

½ cup butter
1 tablespoon finely chopped parsley
1 tablespoon capers
1 tablespoon cider vinegar
salt and white pepper

1 In a small saucepan, melt the butter over medium heat and cook until browned.

2 Remove from the heat and add the parsley, capers and vinegar. Season to taste with salt and pepper and blend thoroughly. Transfer to a bowl, cover and chill for at least 2 hours.

MUSTARD DIP

MAKES: *About 1 cup*

1 cup mayonnaise
2 tablespoons prepared mustard
¼ teaspoon Worcestershire sauce
¼ teaspoon garlic powder
white pepper

In a small bowl, combine the ingredients and stir until blended. Cover and chill for at least 2 hours before serving.

HOT DOG NIBBLES

MAKES: *About 16 servings*

4 cooked lean frankfurters, sliced into ¼-inch slices
½ pound American cheese, cut into ¼-inch cubes
1 can (8 ounces) sliced peaches, drained
1 jar (3 ounces) maraschino cherries, drained
Cheese Dip for Fruit (page 39)
crackers for serving

Thread a piece of hot dog into the center of a toothpick, followed by a cube of cheese, a slice of peach and a cherry. Continue until all the hot dog slices are used. Arrange on a serving tray with the dip and the crackers on the side.

vegetable oil for deep frying
1 cup all-purpose flour
1 large egg, beaten
¾ cup milk
1 teaspoon canola oil
1 clove garlic, minced
4 teaspoons minced white onion
¼ teaspoon celery salt
6 lean frankfurters
Peanut Sauce (recipe follows)

1 Pour the vegetable oil into a deep skillet to a depth of 2 to 3 inches, or use a deep-fat fryer, and heat until hot.

2 In a small bowl, combine the flour, egg, milk, canola oil, garlic, onion and celery salt and mix with a large spoon.

3 Slice the frankfurters into ½- to ¾-inch slices and dip in the batter to coat well. Drop them, 1 at a time, into the hot oil and cook for several minutes until they bob to the surface and are browned on 1 side. Turn and fry the other side until browned. Drain on a wire rack set over paper towels. Serve with toothpicks and the sauce on the side.

HOT DOG-FILLED FRITTERS

MAKES: *About 8 servings*

PEANUT SAUCE

MAKES: *About 1½ cups*

½ cup water
⅓ cup creamy peanut butter
1 small clove garlic, minced
¾ cup orange juice
1 tablespoon packed dark brown sugar
1½ teaspoons light soy sauce
pinch of cayenne pepper

In a small saucepan, combine the water, peanut butter and garlic and bring to a boil over medium heat, stirring. Remove from the heat and stir in orange juice, brown sugar, soy sauce and cayenne. Cool to room temperature, cover and chill until ready to serve.

---

2 tablespoons Herb Butter (recipe follows)
8 lean frankfurters
4 slices white bread, crust removed
4 slices whole-wheat bread, crusts removed
2 teaspoons butter or margarine, melted
16 pimiento-stuffed olives

1 Position the rack in the center of the oven and preheat to 325 degrees F. Lightly grease a baking sheet.

2 Spread the Herb Butter on 1 side of the bread slices. Lay a frankfurter diagonally on each and pull up the corners. Fasten with toothpicks. Brush the outside with the melted butter and place on the baking sheet.

3 Bake for 8 to 10 minutes, or until the bread is toasted. Press an olive onto each end of the toothpicks and serve warm.

COOKING NOTE: **To vary the flavor, use another flavored butter.**

HOT DOG WRAP-UPS

MAKES: *8 servings*

HERB BUTTER

MAKES: *About ½ cup*

½ cup unsalted butter, at room temperature
¼ teaspoon minced fresh marjoram
¼ teaspoon minced fresh rosemary
salt and white pepper

In a small bowl, combine the butter, marjoram and rosemary. Blend gently with a fork and set aside at warm room temperature for at least 2 hours until softened. Stir, season with salt and pepper and chill until ready serve.

INDIA BACON ROLLS

MAKES: *16 Rolls*

16 strips bacon
⅓ cup India-style chutney, such as
    Major Grey's
3 tablespoons Romano cheese

1 Preheat the broiler.

2 Using a small-sized spatula, spread each slice of bacon with chutney, roll up tight and fasten each with a toothpick. Broil for 5 to 6 minutes, turning several times, until the bacon is crisp. Sprinkle with cheese and serve at once.

LETTUCE NEST WITH STUFFED EGGS AND ANCHOVIES

MAKES: *6 to 8 servings*

6 large hard-cooked eggs, cut in half
    and yolks removed
2 tablespoons cappuccino-flavored
    yogurt
3 cups shredded lettuce
12 anchovy fillets, mashed flat
12 capers
pimiento strips

1 In a small bowl, combine the egg yolks and yogurt. Using a small spatula or flat knife, gently push the egg yolk mixture into the depressions in the egg whites.

2 Arrange the lettuce on a plate or platter to resemble a nest and arrange the eggs in it. Lay 1 anchovy fillet across each egg and top with a caper and pimiento strips.

COOKING NOTE: Although this often is served with a vinaigrette dressing drizzled over the top, the yogurt provides good flavor and the dressing is not necessary. Substitute coffee-flavored yogurt for cappuccino-flavored yogurt.

about 8 soft lettuce leaves
½ cup cooked jasmine rice
¼ cup snipped fresh chives
3 tablespoons sour cream
½ teaspoon prepared mustard
½ cup tiny deveined shrimp,
    cleaned and chopped fine
12 thin slices Swiss cheese, halved
    to make strips

1 Thoroughly wash and pat the lettuce leaves dry, lay them between paper towels and chill for about 1 hour.

2 In a small bowl, combine the rice, chives, sour cream, mustard and shrimp and stir until well blended. Cover and chill for about 1 hour.

3 Cut the lettuce leaves into twenty-four strips, each about 1 inch wide and 3½ inches long. Avoid the tough whites veins. Lay on a work surface and spoon about ½ teaspoon of the shrimp filling into the center of each. Roll into tight bundles, tucking in the ends.

4 Lay the cheese strips on the work surface and set a lettuce bundle on each. Wrap the cheese around the bundles, tucking in the edges, and chill for about 1 hour. Serve cold.

LETTUCE SURPRISE

MAKES: *8 servings*

1 cup crumbled liverwurst
1 package (3 ounces) cream cheese,
    at room temperature
½ cup minced green bell pepper
pinch of garlic
salt and pepper
½ cup minced dill pickles
Hot Mustard Sauce (recipe page 29)

1 In a small bowl, combine the liverwurst, cream cheese, bell pepper and garlic and season with salt and pepper. Cover and chill for 1 hour.

2 Using a small melon baller, form the mixture into small balls. Roll each ball in the pickles, lay on a platter in a single layer and chill for about 2 hours. Serve with toothpicks and the sauce on the side.

LIVER BALLS

MAKES: *8 to 10 servings*

MARINATED MUSHROOMS

MAKES: *12 servings*

1 pound fresh mushrooms
½ cup virgin olive oil
3 tablespoons lemon or lime juice
1 clove garlic, mashed
⅛ teaspoon salt
⅛ teaspoon pepper
¼ teaspoon crushed dried chervil

1 Using a sharp knife, cut the stems from the mushrooms so that they are even with the bottom of the crown. Gently scrub the mushroom caps with a soft brush or cloth and put in a large jar with a tight-fitting lid. Discard the stems.

2 In a small saucepan, combine the remaining ingredients and bring to a boil over medium-high heat. Immediately pour the hot oil mixture over the mushrooms. Cover loosely and set aside until cool enough to touch. Tighten the cover and invert the jar until cooled to room temperature. When cool, refrigerate for at least 2 days. Turn top to bottom at least twice a day.

3 To serve, drain and serve with toothpicks.

COOKING NOTE: **This same procedure can be used to marinate small whole canned potatoes.**

MEAL-IN-ONE-TRAY

MAKES: *12 serving*

1 pound fresh asparagus spears
1 to 2 tablespoons butter or margarine
1 small head cauliflower, broken into florets
2 cups thinly sliced cucumbers
1 cup diagonally sliced carrots
2 jars (4.5 ounces each) Green Giant® Whole Mushrooms, drained
1 bottle (8 ounces) Kraft® Italian Dressing or mayonnaise
light- and dark-leaf lettuce
1 jar (6 ounces) marinated artichoke hearts, drained
1 can (5 ounces) pimiento-stuffed olives, drained
1 can (6 ounces) pickled jalapeño peppers, drained
1 can (16.5 ounces) whole pickled beets, drained
1 pound fresh cherry tomatoes
4 ounces sliced mozzarella cheese
4 ounces sliced provolone cheese
4 ounces sliced salami
various breads for serving

1 Trim the tough white portion from the asparagus spears and sauté in butter for 1 or 2 minutes. Drain on a paper towel, dip in ice water and drain on the paper towels a second time.

2 In a saucepan of boiling water set over medium heat, cook the cauliflower for 2 to 3 minutes. Drain and then plunge the florets into ice water. Drain again.

3 Using plastic wrap, individually wrap the asparagus, cauliflower, cucumbers, carrots and mushrooms. Lay the packets in a 3-quart baking pan. Open each packet and drizzle a little salad dressing into each. Refrigerate for 8 hours or overnight. Drizzle a little more dressing over the vegetables after chilling and let sit for 1 hour or longer. Drain the vegetables.

4 Line a large-sized platter or serving tray with a combination of light and dark lettuce leaves and arrange the marinated vegetables and the mushrooms, artichoke hearts, olives, jalapeños, beets and tomatoes on the platter. Serve with the cheeses and salami and the bread on the side.

1 pound ground lamb
1 large egg, beaten
1 cup soft bread crumbs
1 clove garlic, minced
¼ teaspoon crushed dried tarragon
salt and pepper
½ cup sour cream or plain yogurt
2 tablespoons finely chopped celery
2 tablespoons finely chopped
   cucumber
1 tablespoon finely chopped parsley
   or ½ teaspoon crushed dried
   parsley

1 Position a rack in the center of the oven and preheat to 350 degrees F.

2 In a medium bowl, combine the lamb, egg, bread crumbs, garlic and tarragon. Using a 1-inch melon baller, form the mixture into meatballs and place in a 13-by-9-inch baking pan. Bake for 15 to 18 minutes, or until well browned. Drain on paper towels and keep warm.

3 In the same pan, combine the sour cream, celery, cucumber and parsley. Stir just until blended and transfer to a small bowl. Serve the meatballs with toothpicks and the sauce on the side.

MIDDLE EASTERN LAMB BALLS

MAKES: *20 to 24 servings*

---

3 slices white bread
3 slices whole-wheat bread
2 tablespoons Herb Butter, melted
   (see page 49)
1 tablespoon butter or margarine
10 mushrooms, finely chopped
½ teaspoon garlic powder

1 Preheat the oven to 400 degrees F.

2 Using a sharp 1½-inch round cookie cutter, cut each slice of the bread into 4 rounds. Using a pastry brush, lightly coat 1 side of each round with the melted Herb Butter. Place the rounds, butter side down, on an ungreased baking sheet and bake for about 5 minutes, or until the bottoms are light golden brown. Cool on the baking sheet.

3 In a medium skillet, over low heat, melt the butter and cook the mushrooms for about 5 minutes until lightly brown. Sprinkle with garlic powder and stir until incorporated.

4 Spoon about ½ teaspoon of the mushroom mixture onto the unbuttered sides of the bread rounds, pressing gently with the back of the spoon to cover the rounds. Cover with plastic wrap and refrigerate for 8 to 24 hours. Serve chilled or reheated.

COOKING NOTE: **To reheat, broil for 3 to 4 minutes until hot. Garnish each round with a small piece of pimiento just before reheating, if you desire. For variety, use a different flavored butter in place of Herb Butter. Substitute onion powder for the garlic powder. (Do not use garlic or onion salt, or the mushrooms may taste salty.) Just before removing the mushroom mixture from the stove, add a tablespoon of brandy to the mixture and stir well.**

MUSHROOM-GARLIC ROUNDS

MAKES: *24 servings*

NUTTY CHICKEN BALLS

MAKES: *20 servings*

½ cup finely chopped cashews or pecans
2 ounces Cheddar or Colby cheese, at room temperature
½ cup finely diced cooked chicken
1 small white onion, minced
2 tablespoons dry sherry or white port wine
salt and pepper

1 In a shallow dish or pan, spread the chopped nuts in a single layer.
2 In a medium bowl, combine the remaining ingredients and mix well. Using a serving spoon or a small ice cream scoop, form the mixture into balls and roll each in the nuts to coat. Place on a tray, cover and refrigerate for at least 2 hours. Serve cold.

OLIVE-AND-BACON WRAPS

MAKES: *8 servings*

8 large pimiento-stuffed olives
cream cheese
8 strips bacon

1 Preheat the broiler.
2 Using a sharp knife, cut the olives in half and place a dab of cream cheese on 1 half. Rejoin the

halves, using the cream cheese as "glue." Wrap each olive with bacon and fasten with a toothpick. Place on a tray and broil for 3 to 4 minutes or until the bacon is crisp. Serve at once.

ONION-AND-MUSHROOM-STUFFED EGGS

MAKES: *8 servings*

4 large hard-cooked eggs, cut in half and yolks removed
3 tablespoons Mushroom Filling (recipe follows)
¼ cup minced white onion
paprika

In a small bowl, combine the egg yolks, filling and onion. Using a pastry bag fitted with a large fancy tip, press a generous amount of the filling into each egg white half. Sprinkle with paprika and place on a plate, platter or tray. Cover and refrigerate until ready to serve.

MUSHROOM FILLING

MAKES: *About 1½ cups*

½ cup chopped shallots
6 tablespoons unsalted butter or margarine
16 ounces fresh mushrooms, chopped
2 tablespoons chopped parsley
salt and pepper

1 In a skillet, melt the butter over medium heat and sauté the shallots for 3 to 4 minutes until translucent. Add the

mushrooms and cook for 5 minutes, or until soft and limp. Continue to cook for 5 to 10 minutes, or until most of the liquid evaporates. Reduce the heat to low, add the parsley and cook, stirring, until the mushrooms start to brown.

2 Transfer to a bowl and mash lightly with a fork. Serve warm or cover and chill until ready to serve.

COOKING NOTE: **This tastes best if served warm.**

8 strips bacon, cut in half
18 small white cocktail onions
3 tablespoons grated Parmesan
cheese

1 Preheat the broiler.

2 Wrap each onion with a bacon half and fasten with a toothpick. Broil for 3 to 4 minutes until the bacon is crisp. Sprinkle with cheese and serve at once.

BACON-WRAPPED ONION ROLLS

MAKES: *16 rolls*

½ cup light soy sauce
3 tablespoons sherry or white port
wine
2 cloves garlic, minced
¼ teaspoon onion powder
salt and pepper
12 ounces chicken livers, cleaned
and halved
1 can (6.8 ounces) water chestnut
pieces
8 ounces lean bacon strips, halved

1 Position the broiler rack 3 inches from the heat source and preheat the broiler.

2 In a medium saucepan, combine the soy sauce, sherry, garlic and onion powder and bring to a boil over medium heat. Season with salt and pepper. Set aside to cool slightly and then cover and refrigerate for at least 2 hours.

3 Press pieces of liver and water chestnuts together, wrap with bacon and fasten with toothpicks. Broil for 8 or 10 minutes or until the bacon is crisp and the livers are no longer pink. Serve immediately with the sauce.

ORIENTAL-FLAVORED CHICKEN LIVERS

MAKES: *6 servings*

ORIENTAL-FLAVORED MEATBALLS

MAKES: *35 to 40 meatballs*

1 pound ground lean pork
¼ cup ground rice cakes
1 large egg
¼ cup milk
2 tablespoons minced onion
3 tablespoons water
salt and pepper
5 tablespoons butter or margarine
1 cup Oriental-Style Dipping Sauce
  (recipe follows)

1 In a large bowl, thoroughly combine the pork, rice cakes, egg, milk, onion and water. Season to taste with salt and pepper. Using a small melon baller or a spoon, form into small balls.

2 In a large skillet, melt the butter over medium heat. Cook the meatballs for 10 to 12 minutes, turning, until browned on all sides. Drain on paper towels. Serve warm with toothpicks and the sauce on the side.

ORIENTAL-STYLE DIPPING SAUCE

MAKES: *About 1¼ cups*

½ cup soy sauce
½ cup water
3 tablespoons sherry
1 teaspoon minced fresh ginger
1 clove garlic, minced
1 tablespoon dark-brown sugar
½ teaspoon dry mustard

In a small saucepan, combine the ingredients and cook over medium heat, stirring, until the sugar dissolves. Reduce the heat and simmer for 15 to 20 minutes until thickened and the flavors blend. Serve warm.

OYSTER KEBOBS

MAKES: *8 to 10 servings*

2 cups finely ground whole-wheat
  bread crumbs
2 cups finely chopped celery
salt and pepper
40 canned shucked oysters, drained
3 large eggs, beaten
3 tablespoons butter or margarine,
  melted
toast for serving

1 Preheat the broiler.

2 In a small bowl, combine the bread crumbs and celery and season to taste with salt and pepper.

3 Dip the oysters in the egg and then roll in the crumbs until well coated. Thread onto metal skewers, allowing five oysters per skewer. Lay the skewers over a 13-by-9-inch baking pan and brush with melted butter. Broil for 1 to 2 minutes until browned. Turn, brush with butter and cook the other side until lightly browned. Take care not to overcook. Serve at once with toast.

COOKING NOTE: **For variation, wrap each oyster in bacon before threading onto the skewers. If using bamboo skewers rather than metal, soak the bamboo skewers in cold water for at least 30 minutes before using. This prevents burning.**

4 hard-cooked eggs, cut in half and
  yolks removed
¼ cup Cream Cheese Spread (recipe
  follows)
2 tablespoons finely chopped green
  bell pepper
1 tablespoon finely chopped red bell
  pepper
paprika

In a small bowl, combine the egg
yolks, cheese spread, and peppers and mix well with a fork.
Using a pastry bag fitted with a
large-sized fancy tip, press a generous amount of the filling into
each egg white. Sprinkle with
paprika and chill until ready to
serve.

PEPPER-AND-CHEESE-STUFFED EGGS

MAKES: *8 servings*

CREAM CHEESE SPREAD

MAKES: *About 1¾ cups*

1 package (3 ounces) cream cheese,
  softened
½ cup minced pimientos
6 tablespoons mayonnaise
½ cup finely chopped walnuts

1 In a small bowl, using an
electric mixer on medium
speed, blend together the cream
cheese, pimientos, and
mayonnaise.

2 Beat vigorously and stir in
the chopped nuts. Cover and
chill for at least 1 hour.

---

1 package (8 ounces) refrigerated
  biscuits
2 tablespoons butter or margarine
1 clove garlic, minced
1 tablespoon chopped green bell
  pepper
1 tablespoon chopped red bell
  pepper
⅔ cup tomato sauce
1½ cups chopped cooked chicken
2 tablespoons crushed fresh oregano
3 tablespoons grated Parmesan or
  Romano cheese

1 Position the rack in the center
of the oven and preheat to 425
degrees F. Lightly grease a baking sheet.

2 Cut each biscuit slice in half
and lay the halves on the baking
sheet, leaving about 1 inch
between them.

3 In a skillet over medium heat,
melt the butter and sauté the garlic and peppers for 5 to 6 minutes
until tender. Add the tomato
sauce and continue cooking, stirring frequently, for about 10
minute. Remove from the heat
and stir in the chicken and
oregano.

4 Spread the mixture evenly over
the biscuit halves and sprinkle
with cheese. Bake for 8 to 10 minutes, or until the crust starts to
turn a light brown. Serve hot.

PIZZA BITS

MAKES: *20 servings*

PIZZA-FLAVORED FONDUE

MAKES: *8 servings*

2 cans (10½ ounces each) commercial pizza sauce with cheese
2 tablespoons cornstarch
¼ pound pepperoni or Italian sausage meat, finely chopped
1 tablespoon instant minced onion
1 teaspoon snipped fresh oregano
1 package (16 ounces) processed cheese spread, cubed
1 tablespoon snipped fresh parsley
⅛ teaspoon red pepper sauce
breadsticks, mushrooms, cherry tomatoes, celery sticks and green bell pepper slices for dipping

1 In a 2-quart saucepan over medium heat, combine ½ cup of pizza sauce and the cornstarch and heat until just simmering. Add the remaining pizza sauce, the pepperoni, onions and oregano and bring to a boil, stirring constantly for 1 minute.

2 Remove from the heat and stir in the cheese spread, a few cubes at a time, stirring constantly until the cheese is melted and smooth. Add the parsley and pepper sauce.

3 Transfer to a fondue pot to keep warm. Serve with breadsticks, mushrooms, cherry tomatoes, celery and green bell pepper slices for dipping into the fondue.

POTATO LATKES WITH CHIVES

MAKES: *12 latkes*

6 new potatoes, peeled and cut into 1-inch pieces
1 cup water
1 onion, cut into quarters
2 large eggs, beaten
2 tablespoons snipped chives
1 tablespoon all-purpose flour
½ teaspoon salt
½ teaspoon paprika
¼ teaspoon baking powder

1 Grease a skillet or electric griddle and preheat to hot (400 to 450 degrees F).

2 In the container of a blender, process half of the potatoes on high speed for 20 seconds, or until finely grated. Transfer to a bowl.

3 Process the remaining potatoes with the water and onions. Add this mixture to the bowl with the grated potatoes. Add the eggs, chives, flour, salt, paprika and baking powder and mix to make a thick batter.

4 Drop the batter by ¾ cupfuls onto the hot skillet or griddle and cook over medium heat until the edges start to brown. Turn and cook for about 3 minutes longer, or until golden brown. Serve immediately.

COOKING NOTE: **These latkes are delicious with meat, fish or poultry.**

16 small canned white potatoes
2 slices boiled ham, cut into 2 strips
each
2 slices pimento loaf, cut into 2
strips each
2 slices olive loaf, cut into 2 strips
each
2 slices pressed ham, cut into 2
strips each
½ cup Chili Dip (see page 32)

Wrap each potato with a strip of meat and secure with a tooth-pick. Place on a serving tray, cover and chill for until ready to serve. Serve with the dip on the side.

COOKING NOTE: Chili Dip can be served hot or cold with the rolls.

POTATO ROLLS

MAKES: *8 servings*

---

8 large prunes
cream cheese
8 strips bacon

1 Preheat the broiler.

2 Using a sharp knife, cut the prunes in half and place a dab of cream cheese on 1 half. Rejoin the halves, using the cream cheese as "glue." Wrap each prune with bacon and fasten with a tooth-pick. Place on a tray and broil for 3 to 4 minutes until the bacon is crisp. Serve at once.

PRUNE AND BACON WRAPS

MAKES: *8 servings*

RELISH-AND-CHEESE-STUFFED EGGS

MAKES: *8 servings*

4 hard-cooked eggs, cut in half and
    yolks removed
¼ cup Cream Cheese Spread (see
    page 57)
3 tablespoons sweet pickle relish
paprika

In a small bowl, combine the egg
yolks, cheese spread and relish
and mix with a fork. Using a pastry bag fitted with a large-sized
fancy tip, press a generous
amount of filling into each egg
white. Sprinkle with paprika,
cover, and chill until ready to
serve.

RICE-AND-BACON-STUFFED PIMIENTOS

MAKES: *8 to 10 servings*

2 cups cooked white or wild rice
½ cup chopped cooked bacon
¼ cup cooked green peas
8 small-sized whole pimientos,
    cleaned and peeled
buttered bread crumbs
shredded lettuce for garnish

1 Position a rack in the center of
the oven and preheat to 350
degrees F. Lightly grease a baking sheet.

2 In a small bowl, combine the
rice, bacon and peas. Using a
spoon, stuff the mixture into the
pimientos. Secure closed with
toothpicks.

3 Lay the pimientos on the baking sheet and bake for 4 minutes.
Sprinkle with the bread crumbs
and continue baking for 3 to 4
minutes until the crumbs begin
to brown. Cool and then slice
into 1-inch pieces. Serve on a bed
of shredded lettuce.

COOKING NOTE: **Whole pimientos may be difficult to find.
Canned pimientos can be used
in place of the fresh ones.**

12 chicken livers
2 tablespoons ginger-flavored brandy
¼ cup soy sauce
1 can (8 ounces) water chestnuts
12 strips bacon, cut in half

1 Preheat the broiler.

2 Wash the chicken livers and slice in half. Combine the brandy and soy sauce and dip the livers in the sauce.

3 Thread the bacon onto skewers, leaving one end hanging from the skewer. Add a chicken liver and then thread a little more bacon on the skewer. Add a water chestnut and then pick up the end of the bacon and thread it on the skewer. (The bacon will form an "S" around the liver and water chestnut.) Continue in this fashion until all the ingredients are on skewers.

4 Broil for 8 or 10 minutes until the bacon is crisp and the livers are cooked.

RUMAKI
MAKES: *24 servings*

1 package (3 ounces) sliced cooked ham
1 package (3 ounces) sliced cooked chicken
1 package (3 ounces) sliced cooked turkey
2 large stalks celery, thinly sliced
¾ cup sweet pickle relish
¾ cup mayonnaise
1 loaf unsliced Vienna bread or French or Italian bread
¼ cup butter or margarine, at room temperature
1 teaspoon prepared mustard
cherry tomatoes, cut in half
celery leaves

1 Set aside 5 slices of meat to use later. Finely chop the remaining slices and transfer to a bowl. Add the celery, relish and mayonnaise. Cover and refrigerate for 1 hour.

2 Using a sharp knife, cut the top crust horizontally from of the loaf of bread by making 2 long parallel cuts and lifting the top off the bread. Scoop out the bread inside the loaf, leaving a ¾-inch-thick shell. Discard the scooped out bread or reserve for another use.

3 Combine the butter and mustard and use to coat the inside of the loaf. Layer the loaf with the reserved meat slices. Spoon the chilled meat mixture into the loaf and garnish with cherry tomatoes and celery leaves. Slice and serve.

SALAD BOAT
MAKES: *6 servings*

SALAD SANDWICHES

MAKES: *24 servings*

2 cups shredded lettuce
4 carrots, shredded
½ cup golden raisins
½ cup chopped pecans
½ cup light mayonnaise
24 slices pumpernickel bread (not cocktail size)
butter or margarine, at room temperature

1 In a bowl, combine the lettuce, carrots, raisins and pecans with the mayonnaise and toss to mix.

2 Spread the bread slices with butter and top with the salad mixture.

SALMON CAKES

MAKES: *4 servings*

3 large eggs
1 tablespoon all-purpose flour
2 teaspoons lemon juice
¼ teaspoon salt
dash of white pepper
1 can (12 ounces) whole-kernel corn, drained
1 can (7.75 ounces) salmon, drained and flaked
Cheese Sauce (see page 20) or Pimiento Sauce (see page 47)

1 Preheat a skillet over a medium-low heat or preheat an electric griddle.

2 In a medium bowl, using an electric mixer on medium speed, beat together the eggs, flour, lemon juice, salt and pepper. Add the corn and salmon and stir until well mixed.

3 Drop the mixture by generous half cupfuls into the skillet. Flatten slightly with the back of a spoon and cook for about 3 minutes on each side, or until golden brown. Serve warm with the sauce on the side.

COOKING NOTE: **Substitute any vegetable chopped to the same size as the corn for the corn.**

SALMON CHEESE STRIPS

MAKES: *48 servings*

1 package (3 ounces) cream cheese, at room temperature
2 tablespoons mayonnaise
1 can (7.75 ounces) salmon, finely chopped
½ cup chopped celery
¼ teaspoon prepared mustard
dash of Angostura bitters
16 slices white toast, crusts removed and cut into 1½-inch strips

In a bowl, combine the cheese and mayonnaise and mash until smooth. Stir in the salmon, celery, mustard and bitters. Spread on the toast strips and serve.

DRESSING

½ cup mayonnaise
2 teaspoons heavy cream
2 tablespoons salsa
1 tablespoon chopped green bell
pepper
1 tablespoon chopped red bell
pepper
1 tablespoon chopped white onion
2 tablespoons prepared horseradish
2 hard-cooked egg whites, chopped
1 tablespoon sliced pimiento-stuffed
olives
salt and pepper

FILLING

juice of 1 lemon
1 can (16 ounces) salmon, drained
and flaked
2 tomatoes, chopped
2 hard-cooked egg yolks, chopped
6 dark outer lettuce leaves
2 cups shredded lettuce leaves
2 ounces Swiss cheese, diced

1 To prepare the dressing, in the container of a blender, combine all of the ingredients and process on low for 1 to 2 seconds. Transfer to a bowl, cover, and chill for at least 2 hours.

2 To prepare the filling, sprinkle a little lemon juice over the salmon. In a small bowl, combine the tomatoes and egg yolks and stir to mix. Mix in the salmon.

3 Position a lettuce leaf in a cocktail glass, pushing the leaf deep into the glass. Repeat with 6 cocktail glasses. Put about a third of a cup of shredded lettuce into each glass and divide the salmon equally among the glasses. Top with the dressing and garnish with diced cheese.

SALMON COCKTAIL

MAKES: *6 servings*

1 can (7.75 ounces) salmon, flaked
1 teaspoon prepared horseradish
2 tablespoons lemon or lime juice
1 teaspoon finely chopped white
onion
¼ cup mayonnaise
1 package (11 ounces) pastry pie
crust mix
paprika

1 Position a rack in the center of the oven and preheat to 425 degrees F.

2 In a medium bowl, combine the salmon, horseradish, lemon juice, onion and mayonnaise and mix well.

3 Prepare the pastry mix according to the package directions. Divide the dough in half and roll each into a 9-inch diameter circle. Spread the salmon mixture evenly over the two circles and cut each into 16 wedges. Roll each wedge up, beginning at the wide end, and lay on an ungreased baking sheet. Prick each roll with the tines of a fork and sprinkle with paprika. Bake for 12 to 15 minutes or until lightly browned. Cool on a wire rack before serving.

SALMON ROLLS

MAKES: *32 rolls*

SALMON-STUFFED EGGS

MAKES: *8 servings*

8 hard-cooked eggs, cut in half and yolks removed
1 can (3.75 ounces) sockeye red salmon, flaked
½ cup minced celery leaves
½ cup chopped almonds
2 tablespoons minced green bell pepper
¼ teaspoon prepared mustard
mayonnaise
salt and pepper
watercress for garnish

1 In a small bowl, combine the egg yolks, salmon, celery leaves, almonds, bell pepper, mustard, and mayonnaise. Season with salt and pepper. Using a fork, mash until smooth.

2 Fill each egg white half with the mixture, garnish with watercress and serve.

COOKING NOTE: **For a more decorative look, use a pastry bag fitted with a large-sized star tip and pipe the mixture into the egg whites. Sprinkle with additional nuts and garnish each with a slice of kiwi.**

SALMON-STUFFED PIMIENTOS

MAKES: *8 servings*

1½ cups Salmon Filling (recipe follows)
8 small whole pimientos, cleaned and peeled
buttered bread crumbs
shredded lettuce for garnish

1 Position the rack in the center of the oven and preheat to 350 degrees F. Lightly grease a baking sheet.

2 Using a spoon, stuff the filling into the pimientos and secure each with a toothpick. Lay on the baking sheet and bake for about 4 minutes. Sprinkle with bread crumbs and continue to bake until the crumbs begin to brown.

3 Cool and then slice into 1-inch pieces. Serve on a bed of lettuce.

COOKING NOTE: **Whole pimientos may be difficult to find. Canned pimientos can be used in place of the fresh ones.**

SALMON FILLING

MAKES: *About 1¼ cups*

**½ cup flaked canned salmon
½ cup finely chopped deviled ham
¼ cup flaked crabmeat
salt and pepper
mayonnaise**

In a small bowl, combine the ingredients and stir well. Cover and chill for at least 2 hours.

1 can (7.75 ounces) salmon, drained and flaked
2 large hard-cooked eggs, chopped
½ cup chopped celery
¼ cup chopped cucumber
2 tablespoons finely chopped onion
2 tablespoons snipped fresh parsley
⅓ cup mayonnaise
lemon juice
salt and pepper
6 tomatoes
garlic or onion powder

1 Position the rack 3 to 5 inches from the heat and preheat the broiler. Lightly grease a 13-by-9-by-2-inch baking pan.

2 In a small bowl, combine the salmon, eggs, celery, cucumber, onion, parsley and mayonnaise. Season with lemon juice and salt and pepper and mix well.

3 Using a sharp knife, starting at the stem end, cut the core from the tomatoes. Lightly sprinkle the insides with garlic or onion powder and fill each with the salmon mixture. Place the tomatoes in the pan and broil for 5 to 7 minutes, or until heated through. Serve at once.

SALMON-STUFFED TOMATOES
MAKES: *6 servings*

---

3 tablespoons butter or margarine
8 slices dried beef
2 tablespoons prepared mustard
8 large sweet pickles
variety of breads for serving

1 In a skillet over medium heat, melt the butter. Brush the dried beef with mustard. Place a pickle in the center of each slice. Fold the beef over the pickle and fasten with toothpicks.

2 Cook, turning the bundles from side to side, until the beef starts to brown. Serve at once with the bread.

SAUTÉED BEEF-AND-PICKLE WRAPS
MAKES: *8 wraps*

SCRAMBLED VEGETABLES

MAKES: *8 servings*

3 tablespoons virgin olive oil
1 large clove garlic, minced
3 cups shredded green cabbage
2 tomatoes, diced
½ cup chopped celery
½ cup chopped green bell pepper
1 cup Green Giant® Nibblet® frozen corn
1 packet Equal® sweetener
1 teaspoon crushed dried dill
salt and pepper
4 large eggs, lightly beaten
shredded lettuce
Tarragon Dressing (recipe follows)

1 In a large skillet, heat the oil over medium heat. Add the garlic and cook, stirring, for about 1 minute. Add the cabbage, tomatoes, celery, pepper and corn. Sprinkle with sweetener, dill and salt and pepper to taste and cook for 5 to 8 minutes, stirring occasionally, until the vegetables are tender.

2 Pour the eggs over the vegetables. Reduce the heat to low, cover, and cook for 2 to 3 minutes until firm. Invert onto a bed of lettuce and cut into 8 pieces. Serve with the dressing on the side.

TARRAGON DRESSING

MAKES: *About 2 cups*

1 large egg
2 teaspoons crushed dried tarragon
1½ teaspoons crushed dried parsley
1½ teaspoons dry mustard
2 tablespoons lemon juice
4 small cloves garlic, minced
3 finely chopped green onions
⅓ cup tarragon vinegar
1½ cups vegetable oil
salt and pepper

1 In the container of a blender, combine the egg, tarragon, parsley, mustard, lemon juice, garlic and green onions. Blend for about 30 seconds, or until smooth.

2 Add the vinegar. With the blender on low and with a slow swirl in the center of the mixture, slowly add the oil in a steady stream, blending until all the oil is absorbed and the mixture is smooth and pale green. Season with salt and pepper.

SHRIMP PEPPER BOATS

MAKES: *6 servings*

1 package (10 ounces) frozen broccoli florets, chopped
1 can (8.5 ounces) whole new potatoes, drained and chopped
1 can (4.5 ounces) tiny deveined shrimp, rinsed and drained
1 stalk celery, coarsely chopped
½ cup shredded Cheddar cheese
¼ cup Kraft® Salad Dressing or mayonnaise
2 teaspoons lime juice
3 large green bell peppers
lettuce leaves
freshly snipped parsley

1 In a bowl, combine the broccoli, potatoes, shrimp, celery, cheese, salad dressing and lime juice and toss to mix.

2 Cut the peppers in half lengthwise, scoop out the seeds and membrane and place the halves on the lettuce. Fill each pepper half with the shrimp mixture, garnish with the parsley and serve.

COOKING NOTE: **For a variation, substitute crabmeat for the shrimp.**

½ cup creamy peanut butter
¼ cup mango chutney
1 cup Chicken Stock (see page 295)
2 tablespoons light corn syrup
1 large clove garlic, mashed
1 package (16 ounces) Thorn Apple Valley® cocktail sausages

1 In a small saucepan, heat the peanut butter, chutney, chicken stock, corn syrup and garlic over low heat, stirring constantly, until thickened to the consistency of catsup.

2 Add the sausages and cook until heated through. Transfer to a chafing dish and serve with toothpicks on the side.

SOUTHERN-STYLE COCKTAIL SAUSAGES

MAKES: *40 serving*

---

1 pound Cheddar or Colby cheese, grated
1 cup sweet pickle relish
1 cup Blue Cheese Mayonnaise (see page 24)
½ cup chili sauce
¼ cup Dijon mustard
24 lean Oscar Mayer® turkey franks
24 hot-dog rolls

1 Position the rack in the center of the oven and preheat to 350 degrees F.

2 Combine the cheese, relish, mayonnaise, chili sauce and mustard and stir to mix.

3 Cut the frankfurters lengthwise, leaving them attached at one end. Spread the cheese mixture between the halves and lightly press together. Put each frankfurter in a roll.

4 Wrap each roll in aluminum foil and bake for 4 to 5 minutes, or until hot. Serve at once.

COOKING NOTE: You may scoop some bread from the inside of the hot dog rolls so that the frankfurters can be nestled into the rolls. These may be made ahead of time, wrapped in foil and baked just before serving.

SPICY CHEESE-STUFFED HOT DOGS

MAKES: *24 servings*

SWEET-AND-SOUR SMOKIES

MAKES: *60 serving*

½ cup granulated sugar
½ cup packed dark-brown sugar
3 tablespoons cornstarch
pinch of ground cloves
¼ teaspoon ground cinnamon
1½ cups orange juice
¼ cup cider vinegar
2 packages (16 ounces each) Thorn Apple Valley® smoked cocktail sausages

1 In a saucepan, combine the sugars, cornstarch, cloves, cinnamon, orange juice and vinegar.

Cover and cook over medium-low heat, stirring occasionally, until thickened.

2 Add the sausages and simmer for about 5 minutes or until the sausages are heated through. Pour into a chafing dish and serve with toothpicks on the side.

COOKING NOTE: For a little added flavor, place the toothpicks in a jar with a peeled garlic clove, seal tightly, and place in the refrigerator for several days before using.

TORTILLA BITES

MAKES: *72 serving*

1 package (8 ounces) cream cheese, at room temperature
1 can (4 ounces) chopped green chiles, drained
1 jar (4 ounces) chopped pimientos, drained
½ cup chopped ripe olives
twelve 6-inch flour tortillas
Miramontes Salsa (recipe follows)

1 In a medium bowl, combine the cream cheese, chiles, pimientos and olives and mash with a fork to blend.

2 Spread a heaping tablespoonful of the mixture on each tortilla and roll up tight. Place seam side down, cover, and chill for at least 2 hours. Cut each into 1-inch pieces and serve with the salsa on the side.

MIRAMONTES SALSA

MAKES: *About 4 cups*

¼ cup virgin olive oil
2 large green bell peppers, trimmed, seeded and finely chopped
4 small yellow chile peppers, trimmed, seeded and finely chopped
2 large red onions, trimmed and finely chopped
2 large-sized cans (16 ounces each) tomatoes
3 cans (8 ounces each) tomato sauce
salt and pepper

1 In a large heavy skillet, heat 2 tablespoons of the oil until hot. Sauté the peppers and chiles for about 5 minutes until softened. Transfer to a bowl and set aside. Add the remaining oil to the pan, heat, and sauté the onions for about 5 mintues until softened. Return the peppers and chiles to the pan, stirring to blend.

2 Add the tomatoes, tomato sauce and salt and pepper to taste, cover, and cook over low heat for about 2 hours. Cool to room temperature and chill for at least 4 hours before serving.

2 large tomatoes, cut into 4 slices each
5 large hard-cooked eggs, cut into 24 slices
8 large pimiento-stuffed olives, sliced
2 packages (3 ounces each) cream cheese, at room temperature
3 tablespoons Kraft® French Dressing
watercress for garnish

1 Place the tomatoes out on a work surface and lay 3 slices of hard-cooked egg on each slice. Lay several slices of olives on top of the eggs.

2 In a small bowl, combine the cream cheese and dressing and mash with a spoon. Fill a pastry bag fitted with a large star tip with the cheese mixture. Press out a generous amount of the cheese on top of the olives and garnish with a small sprig of watercress. Arrange on a serving tray or platter and serve.

TOMATO-EGG APPETIZER

MAKES: *8 servings*

½ cup deviled ham or liverwurst
3 tablespoons Quick Salad Dressing (recipe follows)
½ teaspoon minced white onion
2 large tomatoes
mayonnaise for garnish
sprigs of parsley for garnish
8 Pepperidge Farm® Melba Toasted Rounds, or toasted bread rounds

1 In a small bowl, combine the ham, salad dressing and minced onion and mash with a fork to form a smooth paste.

2 Using a sharp knife, slice the tomatoes in half crosswise and then make additional cuts to get eight ¼-inch-thick slices from each tomato.

3 Spread the ham mixture on one slice of tomato and top with a second slice. Garnish the top with a dab of mayonnaise and a sprig of parsley. Repeat with all the tomato slices. Place each on a toasted round and serve.

COOKING NOTE: **The sandwiches can be assembled ahead of time, chilled and then placed on the toasted rounds just before serving.**

TOMATO MINI SANDWICHES

MAKES: *8 servings*

QUICK SALAD DRESSING

MAKES: *1 cup*

½ cup mayonnaise
½ cup commercial barbecue sauce
1 tablespoon lemon juice
1 hard-cooked egg, mashed with a fork

In a small bowl, using an electric mixer on medium speed, blend together the mayonnaise, barbecue sauce and lemon juice. Add the egg and stir until blended. Cover and chill for at least 2 hours. Stir before serving.

TORTILLA-WRAPPED CRABMEAT

MAKES: *8 servings*

8 small flour tortillas
1 cup Crab Filling (recipe follows)
2 slices sharp Cheddar cheese, cut
   into 8 strips
shredded lettuce

1 Spoon 2 tablespoons of filling into the center of each tortilla. Roll up the tortillas, folding in the sides as you roll. Lay a strip of cheese over the seam of each bundle and fasten with a toothpick.

2 Arrange the bundles on a microwave-safe dish and microwave on medium (50 percent) power for 4 to 6 seconds, or until the cheese starts to soften (it should not melt). Remove from the microwave and set aside until the cheese sets. Remove the toothpicks and serve on a bed of lettuce.

COOKING NOTE: This can be made with another seafood, meat or cheese filling.

CRAB FILLING

MAKES: *About 1 cup*

1 cup minced crabmeat
2 tablespoons heavy cream
1 tablespoon prepared horseradish
salt and pepper

In a small bowl, combine the ingredients and stir to mix. Cover and chill for at least 2 hours.

TUNA PIZZA

MAKES: *6 servings*

three 9-inch unbaked pizza crusts
½ cup canola oil
⅓ cup chopped white onion
2 large cloves garlic, minced
3 cans (6 ounces each) tomato paste
2 teaspoons crushed fresh oregano
⅓ cup snipped fresh parsley
3 cans (4 .5 ounces each) tuna,
   mashed with a fork
8 ounces mozzarella cheese, grated
4 ounces provolone cheese, grated

1 Position the rack in the center of the oven and preheat to 425 degrees F. Lightly grease 3 baking sheets. Lay a pizza crust on each baking sheet.

2 In a skillet, heat the oil over medium heat and sauté the onion and garlic for 4 to 5 minutes until tender. Add the tomato paste and continue to cook, stirring frequently, for 10 minutes. Remove from the heat and stir in the herbs.

3 Using a serving spoon, spread the sauce evenly over the pizza crusts to the edge, sprinkle on the tuna, and top with the cheese. Bake for 18 to 20 minutes or until the crust starts to turn a light brown. Serve hot.

1 cooked carrot, mashed
1 cooked beet, peeled and mashed
½ cup cooked green beans, mashed
¼ cup Blue Cheese Mayonnaise (see page 24)
salt and white pepper
4 large hard-cooked eggs, cut in half and yolks removed
paprika
shredded lettuce for garnish

1 In a small bowl, using an electric mixer on medium speed, combine the carrot, beets, beans and mayonnaise and beat until smooth. Season with salt and pepper. Add the yolks and mash with a fork until smooth.

2 Using a pastry bag fitted with a star tip, press generous amounts of filling into each egg white. Sprinkle with paprika and arrange on a nest of shredded lettuce leaves. Serve at once or chill until ready.

VEGETABLE-FILLED EGGS

MAKES: *8 servings*

---

1 package (10 ounces) prepared refrigerator biscuits
ten 1-inch cubes Cheddar cheese
ten 1-inch cubes cooked chicken
ten 1-inch cubes cooked ham
10 large pitted ripe olives
1 cup grated romano cheese

1 Position the rack in the center of the oven and preheat to 375 degrees F. Lightly grease a baking sheet.

2 Cut the biscuits into quarters and stretch the dough into small ropes. Wrap 10 of the dough ropes around the cheese cubes. Wrap 10 more ropes around the chicken, 10 around the ham and 10 more around the olives.

3 Spread the grated cheese in a shallow bowl and roll each dough roll in the cheese. Lay on the baking sheet and bake for 6 to 8 minutes, or until golden brown. Serve immediately.

SNACK WRAPS

MAKES: *40 serving*

---

8 cups dry popped popcorn
2 cups Pepperidge Farm® goldfish crackers
1 cup plain croutons, toasted
1 cup miniature unsalted pretzels
2 tablespoons butter or margarine, melted
1 teaspoon Worcestershire sauce
½ teaspoon garlic powder
½ teaspoon onion powder
½ teaspoon chili powder

1 Position the rack in the center of the oven and preheat to 350 degrees F. Lightly grease a 15-by-½-by-10½-inch jelly-roll pan.

2 In a large bowl, combine the popcorn, goldfish, croutons and pretzels and toss to mix.

3 In a cup, stir together the butter, Worcestershire sauce, garlic powder, onion powder and chili powder. Drizzle in a thin stream over the popcorn mix. Spread evenly on the pan and bake for no longer than 15 minutes, until the popcorn is beginning to turn brown. Turn off the oven, stir, and cool in the oven with the door propped open for about 1 hour. Serve or store in an airtight container.

ALL-THE-USUAL SNACK MIX

MAKES: *About 11 cups*

ALMOND PÂTÉ

MAKES: *About 2½ cups*

1 package (8 ounces) ripe Brie cheese, rind removed, at room temperature
¾ cup butter or margarine, at room temperature
½ cup ground almonds
2 tablespoon Amaretto liqueur
crackers or bread for serving

1 Line a 6½-by-4-by-2½-inch loaf pan or oblong dish with waxed paper, leaving enough overhang at the ends to fold back over the top and meet in the middle.

2 In a medium bowl, using an electric mixer on medium speed, beat together the Brie, butter, almonds, and Amaretto. Spoon into the pan, fold the excess waxed paper over it, press, and weight with cans or weights to compact. Chill for at least 2 hours and preferably overnight. Unmold and serve with crackers or bread.

APRICOT CHEESE BALL

MAKES: *8 to 10 servings*

1 package (8 ounces) cream cheese, at room temperature
½ cup ricotta cheese
2 tablespoons finely chopped dried apricots, soaked in brandy and drained
1 tablespoon finely chopped shallot
1 teaspoon lemon juice
½ teaspoon curry powder
½ cup crushed All-Bran® cereal
crackers for serving

1 In a large bowl, and using an electric mixer on medium speed, beat together the cream cheese and ricotta cheese until smooth. Add the apricots, shallot, lemon juice and curry powder and beat until incorporated. Cover and chill for at least 2 hours or until firm.

2 Spread the cereal in a shallow bowl or plate.

3 Shape the cream cheese mixture into a ball and roll in the cereal to cover. Chill for at least 2 hours before serving with crackers.

COOKING NOTE: **Soak the apricots in brandy for at least 20 minutes.**

ASPARAGUS APPETIZERS

MAKES: *12 to 24 servings*

12 ounces asparagus spears, trimmed
1 tablespoon water
2 packages (3 ounces each) cream cheese, at room temperature
1 package (2 ounces) Kraft® blue cheese, crumbled
1 teaspoon lemon juice
crackers for serving

1 Cut the asparagus spears into 1-inch pieces.

2 In a 2-cup microwave-safe bowl, combine the asparagus and water. Cover with plastic wrap, leaving a corner turned back for venting, or a microwave-safe lid and microwave on high (100 percent) power for 4 to 5 minutes, or until tender. Drain.

3 In a bowl, and using an electric mixer on medium speed, beat the cream cheese, blue cheese, and lemon juice until smooth. Spread the cheese mixture on crackers and garnish with the asparagus.

1 cup shredded Swiss or Muenster
   cheese
8 slices crisp bacon, crumbled
3 to 3¼ cups Kraft® real mayonnaise
1 tablespoon grated shallot
¼ teaspoon celery salt
10 slices white bread, crusts
   removed and cut into thirds

1 Position the rack in the center
of the oven and preheat to 325
degrees F. Lightly grease a baking sheet.

2 In a medium bowl, combine
the cheese, bacon, mayonnaise,
shallot and celery salt and blend
with a fork. Spread evenly to the
very edge of the bread slices and
place on the baking sheet. Bake
for 8 to 10 minutes, or until the
cheese melts, and serve
immediately.

BACON-AND-CHEESE FINGERS

MAKES: *About 30 servings*

butter or margarine, at room
   temperature
24 thin slices white bread, crusts
   removed
½ pound bacon, cooked until crisp
   and crumbled
½ cup grated Parmesan or romano
   cheese
¼ cup minced parsley
dash of paprika
dash of cayenne

1 Preheat the broiler or stove-top
grill.
2 Spread the butter on the bread
slices and lay on a work surface.
Down the middle of each slice,

spoon a narrow line of bacon.
Sprinkle with cheese, parsley,
paprika and cayenne.

3 Roll up each slice as tightly as
possible and secure with a toothpick. Broil or grill for 2 to 3 minutes, or until lightly brown. Serve
at once.

**COOKING NOTE: Soak the tooth-
picks in cold water to cover
before using to prevent
scorching.**

BACON ROLLS

MAKES: *About 24 servings*

Bacon Wraps

Makes: *24 servings*

24 thin slices white bread, crust removed
butter or margarine, melted
Blue Cheese Mayonnaise (see page 24)
½ cup finely minced white onion
½ cup grated romano cheese
dash of cayenne
½ pound bacon

1 Position the rack in the center of the oven and preheat to 400 degrees F. Spread a work surface with wax paper.

2 Using a pastry brush, brush one side of the bread slices with the melted butter and lay them on the wax paper, butter side down. Spread the mayonnaise on the upturned sides of the bread. Spoon a narrow line of onions down the center of the bread. Sprinkle with cheese and cayenne.

3 Roll up each slice as tightly as possible and wrap a slice of bacon around each end of the bread roll. Secure both ends with toothpicks. Place on an ungreased baking sheet. Bake for 8 to 12 minutes, or until the bread is cooked through and the bacon is crisp. Serve at once.

Beer-Batter Franks

Makes: *24 servings*

SAUCE
⅓ to ½ cup dry mustard
½ cup distilled white vinegar
½ cup sugar
1 large egg yolk

FRANKFURTERS
¾ cup all-purpose flour
½ cup flat beer
1 tablespoon canola oil
1 large egg white
oil for frying
24 cocktail franks

1 To make the sauce, in a small bowl, whisk the mustard and vinegar together. Cover and let stand at room temperature for at least 8 hours or overnight.

2 In a small saucepan, combine the mustard mixture, sugar and egg yolk and whisk well. Bring to a simmer over low heat and cook until thickened to the consistency of salad dressing. Cover and chill until ready to use. (Makes about 1⅓ cups.)

3 To prepare the franks, in a small size bowl, using an electric mixer on medium speed, beat together the flour, beer and canola oil.

4 In a small bowl, using an electric mixer, beat the egg white until stiff but not dry. Fold into the beer batter.

5 Pour vegetable oil into a large skillet to a depth of ½ inch and heat over high heat until hot.

6 Using a skewer, spear each frank and dip it into the batter, letting the excess drip back into the bowl. One at a time, put the franks in the oil, removing the skewer. Cook franks for about 1 minute on each side until golden brown. Lift from the oil with tongs and drain on paper towels. Serve with the sauce on the side.

1 package (8 ounces) blue cheese, at
   room temperature
½ cup unsalted butter, at room
   temperature
1 large egg
1 teaspoon ground white pepper
1¾ cups all-purpose flour
¾ cup chopped pecans or hazelnuts

1 In a medium bowl, and using an electric mixer on medium speed, beat together the cheese and butter until smooth. Beat in the egg and pepper. Stir in the flour to make a firm dough.

2 Turn the dough out onto a lightly floured surface and form it into a log about 1½ inches in diameter. Wrap with wax paper and chill for at least 2 hours or until firm.

3 Position the rack in the center of the oven and preheat to 425 degrees F.

4 Using a sharp knife, cut the dough into ¼-inch-thick slices and place on an ungreased baking sheet, leaving about 1 inch between each slice. Bake for 8 to 10 minutes, or until lightly browned. Serve immediately.

BLUE CHEESE CRISPS

MAKES: *12 to 16 servings*

---

1 package (8 ounces) cream cheese,
   at room temperature
1 package (4 ounces) crumbled blue
   cheese, at room temperature
6 slices crisp bacon, crumbled
3 tablespoons cream, at room
   temperature
1 tablespoon prepared horseradish
1 teaspoon Worcestershire sauce
Bugles® Snack Cones

1 In a medium bowl, using an electric mixer on medium speed, beat together the cream cheese, blue cheese, bacon, cream, horseradish and Worcestershire sauce, blending until smooth.

2 Form into a ball, cover and chill at least for 2 hours, or until firm.

3 Push as many of the of the Bugle Cones (wide end into the cheese) as possible into the cheese so the cones look like spikes.

BLUE CHEESE HORN BALL

MAKES: *10 to 12 servings*

---

24 cubes (2½ inches each)
   cantaloupe
2 tablespoons lime or lemon juice
24 thin strips (3-by-1-inches each)
   smoked salmon
½ pound seedless green grapes

1 In a bowl, gently toss the cantaloupe with the lime juice to coat.

2 Wrap each melon square with a strip of salmon. Arrange on a tray and garnish with grapes. Cover with plastic wrap and chill for at least 6 hours before serving.

CANTALOUPE WITH SALMON STRIPS

MAKES: *24 servings*

CHEDDAR CHEESE WAFERS

MAKES: *60 servings*

¾ cup all-purpose flour
dash of cayenne
½ cup butter or margarine, at room temperature
2 cups shredded sharp Cheddar cheese
1½ cups Rice Krispies® cereal

1 Position the rack in the center of the oven and preheat to 350 degrees F.

2 In a small bowl, blend together the flour and cayenne.

3 In a large bowl, using an electric mixer on medium speed, beat the butter and cheese together until light and fluffy. Stir in the cereal with a spoon. Gently blend in the dry ingredients until incorporated.

4 Drop by rounded teaspoonfuls onto an ungreased baking sheet and flatten with the back of the spoon. Bake for 10 to 12 minutes, or until the edges are golden brown. Cool on wire racks.

CHEESE AND SAUSAGE SURPRISES

MAKES: *About 36 servings*

½ cup Bisquick® baking mix
½ pound ground Italian sausage
1 cup shredded sharp Cheddar cheese
1 can (6.5 ounces) water chestnuts, drained and quartered

1 Position the rack in the center of the oven and preheat to 400 degrees F.

2 In a medium bowl, combine the baking mix, sausage and cheese. Pinch off small pieces of the dough and roll into balls about the size of large olives.

3 Press a chestnut quarter into the center of each and re-form the ball. Place on an ungreased baking sheet, leaving about ½ inch between them. Bake for 12 to 15 minutes, or until golden brown. Serve immediately.

CHEESE KRISPIES

MAKES: *About 50 servings*

1¾ cups all-purpose flour
2½ cups Rice Krispies® cereal
½ teaspoon cayenne
¼ teaspoon salt
2 cups shredded Cheddar cheese, at room temperature
1 cup butter or margarine, at room temperature

1 Position the rack in the center of the oven and preheat to 350 degrees F. Lightly grease several baking sheets.

2 In a medium bowl, combine the flour, Rice Krispies, cayenne and salt.

3 In a small bowl, using an electric mixer on medium speed, beat together the cheese and butter until smooth. Add the dry ingredients and stir with a spoon to blend to make a soft dough. Pinch off small pieces of the dough and roll into balls about the size of walnuts.

4 Place on the baking sheet, leaving about 1 inch between them, and flatten with the back of a spoon or fork. Bake for 12 to 15 minutes, or until golden brown. Cool on wire racks.

2 cups shredded Cheddar or Tillamook cheese, at room temperature
1 cup butter or margarine, at room temperature
2 cups all-purpose flour
⅛ teaspoon cayenne
1 cup finely chopped salted peanuts

1 In a medium bowl, using an electric mixer on low speed, beat the cheese and butter until fluffy. Add the flour and cayenne and mix with a fork until smooth. Cover and chill for at least 4 hours.

2 Position the rack in the center of the oven and preheat the oven to 400 degrees F.

3 Pinch off small pieces of the dough and roll into balls about the size of walnuts.

4 Spread the peanuts in a shallow bowl or on a plate. Dip each ball in the nuts so that only half of each one is coated with nuts. Place, coated side up, on ungreased baking sheets, leaving about 1½ inches between them. Bake for 12 to 14 minutes, or until golden brown. Cool on wire racks and serve warm or cooled.

CHEESE-PEANUT CRISPIES

MAKES: *About 60 servings*

1 package (3 ounces) cream cheese
¼ cup powdered sugar
1 tablespoon grated orange zest
1 package (8 ounces) whole pitted dates

1 In a medium bowl, combine the cream cheese, sugar, and orange zest and mash with a fork.

2 Spoon the cream cheese into the dates, pressing it into the cavities with the back of the spoon. Cover and chill until ready to serve.

COOKING NOTE: **For variety, add a few drops of vanilla or almond extract to the cream cheese filling.**

CHEESE-STUFFED DATES

MAKES: *24 servings*

CHEESE-FLAVORED PARTY MIX

MAKES: *10 to 12 servings*

3 tablespoons butter or margarine, melted
¼ teaspoon cayenne
1 tablespoon Worcestershire sauce
½ cup grated Parmesan cheese
2 cups fried potato sticks
2 cans (2.8 ounces each) French's® fried onions
2 cups Corn Chex® cereal
1 cup miniature pretzels

1 Position the rack in the center of the oven and preheat to 250 degrees F.

2 In a 13-by-9-inch baking pan, combine the butter, cayenne, Worcestershire sauce and cheese and stir to mix.

3 In a large bowl, toss together the potato sticks, onions, cereal and pretzels. Add to the baking pan and toss to coat. Bake for 45 minutes, stirring every 15 minutes. Cool slightly in the pan before serving.

CHICKEN HORS D'OEUVRES

MAKES: *About 40 servings*

vegetable oil for frying
1 can (11 ounces) condensed Cheddar cheese soup
1 can (5 ounces) chunk white chicken, drained and flaked
1 large egg, lightly beaten
½ cup fine dry bread crumbs, plus more for coating
2 tablespoons finely chopped green bell pepper
2 tablespoons finely chopped onion
¼ teaspoon hot-pepper sauce
¼ cup sour cream
dash of crushed dried tarragon leaves

1 Pour oil into a large skillet or deep-fryer to a depth of 1½ inches and heat until hot (400 degrees F. in a deep-fryer).

2 In a large bowl, blend together ¼ cup of the soup, chicken, egg, bread crumbs, pepper, onion, and pepper sauce. Pinch off small pieces of the mixture and roll into balls about the size of large olives.

3 Gently drop a few of the balls into the oil and fry for 2 to 4 minutes or until browned. Using a slotted spoon, lift from the oil and drain on paper towels. Cover to keep warm. Continue frying the remaining balls.

4 In a small saucepan, combine the remaining soup, the sour cream and tarragon, and heat over medium heat, stirring constantly, until hot and smooth. Serve the sauce with the fried balls.

2 teaspoons canola oil
1½ cups pecan halves
1½ cups Macadamia nuts
1½ cups unsalted almonds
1½ teaspoons chili powder
½ teaspoon cayenne pepper
¾ teaspoon sea salt
½ teaspoon sugar
1 teaspoon lime juice

1 In a large skillet, warm the oil over medium heat. Add the nuts and cook, stirring frequently, for 6 to 8 minutes until browned. Transfer to a plate.

2 Combine the chili powder, cayenne, salt and sugar and cook in the same skillet over medium heat for a few seconds until fragrant. Add the nuts and toss. Sprinkle the lime juice over the nuts and continue to cook, stirring frequently, until the liquid has evaporated. Drain on paper towels and serve warm.

CHILI AND NUTS

MAKES: *About 4½ cups*

2 packages (8 ounces each) cream cheese, at room temperature
1 cup Kraft® crumbed blue cheese
1 tablespoon chopped white onion
⅛ cup finely chopped red bell pepper
⅓ cup chopped parsley for garnish
⅓ cup pimiento strips for garnish
crackers or fresh fruit slices for serving

1 In a medium bowl, using an electric mixer on low speed, beat together the cream cheese, blue cheese, onion and red pepper. Cover and chill for at least 1 hour.

2 Form into a ball, wrap in plastic wrap and chill for at least 2 hours or until firm.

3 Spread the parsley in a shallow bowl or plate and roll the cheese ball in it to cover. Lay the pimiento strips over the ball to look like leaves and serve with crackers or fruit.

CHRISTMAS CHEESE BALL

MAKES: *8 to 12 servings*

2 cups apple-cinnamon flavored cereal
2 cups pecan halves
1 cup Black Diamond® whole almonds
1 cup chow mein noodles
2 large egg whites
1 cup sugar

1 Position the rack to the center of the oven and preheat to 300 degrees F. Lightly grease a baking sheet.

2 In a large bowl, combine the cereal, pecans, almonds and noodles and toss. Spread evenly on the baking sheet.

3 Whisk together the egg whites and sugar. Drizzle over the cereal mixture and stir gently. Bake for 40 minutes, stirring frequently to break apart. Transfer to a wax paper-covered work surface and cool completely before serving.

CINNAMON CEREAL SNACK MIX

MAKES: *18 to 20 servings*

CHEESE TRIANGLES

MAKES: *About 48 servings*

1 pound grated Monterey Jack or Tillamook cheese, at room temperature
1 large egg
¼ teaspoon salt
½ pound phyllo dough sheets
¼ cup butter or margarine, melted

1 Position the rack in the center of the oven and preheat to 400 degrees F. Lightly grease several baking sheets.

2 In a medium bowl, combine the cheese, egg and salt.

3 Unroll the phyllo onto a work surface. Remove 1 sheet and cover the remainder with wax paper and a damp (not wet) towel. Brush the phyllo sheet with melted butter, top with a second sheet and brush it with butter. Cut the sheets into lengthwise strips, about 2 inches wide and about 5 inches long. Spoon 1 tablespoon of the mixture onto one end of the phyllo strip. Fold the corner over to form a triangle and continue folding, as if folding a flag, end over end until you are left with a triangular bundle. Brush the protruding point of dough with butter and tuck into the fold of the triangle to seal. Repeat with remaining phyllo and filling.

4 Place the triangles on baking sheets, leaving about 1 inch between them, and brush with the remaining butter. Bake for 12 to 15 minutes, or until a golden brown and crispy. Serve warm.

COCKTAIL CHEESE BALLS

MAKES: *About 90 balls*

½ cup butter or margarine, at room temperature
½ pound grated Cheddar or Tillamook cheese
1 cup all-purpose flour
1 package Lipton's® dried onion soup mix
¼ cup chopped parsley

1 Position the rack in the center of the oven and preheat to 400 degrees F.

2 In a small bowl, using an electric mixer on medium speed, beat the butter and cheese until smooth. Add the flour, soup mix, and parsley and beat until well mixed.

3 Pinch off pieces of the mixture and roll into balls about the size of large olives.

4 Place the balls on ungreased baking sheets, leaving about 1 inch between them, and bake for 6 to 8 minutes, or until golden brown. Serve hot or cooled.

2 tablespoons butter or margarine
1 large red onion, chopped
⅔ cup apple jelly
⅔ cup firmly packed brown sugar
2 pounds cocktail-size smoked
   sausages
3 apples, cored, peeled and cut into
   wedges
1 tablespoon cornstarch
2 tablespoons warm water

1 In a large skillet, heat the butter over medium-high heat and sauté the onion for about 5 minutes until golden-brown. Add the jelly and brown sugar and stir thoroughly. Add the sausages,
reduce the heat to medium-low, cover and cook for about 20 minutes, stirring occasionally, or until the mixture begins to thicken.

2 Add the apples, and cook, partially covered, for about 10 minutes longer, or until the apples are tender. Combine the cornstarch and warm water and add to the apples, stirring constantly. Cook for 2 to 3 minutes longer, or until thickened. Serve in a chafing dish with cocktail forks or toothpicks on the side.

COCKTAIL SAUSAGE-AND-APPLE APPETIZERS

MAKES: *About 30 servings*

---

4 slices salami
3 tablespoons Beer-and-Cheese
   Spread (recipe follows)
16 small pimiento-stuffed olives

Lay 2 slices of salami on a work surface and spoon half of the spread onto each slice in an even
layer. Lay 2 slices of salami on top of the spread and cut the stacks into quarters. Thread an olive onto a toothpick and insert into the center of each wedge.

COOKED SALAMI WEDGES

MAKES: *16 appetizers*

BEER-AND-CHEESE SPREAD

MAKES: *About 4 cups*

1 pound sharp Cheddar cheese,
   grated
1 pound Swiss Cheese, grated
1½ teaspoons dry mustard
1 small clove garlic, minced
½ teaspoon steak sauce
1 cup beer, at room temperature

In a small bowl, combine the ingredients and blend until smooth and a spreading consistency. Cover and chill for at least 2 hours.

CORN DOGS ON A STICK

MAKES: *10 servings*

vegetable oil for frying
1 cup Corn Bread Mix (recipe follows)
⅓ cup all-purpose flour
⅓ cup water
1 large egg
½ teaspoon dry mustard
¼ teaspoon paprika
10 beef or chicken frankfurters

1 Pour the oil into a heavy skillet or deep-fat fryer to a depth of 2 inches and heat over medium-high heat until hot (365 degrees F. in a deep-fat fryer).

2 In a medium bowl, combine the corn bread mix, flour, water, egg, mustard and paprika and stir to make a smooth, heavy batter.

3 Thoroughly wash and dry the frankfurters and thread each one on a heavy wooden skewer, so that the skewer goes in one end of the frankfurter and out the other. Dip into the batter, allowing the excess to drip back into the bowl. Put the frankfurters into the hot oil, holding them at an angle, and fry for 3 to 4 minutes, turning once, until brown. Drain on paper towels and serve hot or cool.

COOKING NOTE: **Popsicle sticks also work well for this recipe. Soak the skewers in cold water to cover for 10 to 20 minutes before using to prevent scorching.**

CORN BREAD MIX

MAKES: *12 cups*

4 cups all-purpose flour
4 cups yellow cornmeal
1¾ cups nonfat dry milk powder
⅓ cup baking powder
2 teaspoons salt
1¾ cups vegetable shortening

In a bowl, combine the flour, cornmeal, dry milk, baking powder and salt. Using a pastry blender or two knives, cut the vegetable shortening into the dry ingredients until the mixture resembles coarse crumbs. Transfer to an airtight container and store in the refrigerator for up to 3 months.

COOKING NOTE: **Baking powder has a shelf life. If you find the corn bread isn't rising as it should, add ½ teaspoon of fresh baking powder to the mix.**

CRABMEAT-AND-BACON BALLS

MAKES: *About 24 balls*

1 pound fresh crabmeat
¼ teaspoon dry mustard
¼ cup dry sherry
1 cup dry bread crumbs
12 slices lean bacon, halved
3 tablespoons prepared mustard

1 Position the broiler rack 3 inches from the heat source and preheat the broiler.

2 In a large bowl, combine the crabmeat, mustard, sherry and bread crumbs and blend with a fork.

3 Pinch off pieces of the mixture and form into balls about the size of walnuts. Wrap each ball in half a slice of bacon and secure with a toothpick. Broil for about 10 minutes, turning once, until the bacon is crisp. Drain and serve at once or keep warm in a 200 degree F. oven.

COOKING NOTE: **Soak the toothpicks in cold water to cover for 10 to 20 minutes before using to prevent scorching.**

1 pound chocolate almond bark or white chocolate, chopped
1 jar (6 ounces) creamy peanut butter
1 box (9.5 ounces) thin oat crackers

1 In the top of a double boiler, melt the almond bark over low heat, stirring until smooth.

2 Spread the peanut butter evenly over half of the crackers and top with a second cracker. One at a time, dip half of each cracker sandwich into the melted chocolate. Cool of a wax-paper-lined tray. When cool and the chocolate is set, dip the other half. (Keep the chocolate warm over hot water or re-heat if necessary.) Cool before serving.

COOKING NOTE: For variation, dip half of each sandwich in white chocolate and the other half in dark chocolate.

CRACKER-ATTACK SNACKS

MAKES: *10 to 12 servings*

½ cup butter or margarine
1 package (14 ounces) oyster crackers
garlic salt to taste
½ cup grated Parmesan or romano cheese

1 In a large saucepan, melt the butter over low heat. Add the crackers, stirring until the butter is completely absorbed.

2 Remove from the heat, and sprinkle with the garlic salt and cheese, blending until well coated. Serve warm or cool.

CRACKER SNACK

MAKES: *About 3 cups*

3 cups Cheeze-It® crackers
3 cups oyster crackers
2 cups pretzel sticks
2 cups Triscuit® crackers
2 packages (1 ounce each) Hidden Valley Ranch Dressing® mix
½ teaspoon crushed dried oregano
½ cup canola oil

1 In a large bowl, combine the crackers, pretzels and Triscuits. Sprinkle with the dressing mix and toss to coat.

2 In a cup, whisk together the oregano and oil. Drizzle over the dry ingredients and toss. Serve immediately or store in an air-tight container.

CRACKER SNACK MIX

MAKES: *About 10 cups*

CRISP CHEESE WAFERS

MAKES: 3½ to 4 dozen

2 cups shredded sharp Cheddar or
   Colby cheese
⅓ cup butter or margarine, at room
   temperature
1 teaspoon Worcestershire sauce
¼ teaspoon salt
1 cup all-purpose flour

1 In a large bowl, and using an
electric mixer on low speed, beat
together the cheese, butter,
Worcestershire sauce and salt.

2 Add the flour and blend with a
fork to make a stiff dough. Form
into 2 logs, each about 1½ inches

in diameter. Wrap in wax paper
and chill for 8 hours or
overnight.

3 Position the rack in the center
of the oven and preheat to 375
degrees F. Lightly grease two
baking sheets.

4 Slice the logs into ¼-inch slices
and place on the baking sheet,
leaving about ½ inch between
them. Bake for 10 to 12 minutes,
or until a lightly browned. Cool
on wire racks.

CROUTON PARTY SNACKS

MAKES: 10 to 12 servings

½ cup butter or margarine
2 tablespoons Worcestershire sauce
4 cups herb-seasoned croutons
1 cup salted cocktail peanuts
1 cup thin pretzel sticks

1 Position the rack in the center
of the oven and preheat to 300
degrees F.

2 In a small saucepan, melt the
butter over low heat. Remove
from the heat and stir in the
Worcestershire sauce.

3 In large bowl, combine the
croutons, peanuts and pretzels
and toss to mix. Drizzle with the
butter and toss again to coat.
Transfer to a jelly-roll pan or
other shallow pan and spread
evenly. Bake for 12 to 15 minutes,
stirring occasionally, or until
crisped and lightly browned.
Cool and serve immediately or
store in an airtight container.

DEVILED EGGS WITH OLIVES

MAKES: 22 servings

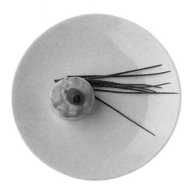

11 large hard-cooked eggs
¼ cup Kraft® real mayonnaise
4 teaspoons Dijon mustard
1 tablespoon prepared horseradish
½ cup chopped ripe olives
stuffed Spanish olives, for garnish

1 Cut a very small piece from
both ends of the egg so they will
sit upright. Using a crinkle or
wavy cutter, make a cut around
the middle (equator) of the egg.
Remove the yolk and reserve the
white halves.

2 In a medium bowl, mash the
egg yolk, egg white trimmings,
mayonnaise, mustard and horseradish until blended. Stir in the
ripe olives. Using a pastry bag
fitted with a star tip, press the
mixture into the egg whites. Garnish each with a stuffed olive. Set
the eggs on a platter and serve.

COOKING NOTE: The eggs can be
cut with a small knife, using a
zigzag motion.

2 cups corn oil
6 large white onions, finely chopped
1 can (17 ounces) stewed tomatoes
1 6-inch stalk celery, chopped finely
1 finely chopped green bell pepper
2 small cloves garlic, minced
dash of cayenne or ground red
   pepper
salt and ground black pepper to
   taste
2 cups long-grain rice
4 cups water
1 cup tomato sauce
¼ cup lemon juice
1 jar (16 ounces) grape leaves, rinsed
   and drained
pinch of garlic salt

1 In a large skillet, heat the oil over medium heat and sauté the onion for 5 to 6 minutes until transparent. Stir in the tomatoes, celery, green pepper, garlic and cayenne. Season to taste with salt and pepper.

2 Reduce the heat to medium-low and cook, stirring frequently, for 5 minutes. Add the rice, 1 cup of water, ½ cup of tomato sauce, and 1 tablespoon of lemon juice. Cover and simmer for 20 to 25 minutes, until the water is absorbed. Transfer to a bowl, cover and chill for 8 hours or overnight.

3 On a work surface, arrange the grape leaves vein-side up. Spoon about a tablespoon of filling on each leaf. Roll up tight, folding in the edges as you go. Place the leaves in a large saucepan, packing tightly, and weight with a heavy plate. (The plate is very important; it keeps the dolmas from unrolling during cooking.) Add the remaining 3 cups of water, ½ cup of tomato sauce, 3 tablespoons of lemon juice and the garlic salt. Simmer over medium-low heat for about 30 minutes until most of the liquid has been absorbed.

4 Transfer the dolmas to a platter or plate and chill for 8 hours or overnight. Serve cold.

COOKING NOTE: To prevent sticking during cooking, diffuse the heat under the dolmas by setting the saucepan in a heavy frying pan or using a flame-tamer or heat-proof trivet.

DOLMAS
MAKES: *100 servings*

8 crisp slices bacon, crumbled
1 tablespoon grated white onion
1½ cups grated Cheddar cheese
½ cup chopped pecans
½ cup Kraft® mayonnaise
pecan halves
crackers for serving

1 In a medium bowl, combine the bacon, onion, cheese, chopped pecans and mayonnaise and stir to mix.

2 With lightly floured hands, form into a ball. Wrap in plastic wrap and chill for at least 4 hours until firm.

3 Press the pecan halves into the ball in a decorative design. Serve with crackers.

EASY CHEESE BALL
MAKES: *8 servings*

FILBERT SLICES

MAKES: *16 servings*

4 slices pumpernickel bread
½ cup shredded sharp Cheddar or
    Wisconsin brick cheese
½ cup chopped filberts

1 Position the broiler rack 4 inches from the heat source and preheat the broiler.

2 Lay the bread slices on a broiler tray and top with cheese and nuts. Broil for 3 to 4 minutes or until the cheese melts. Quarter each bread slice and serve immediately.

FRUIT PARTY MIX

MAKES: *6 servings*

2 cups roasted peanuts
1 cup raisins
1 cup chopped dried apricots
½ cup shredded coconut
1 large egg white
2 tablespoons water
⅔ cup sugar
1 teaspoon ground cinnamon
1 teaspoon ground allspice
½ teaspoon ground ginger
½ teaspoon ground nutmeg

1 Position the rack in the center of the oven and preheat to 275 degrees F. Lightly grease a jelly-roll pan.

2 In a large bowl, combine the peanuts, raisins, apricots, and coconut and toss.

3 In a bowl, whisk the egg white with the water until foamy. Add the sugar, cinnamon, allspice, ginger and nutmeg and beat until blended. Pour over the peanut mixture and toss to coat.

4 Spread evenly in the pan and bake for 50 to 55 minutes, stirring frequently, until the egg white coating solidifies and the nuts are lightly browned. Set the pan on a wire rack and let the mixture cool. Serve when cool or store in an airtight container.

FRUITY SNACK BARS

MAKES: *24 servings*

¾ cup packed dark-brown sugar
½ cup honey
1½ cups creamy peanut butter
1 package (6 ounces) mixed dried
    fruit bits
5 cups Wheaties® cereal

1 In a large saucepan, combine the brown sugar and honey and bring to a boil over medium heat. Remove from the heat and add the peanut butter, stirring until smooth.

2 Reserve ⅓ cup of the fruit bits and stir the remaining bits into the peanut butter. Add the cereal and stir until mixed. Spoon into a 9-inch square pan and press to cover the pan in an even layer. Sprinkle the reserved fruit on top and lay a piece of wax paper directly on the fruit. Press to compact. Chill for at least 2 hours. Peel off the paper and chill for at least 2 hours longer. Cut into bars to serve.

1 pound large mushrooms, cleaned, stems removed and reserved
¼ cup Italian salad dressing
1 cup fine fresh bread crumbs
¼ cup grated romano or Parmesan cheese
1 tablespoon finely chopped cilantro (Chinese parsley)

1 Position the rack in the center of the oven and preheat to 350 degrees F. Lightly grease a 13-by-9-inch baking dish.

2 Chop the mushroom stems finely and transfer to a bowl. Add the salad dressing, bread crumbs, cheese and cilantro and stir to mix. Spoon the filling into the mushroom caps, mounding the filling.

3 Place in the baking dish, add water to a depth of ¼ inch, and bake for 18 to 20 minutes, or until the mushrooms are tender.

FUNGO ITALIANO

MAKES: *About 24 servings*

6 large hard-cooked eggs, chopped
1 tablespoon minced onion or chives
1 cup ground cooked ham
pinch of black pepper
3 tablespoons bourbon
½ cup ground walnuts or pecans

1 In a medium bowl, combine the eggs, onion, ham, pepper and bourbon and mash with a fork until smooth. Pinch off pieces of the mixture and roll into balls about the size of large olives.

2 Spread the nuts in a shallow bowl or a plate. Roll the balls in the nuts to coat. Insert a toothpick into each ball, cover and chill until serving.

HAM-AND-BOURBON BALLS

MAKES: *About 36 appetizers*

1½ cups finely chopped cooked smoked ham
1 cup sour cream or plain yogurt
¼ cup shredded Swiss or Gouda cheese
¼ cup crushed saltine crackers
2 tablespoons melted butter or margarine
1 teaspoon caraway seeds
6 large eggs

1 Position the rack in the center of the oven and preheat to 375 degrees F. Lightly grease an 8-inch-square baking pan.

2 In a medium bowl, combine ham, sour cream, cheese, cracker crumbs, butter, and caraway seeds and mix until blended.

3 In a small bowl, using an electric mixer on high speed, beat the eggs until thick and light colored. Fold the eggs into the ham mixture and pour into the pan. Bake for 15 to 17 minutes, or until browned. Cut into bite-sized squares and serve hot.

HAM-AND-CHEESE SQUARES

MAKES: *12 to 16 servings*

HAM-WRAPPED FRUIT

MAKES: *About 32 servings*

1 package (3 ounces) cream cheese, at room temperature
1 tablespoon orange marmalade
⅓ pound thinly sliced cooked ham, cut into strips, each about 1 inch wide and 4 inches long
2 papayas, peeled, seeded, and cut into eighths
2 kiwi fruit, peeled and sliced

1 In a small bowl, using an electric mixer on medium speed, beat together the cream cheese and marmalade until smooth.

2 Spread the mixture on the ham strips. Place a piece of fruit (either papaya or kiwi) on each ham strip, wrap the ham around the fruit, and secure with a toothpick. Cover with wax paper and chill for at least 2 hours. Serve chilled

HAM-WRAPPED OYSTERS

MAKES: *24 servings*

3 tablespoons prepared horseradish
½ pound thinly sliced ham, cut into strips, each about ¼ inch wide and 3 inches long
2 dozen fresh oysters, shucked
3 tablespoons melted butter or margarine
1 tablespoon lemon juice
¼ teaspoon garlic powder

1 Position the broiler rack 6 inches from the heat source and preheat.

2 Spread the horseradish on the ham strips. Place 1 oyster on each strip and wrap the ham around it, securing each with a toothpick. Arrange on the broiler pan.

3 In a small cup, combine the butter, lemon juice and garlic powder and mix with a fork. Brush the ham rolls with this mixture. Broil for 10 to 15 minutes, or until the oysters are warmed through, brushing occasionally with the remaining lemon-butter. Serve immediately.

COOKING NOTE: **Soak the toothpicks for 10 to 20 minutes in cold water to cover before using to prevent scorching.**

HELP-YOURSELF HAM BALL

MAKES: *1 ball*

2 cans (4 ounces each) deviled ham
3 tablespoons chopped pimiento-stuffed green olives
1 tablespoon prepared brown mustard
Tabasco sauce to taste
1 package (3 ounces) cream cheese, at room temperature
2 teaspoons milk
parsley for garnish
crackers for serving

1 In a medium bowl, combine the ham, olives and mustard and season to taste with Tabasco. Using your hands, form the mixture into a large ball. Cover with plastic wrap and chill for at least 2 hours.

2 In a small bowl, using an electric mixer on medium speed, beat together the cream cheese and milk. Spread over the ball to coat. Cover and chill again until firm. Garnish with parsley and serve with crackers.

COOKING NOTE: **For festive occasions, press whole watercress sprigs over the outside of the ball.**

½ cup butter or margarine
1 cup creamy peanut butter
1½ cups carob chips
1 cup wheat germ
1 cup shredded coconut
1 cup chopped walnuts
½ cup sesame seeds
½ cup sunflower seeds

1 In a small saucepan melt the butter, peanut butter and carob chips over medium heat, stirring constantly.

2 In a large bowl, combine the wheat germ, coconut, walnuts, sesame seeds and sunflower seeds and toss. Drizzle the butter over this mixture and toss to coat. Press into a 13-by-9-inch baking pan, cover with wax paper and press to compress. Chill until firm.

3 Using a sharp knife cut into bars. Wrap each bar in wax paper until ready to eat.

HIGH-PROTEIN SQUARES

MAKES: *About 24 servings*

---

2 tablespoons butter or margarine
½ cup chunky peanut butter
⅓ cup honey
½ cup nonfat dry milk powder
1 teaspoon vanilla extract
2½ cups Cheerios®

1 Liberally butter an 8-inch square baking pan.

2 In a medium bowl, combine the peanut butter and honey and heat, stirring, over medium heat

until smooth and liquefied. Remove from the heat, add the dry milk and vanilla and stir until blended. Add the cereal and fold until all pieces are coated.

3 Transfer to the pan and spread evenly. Cover with wax paper and press the paper against the cereal mixture. Set aside until cool. Cut into squares to serve.

HIKERS' SQUARES

MAKES: *About 16 servings*

---

3 tablespoons butter or margarine, melted
½ teaspoon ground cinnamon
4 cups Nabisco® Frosted Shredded Wheat, loosely crumbled
1 cup miniature pretzels
½ cup honey-roasted mixed nuts
½ cups raisins

1 Position the rack in the center of the oven and preheat to 250 degrees F.

2 In a cup, combine the butter and cinnamon and whisk well.

3 In a large bowl, combine the cereal, pretzels, nuts and raisins. Drizzle the butter over the mixture, tossing until well coated. Spread in a 15½-by-10-by-½-inch jelly-roll pan and bake for 20 minutes. Stir and bake for 5 minutes longer. Remove from the oven. Stir several times during cooling.

CINNAMON-COATED FROSTED WHEAT SNACKS

MAKES: *10 to 12 servings*

HORS D'OEUVRE CREAM PUFFS

MAKES: *48 servings*

½ cup all-purpose flour
¼ teaspoon salt
¼ cup butter or margarine
½ cup water
2 large eggs
¼ cup finely grated Edam cheese, at room temperature
2½ cups Plum-and-Cheese Filling (recipe follows)

1 Position the rack in the center of the oven and preheat to 450 degrees F. Lightly grease 2 baking sheets.

2 In a small bowl, combine the flour and salt and whisk to mix.

3 In a medium saucepan, combine the butter and water and cook over high heat until the butter melts. Reduce the heat to low and add the flour mixture all at once. Stir until smooth and very thick.

4 Remove from the heat, add 1 egg and stir until incorporated. Stir in the cheese, blending until smooth. Add the remaining egg and stir to form a soft dough.

5 Drop the dough by teaspoonfuls onto the baking sheet, leaving about 1 inch between each puff, and bake for 8 minutes. Reduce the heat to 400 degrees F. and bake for about 8 minutes longer, or until the puffs are golden brown. Cool on a wire rack.

6 When cool, cut each puff in half, without making a complete cut but leaving the 2 halves attached. Fill with generous teaspoons of filling and serve.

PLUM-AND-CHEESE FILLING

MAKES: *About 3½ cups*

2½ cups pitted and coarsely chopped fresh plums
2½ teaspoons lemon juice
2½ packages (8 ounces each) cream cheese, at room temperature, cut into pieces
¾ cup chopped pecans

1 In a saucepan, cook the plums, lemon juice and enough water cover over low heat for 5 to 6 minutes, or until the plums are soft.

2 Strain and transfer the plums to the container of a blender or food processor. Process on low speed for 5 to 6 seconds. Add the cream cheese and process on low speed for 4 to 5 seconds longer or until smooth. (If using a blender, this may have to be done in batches.) Transfer to a small bowl and stir in the pecans. Cover and chill for at least 3 hours.

COOKING NOTE: When using this filling on an open-face sandwich, sprinkle a few additional nuts over the spread.

4 cups shredded Cheddar or Colby cheese
4 large eggs, lightly beaten
1 teaspoon minced shallot
4 jalapeño peppers, seeded and chopped

1 Position the rack in the center of the oven and preheat to 350 degrees F.

2 In a medium bowl, combine the cheese, eggs, shallot, and peppers and use a fork to blend. Spread evenly in an 8-inch-square baking pan and bake for 28 to 30 minutes, or until the top is golden brown. Cool on a wire rack for 5 minutes before cutting into 1-inch squares.

JALAPEÑO CHEESE SQUARES

MAKES: *64 squares*

1 package (3 ounces) cream cheese, at room temperature
2 tablespoons Kraft® mayonnaise
1 cup ground cooked chicken
1 cup finely ground almonds
1 tablespoon chopped chutney
1 tablespoon curry powder
½ cup shredded sweetened coconut

1 In a small bowl, combine the cream cheese and mayonnaise and blend. Add the chicken, almonds, chutney and curry powder and blend well.

2 Pinch off small pieces of the mixture and form into balls about the size of walnuts.

3 Spread the coconut in a shallow bowl or plate. Roll the balls in the coconut to coat, cover, and chill until ready to serve.

JAMAICAN CHEESE BALLS

MAKES: *48 to 60 servings*

MATZO BALLS

MAKES: *About 12 servings*

6 large eggs, well beaten
¾ cup water
pinch of salt
3 tablespoons chicken fat, melted
    and cooled to room temperature
3 cups matzo meal

1 In a medium bowl, combine the eggs, water, salt, chicken fat and matzo meal and mix well. Cover and chill for at least 2 hours.

2 Pinch off small pieces of the dough and shape into balls about the size of walnuts.

3 In a medium saucepan, bring 4 cups of water to a boil and cook the balls, covered, for about 15 minutes, or until cooked thorough. Drain and serve.

MICROWAVE SNACK KABOBS

MAKES: *8 to 10 servings*

1 can (13 ounces) chunk pineapple,
    drained, juice reserved
1 tablespoon brown sugar
2 tablespoons low-sodium soy sauce
1 tablespoon apple cider vinegar
1 can (12 ounces) luncheon meat, cut
    into 36 pieces

1 In a small bowl, combine the reserved pineapple juice, brown sugar, soy sauce and vinegar and stir to blend.

2 Using a pastry brush, brush each piece of meat and each piece of pineapple with the brown sugar mixture. Thread a piece of meat and a chunk of pineapple on a toothpick and place on a microwave-safe dish.

3 When 12 toothpicks are filled, heat on high (100 percent) power for 1 to 2 minutes until heated through. Set aside and cover to keep warm. Continue with the remaining ingredients, cooking the kabobs in 2 more batches. Serve hot.

COOKING NOTE: **Luncheon meat may be pork, chicken, veal, or turkey. Spam® is one of the most popular luncheon meats, but all work well in this recipe.**

MUSHROOMS ON TOAST

MAKES: *About 6 servings*

1 jar (4.5 ounces) whole mushrooms,
    drained
¼ cup plus 2 to 3 tablespoons butter
    or margarine, at room
    temperature
1 tablespoon lemon juice
2 tablespoons minced parsley
dash of white pepper
3 slices white bread, lightly toasted
    and cut into 1-inch squares
sprigs of parsley or watercress for
    garnish

1 In a large skillet, melt ¼ cup of butter over medium heat. Add the mushrooms, lemon juice, parsley and white pepper to taste and cook, stirring gently and constantly, until heated through. Transfer to a bowl and set aside.

2 In the same skillet, melt the remaining butter and sauté the toast for 4 to 5 minutes until crisp. Remove from the heat. Set a mushroom on each toast square and spear each with a toothpick. Garnish with parsley or watercress and serve.

¼ cup butter or margarine
¾ pounds fresh mushrooms, cleaned and chopped
1 clove garlic, minced
½ teaspoon dried thyme
⅛ teaspoon ground white pepper
1 tablespoon Amaretto Liquor
1¼ cups toasted almonds, finely ground
2 tablespoons unsalted butter, at room temperature
sliced green onions for garnish
crackers, bread, or vegetable sticks for serving

1 Line a 6½-by-4-by-2½-inch loaf pan with wax paper, allowing enough overhang on both ends so that the paper can be folded over and meets in the center.

2 In a large skillet, heat the butter over medium heat and sauté the mushrooms and garlic for 5 to 6 minutes until the mushrooms release their liquid and most of the liquid evaporates. Stir in the thyme, pepper and Amaretto, reduce the heat and simmer until the mushrooms are dry.

3 Transfer to the container of a blender and process on medium speed for 15 to 20 seconds. Add 1 cup of the almonds and the unsalted butter and process until smooth. Pour into a small bowl and using a spoon, fold in the remaining ¼ cup of almonds. Transfer to the prepared pan, spread evenly and fold the ends of the paper over to meet in the center. Press to compress and weight with a heavy can or another weight. Chill for at least 2 hours or until ready to serve.

4 Invert onto a serving plate or platter, peel off the paper, garnish with green onions and serve with crackers, bread or vegetable sticks.

Mushroom Pâté with Toasted Almonds

MAKES: *About 1½ cups*

½ pound lean ground beef
½ pound chorizo sausage, casing removed and crumbled
1 large red onion, chopped finely
Tabasco sauce to taste
1 can (16 ounces) Old El Paso® refried beans
1 can (4 ounces) whole green chiles, chopped finely
3 cups shredded Colby or Monterey Jack cheese
¾ cup Old El Paso® taco sauce
chopped green onions for garnish
sour cream for serving
8 cups tortilla chips for serving

1 Position the rack in the center of the oven and preheat to 400 degrees F. Lightly grease a 15½-by-10½-inch baking dish.

2 In a medium skillet, cook the beef and sausage over medium heat for 6 to 8 minutes until no longer pink. Add the onion, raise the heat to high, and cook, stirring, for 4 to 5 minutes until the onion is translucent. Remove from the heat, pour off the fat and add the Tabasco. Stir well.

3 Spread the beans in the baking dish, top with the meat and chiles, and sprinkle with cheese to cover completely. Drizzle the taco sauce over the cheese and bake for 20 to 25 minutes, or until the cheese melts and starts to brown. Garnish with green onions and serve with sour cream and tortilla chips.

Nacho Dipping Dish

MAKES: *About 24 servings*

NUT-STUFFED CELERY

MAKES: *About 24 servings*

1 package (3 ounces) cream cheese, at room temperature
2 teaspoons onion juice
¼ teaspoon curry powder
¼ cup finely chopped almonds
1 to 1½ tablespoons heavy cream
9 to 10 celery stalks, cut into 4-inch sticks
¼ cup chopped peanuts

1 In a medium bowl, combine the cheese, onion juice, curry powder and almonds and enough cream for a thick spreadable consistency.

2 Spoon the filling into the celery sticks and smooth to fill the cavity.

3 Spread the peanuts in a shallow bowl or plate. Invert the celery sticks so that nuts adhere to the cream cheese filling. Arrange cheese-side up on a platter, cover with wax paper and chill until ready to serve.

OLIVE-STUFFED CHEESE BALLS

MAKES: *About 24 servings*

1 cup Bisquick® baking mix
1 cup shredded sharp Cheddar or Wisconsin Brick cheese
3 tablespoons milk
2 tablespoons butter or margarine, melted
½ teaspoon crushed dried thyme
½ teaspoon crushed dried oregano leaves
24 large pimiento-stuffed green olives, drained

1 Position the rack in the center of the oven and preheat to 400 degrees F. Lightly grease a baking sheet.

2 In a medium bowl, combine the baking mix, cheese, milk, butter, thyme and oregano and blend until smooth. Pinch off teaspoons of the dough and roll into balls about the size of large walnuts. Push an olive into each ball, pulling the dough around the olive. Place the balls on the prepared baking sheet, leaving about 1 inch between them, and bake for 10 to 12 minutes, or until lightly browned. Serve warm.

ONION TOASTS

MAKES: *About 32 servings*

½ cup Kraft® mayonnaise
2 tablespoons grated Parmesan or romano cheese
2 teaspoons grated green onion
1 teaspoon Dijon mustard
2 tablespoons butter or margarine
8 slices pumpernickel bread, quartered

1 Position the broiler rack 4 inches from the heat source and preheat the broiler.

2 In a small bowl, combine the mayonnaise, cheese, onion and mustard and blend well.

3 In a large skillet, melt the butter over medium-high heat and cook the bread for about 2 minutes until crisp on one side (do not turn over). Spread the cheese mixture on the soft (uncooked) side of the bread and arrange on the broiler tray. Broil for 3 to 4 minutes, or until the mixture browns. Quarter each slice of bread and serve hot.

1 package (3 ounces) cream cheese, at room temperature
1 package (3 ounces) smoked ham slices (10 slices)
10 slender green onions, washed and trimmed

Spread the cheese to the very edge of each slice of ham. Lay an onion at one end and roll the ham around the onion into a tight cylinder. Secure with a toothpick, if necessary. Repeat with the remaining ingredients to make 10 rolls. Cover and chill until ready to serve. Remove the toothpicks before serving.

ONION-STUFFED HAM ROLL

MAKES: *10 servings*

---

4 whole graham crackers, crushed
¼ cup honey
1 cup creamy peanut butter
½ cup nonfat dry milk powder

1 Spread the cracker crumbs in a shallow bowl or plate.
2 In a small bowl, combine the honey, peanut butter, and dry milk and blend until mixed.

Break off small pieces of the mixture and form into balls the size of walnuts. Roll each ball in the cracker crumbs to coat and place on a baking sheet. Cover and chill for at least 4 hours, or until firm.

PEANUTTY SNACK BALLS

MAKES: *15 to 20 balls*

PAKORAS

MAKES: *8 servings*

1 cup dried yellow split peas
vegetable oil for frying
½ cup all-purpose flour
1 teaspoon curry powder
⅛ teaspoon ground allspice
¼ teaspoon salt
⅛ teaspoon Tabasco sauce
½ cup finely chopped white onion
½ cup finely chopped green bell
    pepper
½ cup finely chopped celery
1 tablespoon crushed dried mint
fine dry bread crumbs
chutney for serving

1 Bring a saucepan of water to a boil over high heat and add the peas. Return to a boil, reduce the heat and simmer, partially covered, for about 2 hours until tender. Drain and set aside to cool.

2 Heat the oil in a heavy saucepan or deep-fat fryer until hot (370 degrees F. in the deep-fat fryer).

3 Meanwhile, in a small bowl, combine the flour, curry powder, allspice and salt. Stir into the peas. Add the Tabasco sauce, onion, pepper, celery and mint and stir until incorporated.

4 Spread the bread crumbs in a shallow bowl or plate. Drop teaspoons of the pea mixture into the crumbs and roll to coat.

5 Fry each ball for 2 to 3 minutes, or until a golden brown on all sides. Serve hot with chutney on the side.

COOKING NOTE: **Do not overcrowd the balls in the hot oil.**

PARTY CRUNCH

MAKES: *About 10 cups*

½ cup butter or margarine
1½ teaspoons McCormick® Italian
    seasoning
8 cups Quaker® Oat Square cereal
1½ cups thin pretzel sticks
1½ cups salted peanuts
½ cup grated Parmesan or romano
    cheese

1 Position the rack in the center of the oven and preheat to 325 degrees F. Put the butter in a 13-by-9-inch baking pan and let it melt in the oven as it preheats.

2 Remove the pan from the oven and add the Italian seasoning to the melted butter. Add the cereal, pretzels and peanuts and stir and toss until well coated.

3 Sprinkle with cheese, stir again, and bake for about 20 minutes, stirring occasionally during baking, until the cheese browns lightly. Cool completely before serving.

COOKING NOTE: **This can be stored in large plastic bags secured with a twist tie. Margarine will keep better than butter, so if you plan to make this ahead of time, use margarine.**

2 cups toasted oat cereal
2 cups bite-size crispy wheat
squares
2 cups bite-size crispy rice squares
2 cups pretzel sticks
2 cups mixed nuts
⅔ cup Squeeze Parkay® margarine
1 teaspoon Worcestershire sauce
½ teaspoon garlic salt

1 Position the rack in the center of the oven and preheat to 250 degrees F.

2 In a large bowl, combine the oat cereal, wheat squares, rice squares, pretzels and mixed nuts and toss to mix.

2 In a small bowl, combine the margarine, Worcestershire sauce and garlic salt and blend with a fork. Pour over the cereal mix and toss lightly to coat. Spread the mix evenly in an ungreased 15½-by-10½-inch jelly-roll pan and bake for about 1 hour, stirring occasionally, until lightly browned. Serve at once.

COOKING NOTE: Raisins and peanuts can be used in place of the oat cereal and mixed nuts. Although this tastes best when served warm, it can be stored in large plastic bags secured with twist ties.

PARTY MIX
MAKES: *10 cups*

½ cup butter or margarine
¼ cup low-sodium soy sauce
2 cups blanched Black Diamond®
whole almonds
4 cups salted Spanish (small)
peanuts
2 cups golden raisins
1 can (3 ounces) chow mien noodles
¼ cup toasted sesame seeds
1 can (3½ ounces) shredded
sweetened coconut

1 Position the rack in the center of the oven and preheat to 375 degrees F.

2 In a large skillet, melt the butter on medium-low heat. Add the soy sauce and almonds and cook

for about 3 minutes, stirring continually. Add the peanuts, raisins, noodles and sesame seeds, reduce the heat to low and cook, tossing frequently, for about 10 minutes, or until the noodles have browned.

3 Remove from the heat, fold in the coconut and spread evenly in an 18-by-13-inch baking pan. Bake for 10 minutes until lightly browned. Scrape onto paper towels and cool. Serve at once or store in an airtight container.

PARTY SNACK MIX
MAKES: *About 10 cups*

PEANUT BUTTER-AND-CHEESE TRIANGLES

MAKES: *About 24 servings*

½ cup light corn syrup
2 tablespoons nonfat dry milk powder
½ cup crunchy peanut butter
3 cups Kellogg® Rice Krispies cereal
2 packages (3 ounces) cream cheese, at room temperature
2 cups shredded Cheddar or Tillamook cheese
2 tablespoons butter or margarine, at room temperature

1 Line a 13-by-9-inch baking pan with wax paper and set aside.

2 In a medium saucepan, combine the corn syrup and milk and cook, stirring continuously, until the mixture begins to boil. Remove from the heat and stir in the peanut butter, a tablespoon at a time.

3 Add the Rice Krispies and stir until coated. Spread evenly in the prepared baking pan, cover and chill for at least 2 hours or until firm.

4 In a medium bowl, and using an electric mixer on medium speed, beat the cream cheese, shredded cheese and butter together until smooth.

5 Invert the chilled mixture on a work surface and peel off the wax paper. Cut in half to make 2 rectangles.

6 Reserve ⅓ cup of the cheese mixture and spread the remaining on 1 half. Top with the remaining half, pressing lightly to seal. Cover with wax paper and chill for at least 2 hours, or until very firm.

7 To serve, cut into 1-inch squares and cut each square on the diagonal to form triangles. Serve cold, with a dab of the reserved cheese mixture on each.

PEANUT BUTTER SNACK

MAKES: *6 to 8 servings*

6 tablespoons chunky peanut butter
6 tablespoons honey
6 tablespoons semisweet chocolate chips
Ritz® crackers or Triscuits® for serving

In a bowl, combine the peanut butter and honey and blend with a fork until smooth. Stir in the chocolate chips. Cover and chill for at least 2 hours or until ready to serve. Serve with the crackers.

2 cups shredded Cheddar cheese, at
room temperature
1 cup butter or margarine, at room
temperature
2 cups all-purpose flour
⅛ teaspoon cayenne pepper
1 cup finely chopped, salted Spanish
(small) peanuts

1 In a medium bowl, and using
and electric mixer on low speed,
beat the cheese and butter
together until smooth. Add the
flour and cayenne and blend
until mixed. Form into a ball,
cover and chill for at least 2
hours.

2 Position the rack in the center
of the oven and preheat the oven
to 400 degrees F.

3 Pinch off pieces of the dough
and form into balls about the size
of walnuts.

4 Spread the peanuts in a shallow bowl or plate. Dip each ball
in the nuts to coat one side and
place on an ungreased baking
sheet, nut-side up. Bake for 12 to
14 minutes or until golden
brown. Serve at once.

PEANUT-COVERED CHEESE BALLS

MAKES: *About 60 servings*

36 pitted fresh dates
¼ cup Christian Brother's® brandy
2 tablespoons fresh orange juice
36 pecan halves

1 Put the dates in a glass container with a tight-fitting lid and
add the brandy and orange juice.

Cover and chill for at least 24
hours, turning the container
occasionally.

2 Drain the dates, discarding the
liquid. Push a pecan half into
each date and serve.

PECAN-STUFFED DATES

MAKES: *36 servings*

PETITE ENGLISH MUFFIN PIZZA

MAKES: *8 to 10 servings*

1 can (8 ounces) tomato sauce
2 tablespoons finely minced green bell pepper
1 tablespoon finely minced white onion
¼ teaspoon chervil
4 English muffins, split in half and toasted
four 4-inch-wide slices Provolone or Swiss cheese, cut in half

1 Position the broiler rack 4 inches from the heat source and preheat the broiler.

2 In a small bowl, combine the tomato sauce, pepper, onion and chervil and mix until combined. Spoon onto the muffin halves and broil for 2 to 3 minutes, or until hot.

3 Top each half with a slice of cheese and continue heating until the cheese melts. Remove from the heat, cut into wedges and serve.

PICKLE ROLL-UPS

MAKES: *About 48 servings*

1 package (8 ounces) cream cheese, at room temperature
1 package (6 ounces) sliced smoked ham
8 medium Claussen® whole kosher dill pickles

1 Spread 1 tablespoon of the cheese on each slice of ham. Place 1 pickle on the edge of each slice and roll up tight, pressing the edges to seal. Cover and chill for at least 2 hour.

2 Cut each roll-up into 6 equal slices and serve.

POPCORN CEREAL SNACKS

MAKES: *About 12 cups*

3 cups Kix® cereal
6 cups popped popcorn
¼ teaspoon garlic salt
¼ cup butter or margarine, melted
2 cups French fried shoestring potatoes
1 cup French fried onions

1 Position the rack in the lower third of the oven and preheat to 325 degrees F.

2 In a mixing bowl, combine the Kix, popcorn and garlic salt and toss to mix. Drizzle with butter and toss to coat.

3 Spread evenly in a 13-by-9-inch baking pan and bake for about 5 minutes. Add the potatoes and onions, stir, and bake for about 5 minutes longer or until lightly browned. Serve immediately.

PUMPKERNICKEL CHEESE BALLS

MAKES: *About 24 servings*

1 cup butter or margarine, at room temperature
1¼ cups finely grated Edam or Jarlsberg cheese
1 teaspoon ground cumin
1 teaspoon cumin seeds
pinch of cayenne pepper
ground white pepper
1½ cups fresh pumpernickel bread crumbs

1 In a medium bowl, and using an electric mixer on low speed, beat the butter until light and fluffy. Beat in the cheese, cumin and cumin seeds and season to taste with cayenne and pepper. Cover and chill for about 30 minutes.

2 Spread the bread crumbs in a shallow bowl or plate.

3 Pinch off small pieces of the cheese mixture and form into balls about the size of walnuts. Roll each ball in the bread crumbs until coated. Cover and chill until firm.

QUICK SNACK

MAKES: *About 3 cups*

2 cups flaked sweetened coconut
½ cup chopped pecans
½ cup chopped hazelnuts

In a container with a tight-fitting lid, combine the ingredients. Cover and shake to mix. Store in the refrigerator and eat by the handful when desired.

QUICKIE PEANUT BITES

MAKES: *About 72 servings*

1 loaf thinly sliced whole-wheat bread, crusts trimmed and bread cut into 1½-inch squares
2 cups creamy peanut butter
½ cup canola oil
3 tablespoons brown sugar
1½ cups honey-flavored wheat germ

1 Position the rack in the center of the oven and preheat to 250 degrees F.

2 Place the bread on an ungreased baking sheet and bake for 45 to 50 minutes, or until lightly brown and dry.

3 In a small saucepan, combine the peanut butter, oil and brown sugar and heat, stirring occasionally, over medium heat until smooth.

4 Spread the wheat germ on a large sheet of wax paper. Dip the bread squares in the peanut butter mixture to coat and then in the wheat germ, turning to coat both sides. Dry on wire racks.

RAISIN SNACKS

MAKES: *About 1¼ cups*

1 cup seedless raisins
2 tablespoons plus 2 teaspoons
  sunflower seeds
2 tablespoons plus 2 teaspoons
  flaked coconut
1 tablespoon carob or semisweet
  chocolate chips

In a plastic container with a tight-fitting lid, combine the ingredients and shake to mix. Store in a cool place and eat by the handful when desired.

REAL PARTY SNACKS

MAKES: *About 6 to 7 cups*

1 box (11 ounces) Ritz Bits®
1 box (11 ounces) Ritz Cheese Bits®
1 package (15 ounces) small pretzels
1 jar (6 ounces) dry roasted peanuts
2 packages (1 ounce each) Hidden
  Valley® Ranch Dressing
½ teaspoon lemon pepper
1 cup canola oil

1 In a mixing bowl, combine the Ritz Bits, pretzels and peanuts.

2 In a cup, combine the dressing mix and pepper and sprinkle evenly over the dry ingredients. Sprinkle with oil, about ¼ cup at a time, tossing after each addition. Store in a large container with a tight-fitting lid or serve at once.

RICE BALLS

MAKES: *12 servings*

3 cups canola oil
fine cracker crumbs
1 cup bread crumbs
½ cup Hunt's® tomato sauce
2 cups cooked rice
½ cup grated romano or Parmesan
  cheese
1 cup chopped cooked chicken
2 large eggs
salt and pepper

1 Heat the oil in a large skillet over a medium-low heat until hot (400 degrees F.).

2 Spread the cracker crumbs in a shallow bowl or plate.

3 In a large bowl, combine the tomato sauce, rice, cheese, chicken, bread crumbs and eggs, season to taste with salt and pepper and mix well. Using a small spoon, scoop out balls about the size of walnuts. Roll the balls in the cracker crumbs to coat.

4 Fry the balls, a few at a time, in the hot oil for 3 to 4 minutes, or until browned. Drain on paper towels and serve warm.

2 boxes (10 ounces each) Ritz® Bits
    crackers
1 cup pecan halves
½ cup unsalted butter
1 cup sugar
½ cup light corn syrup
1 teaspoon vanilla extract
1 teaspoon baking soda

1 Position the rack in the center
of the oven and preheat to 250
degrees F.

2 In a bowl, combine the crackers and pecans and spread in a
15½-by-10-by-2-inch jelly-roll
pan.

3 In a small saucepan, melt the
butter over medium heat. Add
the sugar and corn syrup, bring
to a boil, and cook for 5 minutes
without stirring. Remove from
the heat and immediately add
the vanilla and baking soda. Stir
quickly and carefully and pour
over the crackers. Stir to blend
and bake for about 1 hour, stirring every 15 minutes, until
browned and crispy.

4 Lay a piece of wax paper on a
work surface and pour the cracker mixture onto it to cool. When
hard, break into pieces. Serve or
store in an airtight container.

COOKING NOTE: **The sugar and
corn syrup mixture is very hot.
Take care when working with it.**

RITZ BITS SNACKS

MAKES: *About 10 servings*

⅔ cup grated Romano cheese
½ cup Kraft® real mayonnaise
4 chopped green onions, tops only
½ teaspoon garlic powder
½ teaspoon crumbled dried basil
¼ teaspoon crumbled dried oregano
1 package (10 ounces) Pillsbury®
    refrigerated biscuits

1 Position the rack in the center
of the oven and preheat to 400
degrees F.

2 In a bowl, combine the cheese,
mayonnaise, onions, garlic powder, basil and oregano and whisk
to blend.

3 Separate the biscuits and lay
them on a work surface. Roll out
to form circles 5 inches in diameter. Arrange the circles 1 inch
apart on ungreased baking pans.
Spread 1 tablespoon of the mixture on each circle, leaving a ¼-
inch border. Bake for 10 to 12
minutes, or until the biscuits are
golden brown.

COOKING NOTE: **For a cheesier
flavor, sprinkle more romano
over the filling before baking.**

ROMANO ROUNDS

MAKES: *About 10 servings*

SALMON-IN-PASTRY APPETIZER

MAKES: *About 20 servings*

PASTRY

1⅓ cups all-purpose flour
½ teaspoon salt
½ cup vegetable shortening
3 to 4 tablespoons ice water
1 large egg white, beaten

FILLING

2 tablespoons butter or margarine, at room temperature
½ cup chopped green onion, green part only
1 can (7 ounces) salmon, drained and flaked
¼ teaspoon dried dill
3 large egg yolks, beaten
1 cup sour cream or plain yogurt
salt and pepper
Herb Mayonnaise (recipe follows)

1 Position the rack in the center of the oven and preheat to 450 degrees F. Lightly grease two 2½-inch muffin pans.

2 To make the pastry, in a medium bowl, combine the flour and salt and whisk to blend. Add the vegetable shortening and using a pastry blender or two knives, cut it into the dry ingredients until crumbly. Add enough water to make a soft dough.

3 Turn the dough out onto a floured surface and roll to a thickness of about ¼ inch. Using a 3-inch round cookie cutter or upturned glass, stamp out rounds and press each into the muffin cup. Brush with the beaten egg white and bake for 3 to 4 minutes, or until lightly golden. Remove from the oven and reduce the temperature to 350 degrees F.

4 To make the filling, in a small skillet, melt the butter over medium heat. Add the green onions and sauté for 1 to 2 minutes until slightly softened. Add the salmon and cook for only 1 minute longer. Remove from the heat and stir in the dill.

5 In the top of a double boiler set over simmering water, combine the egg yolks and sour cream. Season to taste with salt and pepper and cook for about 15 minutes, or until thickened.

6 Spoon salmon mixture into each shell and spoon the custard over the salmon. Bake for 6 to 8 minutes, or until set. Serve with the mayonnaise on the side.

HERB MAYONNAISE

MAKES: *About ½ cup*

½ cup mayonnaise
⅛ teaspoon lemon juice
1 teaspoon finely chopped parsley
1 teaspoon snipped chives
1 teaspoon crushed dried chervil
pinch of dried thyme

In a small bowl, combine the ingredients and stir until smooth. Cover and chill for at least 24 hours before serving.

COOKING NOTE: **Use different herbs to vary the flavor.**

3 quarter-size slices peeled, fresh ginger

3 green onions, white part only, cut into 1-inch pieces

12 water chestnuts, roughly chopped

1½ pounds medium shrimp, shelled, deveined and coarsely chopped

2 small egg whites

4½ teaspoons dry sherry

4½ teaspoons cornstarch dissolved in ¼ cup cold water

4 thick slices stale white bread, crumbed into bread crumbs

6 cups vegetable oil for deep frying

Sweet-and-Sour Sauce (recipe follows)

1 In the container of a blender, combine the ginger, green onions and water chestnuts and process until puréed (the mixture will be a little chunky). Transfer to the bowl of an electric mixer.

2 Add the shrimp, and using an electric mixer on medium speed, beat to form a paste. Beat in the egg whites and blend thoroughly and then beat in the sherry and dissolved cornstarch. Cover and chill for at least 2 hours.

3 Spread the bread crumbs in a shallow bowl or a plate.

4 Shape the shrimp mixture into small balls the size of walnuts. Roll each in the bread crumbs to coat.

5 In a large heavy skillet or deep-fat fryer, heat the oil until hot (325 degrees F. in a deep-fat fryer). In small batches, fry the shrimp balls for 6 to 8 minutes, turning frequently until lightly browned. Drain on paper towels and cover to keep warm while frying all the balls. Serve with the sauce.

SHRIMP BALLS

MAKES: *48 servings*

SWEET-AND-SOUR SAUCE

MAKES: *1¾ cups*

¼ cup canola oil

6 tablespoons ketchup

6 tablespoons sugar

6 tablespoons red wine vinegar

6 tablespoons pineapple juice

1 tablespoon cornstarch dissolved in 6 tablespoons cold water

¾ teaspoon salt

In a small saucepan, combine the oil and ketchup and cook over medium heat, stirring, until the color deepens. Add the sugar, vinegar, juice, cornstarch and salt and whisk until blended. Cook, stirring constantly, for about 2 minutes until thickened. Transfer to a bowl and cool to room temperature.

---

butter- or garlic-flavored vegetable spray

5 tablespoons Worcestershire sauce

1 teaspoon garlic powder

1 teaspoon onion powder

2 cups Wheat Chex® cereal

2 cups Rice Chex® cereal

2 cups Pepperidge Farm® Cheddar Cheese Fish Crackers

2 cups Pepperidge Farm® Pretzel Fish Crackers

1 cup Multi-grain Cheerios®

1 cup pinenuts

1 Position the rack in the center of the oven and preheat to 250 degrees F. Spray a jelly-roll pan with vegetable oil spray.

2 In a cup, blend together the Worcestershire sauce, garlic powder and onion powder.

3 In a large bowl, combine the Wheat Chex, Rice Chex, Fish crackers, Cheerios and pinenuts. Toss to blend, spraying with the vegetable oil spray until coated. Drizzle with the Worcestershire sauce mixture, tossing to coat.

4 Spread evenly into the pan and bake for about 1 hour until browned and crispy, stirring several times during baking. Spread on a work surface covered with paper towels to cool. Store in a container with a tight-fitting lid.

SPICY SNACK MIX

MAKES: *10 to 11 cups*

SMILES

MAKES: *About 12 servings*

1¼ cups water
7 tablespoons butter or margarine
½ teaspoon Worcestershire sauce
1¼ cups all-purpose flour
3 large eggs
1½ cups grated Gouda or Swiss
  cheese
Cheese Dip for Fruit (see page 39)

1 Position the rack in the center of the oven and preheat to 375 degrees F.

2 In a medium saucepan, combine the water and butter and bring to a boil over high heat. Reduce the heat and simmer until the butter melts. Add the Worcestershire sauce, remove from the heat and immediately add the flour. Using a wooden spoon, stir until blended. (The mixture will be thick.)

3 Add the eggs, one at a time, stirring thoroughly after each addition.

4 Add ¾ cup of the cheese to the dough and stir until mixed. Using a spoon, shape the dough into balls about the size of walnuts. Place on an ungreased baking sheet and sprinkle with the remaining cheese. Bake for 20 to 25 minutes, or until golden brown. Remove from the oven and cool slightly. Serve with the dip on the side.

STUFFED CUCUMBERS

MAKES: *About 18 to 20 servings*

2 cucumbers
sea salt
1 package (3 ounces) cream cheese,
  at room temperature
2 tablespoons minced onion
¼ teaspoon paprika
1 tablespoon Kraft® French dressing
6 tablespoons pimiento cheese
¼ cup minced celery
½ teaspoon Worcestershire sauce
½ cup Kraft® real mayonnaise

1 Score the cucumbers with the tines of a fork by pressing hard and dragging the tines along the length of the cucumber. Using a sharp knife, cut the cucumbers in half lengthwise. (Keep the halves together.) Using a melon baller or spoon, remove the seeds to make in the centers of the cucumbers. Sprinkle with sea salt and place cut side down on a paper towel.

2 In a medium bowl, using an electric mixer on low speed, beat together the cream cheese, onion, paprika and dressing until smooth.

3 In a small bowl, beat together the pimiento cheese, celery and Worcestershire sauce. Add ¼ cup of the mayonnaise to each mixture and beat each until smooth.

4 Fill each cucumber half with one or the other of the spreads. Be sure to use the same filling for each cucumber.

5 Press the cucumber halves together, wrap tightly with plastic wrap and chill for at least 2 hours, or until ready to serve.

6 Unwrap the cucumbers and cut into ½-inch slices and serve.

1 pound Jimmy Dean® Hot Sausage, crumbled
1 pound lean ground beef
½ cup finely chopped shallot
2 pounds Velveeta® cheese, cubed
1 loaf cocktail rye bread
sliced ripe olives

1 Position the rack in the center of the oven and preheat to 350 degrees F.

2 In a large skillet, combine the sausage, beef and shallot and cook over medium heat for about 10 minutes until no longer pink. Add the cheese and cook until the cheese melts.

3 Spread on the bread, top with olives and bake for 5 to 8 minutes, or until bubbling. Serve at once.

COOKING NOTE: Pumpernickel can be used in place of rye bread.

SUPER BOWL, GOTTA HAVE IT SNACK

MAKES: *About 6 to 8 servings*

---

4 cups popped white popcorn
2 cups Post® Sugar Crisp cereal
2 cups miniature marshmallows
1 cup semisweet chocolate chips
1 cup milk chocolate chips
1 cup unsalted peanuts
1 cup golden raisins

In a large bowl, combine the popcorn, cereal, marshmallows, chocolate chips, peanuts and raisins. Store in a large container with a tight-fitting lid until ready to eat by the handful.

SUPER CRUNCH SNACKS

MAKES: *About 12 cups*

SUPER PARTY MIX

MAKES: *12 cups*

1 package (15 ounces) Cherrios®
1 package (17.5 ounces) Rice Chex®
1 package (23.5 ounces) Wheat Chex®
2 cups Pretzel Stix®
2 cans (5 ounces each) salted peanuts
1 teaspoon dried marjoram
1 teaspoon dried savory
1 tablespoon Spice Island® Beau Monde Seasoning
1 tablespoon Spice Island® Old Hickory Smoked Salt
½ teaspoon garlic powder
½ teaspoon onion powder
pinch cayenne
¾ pound butter, diced into small pieces

1 Position the rack in the lowest portion of the oven and preheat to 250 degrees F.

2 In a large bowl, combine the cereals, pretzels and peanuts and toss to mix.

3 In a small bowl, combine the herbs, garlic powder, onion powder and cayenne and mix well. Sprinkle over the cereal mixture and toss to mix. Spread in a large baking pan and dot with butter. Bake for about 45 minutes, stirring frequently but taking care not to break or crush the cereal pieces. Cool in the pan and store in a large plastic bag until ready to eat by the handful.

COOKING NOTE: **It may be necessary to bake this in batches.**

MUENSTER CHEESE-FILLED POCKETS

MAKES: *About 36 servings*

1 package (3 ounces) cream cheese, at room temperature
¼ pound butter or margarine, at room temperature
1 cup all-purpose flour
2 large eggs
2 cups shredded Muenster cheese
1 tablespoon grated white onion
¼ teaspoon Tabasco sauce
black pepper
1 large egg white, slightly beaten
sesame seeds

1 In a medium bowl, combine the cream cheese and butter and mash until smooth. Blend in the flour until incorporated. Form into a ball, wrap in wax paper and chill for at least 2 hours.

2 Position the rack in the center of the oven and preheat to 375 degrees F.

3 In a small bowl, using an electric mixer on medium speed, beat the eggs until thick and light.

Beat in the Muenster cheese, onion and Tabasco. Season with pepper to taste.

4 Lightly flour a work surface and roll out the chilled dough to a thickness of ⅛ inch. Using a 2½-inch round cookie cutter or upturned glass, cut out as many rounds as possible. Gather the scraps of dough, roll out again and cut as many rounds as possible. Repeat until all the dough is used.

5 Drop teaspoonfuls of the cheese filling in the center of each round, fold them in half, and seal the edges together. Brush with the egg white and sprinkle with sesame seeds. Place the turnovers on an ungreased baking sheet, leaving about 1 inch between them. Bake for about 20 to 25 minutes, or until lightly browned. Cool on wire racks and serve warm or at room temperature.

1 cup light-brown sugar
½ cup light corn syrup
½ teaspoon salt
½ cup butter or margarine
6 cups Cheerios®
1 cup golden raisins
1 cup unsalted peanuts
½ teaspoon baking soda

1 Position the rack in the center of the oven and preheat to 250 degrees F. Lightly grease an 18-by-13-inch baking sheet.

2 In a small saucepan, combine the sugar, corn syrup, salt and butter. Bring to a boil over medium heat and cook for 5 minutes.

3 Meanwhile, in a large bowl, combine the cereal, raisins and peanuts.

4 Remove the syrup from the heat, stir in the baking soda and drizzle over the cereal mix, stirring and tossing until coated.

5 Spread in the prepared baking pan and bake for about 15 minutes, until very lightly browned. Serve warm or store in a tightly-lidded container.

SWEET CHEERIOS SNACKS

MAKES: *About 10 cups*

---

24 chicken wings
1 cup low-sodium soy sauce
¾ cup chopped shallot
⅓ cup sugar
4 teaspoons canola oil
1 large clove garlic, minced
1 tablespoon ground ginger

1 Thoroughly wash the chicken wings. Using a sharp knife, disjoint the chicken wings and cut off and discard the tips.

2 In a large bowl, combine the soy sauce, shallot, sugar, oil, garlic and ginger and whisk. Add the chicken and stir to coat. Cover and chill for at least 1 hour or overnight.

3 Position the rack in the center of the oven and preheat to 350 degrees F.

4 Remove the chicken from the marinade and reserve. Place the chicken in a 13-by-9-inch baking pan and bake for 25 to 30 minutes, turning several times and basting with the marinade during the first half of the cooking. Do not disturb during the last 15 minutes of cooking. Serve warm.

TERIYAKI CHICKEN WINGS

MAKES: *48 servings*

---

1 loaf sliced cocktail rye bread
½ cup Garlic Butter (recipe follows)
½ cup grated Parmesan or romano cheese

1 Position the broiler rack 4 inches from the heat source and preheat the broiler. Lightly grease the broiler pan.

2 Broil 1 side of the bread slices until lightly toasted. Spread the untoasted side evenly with Garlic Butter and sprinkle with the cheese. Broil for 2 to 3 minutes until browned. Cut each slice of bread in half on the diagonal and serve hot.

TOASTED RYE SLICES

MAKES: *About 72 servings*

GARLIC BUTTER

MAKES: *About ½ cup*

½ cup unsalted butter
2 cloves garlic, minced
salt and white pepper

In a saucepan, melt the butter over medium heat. Add the garlic and season with salt and pepper, stir, and cook gently for about 5 minutes. Strain into a small bowl, cover, and chill until ready to use.

TROPICAL CHEESE LOG

MAKES: *8 to 12 servings*

1 package (8 ounces) Philadelphia® cream cheese

1 can (8 ounces) crushed pineapple, drained

2 cups shredded Cheddar or Tillamook cheese

½ cup chopped pecans

½ cup chopped dried apricots

2 teaspoons chopped crystallized ginger

crackers

1 In a large bowl, combine the cream cheese and pineapple and mix with a fork until smooth.

Add the Cheddar cheese, pecans, apricots and ginger and stir to mix. Cover and chill for about 2 hours or until firm.

2 Shape into a log about 1½ inches in diameter. Serve on a tray with crackers.

COOKING NOTE: **After shaping, the log can be rolled in toasted sesame seeds, ground nuts or chopped parsley.**

TROPICAL QUICK SNACK

MAKES: *About 5 cups*

1½ cups pecans or unsalted peanuts

½ cup golden raisins

1 cup seedless raisins

½ cup flaked coconut

½ cup dried diced pineapple

½ cup dried diced papaya

½ cup dried cherries or cranberries

In a plastic container with a lid, combine the nuts, raisins, coconut, pineapple, papaya and cherries. Cover and shake to mix. Store until ready to eat by the handful.

TROPICAL SHRIMP BALLS

MAKES: *30 servings*

1 pound medium shrimp, peeled, deveined and very finely chopped

2 large eggs

¼ cup grated coconut

1 tablespoon cornstarch

1 teaspoon ground coriander

1 cup canola oil

1 In a medium bowl, combine the shrimp, eggs, coconut, cornstarch and coriander and mix well. Cover and chill for about 30 minutes.

2 In a wok or heavy skillet, heat the oil until hot. Using a small spoon, break off pieces of the dough and form into balls about the size of walnuts. Cook for about 3 minutes on each side until lightly browned. Drain on paper towels and serve at once.

1½ cups shredded American cheese
1 can (4 ounces) sliced mushrooms, drained
¼ cup Kraft® mayonnaise
1 tablespoon finely chopped white onion
⅛ teaspoon cayenne
2 teaspoons Worcestershire sauce
½ teaspoon prepared mustard
6 Eggo® Frozen Waffles

1 Position the broiler rack so it is 4 inches from the heat source and preheat the broiler.

2 In a medium bowl, combine the cheese, mushrooms, mayonnaise, onion, cayenne, Worcestershire sauce and mustard. Spread on the waffles, leaving a ¼-inch border. Place on an ungreased baking sheet and broil for about 3 minutes, or until the cheese melts. Cut each waffle into 8 wedges and serve warm.

WAFFLE WEDGES
MAKES: *48 servings*

1 cup cooked wild rice
1 package (3 ounces) cream cheese, at room temperature
1 green onion, green part only, sliced
1 teaspoon curry powder
dash of cayenne
½ cup drained, chopped mango chutney (optional)
chopped pecans for garnish

1 In a small bowl, using an electric mixer on medium speed, beat together the rice, cheese, onion, curry and cayenne. Add the chutney and blend well.

2 Form into balls the size of walnuts.

3 Spread the nuts in a shallow bowl or plate.

4 Roll the balls in the nuts, place on a plate or platter, cover, and chill at least 2 hours, or until firm.

COOKING NOTE: **These can be rolled in chopped parsley or toasted sesame seeds instead of nuts. You can use another kind of nut instead of pecans.**

WILD RICE BITES
MAKES: *15 servings*

1 package (8 ounces) cream cheese, at room temperature
½ cup butter or margarine, at room temperature
2 tablespoons finely chopped shallot
1½ teaspoons anchovy paste
1 teaspoon Dijon mustard
1 teaspoon chopped capers
1 teaspoon caraway seeds
1 teaspoon sweet paprika
crackers, cocktail bread or raw vegetables

1 In a bowl, using an electric mixer on low speed, beat together the cheese and butter until smooth. Add the shallots, anchovy paste, mustard, capers, caraway seeds and paprika and beat until smooth. Cover and chill for at least 4 hours.

2 Serve with crackers, bread or vegetables.

AUSTRIAN LIPTAUER SPREAD
MAKES: *About 2 cups*

WONTON BOW TIES WITH SWEET-AND-SOUR SAUCE

MAKES: *50 servings*

SAUCE
4 tablespoons sugar
¼ cup white vinegar
¼ cup catsup
1 cup plus 2 tablespoons water, plus more for sealing
2 tablespoons cornstarch
½ cup chopped green bell pepper
3 tablespoons crushed, drained canned pineapple
1 package (12 ounces) wonton wrappers
oil for frying

1 In a small saucepan, combine the sugar, vinegar, catsup and 1 cup of water and bring to a slow boil over medium heat.

2 In a small cup, combine the 2 tablespoons water and the cornstarch and stir until smooth. Add to the saucepan, stirring until thickened. Add the pepper and pineapple and stir to mix. Set aside.

3 In a large skillet, pour the oil to a depth of ½ inch and heat over high heat until hot.

4 On a work surface, lay several wonton wrappers. Dip a finger in water and rub the water down the center of each one. Crinkle or twist each skin together in the center, where you placed the moisture, to form a bow-tie shape. Repeat with all the wrappers.

5 Fry a few wontons for 2 to 3 minutes until golden brown. Drain on paper towels. Repeat with the remaining wrappers. Serve warm with the sauce.

ZUCCHINI SQUARES

MAKES: *About 100 servings*

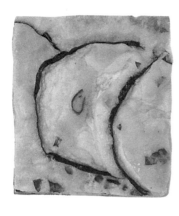

4 cups thinly sliced zucchini
1 cup Bisquick® baking mix
4 large eggs
½ cup finely chopped white onion
½ cup grated Parmesan cheese
½ cup canola oil
2 tablespoons finely chopped parsley
1 small clove garlic, minced
½ teaspoon dried oregano, crumbled
salt and black pepper

1 Position the rack in the center of the oven and preheat to 375 degrees F. Lightly grease a 13-by-9-inch baking dish.

2 In a large bowl, combine the zucchini, baking mix, eggs, onion, cheese, oil, parsley, garlic and oregano and stir to mix. Season to taste with salt and pepper.

3 Spread in the prepared baking dish and bake for 25 to 30 minutes until golden brown and a toothpick inserted in the center of the pan comes out clean. Cool slightly, cut into 1-inch squares and serve.

1 jar (6 ounces) marinated artichokes
1 cup grated Parmesan cheese
¾ cup mayonnaise
pumpernickel cocktail bread

In a bowl, mash the artichokes. Add the cheese and mayonnaise and mix well. Spread on the bread.

COOKING NOTE: **For a thinner spread, use 1 cup of mayonnaise.**

ARTICHOKE SPREAD

MAKES: *12 to 15 servings*

1 large avocado
1 can (7¾ ounces) salmon, flaked
1 tablespoon lemon or lime juice
1 small clove garlic, minced
1 teaspoon onion powder
4 drops hot red-pepper sauce
cocktail bread or crackers

1 Peel the avocado, remove the pit and place the flesh in a bowl and mash. Add the salmon, lemon juice, garlic, onion powder and pepper sauce and mix well. Cover and let stand at room temperature for at least 1 hour. Serve with the bread or crackers.

AVOCADO-AND-SALMON SPREAD

MAKES: *About 12 servings*

1 jar (8 ounces) marinara sauce
12 plain mini bagels, halved
1 pound mozzarella cheese, sliced

1 Position the rack in the center of the oven and preheat to 350 degrees F.

2 Spread the sauce over the bagels and cover each with a slice of cheese. Transfer to a baking sheet and bake for 10 to 12 minutes or until the cheese melts and the bagels are lightly browned.

BAGEL PIZZA SNACKS

MAKES: *About 24 servings*

BLUE CHEESE CRISPS

MAKES: *About 48 servings*

4 ounces blue cheese, crumbled
2 tablespoons butter or margarine, at room temperature
1 tablespoon minced shallot
1 large egg
1 package (3 ounces) cream cheese, at room temperature
2 cups all-purpose flour
¼ teaspoon salt
¾ cup vegetable shortening
3 to 4 tablespoons ice water
grated Cheddar cheese
paprika for topping

1 Position the rack in the center of the oven, and preheat to 425 degrees F.

2 In a bowl, using an electric mixer on medium speed, beat together the blue cheese, butter, shallot, egg and cream cheese until smooth. Cover and freeze for about 5 minutes, or just until firm.

3 In another bowl, combine the flour, salt and shortening. Using a pastry blender or two knives, cut the shortening into the dry ingredients until the mixture resembles coarse crumbs. Sprinkle about 3 tablespoons of ice water over the mixture and blend until the dough holds its shape. Add more ice water, a teaspoon at a time, if necessary. Form into a ball and divide in half.

4 On a lightly floured surface, roll out the dough to form 2 rectangles, each about 12-by-8 inches. Spread half of the filling over 1 side of a rectangle and then fold in half (like a book) and seal the edges, pressing gently on the package to expel any air bubbles. Repeat the with the other rectangle and remaining filling.

5 Using a pastry wheel, cut each rectangle into 1-inch squares and transfer to ungreased baking sheets. Sprinkle with cheese and paprika and bake for 12 to 15 minutes, or until lightly browned and puffy.

BLUE CHEESE- HAZELNUT SPREAD

MAKES: *12 to 15 servings*

2 packages (8 ounces each) cream cheese, at room temperature
8 ounces blue cheese, crumbled
2 teaspoons chopped pimientos
½ cup finely chopped hazelnuts
cocktail bread or crackers

1 In a bowl, using an electric mixer on medium speed, beat the cream cheese until creamy. Add the blue cheese, pimientos and hazelnuts and mix well. Cover and chill for at least 24 hours.

2 Remove from the refrigerator at least 1 hour before using. Spread on the bread or crackers.

COOKING NOTE: **If packed in a small bowl or jar, this keeps in the refrigerator for up to 10 days.**

8 ounces blue cheese, at room
   temperature
1 cup butter or margarine, at room
   temperature
¼ cup Creme de Almond or another
   nut-flavored liqueur
½ cup chopped pecans
cocktail bread or crackers

In a bowl, using an electric mixer
on high speed, beat the cheese
and butter until smooth. Add the
liqueur and pecans and mix well.
Serve with the bread or crackers.

BLUE CHEESE SPREAD

MAKES: *About 15 servings*

1⅓ cup flaked crabmeat
2 teaspoons snipped fresh chives
2 teaspoons brandy
2 teaspoons chili sauce
cocktail bread or raw vegetables

In a bowl, combine the crabmeat,
chives, brandy and chili sauce
and mix well. Cover and chill for
at least 1 hour. Serve with the
bread or vegetables.

BRANDIED CRAB SPREAD

MAKES: *6 to 8 servings*

CHICKEN SPREAD

MAKES: 24 *servings*

4 cans (4¾ ounces each) prepared chicken spread
1½ cups sour cream
½ teaspoon pepper
1 teaspoon dried thyme
4 teaspoons white anisette
12 slices whole-wheat bread, crusts trimmed

In the container of a blender, combine the chicken spread, sour cream, pepper, thyme and anisette and process for 12 to 15 seconds until smooth. Cover and chill for 1 hour. Spread on the bread, cut each in half on the diagonal and serve.

CHILI CHEESE DOGS

MAKES: 12 *servings*

½ pound lean ground beef
1 package Lawry's® Chili Seasoning Mix
1 can (6 ounces) Hunt's® Tomato Paste
1 cup water
1 can (15.5 ounces) kidney beans, drained
1 teaspoon prepared mustard
12 frankfurters
12 frankfurter buns
¾ cup grated Cheddar cheese

1 Position the rack in the center of the oven and preheat to 400 degrees F.

2 In a nonstick skillet, cook the beef over medium-high heat until browned. Drain and discard the fat. Add the seasoning mix, tomato paste, water, beans and mustard and simmer for about 10 minutes, stirring frequently, until heated through.

3 Put a frankfurter in each bun and top each with chili and about 1 tablespoon of cheese. Wrap well in aluminum foil and transfer to a baking pan. Cook for 12 to 15 minute, or until heated through.

CHEESE-AND-PEPPERONI PIE

MAKES: *About 18 servings*

2 large eggs
2 cups milk
2 cups all-purpose flour
1½ teaspoons crushed dried oregano
10 ounces Cheddar cheese, diced
1 stick (6 inches long) pepperoni, diced
1 white onion, chopped
1 green bell pepper, chopped
1 can (4 ounces) chopped mushrooms, drained

1 Position the rack in the center of the oven and preheat to 350 degrees F. Lightly grease a 13-by-9-inch baking pan.

2 In a bowl, whisk the eggs until foamy. Add the milk and whisk to blend. Add the flour and oregano and mix well. Add the cheese, pepperoni, onion, pepper and mushrooms and stir until incorporated. Spread in the pan and bake for 35 to 40 minutes, or until a knife inserted in the center comes out clean. Cut into squares and serve hot.

1 loaf (16 ounces) frozen bread
  dough, thawed
2 cups shredded Cheddar or
  Wisconsin brick cheese
¼ cup butter or margarine, melted
2 large eggs, beaten
3 tablespoons fresh snipped chives
¼ teaspoon garlic powder
¼ teaspoon onion powder

1 Put the dough in a bowl, cover
and set aside in a warm place for
1 to 1½ hours until doubled in
bulk.

2 Position the rack in the center
of the oven and preheat to 350
degrees F.

3 Turn the dough out onto a
lightly floured work surface and
divide in half. Roll each half into
a 10-inch circle and transfer to an
ungreased baking sheet.

4 In a bowl, combine the cheese,
butter, eggs, chives, garlic powder and onion powder and mix
well. Spread over the dough circles and bake for 25 to 30 minutes, or until the edges are
golden brown. Slice into wedges
and serve.

CHEESE PIZZA WITH CHIVES

MAKES: *8 to 10 servings*

---

8 ounces Camembert cheese, at room
  temperature
½ cup butter, at room temperature
¼ cup heavy cream
1 cup diced smoked ham
2 tablespoons finely chopped green
  onions
2 teaspoons snipped chives
cocktail bread or crackers

In a bowl, using an electric mixer
on medium speed, beat the
cheese, butter and cream until
smooth. Add the ham, onions
and chives and mix well. Spread
on the bread or crackers.

CHOPPED HAM-AND-CAMEMBERT SPREAD

MAKES: *15 to 18 servings*

COCKTAIL CHEESE BALL

MAKES: *About 20 servings*

1 cup shredded Cheddar or Colby cheese, at room temperature
2 packages (4 ounces each) blue cheese, crumbled, at room temperature
½ cup Kraft® Thousand Island Dressing
1 large hard-cooked egg, chopped
2 tablespoons diced green bell pepper
2 teaspoons Worcestershire sauce
⅛ teaspoon hot red-pepper sauce
1 cup chopped pimiento-stuffed olives
crackers

1 In a bowl, combine the cheeses, dressing, egg, pepper, Worcestershire sauce and pepper sauce and mash until soft and well mixed. Form into a ball, wrap in plastic and chill for 2 to 3 hours or until firm.

2 Spread the olives in a shallow dish and roll the cheese ball in them to coat. Transfer to a platter and serve with crackers.

CREAM CHEESE SPIRALS

MAKES: *About 60 servings*

⅔ cup Wish-Bone® Russian Dressing
1 package (8 ounces) cream cheese, at room temperature
1 cup finely chopped walnuts
1 loaf (16 ounces) unsliced white bread, crusts trimmed and cut lengthwise into 8 slices

1 In a bowl, combine the dressing, cream cheese and walnuts and mash until smooth.

2 Lay the bread slices on a work surface and, with a rolling pin, roll as thin as possible. Spread with the cream cheese mixture and roll tightly into cylinders, starting on a long side. Wrap in plastic wrap and chill for 1 to 2 hours or until firm. Slice into ½ inch slices and serve.

DEVILED HAM NUT BALL

MAKES: *16 to 20 servings*

2 packages (8 ounces each) cream cheese, at room temperature
2 cups shredded sharp Cheddar cheese, at room temperature
1 can (2¼ ounces) deviled ham
2 tablespoons chopped pimiento
2 teaspoons Worcestershire sauce
2 teaspoons grated white onion
1 teaspoon dry mustard
1 teaspoon lemon juice
¾ teaspoon paprika
2 drops hot red-pepper sauce
2 cups chopped pecans, walnuts or hazelnuts
crackers

1 In a bowl, using an electric mixer on medium speed, beat together the cream cheese, Cheddar cheese and ham until smooth. Add the pimiento, Worcestershire sauce, onion, mustard, lemon juice, paprika and pepper sauce and mix well. Cover and chill for 2 to 3 hours or until firm.

2 Divide in half and shape into 2 balls.

3 Spread the nuts in a shallow dish and roll each ball in them to coat. Transfer to a platter and serve with crackers.

COOKING NOTE: **For variety, coat each ball in a different kind of nut.**

EDAM CHEESE BOWL

MAKES: *8 to 10 servings*

1 round (26 ounces) Kraft® Edam Cheese, at room temperature
¼ cup butter or margarine, at room temperature
3 tablespoons sherry or white port wine
crackers or cocktail bread

1 Slice the top quarter from the cheese round and scoop out the interior cheese, leaving a ½-inch shell.

2 Shred the scooped out cheese and the cheese from the top and transfer to a bowl. Add the butter and sherry and, using an electric mixer on low speed, beat until smooth. Spoon into the shell, cover and chill for at least 2 hours. Serve with crackers or bread.

COOKING NOTE: **To avoid cracking, make sure the waxed coating on the Edam is at room temperature before cutting the cheese and scooping it out.**

EGG SPREAD

MAKES: *About 4 servings*

4 large hard-cooked eggs, mashed
1 teaspoon prepared mustard
dash of Worcestershire sauce
1 teaspoon catsup
½ teaspoon onion powder (optional)
salt and pepper
2 slices whole-wheat or rye bread,
   crusts trimmed

In a bowl, using an electric mixer on medium speed, beat the eggs, mustard, Worcestershire sauce, catsup, onion powder and salt and pepper to taste until well mixed. Cover and chill for at least 1 hour. Spread on the bread, cut in half on the diagonal and serve.

FARMER'S COTTAGE CHEESE SPREAD

MAKES: *6 to 8 servings*

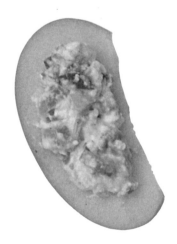

½ cup large-curd cottage cheese
¼ cup plus 2 tablespoons minced
   celery
¼ cup plus 1 tablespoon minced
   green onions
2 tablespoons minced pitted green
   olives
¼ teaspoon paprika
salt and pepper
whole-wheat bread or fresh fruit

In a bowl, using an electric mixer on medium speed, beat the cottage cheese, celery, green onions, olives and paprika until smooth. Season with salt and pepper, cover and chill for at least 1 hour. Spread on the bread or fruit.

COOKING NOTE: This is especially good spread on sliced pineapple, apples or pears.

¼ cup butter or margarine
2 quarts fresh popped white corn
1 tablespoon garlic powder
1 tablespoon grated romano cheese

1 In a small saucepan, melt the butter over low heat.

2 Put the popcorn in a bowl and pour the hot butter over it, stirring as you pour. Add the garlic powder and cheese and toss gently until the popcorn is well coated.

GARLIC-AND-CHEESE POPCORN

MAKES: *About 12 servings*

2 packages (3 ounces each) cream cheese, at room temperature
¼ cup butter or margarine, at room temperature
1 tablespoon finely minced white onion
½ teaspoon dried sage
½ dried savory
2 tablespoons lemon or lime juice
cocktail bread or raw vegetables

In a bowl, using an electric mixer on medium speed, beat the cream cheese and butter until smooth. Add the onion, sage, savory and lemon juice and beat until well mixed. Cover and chill for at least 1 hour. Serve with the bread or vegetables.

HINT-OF-HERBS CREAM CHEESE SPREAD

MAKES: *6 to 8 servings*

HOLIDAY CHEESE LOGS

MAKES: *About 36 servings*

2 packages (8 ounces each) cream cheese, at room temperature
2 cups shredded Cheddar cheese
2 cups shredded Gouda cheese
¼ cup De Kuyper® Ginger Flavored Brandy
3 tablespoons toasted sesame seeds
½ cup coarsely chopped pecans
½ cup chopped parsley
crackers, raw vegetables or fresh fruit

1 In a bowl, using an electric mixer on low speed, beat together the cream cheese, Cheddar and Gouda until blended. Add the brandy and beat until smooth. Cover and chill for at least 1 hour.

2 Spread the sesame seeds in a shallow dish, the pecans in another bowl and the parsley in a third bowl.

3 Divide the cheese mixture in thirds and shape each portion into a log about 2 inches in diameter. Roll 1 log in the sesame seeds to coat, roll 1 log in the pecans, and roll the third log in the parsley. Wrap each in plastic wrap and chill for at least 8 hours or until firm. Serve with crackers, vegetables or fruit.

HONEY-NUT SPREAD

MAKES: *About 4 servings*

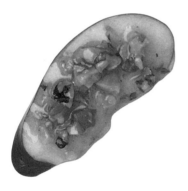

½ cup honey
2 tablespoons lemon or lime juice
2 tablespoons chopped walnuts or pecans
whole-wheat bread or fresh fruit

In a bowl, combine the honey, lemon juice and nuts and stir until smooth. Cover and chill for at least 2 hours. Spread on the bread or fruit.

LOBSTER SPREAD

MAKES: *4 to 6 servings*

1 cup minced cooked lobster
1 tablespoon unsalted butter, melted
1 tablespoon mayonnaise
1 tablespoon French dressing
1 teaspoon lemon juice
salt and pepper
pumpernickel cocktail bread or wheat crackers

In a bowl, using an electric mixer on low speed, beat the lobster, butter, mayonnaise, dressing, lemon juice and salt and pepper until blended. Cover and chill for at least 1 hour. Serve with the bread or crackers.

10 small eggs
2 tablespoons black tea leaves
2 tablespoons salt
1 tablespoon black pepper
5 whole star anise
2 tablespoons soy sauce

1 In a saucepan, combine the eggs and enough water to cover and bring to a boil over medium-high heat. Reduce the heat and simmer for about 10 minutes. Drain and run under cold running water. Using a spoon, gently tap the eggs to crack them all over without removing the shells.

2 Return to the pan, add more water to cover, the tea, salt, pepper, star anise and soy sauce and bring to a boil over medium-high heat. Reduce the heat and simmer for about 20 minutes. Drain, peel the shells and serve the eggs.

MARBLEIZED TEA EGGS

MAKES: *About 10 servings*

---

1 pound hot chorizo sausage, crumbled
1 jar (8 ounces) Mexican-Style Cheese Whiz®
2 cups Bisquick® Baking Mix
1 tablespoon butter or margarine, at room temperature
1 tablespoon crushed dried oregano
½ teaspoon crushed dried basil
1 teaspoon garlic powder
melted butter

1 Position the rack in the center of the oven and preheat to 350 degrees F. Lightly grease a baking sheet.

2 In a bowl, combine the sausage and cheese and mix well. Add the baking mix, butter, oregano, basil and garlic powder and knead by hand to make a heavy dough.

3 Pinch off pieces of the mixture and form into balls about the size of walnuts. Transfer to the baking sheet, brush with butter and bake for 18 to 20 minutes, or until browned.

MEXICAN PIZZA BALLS

MAKES: *About 36 servings*

NUT-FLAVORED CRAB SPREAD

MAKES: *About 6 servings*

¾ cup minced flaked crabmeat
2 large hard-cooked eggs, mashed
2 tablespoons melted butter
2 teaspoons hazelnut-flavored
   brandy
crackers or raw vegetables

In a bowl, using an electric mixer on low speed, beat the crabmeat, eggs, butter and brandy until smooth. Cover and chill for at least 1 hour. Serve with the crackers or vegetables.

NUTTY CHEESE WAFERS

MAKES: *30 to 36 servings*

16 ounces Colby cheese, shredded
2 packages (3 ounces each) cream
   cheese, at room temperature
1 cup finely chopped pecans
2 large cloves garlic, mashed
paprika

1 In a bowl, using an electric mixer on medium speed, beat together the cheese, cream cheese, pecans and garlic until blended.

2 Turn the mixture out onto a work surface and form into a log about 1½ inches in diameter. Roll in paprika to coat, wrap in wax paper and chill for at least 2 hours or until firm. Cut into ¼-inch slices and serve.

PINEAPPLE-CREAM CHEESE SPREAD

MAKES: *About 6 servings*

1 package (3 ounces) cream cheese,
   at room temperature
½ cup crushed pineapple, drained
¼ cup finely chopped pecans
cocktail bread or crackers

In a bowl, using an electric mixer on medium speed, beat the cream cheese until fluffy. Reduce

to low speed, add the pineapple and pecans and beat until blended. Cover and chill for at least 1 hour. Serve with the bread or crackers.

PLAIN CRAB SPREAD

MAKES: *About 6 servings*

1 cup minced flaked crabmeat
2 tablespoons heavy cream
1 tablespoon prepared horseradish
cocktail bread or crackers

In a bowl, using an electric mixer on low speed, beat the crabmeat, cream and horseradish until smooth. Cover and chill for at least 1 hour. Serve with the bread or crackers.

QUICK CLUB SUPPER

MAKES: *About 12 servings*

12 beef or chicken frankfurters
¼ cup butter or margarine
1 cup sliced Bermuda onion
½ cup minced green bell pepper
3 cans (15.5 ounces each) spaghetti in tomato sauce with cheese
1½ cans (12 ounces each) whole-kernel corn
salt and pepper
1 cup grated Parmesan cheese

1 Position the rack in the center of the oven and preheat to 350 degrees F.

2 Slice the frankfurters diagonally into 1½-inch-thick slices.

3 In a saucepan, heat the butter over medium heat until melted. Add the onion and frankfurters and cook, stirring, for about 5 minutes or until the onions are transparent. Add the peppers and cook for about 1 minute more. Add the spaghetti and corn, season with salt and pepper and mix well. Spoon into a 13-by-9-inch baking pan, sprinkle with cheese and bake for 30 to 40 minutes, or until very hot.

SHERRIED CREAM CHEESE SPREAD

MAKES: *6 to 8 servings*

2 packages (3 ounces each) cream cheese, at room temperature
¼ cup plus 1 tablespoon sherry
1 small orange, peeled, diced and seeds removed
¼ teaspoon paprika
cocktail bread or raw vegetables

In a bowl, using an electric mixer on medium speed, beat the cream cheese, sherry, orange and paprika until blended. Cover and chill for at least 1 hour. Spread on the bread or vegetables.

SPICED FAVA BEANS

MAKES: *About 20 servings*

3 cups fresh fava beans, trimmed
2 whole star anise
salt and pepper
sea salt

In a saucepan, combine the beans, anise and salt and pepper to taste with enough cold water to cover and bring to a boil over high heat and cook for about 15 minutes until tender. Drain, transfer to a bowl, sprinkle with sea salt, cover and chill for at least 2 hours until cold.

SPINACH BARS

MAKES: *12 servings*

1 cup milk
¼ cup butter or margarine, melted
2 large eggs
½ cup finely chopped shallot
1 cup all-purpose flour
1 teaspoon baking powder
1 cup chopped fresh spinach
1 pound shredded Cheddar cheese

1 Position the rack in the center of the oven and preheat to 350 degrees F. Lightly grease a 13-by-9-inch baking pan.

2 In a bowl, using an electric mixer on medium speed, combine the milk, butter, eggs, shallot, flour and baking powder and mix well. Add the spinach and cheese and stir to mix. Spread into the pan and bake for 30 to 35 minutes, or until a golden brown. Cool set on a wire rack and cut into small squares for serving.

SAUSAGE PIZZA

MAKES: *About 6 servings*

2 links chorizo sausage, crumbled
1 can (10 ounces) refrigerated pizza dough
1 cup shredded mozzarella cheese
1 cup shredded provolone cheese
2 small yellow summer squash, diced
1 red bell pepper, chopped
½ cup sliced green onion

1 Position the rack in the lowest position in the oven and preheat to 425 degrees F.

2 In a skillet, cook the sausage over medium-high heat for 5 or 6 minutes until cooked. Drain.

3 Prepare the pizza dough according to the package directions and fit into a 12-inch pizza pan. Sprinkle ½ cup of each cheese over the crust, top with sausage, squash, pepper and onion. Sprinkle with the remaining cheese and bake for 18 to 24 minutes, or until the crust is golden brown. Cut into wedges to serve.

1 can (4½ ounces) small shrimp
3 tablespoons mayonnaise
1 tablespoon finely chopped celery
1 tablespoon prepared chili sauce
2 teaspoons snipped chives
cocktail bread or crackers

1 Drain the shrimp and transfer to a sieve. Rinse under cold running water and spread on paper towels to dry.

2 In a bowl, combine the mayonnaise, celery, chili sauce and chives and mix well. Cover and chill for at least 2 hours. Serve with the bread or crackers.

SHRIMP SPREAD

MAKES: *About 6 servings*

¾ pound smoked fish, flaked
1 package (8 ounces) cream cheese, at room temperature
3 tablespoons heavy cream or evaporated milk
1 tablespoon lemon or lime juice
1 small clove garlic, minced
dash liquid smoke (optional)
rye or pumpernickle cocktail bread

In a bowl, combine the fish, cream cheese, lemon juice, garlic and liquid smoke and mix well. Cover and chill for at least 2 hours. Spread on the bread.

SMOKED FISH SPREAD

MAKES: *12 to 15 servings*

2 cups shredded Tillamook or Cheddar cheese, at room temperature
2 tablespoons white port wine or sherry
2 tablespoons butter or margarine, at room temperature
1 teaspoon minced shallot
1 teaspoon prepared brown mustard
1 large egg, lightly beaten
one 12- to 15-inch loaf French bread, halved lengthwise
2 small tomatoes, diced

1 Position the rack in the center of the oven and preheat to 400 degrees F.

2 In a bowl, combine the cheese, sherry and butter and mash to mix. Add the shallot, mustard and egg and stir well. Spread over the bread halves and transfer to an ungreased baking sheet and tent with aluminum foil. Bake for 8 to 10 minutes, or until the cheese melts and the bread is heated through. Cut each piece into slices and serve warm, garnished with tomatoes.

TILLAMOOK SURPRISE

MAKES: *About 8 servings*

TROPICAL COCONUT SPREAD

MAKES: *6 to 8 servings*

1 package (8 ounces) cream cheese, at room temperature
2 tablespoons pineapple preserves
⅓ cup flaked coconut
fresh fruit or crackers

In a bowl, combine the cream cheese and preserves and mash until blended. Add the coconut and stir to blend. Cover and chill for at least 1 hour. Serve with the fruit or crackers.

COOKING NOTE: **This is good served on fruit quick bread, such as banana bread or cranberry bread.**

TUNA FISH SPREAD

MAKES: *6 to 8 servings*

1 can (6½ ounces) albacore tuna, flaked
1 package (3 ounces) cream cheese, at room temperature
¼ teaspoon chopped dried chiles
3 or 4 slices whole-wheat bread, crusts trimmed

In a bowl, combine the tuna, cream cheese and chiles and mix well. Cover and chill for at least 1 hour. Spread on the bread and cut in half on the diagonal.

ORIENTAL EGG BALLS
MAKES: *24 to 30 servings*

vegetable oil
½ pound ham, finely chopped
1 tablespoon chopped white onion
3 large eggs, lightly beaten
3 slices white bread, crusts trimmed and bread cubed
2 tablespoons all-purpose flour
1 cup uncooked vermicelli, broken into ½-inch lengths

1 In a large skillet or deep-fat fryer, pour the oil to a depth of 2 inches and heat over medium-high heat until hot (375 degrees F. in a deep-fat fryer).

2 In a bowl, combine the ham, onion, eggs and bread and blend. Add enough flour to make a thick mash and mix until well incorporated.

3 Spread the vermicelli in a shallow dish. Pinch off pieces of the egg mixture and form into balls about the size of walnuts. Roll the balls in the vermicelli to coat and fry for 3 or 4 minutes or until golden brown. Drain on paper towels and serve hot.

WALNUT NIBBLIES
MAKES: *18 to 20 servings*

3 cups walnut halves
1½ tablespoons butter or margarine
2 tablespoons finely grated romano cheese

1 Position the rack in the center of the oven and preheat to 350 degrees F.

2 Spread the walnuts evenly on a jelly-roll pan and dot with butter. Bake for 18 to 20 minutes, or until golden brown, stirring or shaking the pan frequently so that the nuts are evenly coated with the butter.

3 Sprinkle the cheese over the nuts, toss gently and cool on a double thickness of paper towels to room temperature.

COOKING NOTE: For the most even distribution, put the cheese in a small mesh strainer for sprinkling the nuts.

ARTICHOKE HEART APPETIZERS
MAKES: *About 36 servings*

2 cans (8 ounces each) refrigerated crescent dinner rolls
¾ cup shredded mozzarella cheese
¾ cup grated Parmesan cheese
½ cup Kraft® French or Italian Dressing
1 can (14 ounces) water-packed artichoke hearts, drained and chopped
1 can (4 ounces) green chiles, chopped

1 Position the rack in the center of the oven and preheat to 375 degrees F.

2 Separate the dough into rectangles and press into a jelly-roll pan, smoothing along the perforations to cover the bottom of the pan. Bake for about 10 minutes, or until lightly browned.

3 In a bowl, combine the cheeses, dressing, artichoke hearts and chiles and mix well. Spread over the crust and bake for about 15 minutes longer or until the cheese melts. Let cool for about 5 minutes before cutting into squares.

BAGEL PIZZA BITES

MAKES: *About 10 servings*

2 teaspoons olive oil
1 onion, finely chopped
1 can (8 ounces) tomato sauce
½ teaspoon crushed dried oregano
¼ teaspoon garlic powder
salt and pepper
10 mini bagels, halved
1 cup shredded mozzarella cheese
2 cans (4 ounces each) sliced
    mushrooms

1 In a skillet, heat the olive oil over medium heat and cook the onion for about 5 minutes until softened and lightly browned. Add the tomato sauce, oregano and garlic powder. Season with salt and pepper and mix well. Reduce the heat and simmer for about 25 minutes until the flavors blend. Cool to room temperature.

2 Position the broiler rack about 6 inches from the heat source and preheat the broiler.

3 Spread the sauce over the bagel halves, sprinkle with mozzarella cheese and top with mushrooms. Transfer to a broiling pan and broil for 3 or 4 minutes or until the cheese bubbles. Serve hot.

BAKED SHRIMP

MAKES: *About 4 servings*

½ cup peanut oil
2 cloves garlic, minced
2 tablespoons Creole seasoning
2 tablespoons grapefruit juice
1 tablespoon honey
1 tablespoon soy sauce
1 pound large shrimp, peeled and
    deveined
lemon wedges
pumpernickel bread

1 In a baking dish, combine the oil, garlic, seasoning, grapefruit juice, honey and soy sauce and mix well. Add the shrimp, toss to coat, cover and chill for at least 1 hour and no longer than 4 hours.

2 Position the rack in the center of the oven and preheat to 450 degrees F.

3 Bake the shrimp for 8 to 10 minutes or until the shrimp turns pink and is cooked through. Serve garnished with lemon wedges and with the bread.

BARBECUED GARLIC

MAKES: *About 8 servings*

8 large heads garlic
¼ cup butter or margarine
4 sprigs fresh rosemary
French bread, sliced

1 Prepare a charcoal or gas grill.

2 Peel the papery outer skins from the garlic, leaving the cloves intact. Put 2 heads in the center of a large square of aluminum foil. To each, add 1 tablespoon of butter and a sprig of rosemary. Fold the foil into a secure packet.

3 Grill the packets for about 40 minutes, or until the garlic cloves are softened. Unwrap the garlic heads, separate into cloves and serve squeezed on the bread.

1 package (10 count) refrigerator
   biscuits
¼ cup butter or margarine
3 tablespoons crumbled blue cheese

1 Position the rack in the center
of the oven and preheat to 400
degrees F. Lightly grease a baking sheet.

2 Separate the biscuits and cut
each into quarters. Transfer to the
baking sheet.

3 In a saucepan, combine the
butter and cheese and cook over
low heat, stirring, until the butter
melts and blends with the cheese.
Drizzle over the biscuits and
bake for 12 to 15 minutes or until
golden.

BLUE CHEESE BALLS

MAKES: *About 40 servings*

1 pound fresh mushrooms, about 1½
   inches in diameter
¼ cup sliced green onion
2 tablespoons butter or margarine
1 package (4 ounces) crumbed blue
   cheese
1 package (3 ounces) cream cheese,
   at room temperature

1 Position the broiler rack about
6 inches from the heat source and
preheat the broiler.

2 Remove the stems from the
mushrooms and finely chop the
stems. Transfer to a skillet, add

the onion and butter and cook
over medium heat for about 5
minutes until the onions soften.
Transfer to a bowl, add the blue
cheese and cream cheese and mix
well.

3 Spoon the mixture into the
mushroom caps, transfer to a
broiling pan, stuffed side up, and
broil for 2 or 3 minutes or until
lightly browned and heated
through.

BLUE CHEESE MUSHROOMS

MAKES: *About 6 servings*

BRAISED CUCUMBERS

MAKES: *About 6 servings*

2 tablespoons canola oil
6 cucumbers, peeled and cut into
    1-inch cubes
2 tablespoons soy sauce
1 teaspoon sugar

In a skillet, heat the oil over medium-high heat for about 1 minute. Add the cucumbers and stir-fry for 1 or 2 minutes, tossing so that each cube is coated. Add the soy sauce and stir fry about 2 minutes longer. Add the sugar, reduce the heat, cover and simmer for 15 to 20 minutes, stirring occasionally, until softened. Cool for about 5 minutes before serving.

BRAUNSCHWEIGER BALL

MAKES: *6 to 8 servings*

1 package (8 ounces) cream cheese,
    at room temperature
1 pound braunschweiger, at room
    temperature
¾ cup finely chopped dill pickles
¼ cup Kraft® Real Mayonnaise
¼ cup chopped onion
2 tablespoons dill pickle juice
1 tablespoon Worcestershire sauce
¼ teaspoon garlic salt
3 drops hot red-pepper sauce
½ cup chopped unsalted peanuts
crackers

1 In a bowl, combine half of the cream cheese, the braunschweiger, pickles, mayonnaise, onion, pickle juice, Worcestershire sauce, garlic salt and pepper sauce and mix well. Form into a ball, cover and chill for at least 3 hours.

2 Spread the remaining cream cheese over the ball and garnish with nuts. Cover and chill for at least 1 hour longer. Serve with crackers.

COOKING NOTE: **Braunschweiger is a type of liver sausage. Use any liverwurst if you cannot find braunschweiger.**

CHICKEN FLAUTAS

MAKES: *About 12 servings*

3 cups finely diced cooked chicken
1 cup water
1 package chicken taco seasoning
    mix
vegetable oil
12 (7-inch) flour tortillas
sour cream

1 In a large skillet, combine the chicken, water and seasoning mix and bring to a boil over high heat. Reduce the heat and simmer for about 10 minutes, stirring, until the mixture thickens.

2 In another skillet, pour the oil to a depth of about ½ inch and heat over medium-high heat until hot.

3 Spoon the chicken mixture down the center of each tortilla and roll to form a tight roll. Using tongs, fry the tortillas in the oil, seam-side down, to seal. Turn and brown on all sides. Drain on paper towels. You will have to cook the flautas in batches. Serve with sour cream on the side.

2 pound lean ground beef
3 cloves garlic, crushed
1 teaspoon pepper
½ teaspoon ground allspice
¼ teaspoon salt
½ cup club soda

1 In a large bowl, combine the beef, garlic, pepper, allspice and salt and mix until compact. Add the soda, a little at time, kneading between each addition, until smooth and elastic.

2 Pinch off pieces of the mixture and form into logs about 3 or 4 inches long and 1 inch in diameter. Transfer to a plate, cover and chill for at least 24 hours.

3 Let the logs stand at room temperature for 1 hour before cooking.

4 Position the broiler rack about 6 inches from the heat source and preheat the broiler.

5 Broil the logs for about 10 minutes, turning frequently, until browned. Take care the logs do not break apart.

CARNATZLACH

MAKES: *About 6 servings*

---

2 cups grated sharp Cheddar cheese
1 cup all-purpose flour
½ cup butter or margarine, at room temperature
1 jar (4 ounces) pimiento-stuffed olives

1 In a bowl, combine the cheese, flour and butter and mix well. Pinch off pieces of the mixture and form into balls about the size of walnuts. Flatten each ball and press an olive in the center. Fold the cheese mixture around the olive and seal to enclose the

olive. Repeat until all the ingredients are used. Transfer to a freezer-safe plate, cover with wax paper and freeze for at least 4 hours or until very firm.

2 Position the rack in the center of the oven and preheat to 375 degrees F. Lightly grease a baking sheet.

3 Transfer the balls to the baking sheet and bake for 8 to 10 minutes or until golden brown. Cool on wire racks.

CHEDDAR CHEESE APPETIZERS

MAKES: *About 6 servings*

1½ cups all-purpose flour
¼ teaspoon salt
½ cup chopped walnuts or pecans
⅔ cup butter or margarine
3 or 4 tablespoons ice water
2 rounds (4½ ounces each) Brie cheese

1 Position the rack in the center of the oven and preheat to 425 degrees F.

2 In a bowl, combine the flour, salt and walnuts and using a pastry blender or two knives, cut the butter into the dry ingredients until the mixture resembles coarse crumbs. Sprinkle about 3 tablespoons of ice water over the mixture and blend until the

dough holds its shape. Add more ice water, a teaspoon at a time, if necessary. Form into a ball and divide into quarters.

3 On a lightly floured surface, roll each piece of dough into a 6-inch circle. Put a round of Brie in the center of 1 circle and top with another circle. Using a fork, crimp the edges of the pastry to seal. Repeat with the other round of Brie and remaining circles of pastry. Transfer to an ungreased baking sheet and bake for 20 to 25 minutes or until lightly golden. Cool on wire racks for about 30 minutes. Cut into wedges to serve.

BRIE IN WALNUT PASTRY

MAKES: *About 16 servings*

CHICKEN HORS D'OEUVRES

MAKES: *About 35 servings*

1 package (3 ounces) cream cheese, at room temperature
1 can (5 ounces) chicken spread
⅓ cup diced unpeeled apples
¼ cup chopped walnuts or pecans
¼ cup plus 1 tablespoon chopped parsley
½ teaspoon Worcestershire sauce
pinch of cayenne
toasted wheat germ

1 In a bowl, using an electric mixer on low speed, beat the cream cheese until smooth. Add the chicken spread, apples, walnuts, parsley, Worcestershire sauce and cayenne and beat until mixed. Cover and chill for at least 2 hours.

2 Spread the wheat germ in a shallow dish. Pinch off pieces of the chicken mixture and form into balls about the size of walnuts and roll in the wheat germ to coat. Transfer to a platter, cover and chill for at least 1 hour.

CHICKIE CHEESE BALLS

MAKES: *About 30 servings*

1 cup finely chopped cooked chicken
⅓ cup shredded Gruyere cheese
¼ cup finely chopped celery
3 tablespoons mayonnaise
1 tablespoon chopped parsley
¼ teaspoon crushed dried tarragon
hot pepper sauce
salt and pepper

1 Position the rack in the center of the oven and preheat to 350 degrees F. Lightly grease a baking sheet.

2 In a bowl, combine the chicken, cheese, celery, mayonnaise, parsley and tarragon and season with pepper sauce and salt and pepper and mix well. Pinch off pieces of the mixture and form into balls about the size of walnuts and transfer to the baking sheet. Bake for 8 to 10 minutes or until lightly browned.

CLAM HOT CAKES

MAKES: *About 24 servings*

1½ cups all-purpose flour
1½ teaspoons baking powder
¼ teaspoon salt
1 large egg
½ cup milk
2 tablespoons butter or margarine, melted
1 teaspoon instant minced onions
¼ teaspoon pepper
1 can (10 ounces) minced clams, drained and liquid reserved

1 In a bowl, combine the flour, baking powder and salt and whisk well.

2 In another bowl, using an electric mixer on high speed, beat the egg until light colored. Add the milk, butter, onion, pepper and reserved clam liquid and mix well. Add the dry ingredients and beat until smooth. Add the clams and stir gently to mix.

3 Preheat a nonstick skillet or griddle and drop the batter by tablespoonfuls onto the hot skillet and cook for 2 or 3 minutes, turning once, until golden brown.

1 pound firm tofu
3 or 4 ounces peanut sauce mix

1 Position the rack in the center of the oven and preheat to 350 degrees F.

2 Cut the tofu in quarters and spread the sauce mix on all sides. Transfer to an ungreased baking sheet and bake for 12 to 15 minutes or until heated through.

COOKING NOTE: Peanut sauce mix is available in Asian markets.

COAT-AND-BAKE TOFU
MAKES: *4 servings*

2 packages (3 ounces each) Roquefort cheese
1 package (4 ounces) shredded Cheddar cheese
1 package (8 ounces) cream cheese, at room temperature
1 package (about 3.5 ounces) flaked coconut

1 In a bowl, using an electric mixer on medium-high speed, beat the cheeses until smooth. Cover and chill for at least 1 hour.

2 Spread the coconut in a shallow bowl. Pinch off pieces of the cheese mixture and form into balls about the size of walnuts and roll in the coconut to coat.

COCONUT-AND-CHEESE BALLS
MAKES: *About 12 servings*

3 packages (8 ounces each) cream cheese, at room temperature
2 tablespoons Kraft® Real Mayonnaise
dash of hot red-pepper sauce
1 teaspoon lemon juice (optional)
¼ cup finely chopped green onion
¼ cup finely chopped celery
dash of paprika
salt and pepper
1 can (16 ounces) pitted ripe olives, drained and finely chopped
1 can (8 ounces) crabmeat, drained and flaked
nacho cheese-flavored tortilla chips

1 In a bowl, using an electric mixer on medium-high speed, beat together the cream cheese, mayonnaise and pepper sauce until smooth. The mixture should be just a little thicker than mayonnaise. Add the lemon juice to thin it, if necessary.

2 Add the onion and celery, season with paprika, salt and pepper and mix well. Add the olives and crabmeat and fold gently to mix. Serve with tortilla chips.

COLD CRAB AND NACHOS
MAKES: *About 16 servings*

COLD NOODLE SALAD WITH PEANUT BUTTER

MAKES: *About 6 servings*

2 tablespoons sesame oil
½ pound Asian noodles, cooked and kept warm
½ cup creamy peanut butter
¼ cup plus 2 tablespoons water
¼ cup plus 2 tablespoons soy sauce
3 tablespoons red wine vinegar
1 tablespoon sugar
½ teaspoon dried red pepper flakes
6 stalks celery, very thinly sliced

1 In a bowl, sprinkle 1 tablespoon of the oil over the noodles, tossing to coat. Cover and chill for at least 1 hour.

2 In a bowl, combine the peanut butter with the water, adding the water a tablespoon at a time and stirring until smooth. Add the remaining oil, the soy sauce, vinegar, sugar and pepper flakes and stir until well mixed.

3 Add the peanut butter to the noodles and toss gently. Top with the celery and serve.

CRAB LOUIS

MAKES: *4 servings*

¾ cup chili sauce
½ cup mayonnaise
1 teaspoon finely chopped onion
½ teaspoon sugar
¼ teaspoon Worcestershire sauce
salt and white pepper
bibb lettuce
2 cups cooked crabmeat
4 tomatoes, quartered
4 large hard-cooked eggs, quartered
24 pimiento-stuffed olives

1 In the container of a blender, combine the chili sauce, mayonnaise, onion, sugar and Worcestershire sauce and process until smooth. Season to taste with salt and pepper and process again to mix.

2 Divide the lettuce among 4 plates. Top with crabmeat, tomatoes and eggs and spoon the sauce over evenly. Garnish with olives and serve.

1 cup finely diced green onion
1 avocado, finely diced
2 large eggs
½ cup mild salsa
salt and pepper
2 pounds fresh crabmeat
¼ cup dried bread crumbs
vegetable oil
all-purpose flour
1 small green bell pepper, finely
   sliced

1 In a bowl, combine the onions and avocado and mix well.

2 In another bowl, combine the eggs and salsa, season with salt and pepper and stir well. Add the crabmeat and bread crumbs and stir until well mixed. Mix with the avocado mixture.

3 Pinch off pieces of the mixture and form into balls about the size of walnuts and transfer to a baking sheet lined with parchment paper. Cover and chill for at least 4 hours.

4 In a heavy skillet or deep-fat fryer, pour the oil to a depth of 2 inches and heat over medium-high heat until hot (375 degrees F. in a deep-fat fryer).

5 Spread the flour in a shallow dish and roll the balls in the flour to coat. Fry for 3 or 4 minutes or until golden brown. Drain on paper towels. You will have to cook the fritters in batches. Serve warm, garnished with peppers.

CRAB-AND-AVOCADO FRITTERS

MAKES: *About 48 fritters*

1½ cups Kraft® Real Mayonnaise
½ cup sour cream
⅓ cup lemon juice
¼ cup sugar
1 large red onion, thinly sliced
2 tablespoons crushed dried dill
2 pounds medium-sized cooked
   shrimp, shelled and deveined

In a bowl, combine the mayonnaise, sour cream, lemon juice, sugar, onion and dill and mix well. Add the shrimp and toss to coat. Cover and chill for at least 8 hours. Serve with toothpicks on the side.

DILLED SHRIMP

MAKES: *8 to 10 servings*

HAM-AND-CHEESE CELERY STICKS

MAKES: *About 12 servings*

1 can (2¼ ounces) deviled ham
1 package (3 ounces) cream cheese, at room temperature
½ teaspoon spicy prepared mustard
½ teaspoon hot red-pepper sauce
4 stalks celery, cut into 3-inch lengths
pickle relish for garnish

In a bowl, combine the ham, cream cheese, mustard and pepper sauce and mix well. Press into the indentation in the celery lengths. Cover and chill for at least 1 hour.

JALAPEÑOS STUFFED WITH CHORIZO AND CREAM CHEESE

MAKES: *About 6 servings*

1 tablespoon vegetable oil
1 tablespoon finely minced onion
1 clove garlic, minced
3 ounces chorizo sausage, crumbled
2 tablespoons cream cheese, at room temperature
1 tablespoon sour cream
salt
12 jalapeño peppers, halved horizontally and seeded

1 In a skillet, heat the oil over medium heat and cook the onion and garlic for about 3 minutes until the onions are transparent. Add the sausage and cook for about 5 minutes, stirring, until heated through. Cool slightly.

2 Add the cream cheese and sour cream. Season with salt and mix well. Spoon into the jalapeños, cover and chill for at least 30 minutes.

¼ cup butter or margarine
2 tablespoons grated American cheese
1 tablespoon heavy cream
1 tablespoon chopped parsley
1 teaspoon prepared mustard
6 slices white or pumpernickel bread, crusts trimmed

1 Position the broiler rack about 6 inches from the heat source and preheat the broiler.

2 In a bowl, using an electric mixer on medium speed, beat the butter until smooth. Add the cheese, cream, parsley and mustard and mix well. Spread on the bread and cut each slice into thirds. Transfer to a broiling pan and cook for 3 or 4 minutes or until golden brown.

PARSLEY STRIPS
MAKES: *18 servings*

---

vegetable oil
2 cups ground cooked ham
1 can (7 ounces) whole-kernel corn, drained
2 large eggs, lightly beaten
¼ cup mayonnaise
1 teaspoon prepared mustard
2 cups Cheese It® cracker crumbs

1 In a skillet or deep-fat fryer, pour the oil to a depth of about 2 inches and heat over medium-high heat until hot (375 degrees F. in a deep-fat fryer).

2 In a bowl, combine the ham, corn, eggs, mayonnaise and mustard and mix well. Add 1 cup of the cracker crumbs and stir until blended.

3 Spread the remaining cup of crumbs in a shallow dish. Pinch off pieces of the mixture and form into balls about the size of walnuts and roll in the crumbs to coat completely. Fry, a few balls at a time, for 2 or 3 minutes or until golden brown. Drain on paper towels and serve warm.

PARTY NIBBLES
MAKES: *24 to 36 servings*

PINEAPPLE-PECAN CHEESE BALL

MAKES: *8 to 10 servings*

1 package (8 ounces) cream cheese
1 can (15 ounces) crushed pineapple, drained
2 cups finely chopped pecans
¼ cup chopped green bell pepper
2 tablespoons finely chopped white onion
2 cans (8 ounces each) sliced pineapple, drained
½ cup pecan halves for garnish
maraschino cherries for garnish
crackers

1 In a bowl, combine the cream cheese, crushed pineapple, chopped pecans, pepper and onion and mix well. Cover and chill for at least 1 hour.

2 Form into a ball and wrap in plastic wrap. Chill for at least 30 minutes longer before serving.

3 Press the pineapple slices into the sides of the ball and press the walnut halves between the slices and a cherry in the center of each slice. Serve with crackers.

SAVORY SWISS CHEESE BITES

MAKES: *6 to 8 servings*

1 cup water
½ cup butter or margarine
¼ teaspoon salt
1 cup all-purpose flour
4 large eggs
1 cup shredded Swiss cheese

1 Position the rack in the center of the oven and preheat to 400 degrees F. Lightly grease a baking sheet.

2 In a saucepan, combine the water, butter and salt and heat over high heat, stirring, until the butter melts and the mixture boils. Add the flour all at once and stir vigorously until the mixture holds together and pulls away from the sides of the pan. Remove from the heat and add the eggs, 1 at a time, stirring well after each addition until smooth. Return the pan to the heat and add the cheese, stirring until blended.

3 Drop the batter by teaspoonfuls onto the baking sheet and bake for 18 to 20 minutes our until puffed and golden. Cool on wire racks for about 5 minutes before serving.

Chapter 3

COMPANY'S COMING CANAPÉS

The word that best describes this chapter is versatility. Whenever you set out to make canapés or small cocktail sandwiches, be prepared to mix and match flavors with glorious abandon. Included here are recipes appropriate for creating a kaleidoscope of colorful, tasty foods sure to charm guests. Use the flavored butters and spreads as little or as generously as you personally prefer. They transform a simple slice of white or wheat bread into something truly spectacular—and very deftly turn you into a host or hostess with a reputation for great food.

ANCHOVY-AND-CHEESE CANAPÉS

MAKES: *32 canapés*

¾ cup Cheese-and-Green Olive
   Filling (recipe follows)
32 melba toast rounds
64 anchovy fillets

1 Position a rack in the center of
the oven and preheat to 450
degrees F.

CHEESE-AND-GREEN OLIVE FILLING

MAKES: *About ⅔ cup*

¼ cup mayonnaise
2 tablespoons cream cheese, at
   room temperature
5 tablespoons thinly sliced
   pimiento-filled green olives.

2 Spread a generous amount of
the filling on the rounds and
transfer to a baking sheet. Bake
for 2 to 4 minutes until the filling
bubbles. Crisscross the anchovy
fillets over the filling and serve.

In a bowl, combine the mayonnaise and cream cheese and
blend well. Add the olives and
stir until well mixed. Cover and
chill for at least 1 hour.

HAM-AND-CHUTNEY-FILLED EGG CANAPÉS

MAKES: *8 canapés*

1 package (3 ounces) cream cheese,
   at room temperature
8 slices white bread, cut into 2½-
   inch ovals
4 hard-cooked eggs, cut in half
   lengthwise
1 cup Ham-and-Chutney Sandwich
   Filling (recipe follows)
ripe olive slices, for garnish
shredded lettuce

1 Spread the cream cheese over
the bread.

HAM-AND-CHUTNEY SANDWICH FILLING

MAKES ABOUT: *2 cups*

1 cup chopped boiled ham
1 cup plum or fruit chutney

2 Remove and the yolks from the
eggs and spoon the filling into
the whites. Set the eggs on the
bread. Surround the eggs with
olive slices and place on a bed of
lettuce. Chill until ready to serve.

COOKING NOTE: **Reserve the
yolks for another use.**

In a small bowl, combine the
ham and chutney and stir to
blend. Cover and chill for at
least 2 hours.

2 tablespoons lemon juice
8 thin apple slices, halved
8 slices white bread, toasted
¼ cup Cheese Butter (recipe follows)
1 cup Apple-and-Cheese Filling
   (recipe follows)
celery leaves, for garnish

1 Brush the lemon juice over both sides of the apples slices and set aside.

2 Using decorative cookie cutters, cut the bread into various shapes.

3 Spread the butter evenly over the bread, spreading to the edge, and top with a layer of filling. Garnish with the apples and celery leaves.

APPLE-AND-CHEESE CANAPÉS

MAKES: *8 canapés*

CHEESE BUTTER

MAKES: *About ¾ cup*

½ cup unsalted butter
¼ cup grated Parmesan or Romano
   cheese

In a small bowl or cup, mash the butter until soft and creamy. Add the cheese and fold thoroughly.

APPLE-AND-CHEESE FILLING

MAKES: *About 1¼ cups*

½ cup Roquefort cheese
2 tablespoons butter, at room
   temperature
1 apple, peeled, cored and finely
   chopped
1 tablespoon black currants
   (optional)

In a bowl, combine the cheese and butter and stir until smooth. Add the apple and currants and stir until mixed. Cover and chill for at least 1 hour.

---

8 slices dark rye or pumpernickel
   bread, crusts trimmed
3 tablespoons Black Butter (see page
   48)
8 slices smoked turkey
3 tablespoons Mustard Dip (see
   page 48)
3 tablespoons chopped pimento
3 tablespoons chopped green olives
2 hard-cooked eggs, thinly sliced

Butter the bread and then lay a slice of turkey on each slice of bread. Spoon a line of dip down the center of each slice and sprinkle a row of pimientos on 1 side of the dip and a row of olives on the other. Place a slice of egg in the center and serve.

BLACK RUSSIAN CANAPÉS

MAKES ABOUT: *8 canapés*

BACON-AND-ENDIVE FILLED CANAPÉS

MAKES: *16 canapés*

8 slices white bread, toasted
¼ cup Egg Spread with Peanut Butter (recipe follows)
1 cup Bacon-Endive Sandwich Filling (see page 31)
¼ cup bacon bits

Cut the bread into 16 squares or triangles and spread with the egg spread. Spread a layer of the filling on top and garnish with bacon bits. Serve at once.

EGG SPREAD WITH PEANUT BUTTER

MAKES: *About 1 cup*

3 large hard-cooked eggs, mashed
3 tablespoons minced sweet pickles
2 tablespoons creamy peanut butter
½ teaspoon prepared mustard mayonnaise

In a bowl, using an electric mixer on medium speed, combine the eggs, pickles, peanut butter and mustard and beat to mix. Add enough mayonnaise to bind and beat until all the ingredients are incorporated. Cover and chill for at least 1 hour.

BAKED BEAN CANAPÉS

MAKES: *8 canapés*

½ cup canned baked beans
1 tablespoon salsa
2 tablespoons Bean Butter (recipe follows)
8 slices white bread
8 strips bacon
8 small jalapeño peppers, stemmed (optional)

1 Position a rack in the center of the oven and preheat to 400 degrees F.

2 In small bowl, combine the beans and salsa.

3 Spread the bean butter on the bread, spreading it to the edge. Trim the crusts and roll each slice into a cylinder. Wrap a strip of bacon around each bread roll and fasten with toothpicks. Lay the rolls in a baking dish and bake for 4 to 6 minutes, or until the bacon is crisp. Garnish each roll by threading a small pepper on the end of each toothpick. Serve with the salsa mixture on the side.

BEAN BUTTER

MAKES: *About ¾ cup*

¼ cup unsalted butter
½ cup canned baked beans, mashed

In a small bowl or cup, mash the butter until soft and creamy. Add the baked beans and fold until blended.

3 tablespoons Pimiento Butter
(recipe follows)
4 slices cracked-wheat bread
4 thin slices bologna
8 slices sweet pickles
8 pimiento-stuffed olives

1 Position the rack in the center of the oven and preheat to 400 degrees F. Lightly grease a baking sheet.

2 Spread the butter on the bread and top with a slice of bologna. Transfer to the baking sheet and bake for 3 to 4 minutes, or until the bologna starts to curl at the edges.

3 Slice in half on the diagonal and put a pickle slice in the center of each triangle. Attach an olive to each with a toothpick. Serve warm.

BOLOGNA CANAPÉS
MAKES: *8 canapés*

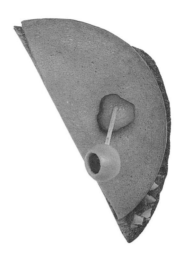

PIMIENTO BUTTER
MAKES: *About ¼ cup*

¼ cup unsalted butter
1 tablespoon chopped pimiento

In a small bowl or cup, mash the butter until soft and creamy. Add the pimiento and stir until blended.

---

2 tablespoons Onion Butter (recipe follows)
8 slices cocktail rye bread
½ cup Cheese-and-Nut Filling (recipe follows)
¼ cup chopped or sliced Brazil nuts

1 Position a rack in the center of the oven and preheat to 400 degrees F. Lightly grease a baking sheet.

2 Spread the butter evenly over the bread, spreading to the edge. Spread the filling over the butter and transfer to the baking sheet. Bake for 3 to 4 minutes, or until the cheese melts. Sprinkle with nuts and slice the toast in half. Serve warm.

BRAZIL NUT CANAPÉS
MAKES: *16 canapés*

ONION BUTTER
MAKES: *About ¼ cup*

¼ cup unsalted butter, softened
1 tablespoon finely chopped white onions or snipped chives

In a small bowl or cup, mash the butter until soft and creamy. Add the onions or chives and blend well.

CHEESE-AND-NUT FILLING
MAKES: *About 1¼ cup*

¼ cup mayonnaise
¼ cup shredded provolone cheese
2 tablespoons chopped walnuts
2 tablespoons chopped pecans
dash of Worcestershire sauce

In the container of a blender, combine the mayonnaise, cheese and nuts and process at slow speed for 2 to 5 seconds, or until nearly smooth. Season to taste with Worcestershire sause. Transfer to a bowl, cover, and chill for at least 2 hours.

CARROT-AND-PICKLE CANAPÉS

MAKES: *16 canapés*

¼ cup Roquefort Cheese Butter (see page 18)
4 slices honey whole-wheat bread, toasted, crusts trimmed
1 cup Pickle-and-Carrot Filling (recipe follows)
2 kosher dill pickles, sliced lengthwise into thin strips
chopped parsley for garnish
whole chives for garnish

Spread the butter on the bread, spreading to the edges. Spread a layer of filling over the butter and cut the bread into quarters. Lay a pickle slice on each quarter and garnish with parsley and chives.

PICKLE-AND-CARROT FILLING

MAKES: *About 2 cups*

1 cup grated carrots
½ cup finely chopped sweet pickles
½ cup mayonnaise

In a small bowl, combine the carrots, pickles, and mayonnaise and stir well. Cover and chill until ready to use.

CAVIAR-AND-SHRIMP CANAPÉS

MAKES: *16 canapés*

8 cooked jumbo shrimp
½ cup French salad dressing
16 slices cocktail bread, toasted
1 tablespoon lemon juice
¼ cup mayonnaise
1 jar (2 ounces) caviar (red or black)
lemon wedges for garnish
shredded lettuce

1 Split the shrimp along the inside curl so that they are in 2 pieces. Transfer to a bowl and add the salad dressing. Toss gently, cover and chill for at least 2 hours and not longer than 4 hours.

2 Brush the toast with lemon juice and then spread with mayonnaise. Place a shrimp half on top, flat side down, and pull the ends in to accentuate the curve. Place a ½ teaspoon of caviar in the curve of the shrimp and garnish with a wedge of lemon. Serve on a bed of lettuce.

CAVIAR CANAPÉS

MAKES: *16 canapés*

16 small round plain crackers
2 tablespoons lemon juice
1 cup Plain Caviar Filling (recipe follows)
thinly cut lemon wedges

Brush each cracker with lemon juice and put, brushed side up, on a tray. Spoon a dab of filling in the center of each and garnish with a lemon wedge. Chill until ready to serve.

PLAIN CAVIAR FILLING

MAKES: *About 1 cup*

6 ounces black or red caviar
2 tablespoons minced white onions
2 tablespoons lemon juice

In a bowl, combine the caviar, onions and lemon juice and stir gently. Cover and chill for at least 1 hour.

1 package (3 ounces) cream cheese, at room temperature
¼ cup undiluted cream of celery soup
1 cup chopped salami slices
20 Rye Krisp® crackers
buttered bread crumbs, for garnish

1 Position a rack in the center of the oven and preheat to 350 degrees F. Lightly grease a baking sheet.

2 In a small bowl, combine the cream cheese, soup and salami and blend thoroughly. Heap the mixture into the center of each of the crackers and transfer the crackers to the baking sheet. Sprinkle with bread crumbs and bake for 3 to 4 minutes, or until the crumbs are browned. Serve warm.

COOKING NOTE: **Do not use dry Italian-style salami**

CELERY CANAPÉS

MAKES: *20 canapés*

¼ cup Olive Butter (recipe follows)
8 ½-inch thick slices Italian bread
1 cup Cheese-and-Green Olive Filling (see page 142)
chopped parsley for garnish
16 pimiento-stuffed olives, thinly sliced

Spread the butter on the bread and spread a layer of filling over the butter. Sprinkle with parsley and arrange olive slices on the top. Cover and chill for at least 1 hour.

CHEESE-AND-OLIVE CANAPÉS

MAKES: *8 canapés*

OLIVE BUTTER

MAKES: *About ¼ cup*

¼ cup unsalted butter
2 tablespoons finely chopped ripe or green olives
¼ teaspoon lemon or lime juice

In a small bowl or cup, mash the butter until soft and creamy. Add the olives and lemon juice and fold to blend.

CHEESE-AND-TOMATO CANAPÉS

MAKES: *12 canapés*

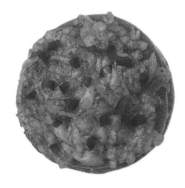

12 3½-inch rounds white bread
3 tablespoons olive oil
6 ounces American cheese, at room temperature
¼ teaspoon salt
pinch of paprika
2 large tomatoes, sliced into 12 slices
diced green bell pepper or tomato

1 Position the rack in the center of the oven and preheat to 375 degrees F.

2 In a skillet, heat 1 tablespoon of oil over medium-high heat and sauté the bread rounds for 1 to 2 minutes on one side only until lightly brown on the bottom.

3 Force the cheese though a ricer and transfer to a bowl. Add the salt and paprika and set aside.

4 Brush the remaining 2 tablespoons olive oil on the untoasted sides of the bread rounds and top each with a tomato slice. Sprinkle with the cheese mixture and transfer to a baking sheet. Bake for 3 to 4 minutes, or until the cheese melts. Garnish with the peppers or tomatoes and serve.

COOKING NOTE: **If you do not have a ricer, coarsely grate the cheese.**

CHEESE CANAPÉS WITH NUTS AND RAISINS

MAKES: *32 canapés*

16 slices white bread
¼ cup Sesame Seed Butter (recipe follows)
1 cup Cheese-and-Nut Filling with Raisins (recipe follows)
32 pecan halves
32 mint leaves

Using a crescent-shaped cookie cutter, cut out 32 bread crescents. Spread each with butter, spreading to the edges. Mound a spoonful of filling in the center of the crescents and press a pecan half and mint leaf into each mound. Serve at once.

SESAME SEED BUTTER

MAKES: *About ¼ cup*

¼ cup unsalted butter
2 tablespoons toasted sesame seeds

In a small bowl or cup, mash the butter until soft and creamy. Add the sesame seeds and fold until well mixed.

CHEESE-AND-NUT FILLING WITH RAISINS

MAKES: *About 1¼ cup*

½ cup grated Gruyere cheese
¾ cup ground walnuts
2 tablespoons Brie cheese, mashed
salt and pepper
½ cup seedless raisins
chopped walnuts for garnish

In a bowl, use a spoon to combine the Gruyere cheese, ground nuts, and Brie cheese and season to taste with salt and pepper. Blend well, cover, and chill for at least 1 hour. Sprinkle the raisins and chopped walnuts on the chilled mixture, pressing them lightly into the surface and use immediately.

8 slices white bread, toasted
¼ cup Olive Butter (see page 147)
1 cup Cheese-and-Green Olive
    Filling (see page 142)
¼ cup bacon bits
8 thin lemon slices, halved

Cut each slice of toasted bread in half to make 16 rectangles or tri-angles. Spread the butter on the bread, spreading it to the edge. Spread a layer of filling over the top and garnish with bacon bits. Lay a slice of lemon on each canapé, cover, and chill until ready to serve.

CHEESE CANAPÉS WITH OLIVES

MAKES: *16 canapés*

3 tablespoons Anchovy Butter (see
    page 17)
8 slices home-style white bread,
    crusts trimmed
8 slices chicken
anchovy paste, for garnish
rolled anchovy fillets, for garnish

1 Spread the butter on the bread, spreading it to the edge. Using a 2- to 2½-inch round cookie cut-ter, cut at least 16 rounds from the bread.

2 Cut an equal number of rounds from the chicken. Lay a chicken round on each slice of bread. Put a dab of anchovy paste in the center of the chicken and a rolled anchovy fillet in the center of the paste. Serve at once.

CHICKEN CANAPÉS

MAKES: *16 canapés*

½ cup Roquefort Cheese Butter (see
    page 18)
8 melba toast rounds
1 cup sautéed chicken livers,
    chopped fine
¼ cup chopped crisp fried bacon
8 slices cucumber, each cut into 8
    wedges
8 cherry tomatoes, sliced thin

1 Spread the butter on the toast rounds.

2 In a small bowl, combine the chicken livers and bacon and mix well. Spread on the rounds. Lay the cucumber wedges around the edge of the rounds with the points towards the center. Place a cherry tomato in the center and serve at once.

CHICKEN LIVER-AND-BACON CANAPÉS

MAKES: *8 canapés*

COOKED TONGUE CANAPÉS

MAKES: *8 canapés*

¼ cup Cheese Butter (see page 143)
8 slices white bread, toasted, cut into 3-inch squares
8 thin slices cooked tongue
2 tablespoons tomato sauce
2 hard-cooked eggs, sliced

Spread the butter on the bread, spreading it to the edge. Lay a slice of tongue on each slice and brush with tomato sauce. Set an egg slice in the center of the canapé, cover, and chill until ready to serve.

COTTAGE CHEESE STACKS

MAKES: *16 canapés*

1 small cucumber, peeled and cut into a 2-inch pieces
16 slices white bread
¼ cup Pimiento Butter (see page 145)
1¼ cups Cottage Cheese Filling (see page 34)
16 tomato slices
watercress sprigs for garnish

1 Using a melon baller, remove the core from the cucumber and slice it into very thin slices; each slice should have a hole in the center.

2 Using a round scallop-shaped cookie cutter, cut 16 rounds from the bread and spread each round with the butter, spreading it to the edge. Spread 1 cup of the filling on the rounds and top each with a tomato slice. Set a cucumber slice on each tomato and dollop a little of the remaining ¼ cup of filling in the hole of each cucumber slice. Garnish with watercress sprigs.

CRAB CANAPÉS WITH MUSHROOMS

MAKES: *18 canapés*

2 tablespoons Anchovy Butter (see page 17)
9 slices buttermilk or white bread
8 ounces cooked crabmeat, flaked
2 cans (4 ounces each) sliced mushrooms, drained
¼ cup heavy cream
4 drops hot pepper sauce
dash of cayenne
½ cup grated Romano cheese
buttered bread crumbs for garnish

1 Position a rack in the center of the oven and preheat to 425 degrees F. Lightly grease a baking sheet.

2 Spread the butter on the bread. Using a diamond-shaped cookie cutter, cut 2 diamond shapes from each slice of bread.

3 In a small bowl, combine the crabmeat, mushrooms, cream, pepper sauce and cayenne and blend well. Spread on the bread, sprinkle with the cheese and bread crumbs and transfer to the baking sheet. Bake for 8 to 10 minutes, or until the crumbs are browned. Serve warm.

¼ cup Blue Cheese Butter (recipe follows)
16 slices Swedish rye bread with caraway seeds
1¼ cups Crab Filling (recipe follows)
8 lemon slices, halved
8 lime slices, halved
watercress sprigs for garnish
parsley sprigs for garnish

1 Using a spatula, spread the butter on the bread, spreading it to the edges. Top with a layer of filling and cut each slice in half.

2 Lay a lemon slice on half the canapés and a lime slice on the rest. Garnish with watercress and parsley.

CRAB-FILLED CANAPÉS

MAKES: *32 canapés*

BLUE CHEESE BUTTER

MAKES: *About ¼ cup*

¼ cup unsalted butter
2 tablespoons crumbled blue cheese
1 teaspoon snipped chives

In a small bowl or cup, mash the butter until soft and creamy. Add the cheese and chives and fold to blend.

CRAB FILLING WITH HORSERADISH

MAKES: *About 1 cup*

1 cup minced cooked crabmeat
2 tablespoons heavy cream
1 tablespoon prepared horseradish
salt and pepper

In a small bowl, combine the crabmeat, cream, and horseradish and season to taste with salt and pepper. Cover and chill for at least 2 hours.

---

16 slices Russian rye bread
¼ cup Anchovy Butter (see page 17)
1¼ cups Olive, Prune and Cucumber Filling (recipe follows)
16 slices cooked beets
sprigs of parsley for garnish
sprigs of mint for garnish

1 Spread the butter on the bread, spreading it to the very edge. Top with a layer of filling and center a beet slice in the middle.

2 Cut each slice of bread in half on the diagonal and serve garnished with parsley and mint.

CUCUMBER-AND-OLIVE CANAPÉS

MAKES: *32 canapés*

OLIVE, PRUNE AND CUCUMBER FILLING

MAKES: *About 1½ cups*

2 packages (3 ounces each) cream cheese, at room temperature
¼ cup finely chopped pitted ripe or green olives
¼ cup finely chopped pitted stewed prunes
¼ cup finely chopped cucumbers
¼ cup finely chopped pecans

In a small bowl, using an electric mixer on slow speed, beat together the cream cheese, olives, prunes, cucumbers, and pecans until smooth. Cover and chill for at least 2 hours.

CRAB STACK CANAPÉS

MAKES: *12 canapés*

4 slices honey whole-wheat bread
4 slices white bread
¼ cup Crabmeat Butter (recipe follows)
2 cups Crabmeat Filling (recipe follows)
1 cup Cheese-and-Nut Filling (see page 145)
2 tablespoon snipped fresh parsley
black olive slices

1 Spread the bread with butter, spreading it to the edge. Top with a layer of crabmeat filling.

2 Using a 2-inch round or scallop-shaped cookie cutter, cut 3 rounds from each slice of bread. Stack 1 round on top of another, alternating brown and white colors. Each stack should have 2 rounds. Press gently with a spatula to adhere.

3 Spread the cheese filling around the sides of the stacks, cover, and chill for at least 2 hours. Place an olive slice in the center of each canapé and sprinkle with parsley.

CRABMEAT BUTTER

MAKES: *About 2 cups*

1 cup unsalted butter
1 cup minced cooked crabmeat
dash of paprika
1 tablespoon lemon juice

In a small bowl or cup, mash the butter until soft and creamy. Add the crabmeat, paprika, and lemon juice and mix well.

CRABMEAT FILLING

MAKES: *About 1½ cups*

1⅓ cup flaked cooked crabmeat
2 teaspoons minced green bell pepper
2 teaspoons minced red bell pepper
2 teaspoons Worcestershire sauce
2 teaspoons salsa
salt and pepper

In a small bowl, combine the crabmeat, peppers, Worcestershire sauce, and salsa and season to taste with salt and pepper. Mix well, cover, and chill for at least 2 hours.

DARK-AND-LIGHT CANAPÉS

MAKES: *16 canapés*

8 slices sourdough bread, toasted, crusts trimmed
5 tablespoons Black Butter (see page 48)
8 slices Cheddar cheese, cut into ¼-inch-wide strips
chopped parsley for garnish

Spread the butter on the toast and cut in half. Form patterns on top of the toast with the cheese strips. Garnish with parsley and serve at once.

COOKING NOTE: These can be decorated effectively by arranging the strips in a tic-tac-toe pattern.

1 can (12 ounces) crabmeat, flaked
½ cup Kraft® Salad Dressing or
    mayonnaise
2 teaspoons grated fresh horseradish
1 teaspoon Worcestershire sauce
½ teaspoon prepared Dijon mustard
8 shallow commercial pastry shells
    or homemade croustades
½ cup Curry Sauce (recipe follows)
2 tablespoons buttered bread
    crumbs

1 Position a rack in the center of
the oven and preheat to 400
degrees F. Lightly grease a baking sheet.

2 In a small bowl, combine the
crabmeat, salad dressing, horseradish, Worcestershire sauce and
mustard and mix well.

3 Spoon generous amounts into
each croustade and transfer the
croustades to the baking sheet.
Spoon curry sauce over the tops
and sprinkle with bread crumbs.
Bake for 3 to 4 minutes, or until
browned.

CURRIED CRABMEAT CANAPÉS

MAKES: *8 canapés*

CURRY SAUCE

MAKES: *About 1 cup*

1 cup half-and-half
1½ tablespoons flour, cornstarch or
    arrowroot
2 teaspoons curry powder
salt and pepper

In a small saucepan, combine
the half-and-half and flour and
stir to remove lumps. Cook

over medium heat until boiling.
Reduce the heat and cook, stirring constantly, for 2 to 3 minutes longer until thickened.
Add the curry powder, season
with salt and pepper, and cook,
stirring, just until smooth and
well blended.

¼ cup Anchovy Butter (see page 17)
16 slices Russian rye bread
1 cup Eastern Mediterranean Filling
    (recipe follows)
one ½-inch-thick slice cooked
    eggplant, diced
mint leaves for garnish

Spread the butter on the bread,
spreading it to the edge. Spread 8
slices with a layer of filling and

sprinkle eggplant over each one.
Garnish by gently pushing several mint leaves into the filling. Top
with the remaining 8 slices of
bread. Cut the sandwiches in half
on the diagonal and serve at
once.

EASTERN MEDITERRANEAN-FLAVORED CANAPÉS

MAKES: *16 canapés*

EASTERN MEDITERRANEAN FILLING

MAKES: *About 1 cup*

3 tablespoons cream cheese, at
    room temperature
2 teaspoons Roquefort cheese
3½ tablespoons chopped pistachio
    nuts
⅓ cup chopped pitted black olives
⅓ cup chopped pitted dates

In a small bowl or cup, whisk
the cheeses until creamy. Add
the nuts, olives, and dates and
stir well. Cover and chill for at
least 1 hour.

DOUBLE HAM CANAPÉS

MAKES: *8 canapés*

8 slices extra-sour rye bread
2 tablespoons Mustard Butter (recipe follows)
½ cup Ham Sandwich Filling (recipe follows)
¼ cup Chili-Sauce Butter (recipe follows)
buttered bread crumbs

1 Position a rack in the center of the oven and preheat to 400 degrees F. Lightly grease a baking sheet.

2 Using a 2- to 2½-inch round cookie cutter, cut 16 rounds from the bread.

3 Spread mustard butter on 8 of the rounds. Spread a layer of filling over 4 of these and top with the remaining buttered rounds to make 4 sandwiches. Press lightly and transfer to the baking sheet.

4 Spread the chili butter over the 8 remaining rounds and spread a layer of filling over 4 of these and top with the remaining buttered rounds to make 4 sandwiches. Press lightly and transfer to the baking sheet.

5 Sprinkle all 8 sandwiches with bread crumbs and bake for 3 to 4 minutes, or until the crumbs brown. Serve warm.

COOKING NOTE: **Grated cheese can be substituted for the bread crumbs.**

MUSTARD BUTTER

MAKES: *About ¼ cup*

¼ cup unsalted butter
2 teaspoons prepared mustard

In a small bowl or cup, mash the butter until soft and creamy. Add the mustard and blend thoroughly.

HAM SANDWICH FILLING

MAKES: *About 1 cup*

1 cup minced boiled ham
¼ cup heavy cream
pinch of ground cloves
pinch of mace

In a small bowl, combine the ham, cream, cloves and mace and stir to mix. Cover and chill for at least 2 hours.

CHILI-SAUCE BUTTER

MAKES: *About ¼ cup*

¼ cup unsalted butter
1 tablespoon bottled chili sauce

In a small bowl or cup, mash the butter until soft and creamy. Add the chili sauce and blend well.

8 slices whole-wheat bread, crusts trimmed
2 tablespoons Mushroom Butter (recipe follows)
¾ cup Spinach-and-Egg Filling (recipe follows)

1 Using small decorative cookie cutters, cut the bread into various shapes, such as hearts, clubs, spades and diamonds to make 32 pieces.

2 Spread the butter on the bread, spreading it to the edges. Top with a layer of filling and serve at once.

EGG SALAD CANAPÉS
MAKES: *32 canapés*

MUSHROOM BUTTER
MAKES: *About ½ cup*

¼ cup unsalted butter
¼ cup finely chopped mushrooms

In a small bowl or cup, mash the butter until soft and creamy. Add the mushrooms and blend thoroughly.

SPINACH-AND-EGG FILLING
MAKES: *About 1½ cups*

½ cup chopped fresh spinach
2 tablespoons chopped celery leaves
1 small red onion, diced
4 hard-cooked eggs, mashed
mayonnaise
salt and pepper

In a bowl, combine the spinach, celery, onion and eggs and stir to mix. Add enough mayonnaise to bind and season to taste with salt and pepper. Cover and chill for at least 1 hour.

---

1 tablespoon butter or margarine
4 large eggs, lightly beaten
2 tablespoons Watercress Butter (recipe follows)
8 slices white bread, crusts trimmed
2 cherry tomatoes, thinly sliced

1 Position a rack in the center of the oven and preheat to 425 degrees F.

2 In a skillet, heat the butter over medium heat. Add the eggs and reduce the heat to medium-low. Cook for 5 to 6 minutes, stirring, until the eggs scramble. Do not let the eggs dry out. Set aside to cool.

3 Spread the butter on the bread, spreading it to the edges. Spoon the eggs on the bread and roll each slice into a loose roll, securing with toothpicks. Transfer to a baking sheet and bake for 3 to 4 minutes or until the bread is lightly toasted. Thread a tomato slice on each toothpick and serve warm.

EGG-STUFFED CANAPÉS
MAKES: *8 canapés*

WATERCRESS BUTTER
MAKES: *About ¼ cup*

¼ cup unsalted butter
2 tablespoons minced fresh watercress

In a small bowl or cup, mash the butter until soft and creamy. Add the watercress and stir until blended.

FINNAN HADDIE CANAPÉS WITH MUSHROOMS AND ONIONS

MAKES: *12 canapés*

3 tablespoons butter or margarine
1½ teaspoons minced onion
2 tablespoons minced mushrooms
2 tablespoons all-purpose flour
⅔ cup half-and-half
2 tablespoons grated Swiss cheese
2 large egg yolks, lightly beaten
1 cup flaked finnan haddie
dash of cayenne
6 plain bagels
½ cup grated Romano cheese
buttered bread crumbs for garnish

1 Position a rack in the center of the oven and preheat to 400 degrees F. Lightly grease a baking sheet.

2 In a skillet, melt the butter over medium-high heat. Add the onion and mushrooms and sauté for 3 to 5 minutes until softened.

Add the flour and stir until the flour is absorbed and the mixture is free of lumps of flour.

3 Add the half-and-half and, stirring constantly, cook over high heat until boiling. Remove from the heat and add the Swiss cheese and egg yolks, stirring to mix. Add the finnan haddie and season to taste with cayenne.

4 Cut the bagels in half and spread with the finnan haddie mixture. Transfer to the baking sheet and sprinkle with Romano cheese and bread crumbs. Bake for 3 to 5 minutes, or until the crumbs are browned. Serve warm.

COOKING NOTE: Finnan haddie is lightly salted and smoked haddock and is sold whole or in fillets.

HALF-AND-HALF CANAPÉS

MAKES: *8 canapés*

8 slices white bread
¼ cup Salmon Spread (recipe follows)
¼ cup Olive Butter (see page 147)
8 2½-inch-long strips pimiento
8 walnut halves
8 green olive slices

1 Using a 2½-inch round cookie cutter or upturned glass, cut 8 rounds from the bread. Toast the rounds until lightly browned on both sides.

2 Spread the salmon spread over 4 toasted rounds, spreading it only over half of the round. Spread the butter over the other half of the rounds. Lay a pimiento strip down the center to mark the division between the toppings. Garnish with a walnut half on the olive side and an olive slice on the salmon side. Cover and chill until ready to serve.

SALMON SPREAD

MAKES: *About 1¼ cups*

1 cup flaked salmon
¼ cup mayonnaise
2 tablespoons chopped kosher pickles
salt and pepper

In a small bowl, combine the salmon, mayonnaise, and pickles and stir to mix. Season to taste with salt and pepper, cover, and chill for at least 2 hours.

1 loaf fresh white bread, unsliced
¼ cup Horseradish Butter (recipe
  follows)
½ cup Ham-and-Cheese Spread
  (recipe follows)
6 pimiento-stuffed olives, finely
  chopped

1 Slice the crust from the bread
loaf and slice the loaf in half
lengthwise and then cut one ¼-
inch slice as long as the bread
loaf. Reserve the remaining bread
for another use.

2 Spread the butter over the
bread slice. Top with a layer of
the spread. Sprinkle the olives
over the bread. Starting at the
narrow end, roll the slice into a
cylinder. Wrap in a damp paper
towel and chill for at least 2
hours.

3 Slice the cylinder into 8 slices
and serve.

HAM-AND-CHEESE PINWHEEL CANAPÉS

MAKES: *8 canapés*

HORSERADISH BUTTER

MAKES: *About ¼ cup*

¼ cup unsalted butter
1 tablespoon prepared horseradish

In a small bowl or cup, mash
the butter until soft and creamy.
Fold in the horseradish and mix
until blended.

HAM-AND-CHEESE SPREAD

MAKES: *About 1¼ cups*

1 can (4½ ounces) deviled ham
½ cup shredded Swiss cheese
3 tablespoons mayonnaise
¾ teaspoon Worcestershire sauce

In a small bowl, combine the
ham, cheese, mayonnaise and
Worcestershire sauce. Using an
electric mixer on low speed,
beat until well blended and
smooth. Cover and chill for at
least 1 hour.

---

2 tablespoons Olive Butter (see page
  147)
8 slices white bread, crusts trimmed
½ cup Corned Beef Filling (recipe
  follows)
2 tablespoons minced mushrooms

1 Position a rack in the center of
the oven and preheat to 425
degrees F.

2 Spread the butter on the bread,
spreading it all the way to the
edge.

3 In a small bowl, combine the
filling and mushrooms and stir to
mix. Spread on the bread and roll
each slice into a cylinder, securing each with a toothpick. Transfer to a baking sheet and bake for
3 to 5 minutes, turning once,
until lightly browned. Serve
warm.

HOT CORNED BEEF CANAPÉS

MAKES: *8 canapés*

CORNED BEEF FILLING

MAKES: *About 1 cup*

1 cup minced canned corn beef
pinch of ground cloves
pinch of mace
¼ cup heavy cream

In a small bowl, combine the
corned beef, cloves, mace, and
cream and mix well. Cover and
chill for at least 2 hours.

HOT LIVER CANAPÉS

MAKES: *8 canapés*

2 cans (4.5 ounces each) liverwurst
3 tablespoons heavy cream or sour cream
½ teaspoon minced white onion
salt and white pepper
2 tablespoons Onion Butter (see page 145)
8 slices white bread, crusts trimmed

1 Position a rack in the center of the oven and preheat to 450 degrees F.

2 In a small bowl, combine the liverwurst, cream and onion and mash to mix. Season to taste with salt and pepper.

3 Spread the butter on the bread, spreading it to the edges. Top with a layer of the liverwurst mixture and roll each slice into a cylinder, securing each with a toothpick. Transfer to a baking sheet and bake for 3 to 5 minutes, until lightly browned. Serve warm.

HOT TONGUE CANAPÉS

MAKES: *32 canapés*

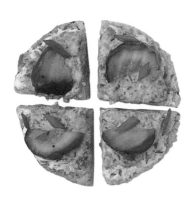

2 tablespoons Onion Butter (see page 145)
8 English muffin halves, toasted
¾ cup Tongue Filling (recipe follows)
buttered bread crumbs
32 slices bread-and-butter pickles

1 Position a rack in the center of the oven and preheat to 400 degrees F. Lightly grease a baking sheet.

2 Spread the butter on the English muffins and top with a layer of the filling, sprinkle with the bread crumbs and transfer to the baking sheet. Bake for 3 to 5 minutes, or until the bread crumbs are lightly browned. Slice each muffin into quarters and top each with a pickle. Serve warm.

TONGUE FILLING

MAKES: *About 1¼ cups*

1 cup finely chopped cooked tongue
2 tablespoons heavy cream
1 large egg yolk
3 drops hot pepper sauce

In a small bowl, combine the tongue, cream, egg yolk and pepper sauce and mash until blended.

2 tablespoons Apricot Butter (recipe follows)
2 slices honey whole-wheat bread, crusts trimmed
2 slices white bread, crusts trimmed
1 cup Ham-and-Chutney Sandwich Filling (see page 142)
8 slices canned peaches
8 slices canned apricots

Spread the butter on the bread, spreading it to the edges. Top with a layer of the filling. Cut each slice of bread into quarters and top 8 with a peach slice and 8 with an apricot slice. Serve at once.

INDIAN-STYLE HAM CANAPÉS

MAKES: *16 canapés*

APRICOT BUTTER

MAKES: *About ¾ cup*

¼ cup unsalted butter
½ cup mashed stewed apricots

In a small bowl or cup, mash the butter until soft and creamy. Fold in the apricots, blending thoroughly.

COOKING NOTE: **To stew the apricots, combine fresh or canned apricots with a little water and cook over medium heat until soft and the consistency of applesauce. Cool.**

---

8 slices white bread
¼ cup Blue Cheese Butter (see page 151)
1 cup Angel Whip Liver-and-Bacon Filling (recipe follows)
8 slices kiwi fruit

1 Using a 2½-inch round cookie cutter or upturned glass, cut 8 rounds from the bread. Toast the rounds until lightly browned on both sides.

2 Spread the butter on the bread, spreading it to the edges. Top with a layer of the filling. Place a slice of kiwi fruit in the center of each round, cover, and chill until ready to serve.

LIVER-AND-BACON CANAPÉS

MAKES: *8 canapés*

ANGEL WHIP LIVER-AND-BACON FILLING

MAKES: *About 1¼ cups*

½ cup heavy cream
4 chicken livers, cooked and diced
4 crisp strips bacon, chopped
½ cup crumbled blue cheese
salt and pepper

In a bowl, using an electric mixer on high speed, beat the heavy cream until stiff. Fold in the liver, bacon, and cheese just until mixed. The mixture will be textured. Cover and chill for at least 1 hour before using

LIVER-AND-CARROT CANAPÉS

MAKES: *8 canapés*

2 slices whole-wheat bread, crusts trimmed
2 slices white bread, crusts trimmed
2½ tablespoons Onion Butter (see page 145)
1 cup Liver-and-Carrot Filling (recipe follows)
⅓ cup finely chopped sweet pickles

Spread the butter on the bread slices. Top with a layer of the filling. Spoon a narrow strip of pickles diagonally from corner to corner. Beginning at another corner, cut the bread slices in half on the diagonal. Serve immediately.

LIVER-AND-CARROT FILLING

MAKES: *About 1¼ cups*

3 ounces cooked calves liver, ground
¾ cup grated carrots
1 package (3 ounces) cream cheese, at room temperature
salt and pepper

In a medium bowl, combine the liver, carrots and cream cheese. Mix well and season with salt and pepper. Cover and chill for at least 1 hour.

LIVER-AND-MUSHROOM CANAPÉS

MAKES: *16 canapés*

¼ cup Mushroom Butter (see page 155)
4 slices white bread, toasted, crusts trimmed
1 cup Liver-and-Mushroom Filling (recipe follows)
⅓ cup finely chopped sweet pickles
4 large white mushrooms, cleaned and stemmed
shredded lettuce for garnish

1 Spread the butter on the toast, spreading it to the edges. Top with a layer of filling and then spoon pickles in the center of each. Set the mushroom, stem side down, on the pickles.

2 Cut the bread into quarters by making 2 diagonal slices, both intersecting the mushroom cap. Serve on a bed of shredded lettuce.

LIVER-AND-MUSHROOM FILLING

MAKES: *About 1¼ cups*

3 ounces cooked calves liver, mashed
½ cup finely chopped fresh white mushrooms
¼ cup heavy cream
salt and pepper

In a bowl, combine the liver, mushrooms and cream, season with salt and pepper and blend until smooth. Cover and chill for at least 1 hour.

2 tablespoons Lobster Butter (recipe follows)
4 slices white bread
1¼ cups Roquefort Cheese-and-Nut Filling with Chopped Olives (recipe follows)
2 tablespoons chopped pecans or walnuts

Spread the butter on the bread, spreading it to the edges. Top with a layer of filling. Using a 2-inch round or scalloped cookie cutter, cut three rounds from each slice of bread. Sprinkle with chopped nuts and serve.

LOBSTER-FLAVORED ROQUEFORT CHEESE CANAPÉS

MAKES: *12 canapés*

ROQUEFORT CHEESE-AND-NUT FILLING WITH CHOPPED OLIVES

MAKES: *About 1¼ cups*

1¾ ounces Roquefort cheese
¾ cup ground walnuts
⅓ cup chopped green olives
salt and pepper

In a medium bowl, mash the cheese against the side of the bowl. Add the walnuts and olives, season with salt and pepper and stir until well mixed. Cover and chill for at least 1 hour.

LOBSTER BUTTER

MAKES: *About ¾ cup*

¼ cup unsalted butter
½ cup flaked lobster meat
⅛ teaspoon lemon juice

In a small bowl or cup, mash the butter until soft and creamy. Add the lobster and lemon juice and fold to mix.

---

2 tablespoons Onion Butter (see page 145)
8 slices buttermilk or white bread, toasted
¼ cup Blue Cheese Mayonnaise (see page 24)
12 thin white onion slices, halved
12 slices processed Swiss cheese, halved
1 tablespoon finely chopped sweet pickles

1 Position a rack in the center of the oven and preheat to 400 degrees F. Lightly grease a baking sheet.

2 Using a 2- to 2½-inch cookie cutter, cut 24 bread rounds.

3 Spread the butter on the rounds and top with a slice of onion and a dab of mayonnaise. Lay a cheese slice on top of the mayonnaise. Transfer to the baking sheet and bake for 3 to 4 minutes, or until the cheese melts. Sprinkle with chopped pickle and serve warm.

MELTED SWISS CHEESE CANAPÉS

MAKES: *24 canapés*

MIDDLE-EASTERN CANAPÉS

MAKES: *4 canapés*

¼ cup Bean Butter (see page 144)
4 slices whole-wheat bread, toasted, crusts trimmed
1 cup Middle-Eastern Cheese Filling (recipe follows)
4 whole pitted dates
2 tablespoons Cheese-and-Green Olive Filling (see page 142)
¼ cup shredded lettuce
2 tablespoons ground pistachio nuts
lemon wedges for garnish

1 Spread a layer of Bean Butter on the bread, spreading it to the edges. Top with a layer of cheese filling.

2 Fill the cavities of the dates with the olive filling. Arrange approximately a tablespoon of lettuce on each slice of bread and set a date in the center of the lettuce. Sprinkle with pistachios and serve garnished with lemon wedges.

MIDDLE-EASTERN CHEESE FILLING

MAKES: *About 2¼ cups*

1 package (8 ounces) cream cheese, at room temperature
¼ cup finely chopped pitted dates
½ cup finely chopped fresh dates
¼ cup golden raisins, soaked for about 15 minutes in warm water, drained
1 teaspoon lemon juice

In a medium bowl, using a eletric mixer on medium speed, combine the cream cheese, dates, raisins and lemon juice and beat until smooth. Cover and chill for at least 2 hours.

MINCED BEEF CANAPÉS

MAKES: *16 canapés*

4 slices whole-wheat bread, crusts trimmed and toasted
1 tablespoon olive oil
2 tablespoons butter or margarine
2 tablespoons minced white onion
¼ cup Chili-Sauce Butter (see page 154)
1 cup Minced Beef and Chive Filling (recipe follows)
sliced pimento-stuffed olives for garnish

1 Brush 1 side of the warm toast with olive oil.

2 In a small skillet, melt the butter over medium heat, add the onion and sauté for about 5 minutes until the onion begins to brown. Drain on paper towels.

3 Spread a layer of chili butter on the toast over the olive oil. Top with a layer of the filling and sprinkle with onions. Cut into quarters and garnish with olives.

MINCED BEEF WITH CHIVE FILLING

MAKES: *About 1½ cups*

1 jar (2½ ounces) minced chipped beef
2 tablespoons snipped chives
¼ cup mayonnaise
salt and pepper

In a medium bowl, combine the chipped beef, chives and mayonnaise and season with salt and pepper and blend until smooth. Cover and chill for at least 1 hour.

4 slices Swedish rye bread, crusts trimmed and toasted
1 tablespoon olive oil
1¼ cups Minted Chopped Lamb Filling (recipe follows)
16 mint leaves

1 Brush 1 side of the warm toast with olive oil.

2 Using a spatula, spread the filling over the toast, spreading it to the edges. Cut into quarters and place a mint leaf on each canapé.

MINT LAMB CANAPÉS

MAKES: *16 canapés*

MINTED CHOPPED LAMB FILLING

MAKES: *About 1¼ cups*

10 ounces cooked lamb, finely chopped (about 1¼ cups)
2 teaspoons crushed fresh mint
2 tablespoons mayonnaise
salt and pepper

In a bowl, combine the lamb, mint and mayonniase and season to taste with salt and pepper and mix well. Cover and chill for at least 1 hour.

---

1 to 2 tablespoons butter or margarine, melted
16 Rye-Krisp® crackers
2 tablespoons Eggplant Dip (recipe follows)
1 cup Eastern Mediterranean Filling (see page 153)
snipped fresh parsley for garnish
chopped pistachio nuts for garnish
sliced pimiento-stuffed olives for garnish
grape leaves (optional)

1 Brush the butter over the crackers and then spread with a layer of dip. Top with a layer of filling.

2 Garnish with parsley, nuts and olives. Serve on a bed of grape leaves, if desired.

MOROCCAN-FLAVORED CANAPÉS

MAKES: *16 canapés*

EGGPLANT DIP

MAKES: *About 2¾ cup*

⅔ cup olive or canola oil
1 small clove garlic, mashed
2 1-pound eggplants, peeled and diced
1 onion, chopped
1 package (3 ounces) cream cheese, at room temperature
3 tablespoons tarragon vinegar
1 teaspoon fresh lemon juice
1 tablespoon snipped fresh chives

1 In a skillet, heat the oil and garlic over medium heat. Add the eggplant, onions and garlic and cook, stirring, for 12 to 15 minutes until browned.

2 Transfer to a food processor and process until smooth. Add the cheese, vinegar and lemon juice and process until smooth. Transfer to a bowl and add the chives. Stir to mix. Cover and chill for at least 2 hours.

MUSHROOM CANAPÉS

MAKES: *8 canapés*

¼ cup Mushroom Butter (see page 155)

8 ½-inch thick slices Italian bread

1 cup Mushroom Filling (see page 54)

snipped fresh parsley for garnish

Spread the butter over the bread and top with a layer of filling. Garnish with parsley and serve.

OLIVE CANAPÉS

MAKES: *24 canapés*

⅓ cup Olive Butter (see page 147)

8 slices white bread, cut into 2- to 2½-inch squares

3 tablespoons finely chopped ripe olives

8 slices pimiento-stuffed olives

1 Spread the butter on the bread, spreading it to the edges. Using the tip of a spatula, create a diagonal line of chopped olives between 2 corners of each square. Create another line from the opposite corners so that the lines cross.

2 Place an olive slice on each canapé in the intersection of the 2 lines. Cover and chill until ready to serve.

OLIVE, PRUNE AND CUCUMBER CANAPÉS

MAKES: *16 canapés*

4 slices white bread, crusts trimmed and toasted

1 tablespoon olive oil

4 thin slices smoked ham

1¼ cup Olive, Prune and Cucumber Filling (see page 151)

chopped parsley or chives for garnish

1 Brush the warm toast with olive oil.

2 Lay a slice of ham on each of the slices and top with a layer of filling. Sprinkle with parsley and cut into quarters and serve.

2 large bananas, thinly sliced
2 tablespoons lemon juice
4 slices honey whole-wheat bread, crusts trimmed and toasted
¼ cup Chutney Butter (see page 37)
1¼ cup Peanut Surprise with Bananas Filling (recipe follows)
parsley for garnish

1 Brush the banana slices with lemon juice and set aside.

PEANUT SURPRISE WITH BANANAS FILLING

MAKES: *About 1½ cups*

1 package (3 ounces) cream cheese, at room temperature
¼ cup chunky peanut butter
2 large bananas, mashed

2 Spread the butter on the toast, spreading it to the edges. Top with a layer of filling and cut the toast into rectangular quarters. Press several banana slices in an overlapping row down the center of each quarter. Garnish with parsley and serve.

In a bowl, using an electric mixer on high speed, combing the the cream cheese, peanut butter and bananas and beat until smooth. Cover and chill for at least 2 hours.

COOKING NOTE: **For sweet preparations where the filling is used as a topping, try pouring chocolate syrup over it.**

PEANUT-AND-BANANA CANAPÉS

MAKES: *16 canapés*

¼ cup Molasses Butter (recipe follows)
4 slices white bread, crusts trimmed and toasted
1¼ cup Peanut Brittle Filling (recipe follows)
chopped peanuts for garnish

MOLASSES BUTTER

MAKES: *About ¾ cup*

¼ cup unsalted butter
½ cup molasses

PEANUT BRITTLE FILLING

MAKES: *About 1¼ cups*

¼ cup unsalted butter
1 cup finely crushed peanut brittle
milk

Spread the butter on the toast. Top with a layer of the filling and sprinkle with nuts. Cut in half on the diagonal and serve.

In a bowl, mash the butter until soft and creamy. Add the molasses and fold until well blended.

In a bowl, mash the butter until soft and creamy. Add the peanut brittle and enough milk to bind and stir until well mixed. Cover and chill for at least 1 hour.

COOKING NOTE: **For richer, sweeter flavor, substitute brandy for milk.**

PEANUT BRITTLE CANAPÉS

MAKES: *8 canapés*

PEANUT BUTTER-AND-CARROT CANAPÉS

MAKES: *16 canapés*

¼ cup Ham Butter (recipe follows)
4 slices honey whole-wheat bread, crusts trimmed
1¼ cups Peanut Butter-and-Carrot Filling (recipe follows)
½ cup thinly sliced carrots
carrot greens for garnish.

Spread the butter on the bread, spreading it to the edges. Top with a layer of filling and cut the bread into rectangular quarters. Press several carrot slices in an overlapping row down the center of each quarter. Garnish with carrot greens and serve.

HAM BUTTER

MAKES: *About 1 cup*

½ cup unsalted butter
¼ pound cooked ham, chopped very fine
2 large hard-cooked eggs, mashed

In a bowl, mash the butter until soft and creamy. Fold in the ham and eggs and blend thoroughly.

PEANUT BUTTER-AND-CARROT FILLING

MAKES: *About 1¼ cups*

1 cup creamy peanut butter
½ cup grated carrots

In a bowl, mash the peanut butter until smooth and creamy. Add the carrots and stir until well mixed. Cover and chill for at least 1 hour.

COOKING NOTE: **For chunkier texture, use chunky peanut butter.**

PEANUT-AND-HAM CANAPÉS

MAKES: *16 canapés*

¼ cup Ham Butter (see above)
4 slices honey whole-wheat bread, crusts trimmed
1¼ cups Peanut Filling (recipe follows)
8 large strawberries, halved
chopped peanuts, for garnish

Spread the butter on the bread, spreading it to the edges. Top with a layer of filling and cut the bread into quarters. Press a strawberry half in the center of each quarter, sprinkle with chopped peanuts and serve.

PEANUT FILLING

MAKES: *About 1¼ cups*

1 package (3 ounces) cream cheese, at room temperature
1 cup coarsely chopped salted peanuts
½ cup chopped parsley

In a bowl, mash the cheese until smooth and creamy. Add the peanuts and parsley and stir until well mixed. Cover and chill for at least 1 hour.

16 small round crackers
1 cup Plum-and-Cheese Filling (see page 90)
2 tablespoons chopped pecans or walnuts

Spread the crackers with filling. Sprinkle with chopped nuts, cover and chill for at least 1 hour. Serve chilled.

PLUM-AND-CHEESE CANAPÉS

MAKES: *16 canapés*

---

2 tablespoons Mustard Butter (see page 154)
8 slices white bread, crusts trimmed
1 cup Prune Filling (recipe follows)
1 carrot, shredded
2 tablespoons chopped pecans or walnuts

Spread the butter on the bread. Top with the filling and sprinkle with shredded carrots and nuts. Cut into quarters, cover and chill for at least 1 hour. Serve chilled.

PRUNE CANAPÉS

MAKES: *32 canapés*

PRUNE FILLING

MAKES: *About 1¾ cups*

1 cup stewed pitted prunes
½ cup mayonnaise
¼ cup finely chopped walnuts

In a bowl, using an electric mixer on medium speed, combine the prunes and mayonnaise and beat until smooth. Add the walnuts and stir to mix. Add more mayonnaise if necessary to bind. Cover and chill for at least 1 hour.

---

2 tablespoons olive oil
4 slices honey whole-wheat bread
1 package (3 ounces) cream cheese, softened
1 tablespoon mayonnaise
1 teaspoon chopped anchovies
½ teaspoon chopped parsley

1 In a skillet, heat the oil over medium-high heat and sauté the bread for 1 or 2 minutes on each side until lightly browned. Using a 2½- or 3-inch round cookie cutter, cut the bread into 8 rounds.

2 In a bowl, combine the cream cheese and mayonnaise and blend well. Add the anchovies and parsley and stir to mix. Heap teaspoons of the filling on each round and smooth each heap into the shape of a pyramid. Chill for at least 2 hours before serving.

PYRAMID CANAPÉS

MAKES: *8 canapés*

SALMON CANAPÉS

MAKES: *12 canapés*

8 slices white bread
¼ cup Lobster Butter (see page 161)
2 cups Salmon Filling (see page 64)
2 tablespoons chopped dill

1 Spread the butter on the bread, spreading it to the edges. Top with a layer of filling.

2 Using a 2-inch round or scalloped cookie cutter, cut bread into 24 rounds. Stack 2 rounds on top of each other and press gently. Sprinkle with dill, cover and chill for at least 2 hours. Serve chilled.

SARDINE CANAPÉS

MAKES: *8 canapés*

2 tablespoons Mustard Butter (see page 154)
8 slices buttermilk or other white bread, crusts trimmed
8 sardines fillets

1 Position a rack in the center of the oven and preheat to 400 degrees F. Lightly grease a baking sheet.

2 Spread the butter on the bread and lay a sardine fillet across each slice. Roll into cylinders and secure with toothpicks. Transfer to the baking sheet and bake for 3 or 4 minutes, or until lightly browned. Serve warm.

COOKING NOTE: Substitute any cheese spread in the book or the Cheese Butter on page 143 for the Mustard Butter.

SHRIMP-FLAVORED HAM CANAPÉS

MAKES: *8 canapés*

4 slices honey whole-wheat bread, crusts trimmed
2 tablespoons Shrimp Butter (recipe follows)
1 cup Ham Sandwich Filling (see page 154)
3 large radishes, thinly sliced

Using a diamond-shaped cookie cutter, cut 2 diamonds from each slice of bread. Spread the butter on the bread, spreading it to the edges. Top with a layer of filling and arrange 2 or 3 radish slices in the center of each diamond. Serve immediately.

SHRIMP BUTTER

MAKES: *About ½ cup*

¼ cup unsalted butter
¼ cup cooked minced shrimp

In a bowl, mash the butter until soft and creamy. Add the shrimp and fold until well blended.

8 slices white bread, crusts trimmed
  and toasted
¼ cup Lemon Butter (recipe follows)
32 smoked oysters
3 tablespoons Caviar Spread (see
  page 22)

Cut the bread into quarters and
spread with the butter. Set a
smoked oyster in the center of
each quarter. Dab a little spread
around each oyster and serve
immediately.

SMOKED OYSTER CANAPÉS

MAKES: *32 canapés*

LEMON BUTTER

MAKES: *About ½ cup*

½ cup butter or margarine
2 tablespoons lemon juice
white pepper

In a small saucepan, melt butter
over medium heat. Remove
from the heat, add the lemon
juice and pepper to taste and
whisk well. Cover and chill for
at least 1 hour.

¼ cup Ham Butter (see page 166)
8 slices honey whole-wheat bread
2 cups Spicy Chicken Sandwich
  Filling (see page 23)
2 tablespoons chopped parsley
sliced pimiento-stuffed olives

1 Spread the butter on the bread,
spreading it to the edges. Top
with a layer of filling.

2 Using a 2-inch round or scalloped cookie cutter, cut the bread
into 24 rounds. Make 12 stacks of
2 rounds each, gently pressing to
adhere. Put an olive slice in the
center of each stack and garnish
with parsley. Cover and chill for
at least 2 hours and serve chilled.

SPICY CHICKEN CANAPÉS

MAKES: *12 canapés*

---

1 cup finely chopped boiled ham
½ cup grated Swiss cheese
½ teaspoon prepared horseradish
½ teaspoon garlic-flavored Dijon
  mustard
½ cup undiluted condensed tomato
  soup
4 slices honey-and-oat bran bread,
  crusts trimmed and toasted
buttered bread crumbs

1 Position the rack in the center
of the oven and preheat to 400
degrees F. Lightly grease a baking sheet.

2 In a small bowl, combine the
ham, cheese, horseradish, mustard and soup and mix well.
Spread on the bread and cut the
bread slices into rectangular
quarters. Transfer to the baking
sheet, sprinkle with the bread
crumbs and bake for 3 or 4 minutes until lightly browned. Serve
warm.

TOMATO-FLAVORED CANAPÉS WITH HAM

MAKES: *16 canapés*

SWEETBREAD CANAPÉS

MAKES: *8 canapés*

2 tablespoons Cheese Butter (see page 143)
8 slices cocktail rye bread
¾ cup Egg-and-Sweetbread Filling (recipe follows)
8 cooked asparagus tips

Spread the butter on the bread, spreading it to the edges. Spread the Egg-and-Sweetbread Filling in an even layer on top of the Cheese Butter. Top each with an asparagus tip and serve.

EGG-AND-SWEETBREAD FILLING

MAKES: *About 2 cups*

4 large hard-cooked eggs, mashed
1 tablespoon cream cheese, at room temperature
1 teaspoon mayonnaise
¼ teaspoon ketchup
½ cup thinly sliced cooked sweetbreads
¼ cup chopped pressed ham
Worcestershire sauce
salt and pepper

In a bowl, combine the eggs, cream cheese, mayonnaise and ketchup and stir well. Add the sweetbreads and ham, season to taste with Worcestershire sauce and salt and pepper and stir well. Cover and chill for at least 1 hour.

TUNA ROUNDS

MAKES: *24 canapés*

2 tablespoons unsalted butter
8 slices white bread, crusts removed
½ cup Tuna Fish Filling (recipe follows)
2 tablespoons grated Parmesan cheese

1 Position a rack in the center of the oven and preheat to 500 degrees F.

2 In a skillet, melt the butter over low heat and sauté the bread for 1 or 2 minutes on each side until

lightly browned. Using a 2-inch round cookie cutter, cut 24 bread rounds.

3 Spread the filling over the bread and sprinkle with cheese. Transfer to a baking sheet and bake for 3 or 4 minutes until the cheese melts and begins to brown. Serve immediately.

TUNA FISH FILLING

MAKES: *About 1¼ cups*

½ cup flaked canned tuna
½ cup minced cooked beets
¼ cup French dressing

In a bowl, combine the tuna, beets and dressing and mix well. Cover and chill for at least 2 hours.

¼ cup Anchovy Butter (see page 17)
4 slices honey whole-wheat bread
4 slices white bread
2 cups Tuna Sandwich Filling
  (recipe follows)
sliced pimiento-stuffed olives
2 tablespoons chopped parsley

1 Spread the butter on the bread, spreading it to the edges. Top with a layer of filling.

2 Using a 2-inch round cookie cutter, cut 24 bread rounds. Make 12 double stacks, each with a round of whole-wheat bread and a round of white bread. Press gently to adhere. Garnish with an olive slice and parsley. Cover and chill for at least 2 hours. Serve chilled.

Tuna Stack Canapés

MAKES: *12 canapés*

Tuna Sandwich Filling

MAKES: *About 2 cups*

2 cups flaked canned tuna
¼ cup pickle relish
4 teaspoons chopped parsley
1 tablespoon lemon or lime juice
mayonnaise or softened cream
  cheese

In a bowl, combine the tuna, relish, parsley and lemon juice and stir to mix. Add enough mayonnaise or cream cheese to bind. Cover and chill for at least 2 hours.

½ cup Cream Cheese Spread (see page 57)
8 slices cocktail pumpernickel or rye bread
8 thin slices smoked turkey
8 sweet pickle slices

Spread the cheese spread on the bread, spreading it to the edges. Top with a slice of turkey and a pickle slice. Cover and chill for at least 2 hours. Serve chilled.

Turkey-and-Cream Cheese Canapés

MAKES: *8 canapés*

EGG-AND-ANCHOVY CANAPÉS

MAKES: *8 canapés*

8 slices white bread
⅓ cup Anchovy Butter (see page 17)
4 large hard-cooked eggs
chopped parsley for garnish

1 Using a 2- to 2½-inch round cookie cutter, cut 8 rounds from the bread. Spread the butter on the rounds, spreading it to the edges.

2 Slice the eggs into thin slices to form round circles with the egg yolk in the center. (Discard the ends that are all egg whites.) Lay the egg rounds on the bread to form overlapping petal-like patterns. Garnish with parsley and serve at once.

CHRISTMAS EVE CANAPÉS

MAKES: *32 canapés*

1 cup shredded Swiss cheese
1 cup Kraft® Real Mayonnaise
1 package (3 ounces) cream cheese, at room temperature
½ cup sour cream
2 tablespoons prepared mustard
1 tablespoon lemon juice
1 package (6 ounces) frozen crabmeat, thawed and drained
8 slices white or whole-wheat bread, crusts trimmed, quartered

1 Position the broiler rack so that it is about 5 inches from the heat source and preheat the broiler.

2 In a bowl, using an electric mixer on medium speed, blend together the Swiss cheese, mayonnaise, cream cheese, sour cream, mustard and lemon juice until smooth. Add the crabmeat and fold until well mixed. Spread on the bread and transfer to a broiling pan. Broil for 3 or 4 minutes or until the cheese bubbles. Serve warm.

BACON-AND-PEANUT BUTTER CANAPÉS

MAKES: *32 canapés*

3 tablespoons creamy peanut butter
1½ tablespoons mayonnaise or Kraft® Salad Dressing
1½ tablespoons chili sauce
3 strips crisp bacon, crumbled
8 slices white bread, lightly toasted
4 pimiento-stuffed olives, sliced
coarsely crushed salted peanuts for garnish

In a bowl, combine the peanut butter, mayonnaise, chili sauce and bacon and mix well. Spread on the toast and cut into quarters. Garnish with olives and sprinkle with peanuts.

1 can (16 ounces) refried beans
2 tablespoons chopped green onions
   (scallions), green portions only
2 tablespoons catsup
1 teaspoon Worcestershire sauce
½ teaspoon Dijon mustard
½ teaspoon liquid smoke
Corn Bread (recipe follows)
5 or 6 lettuce leaves
2 packages (3 ounces each) sliced
   ham or corned beef
8 slices Velveeta® Cheese

1 In a bowl, combine the beans, onions, catsup, Worcestershire sauce, mustard and liquid smoke and mix well. Spread over the cornbread still in the pan and cut the bread into 30 squares, each about 2- to 2½-inches square.

2 Transfer to a platter and cut the lettuce leaves so that a piece of lettuce fits over each square. Cut the ham to fit over the lettuce.

3 Using a decorative cookie cutter, cut out 30 shapes from the cheese and set these on top of the ham. Cover and chill for at least 1 hour.

CORN BREAD CANAPÉS

MAKES: *30 canapés*

CORN BREAD

MAKES: *24 to 36 servings*

1 cup all-purpose flour
1 cup yellow cornmeal
1 cup milk
¼ cup vegetable shortening
1 large egg
2 tablespoons sugar
1 tablespoon plus 1 teaspoon
   baking powder
½ teaspoon salt

1 Position the rack in the center of the oven and preheat to 400 degrees F. Lightly grease a jelly roll pan.

2 In a bowl, using an electric mixer on medium speed, beat together the flour, corn meal, milk, shortening, egg, sugar, baking powder and salt until smooth. Pour in the pan and bake for 10 to 12 minutes, or until golden brown. Cool in the pan set on a wire rack.

1 cup butter or margarine, at room
   temperature
1 teaspoon curry powder
¼ teaspoon cayenne
⅛ teaspoon pepper
1 cup finely chopped almonds
36 unsalted Saltine® Crackers
3 cans (2 ounces each) rolled
   anchovy fillets
pinch of paprika

1 In a bowl, combine the butter, curry powder, cayenne and pepper and mash until blended. Add the almonds and blend well.

2 Spread on the crackers, top with anchovies and sprinkle with paprika.

CURRIED ANCHOVY CANAPÉS

MAKES: *36 canapés*

HERBED CHEESE CANAPÉS

MAKES: *12 to 14 canapés*

½ pound Camembert, at room temperature
½ cup butter or margarine, at room temperature
1 tablespoon chopped white onions
½ teaspoon anchovy paste
1 teaspoon sweet paprika
¾ teaspoon crushed caraway seeds
¼ teaspoon dry mustard
2 red or green bell peppers, halved or quartered
6 or 7 thin slices pumpernickel bread

1 In a bowl, using an electric mixer on medium speed, beat together the cheese, butter, onions, anchovy paste, paprika, caraway seeds and mustard until smooth. Cover and chill for at least 2 hours.

2 Using ½-inch decorative cutters, cut shapes from the peppers, making sure to cut at least 12 or 14 shapes.

3 Spread the cheese butter on the bread and cut each in half diagonally. Set a pepper shape in the center of each and serve.

HAM CANAPÉS

MAKES: *6 canapés*

1 cup shredded Swiss or Tybo cheese
1 cup diced smoked ham
¼ cup chopped red bell pepper
¼ cup chopped green bell pepper
½ cup sour cream or plain yogurt
½ cup Kraft® Real Mayonnaise
1 envelope Good Seasons® Italian Dressing mix
¼ teaspoon garlic powder
6 slices cocktail rye bread

1 In a bowl, combine the cheese, ham, peppers, sour cream, mayonnaise, dressing mix and garlic powder and mix well. Cover and chill for at least 2 hours.

2 Spread on the bread, spreading to the very edge, and serve.

COOKING NOTE: **For hot canapés, arrange the assembled canapés on a baking sheet and heat in a preheated 400 degree F. oven for 3 to 5 minutes, or until heated through. Serve immediately.**

Chapter 4

SMALL SALADS

Salad is a snack worth noting. Most people don't immediately think of salads when they conjure up snacks, but not to do so is a shame. Here, I introduce ingredients that turn ho-hum salads into incredible, full-flavored and colorful treats. These are designed as snack salads, not salads meant to fill bowls and feed hordes of hungry guests. Instead, these are little tastes of delectable freshness.

A VERY SPECIAL FRUIT SALAD

MAKES: *4 to 6 servings*

1 cup Fruit Salad Dressing (recipe follows)
2 tablespoons orange juice
¼ teaspoon crushed crystallized ginger
2 oranges, peeled and sectioned
2 kiwi fruit, peeled and thinly sliced
1 cup fresh red raspberries
2 cups cubed, seeded watermelon
crushed pecans or hazelnuts for garnish

1 In a bowl, combine the dressing, orange juice and ginger and whisk well.

2 On salad plates, arrange equal amounts of the fruit and spoon the dressing in a straight line across the top of each serving. Sprinkle with nuts and serve.

FRUIT SALAD DRESSING

MAKES: *About 2¼ cups*

2 large egg yolks
1 tablespoon orange juice
2 teaspoons grated orange zest
1 tablespoon lemon juice
1½ teaspoon grated lemon zest
2 tablespoons all-purpose flour
1 cup sugar
1 cup heavy cream, whipped

1 In a small saucepan, whisk the yolks until blended. Add the juices and zest, flour and sugar and whisk well. Cook over low heat, stirring constantly, for about 5 minutes until thickened.

2 Cool to room temperature and fold in the whipped cream. Cover and chill for about 30 minutes before using.

APPLE-AND-CELERY SALAD

MAKES: *8 servings*

2 cups diced celery
2 cups diced tart apples
1 cup chopped pecans
¾ cup Blue Cheese Mayonnaise (see page 24)
8 leaves butter or Boston lettuce

In a bowl, combine the celery, apples, pecans and mayonnaise and toss until well coated with mayonnaise. Press the lettuce leaves into 8 small dessert cups and fill with the mixture. Chill for at least 1 hour and serve.

3½ cups apple cider
1 package (4 ounces) lemon-flavored gelatin
1 tablespoon lemon juice
1 cup seedless green or red grapes, halved
1 stalk celery, chopped
large lettuce leaves
Blue Cheese Mayonnaise (see page 24)

1 In a saucepan, bring 2 cups of the cider to a boil over medium heat. Remove from the heat and add the gelatin, stirring until completely dissolved. Add the remaining cider and the lemon juice. Cover and refrigerate for about 1 hour until thickened but not set.

2 Add the grapes and celery to the thickened gelatin and stir until well distributed throughout the gelled mixture. Pour into custard cups and chill for at least 2 hours, or until firm.

3 Arrange the lettuce leaves on a platter. Unmold the gelatin by wrapping a warm, well-wrung damp towel around the outside of the mold for a few seconds and then inverting onto the lettuce leaves. Serve with the mayonnaise on the side.

APPLE CIDER SALAD

MAKES: *6 servings*

¾ cup apple jelly
1 teaspoon chopped fresh mint
½ cup apple-flavored yogurt
1 tablespoon powdered sugar
2 tablespoons finely diced celery
2 tart apples, thinly sliced
2 tablespoons lemon juice
6 large lettuce leaves
1 can (11 ounces) mandarin orange segments, drained
6 small clusters seedless green or red grapes

1 In the top of a double boiler set over simmering water, combine the jelly and mint and cook, stirring, until smooth. Remove from the heat and immediately stir in the yogurt, sugar and celery. Cover and chill for at least 2 hours until gelled.

2 Brush the apple slices with the lemon juice. Lay the lettuce leaves on a platter and fill each with apples, mandarin segments and grape clusters. Serve with the gelled yogurt on the side.

COOKING NOTE: **You can substitute drained canned mango slices for the mandarin orange segments.**

APPLE SALAD WITH ORANGES AND GRAPES

MAKES: *6 servings*

ARTICHOKE-SHRIMP SALAD

MAKES: *4 servings*

8 ounces cooked small shrimp
¼ cup lime juice
1 green bell pepper, finely diced
1 tablespoon chopped red onion
1 tablespoon finely chopped parsley
1 tablespoon safflower oil
2 dashes hot-pepper sauce
salt and pepper
4 canned artichoke bottoms, drained
shredded lettuce

1 In a glass bowl, combine the shrimp and lime juice. Cover and chill for no longer than 2 hours.

2 Drain the shrimp and discard the lime juice. Add the pepper, onion, parsley, oil and hot-pepper sauce. Season to taste with salt and pepper.

3 Scoop out the artichoke bottoms if necessary and spoon the shrimp mixture into the natural cavities. Arrange on a bed of lettuce and serve.

AVOCADO SALADS

MAKES: *6 servings*

3 large avocados
1 can (16 ounces) grapefruit
    segments, drained
1 can (11 ounces) mandarin orange
    segments, drained
1 small banana, thinly sliced
¼ cup honey
2 tablespoons lemon juice
crushed pecans or walnuts

1 Using a sharp knife, cut the avocados in half lengthwise and remove the pits. Using a melon baller, scoop the flesh from the avocados. Reserve the shells.

2 In a bowl, combine the avocado balls, grapefruit, oranges and banana.

3 In a cup, combine the honey and lemon juice and mix well. Spoon over the fruit mixture and fold gently to coat. Spoon into the avocado shells, sprinkle with the nuts and serve.

AVOCADO SALAD WITH TUNA

MAKES: *4 servings*

2 avocados
2 tablespoons plus 2 teaspoons
    lemon juice
1 can (7 ounces) tuna, drained and
    flaked
1 small red onion, chopped
3 tablespoons canola oil
1 tablespoon oyster sauce
½ teaspoon dried oregano
2 tablespoons chopped fresh parsley
salt and black pepper
romaine lettuce leaves

1 Using a sharp knife, cut the avocados in half, removing the pits. Brush the flesh with 2 teaspoons of the lemon juice to keep them from discoloring.

2 In a bowl, combine the tuna and onion. Cover and chill for about 1 hour.

3 In a small bowl, combine the oil, oyster sauce, remaining lemon juice, oregano and parsley and mix well. Season to taste with salt and pepper. Pour over the tuna and toss lightly.

4 Spoon the tuna mixture into the avocado halves Arrange the lettuce on a platter and arrange the avocados on the platter.

2 packets unflavored gelatin
2 cups Chicken Stock (see page 295)
⅛ teaspoon soy sauce
¼ cup chopped fresh parsley
2 tablespoons packed light-brown
 sugar
1 tablespoon ground ginger
pinch of garlic powder
2 cans (4½ ounces each) chunk
 chicken, flaked
sprigs of parsley for garnish

1 In a cup, sprinkle the gelatin over ½ cup of Chicken Stock and set aside to soften.

2 In a saucepan, bring the remaining 1½ cups of stock to a boil. Remove from the heat and stir in the gelatin, soy sauce, parsley, brown sugar, ginger and garlic powder. Stir to mix.

3 Evenly divide the chicken among twelve 2½-inch muffin cups. Pour the stock evenly over the chicken and chill for at least 4 hours or until firm.

4 When ready, unmold and serve, garnished with parsley sprigs.

CHUNK CHICKEN IN ASPIC

MAKES: *12 servings*

2 packets unflavored gelatin
3 cups warm canned, low-sodium
 beef stock
1½ cups chopped cooked beef
1 pimiento or roasted red pepper,
 minced
½ cup chopped broccoli
pinch of garlic powder
lettuce
chopped parsley
mayonnaise

1 In a cup, sprinkle the gelatin over ¼ cup of Beef Stock and set aside for a few minutes to soften.

2 In a large saucepan, combine the remaining 2¾ cups of stock and the softened gelatin mixture, stirring to blend, and heat over medium-high heat until very hot. Cool at room temperature for about 1 hour or until the mixture starts to thicken.

3 Using a large spoon, stir the beef, pimiento, broccoli and garlic powder into the stock and stir to distribute evenly. Pour into 8 custard cups or into eight 3-inch muffin cups and chill for at least 4 hours until firm.

4 Unmold and serve on a bed of lettuce and garnished with parsley. Serve with mayonnaise on the side.

BEEF IN ASPIC

MAKES: *8 servings*

BANANA SALAD

MAKES: *8 servings*

4 large bananas
2 tablespoons lemon juice
1 cup heavy cream, whipped
½ cup mayonnaise or Kraft® Salad Dressing
1½ cups miniature marshmallows
1 can (2 ounces) pimientos, puréed with juice
watercress for garnish
French dressing

1 Cut the bananas into thin slices and brush with the lemon juice. Transfer to a bowl and add the whipped cream, mayonnaise, marshmallows and pimientos and stir gently. Spoon into a 9-inch square metal pan and freeze for at least 4 hours or until firm.

2 Cut into squares and serve garnished with watercress with the French dressing on the side.

CALIFORNIA COLESLAW

MAKES: *4 servings*

1 small head cabbage, shredded
1 small white onion, chopped
1 green bell pepper, seeded and chopped
1 red bell pepper, seeded and chopped
1 small carrot, grated
3 tablespoons minced parsley
½ cup cider vinegar
3 tablespoons sugar
½ cup canola oil
salt and pepper

1 In a bowl, combine the cabbage, onion, green and red peppers, carrot and parsley and toss to mix.

2 In a small bowl, combine the vinegar, sugar and oil and season with salt and pepper. Pour over the cabbage mixture and toss to mix. Cover and chill for at least 2 hours before serving.

CARROT-RAISIN SALAD

MAKES: *8 servings*

1 cup raisins
1½ cups shredded carrots
½ cup sliced celery
½ cup chopped hazelnuts
dash of cayenne
¼ cup mayonnaise or Kraft® Salad Dressing, plus more for garnish
8 sugar ice-cream cones

1 In a small bowl, combine the raisins with enough hot water to cover and set aside for about 5 minutes to plump. Drain, discard the water and dry the raisins between paper towels. Transfer to a large bowl.

2 Add the carrots, celery, hazelnuts and cayenne to the bowl and stir to mix. Add the mayonnaise and toss until well coated. Cover and chill for at least 1 hour.

3 Spoon the salad into the cones and garnish each with a dab of mayonnaise.

COOKING NOTE: As an alternative, the salad can be served on lettuce leaves with the cones on the side.

4 large cooked chicken breasts, skin removed
6 large peaches, pitted and peeled
2 stalks celery, sliced
1 cup walnut halves
1 package (8 ounces) cream cheese with pineapple
¼ teaspoon ground coriander

1 Cut the chicken breast meat into 1-inch cubes and transfer to a bowl.

CHICKEN BISTRO SALAD

MAKES: *8 servings*

2 Chop 2 peaches into small cubes and add to the bowl. Add the celery and walnuts and stir gently to mix thoroughly.

3 Cut the remaining 4 peaches into large chunks and put in a blender or food processor. Process on low speed for 3 to 4 seconds until smooth. Add the cream cheese and coriander and pulse to mix. Add to the chicken and toss lightly to coat. Cover and chill until ready to serve.

---

2 large ripe tomatoes, seeded and chopped
¾ cup chopped green onions
¼ cup chopped fresh cilantro (Chinese parsley)
2 tablespoons chopped pickled jalapeño peppers
1 cup mayonnaise
3 tablespoons fresh lime juice
1 teaspoon chili powder
1 teaspoon ground cumin
2 pounds small red potatoes, cooked and sliced ¼-inch thick
2 cups shredded cooked chicken
1 large red bell pepper, seeded and diced
lettuce leaves
tortilla chips for garnish
paper-thin lime slices for garnish

1 In a bowl, combine the tomatoes, onions, cilantro and jalapeño peppers and mix well and set aside.

CHICKEN-POTATO SALAD

MAKES: *8 servings*

2 In small bowl, combine the mayonnaise, lime juice, chili powder, and cumin and mix well.

3 In another bowl, combine the potatoes, chicken and pepper and stir. Add the mayonnaise dressing and about half of the tomato mixture and toss. Cover and chill for at least 1 hour. Cover and chill the remaining tomato mixture.

4 Line a platter with lettuce leaves and spoon the salad over the lettuce. Serve with tortilla chips and garnished with lime slices.

CHICKEN SALAD

MAKES: *6 servings*

½ head lettuce, torn into bite-size pieces
2 cups diced cooked chicken
3 slices ham, torn into shreds
1 can (16 ounces) cut green beans, drained
1 can (15½ ounces) kidney beans, drained
1 can (14 ounces) artichoke hearts, drained and halved
1 package (4 ounces) sunflower seeds
1 tablespoon chopped parsley
½ cup Italian salad dressing
few drops of red pepper sauce

1 Place the lettuce in a serving bowl and add the chicken, ham, green beans, kidney beans, artichoke hearts and sunflower seeds. Sprinkle with parsley, cover and chill for about 30 minutes.

2 In a small cup, combine the dressing and pepper sauce and whisk to mix. Drizzle over the chilled salad and serve at once.

COOKING NOTE: **Serve shredded mozzarella or Swiss cheese on the side to heighten the flavor.**

CONFETTI PASTA SALAD

MAKES: *4 to 6 servings*

1 cup Blue Cheese Mayonnaise (see page 24)
3 tablespoons cider vinegar
2 tablespoons honey
1 tablespoon milk
1½ teaspoons dry mustard
salt and pepper
1½ cups rotelle pasta, cooked and drained
2 cups finely shredded red cabbage
1 cup shredded carrots
1 large green bell pepper, seeded and cut into strips
Boston lettuce leaves
melba toast

1 In a large bowl, combine the mayonnaise, vinegar, honey, milk and mustard and blend thoroughly. Season to taste with salt and pepper.

2 Add the pasta, cabbage, carrots and pepper and mix until coated. Cover and chill for at least 1 hour before serving.

3 Line a platter with lettuce leaves and spoon the salad on the lettuce. Serve with melba toast on the side.

COTTAGE CHEESE SALAD BALL

MAKES: *6 to 8 servings*

1 cup small-curd cottage cheese
1 cup minced canned salmon
½ cup minced celery
¼ cup finely chopped sweet pickles
½ cup mayonnaise
salt and pepper
wheat crackers

In a large bowl, combine the cottage cheese, salmon, celery, pickles and mayonnaise and season to taste with salt and pepper. Mix well and then form into a large ball. Cover and chill for at least 2 hours. Serve with crackers.

1 package unflavored gelatin
¼ cup cold milk
1½ cups cottage cheese
½ teaspoon crushed dried dill
½ teaspoon instant minced onion
1 can (16 ounces) red salmon, flaked
 (bone and skin removed)
½ cup sour cream or plain yogurt
¼ cup minced celery
1½ teaspoons lemon juice
2 tablespoons cold water
lettuce for garnish
tomato wedges for garnish
sliced hard-cooked eggs for garnish

1 In the top of a double boiler, sprinkle half the gelatin over the milk and let it soak for about 2 minutes to soften. Set over hot water and cook over medium-low heat for about 5 minutes until the gelatin dissolves. Add the cottage cheese, dill and onion and mix well.

2 Transfer the mixture to a lightly oiled 1-quart loaf pan or mold, cover and chill for about 10 minutes, or until the mixture just begins to set.

3 In a bowl, combine the salmon, sour cream, celery and lemon juice and set aside.

4 Put the water in the top of the double boiler and sprinkle with the remaining gelatin and let it soak for about 2 minutes to soften. Set over hot water and cook over medium-low heat for about 3 minutes until the gelatin dissolves.

5 Combine the salmon and gelatin mixtures and pour this mixture over the cottage cheese. Cover and chill for at least 3 hours, or until firm.

6 Line a platter with lettuce leaves. Wrap the outside of the mold with a warm, damp towel and invert onto the lettuce. Serve garnished with tomato wedges and sliced eggs.

COTTAGE CHEESE SALAD WITH SALMON

MAKES: *4 servings*

⅔ cup mayonnaise
⅓ cup sour cream or plain yogurt
¼ cup chopped fresh cilantro
 (Chinese parsley)
2 tablespoons milk
2 tablespoons lemon or lime juice
1 jalapeño pepper, seeded and
 minced
salt and pepper
1½ cups radiatore pasta, cooked,
 rinsed and drained
2 large tomatoes, diced
1 yellow bell pepper, seeded and cut
 into match sticks
1 small zucchini, quartered
 lengthwise and sliced paper thin
4 green onions, chopped (green
 parts only)

In a bowl, combine the mayonnaise, sour cream, cilantro, milk, lemon juice and jalapeño and season to taste with salt and pepper. Add the pasta, tomatoes, pepper, zucchini and onions and toss well. Cover and chill for at least 1 hour before serving.

CREAMY RADIATORE SALAD

MAKES: *6 to 8 servings*

DRUM MAJOR'S SALAD

MAKES: *8 servings*

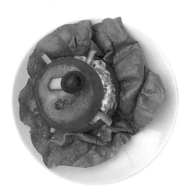

1 package (8 ounces) cream cheese
½ cup mayonnaise
¼ cup chopped walnuts or pecans
¼ cup chopped ripe olives
4 large tomatoes, sliced ¼-inch thick
1 large green pepper, seeded and cut
   into ¼-inch strips
chard leaves
celery stalks
pitted ripe olives
mayonnaise

1 In a bowl, combine the cream cheese and mayonnaise and mash until smooth. Add the nuts and olives and mix well.

2 Spread about 1 tablespoon of the cream cheese mixture on half of tomato slices and lay 2 strips of the pepper over the top to form an x. Top with a second tomato slice to make sandwiches.

3 Line a platter with chard leaves and set the tomato sandwiches on them.

4 Cut the celery into ¼-inch thick stalks that are about 4 inches long. Press an olive into one end of the celery sticks and lay 2 over the top of the sandwiches to form an x. Secure them with toothpicks. Serve with mayonnaise on the side.

FARMER'S SALAD

MAKES: *8 servings*

2 cups diced cooked potatoes
1 cup cooked baby lima beans
½ cup chopped celery
½ cup raisins
⅓ cup shredded carrots
⅓ cup diced cooked beets
4 large hard-cooked eggs, sliced
½ cup minced green onions
salt and pepper
1 cup French dressing
½ cup Blender Mayonnaise (recipe
   follows)
lettuce leaves for garnish
sliced tomatoes for garnish

1 In a large bowl, combine the potatoes, beans, celery, raisins, carrots, beets, eggs and green onions. Season with salt and pepper. Add the dressing and stir until well mixed. Cover and chill for at least 2 hours.

2 Add the mayonnaise and fold until mixed. Arrange lettuce leaves in small bowls and spoon scoops of the salad into the center. Garnish with tomatoes.

BLENDER MAYONNAISE

MAKES: *About 2 cups*

1 large egg
¾ teaspoon salt
½ teaspoon dry mustard
¼ teaspoon paprika
pinch of cayenne
1 tablespoon cider vinegar
1 cup canola oil
1 tablespoon lemon juice

In a container of a blender, combine the egg, salt, mustard, paprika and cayenne and process for 1 or 2 seconds until smooth. Add the vinegar and process until mixed. With the blender running, slowly add the oil in a steady stream. As the mayonnaise thickens, add the lemon juice, a little at a time, until incorporated. Use at once or cover and refrigerate for up to 2 days.

1½ cups shredded green cabbage
1½ cups shredded red cabbage
¼ cup chopped green onions
½ cup thinly sliced green bell
 pepper
1 cup chopped cashews
½ cup rice vinegar
2 tablespoons sesame oil
1 teaspoon cumin
1 tablespoon grated orange zest
sliced red bell pepper for garnish
sliced hard-cooked eggs for garnish
sliced pimiento-stuffed olives for
 garnish

1 In a large bowl, combine the cabbage, onions, green pepper, and cashews and toss to mix.

2 In another bowl, combine the vinegar, oil, cumin and orange zest. Pour over the vegetables and toss to blend. Cover and chill for at least 4 hours.

3 Serve garnished with peppers and egg slices. Position an olive slice in the center of each egg slice on top of the yolk.

FESTIVE CABBAGE SLAW

MAKES: *4 servings*

---

1 can (16 ounces) jelled cranberry
 sauce
1 cup canned apple pie filling
1 cup sour cream or plain yogurt
1 tablespoon lemon juice
3 tablespoons powdered sugar
lettuce leaves
lemon slices for garnish
fresh cranberries for garnish

1 In a large bowl, combine the cranberry sauce and apple filling and gently mix, taking care not to mash the apples.

2 In another bowl, combine the sour cream, lemon juice and sugar and stir to mix. Add the cranberry mixture and stir well. Pour into an 8-by-4-inch loaf pan, cover and freeze for at least 4 hours or until firm.

3 Line a platter with lettuce leaves. Wrap the outside of the mold with a warm, damp towel and invert the loaf on the platter. Let stand at room temperature for about 10 minutes before serving garnished with lemon slices and cranberries.

FROZEN CRANBERRY SALAD

MAKES: *6 servings*

FROZEN FRESH FRUIT SALAD

MAKES: *8 servings*

1 packet unflavored gelatin
¼ cup cold water
3 tablespoons lemon or lime juice
½ cup sugar
1 cup drained crushed pineapple
1 cup diced fresh apricots
1 cup diced fresh peaches
2 large bananas, sliced
2 cups Ginger Dressing (recipe follows)
1 cup heavy cream, whipped

1 In the top of a double boiler, sprinkle the gelatin over the water and let it soak for about 5 minutes to soften. Set over hot water and cook over low heat for about 5 minutes, whisking, until the gelatin dissolves. Stir in the lemon juice, sugar, pineapple, apricots, peaches and bananas and stir gently until the mixture thickens.

2 Remove from the heat, add 1 cup of the dressing and the whipped cream and stir gently. Pour into a 13-by-9-inch metal pan and freeze for at least 4 hours or until firm.

3 To serve, cut into squares or fancy shapes and serve with the remaining cup of dressing.

GINGER DRESSING

MAKES: *About 1⅓ cup*

½ cup mayonnaise
½ cup honey
2 tablespoons finely chopped crystallized ginger
1 tablespoon lime juice
1 tablespoon canola oil
½ teaspoon grated lime zest

In the container of a blender, combine the ingredients and process for 20 to 30 seconds until smooth. Cover and chill for at least 2 hours.

GARDEN SALAD MOLD

MAKES: *4 servings*

1 package (3 ounces) lemon-flavored gelatin
1 cup boiling water
½ teaspoon crushed dried chervil
½ teaspoon crushed dried tarragon leaves
1 cup sour cream or plain yogurt
2 tablespoons tarragon vinegar
salt
¾ cup finely diced celery
½ cup finely diced radishes
½ cup finely diced cucumbers
¼ cup finely diced green bell pepper
¼ cup finely diced green onion
lettuce leaves
1 cup Ginger Dressing (see above)

1 In the top of a double boiler, sprinkle the gelatin over the water and set aside for about 2 minutes to soften. Set over hot water, add the chervil and tarragon and cook over low heat for about 5 minutes, whisking, until the gelatin dissolves. Cover and chill for about 30 minutes until thickened.

2 Add the sour cream and vinegar to the gelled mixture and season with salt. Stir well. Add the celery, radishes, cucumbers, peppers and onions and fold until incorporated. Pour into 4 custard cups or decorative molds. Cover each and chill for at least 2 hours, or until set firm.

3 Line serving plates with lettuce leaves and unmold the salads on top of the leaves. If necessary, wrap the bottoms of the molds with warm, damp towels to help with the unmolding. Serve with the dressing on the side.

1 can (16 ounces) fruit cocktail, drained, juice reserved
1 can (16 ounces) apricot halves, drained, juice reserved
1 can (16 ounces) pineapple chunks, drained, juice reserved
4 ounces miniature marshmallows
1 packet unflavored gelatin
1 jar (4 ounces) maraschino cherries, diced, juice reserved
1 package (3 ounces) cream cheese, at room temperature
½ cup Banana Dressing (recipe follows)
¾ cup heavy cream, whipped
dried apricots for garnish
mint sprigs for garnish

1 In a bowl, combine the fruit cocktail, apricot halves, pineapple and marshmallows. Stir gently and set aside.

2 In a saucepan, combine the reserved juices from the fruit and the gelatin and stir to mix. Let the gelatin soften in the liquid for about 2 minutes. Cook over medium heat, stirring constantly, for about 5 minutes until the gelatin dissolves.

3 Remove from the heat, cool slightly and pour over the fruit. Cover and chill for about 30 minutes until slightly thickened. Add the cherries and their juice and stir to mix.

4 In another bowl, combine the cream cheese and dressing and blend until incorporated. Add to the fruit and mix well. Cover and chill for about 1 hour or until very thick but not completely set.

5 Fold the whipped cream into the jelled mixture. Pour into an 11-by-7-inch metal dish and freeze for at least 4 hours or until firm. Cut into squares and serve garnished with dried apricots and mint sprigs.

FROZEN FRUIT SALAD
MAKES: *8 servings*

BANANA DRESSING
MAKES: *About 2 cups*

2 large bananas, sliced
1 cup sour cream or banana-flavored yogurt
2 tablespoons packed light-brown sugar
2½ teaspoons fresh lemon juice

In the container of a blender, combine all the ingredients and process for 15 to 20 seconds until smooth. Cover and refrigerate for at least 2 hours.

2 small avocados, peeled, pitted and thinly sliced
2 green onions, thinly sliced
1 cucumber, thinly sliced
½ pound Cheddar cheese, cut into ½-inch cubes
4 Romaine lettuce leaves, torn into pieces
2 tablespoons lemon or lime juice
lemon wedges for garnish
Herb Dressing (see page 304) or Ginger Dressing (see page 186)
crackers

1 In a bowl, combine the avocados, onions, cucumber, cheese, lettuce and lemon juice and toss well. Cover and chill for about 1 hour.

2 Serve garnished with lemon wedges and with the dressing and crackers on the side.

GARDEN SALAD WITH CHEESE
MAKES: *4 servings*

GARDEN SALAD WITH HOT DOGS

MAKES: *8 servings*

8 Ball Park® lean frankfurters
1½ cups cooked elbow macaroni
4 stalks celery, sliced
1 large cucumber, peeled and diced
⅓ cup minced green bell pepper
1 small red onion, minced
8 large pitted black olives, sliced
4 large hard-cooked eggs, chopped
1 cup Quick Salad Dressing (see page 69)
2 teaspoons prepared mustard
salt and pepper

1 Slice the frankfurters on the diagonal into ¼-inch-thick slices. Transfer to a bowl and add the macaroni, celery, cucumber, peppers, onion, olives and eggs.

2 In a cup, combine the salad dressing and mustard and whisk to mix. Pour over the salad and toss until well coated. Season with salt and pepper and chill for at least 1 hour before serving.

GREEN BEAN-AND-TOMATO SALAD WITH SALAMI

MAKES: *4 servings*

1 pound fresh green beans, trimmed and cut into 3-inch-long pieces
½ pound salami, unsliced
¼ cup sliced green onion
3 tomatoes, peeled
Herb Dressing (see page 304) or Tarragon Dressing (see page 66)

1 In a steaming basket set over simmering water, steam the green beans over medium heat for about 10 minutes until tender. Drain and transfer to a bowl.

2 Cut the salami into 2-inch pieces and then cut these pieces into matchsticks. Add the salami and onion to the beans and toss.

3 Cut the tomatoes into wedges and add to the bowl. Pour the dressing over the salad and toss to coat. Cover and refrigerate for at least 2 hours before serving.

COOKING NOTE: **You can use another flavor of salad dressing, according to your taste.**

1 package (3 ounces) lemon-flavored
  gelatin
1 cup boiling water
2 tablespoons rice wine vinegar
1 can (12 ounces) corned beef
2 stalks celery, chopped
1 green bell pepper, chopped
1 small white onion, finely chopped
3 large hard-cooked eggs, chopped
1 cup mayonnaise
2 teaspoons prepared horseradish
½ teaspoon salt
lettuce leaves

1 In a bowl, sprinkle the gelatin over the water and set aside for about 5 minutes, stirring occasionally, until the gelatin dissolves. Stir in the vinegar and then set the bowl in a larger bowl or sink filled with ice for about 1 hour until thickened.

2 Meanwhile, put the corned beef in a metal bowl and break into pieces with a fork. Add the celery, pepper, onion, eggs, mayonnaise, horseradish and salt and stir to mix. Cover and freeze while the gelatin thickens.

3 Scrape the corned beef mixture into the gelatin and stir to combine. Pour into 6 custard cups or decorative molds and chill for about 2 hours or until set.

4 Line serving plates with lettuce leaves and unmold the salads on top of the leaves. If necessary, wrap the bottoms of the molds with warm, damp towels to help with the unmolding.

HEARTY CORNED BEEF SALAD

MAKES: *6 servings*

---

1 packet unflavored gelatin
½ cup dry white wine
2 cups small-curd cottage cheese
½ cup crumbled blue cheese
2 tablespoons finely minced green
  onion
1½ teaspoons prepared horseradish
2 tablespoons finely minced fresh
  chervil
1 cup sour cream
lettuce leaves

1 In the top of a double boiler, sprinkle the gelatin over the wine and set aside for about 2 minutes to soften. Set over hot water and cook over low heat for about 5 minutes, whisking, until the gelatin dissolves. Remove from the heat and set aside.

2 In a bowl, combine the cottage cheese and blue cheese and mash with a fork until smooth and creamy. Add the onion, horseradish, chervil and sour cream and blend until smooth. Add the gelatin and wine mixture and stir well.

3 Pour into a lightly oiled mold and chill for at least 4 hours or until firm.

4 Line a platter with lettuce leaves and unmold the salad on top of the leaves. If necessary, wrap the bottom of the mold with a warm, damp towel to help with the unmolding.

HORSERADISH-FLAVORED SALAD MOLD

MAKES: *4 to 6 servings*

LIME SALAD WITH RUM

MAKES: *8 servings*

1 package (3 ounces) lime-flavored gelatin
1 cup boiling water
1 can (6 ounces) frozen lime juice concentrate
½ cup light rum
1 can (20 ounces) crushed pineapple, drained, juice reserved
melon balls, such as watermelon, cantaloupe or muskmelon

1 In a bowl, combine the gelatin and water and stir until the gelatin dissolves. Add the concentrate, rum and 1¼ cup of the reserved juices from the pineapple and stir well. Chill for about 1 hour, or until thickened.

2 Add the pineapple and stir until incorporated. Pour into 8 custard cups or decorative molds and chill for at least 4 hours or until firm.

3 Unmold onto serving plates. If necessary, wrap the outside of the molds with a warm, damp towel to help with the unmolding. Serve circled with melon balls.

COOKING NOTE: Press the pineapple firmly to extract as much juice as possible. One can should yield at least 1¼ cups and may yield 1½ cups. You could use 10 custard cups for 10 smaller servings

CHILLED MACARONI-AND-CHEESE SALAD

MAKES: *8 to 10 servings*

2 cups uncooked small shell macaroni
3 tablespoons Italian dressing
1 cup cubed sharp Cheddar cheese
3 large hard-cooked eggs, chopped
1 cup cooked peas
½ cup chopped celery
½ cup sliced green onion, green portions only
⅓ cup Kraft® Real Mayonnaise or other mayonnaise
1 tablespoon prepared mustard
1½ teaspoons prepared horseradish
½ teaspoon Worcestershire sauce
salt and pepper
lettuce leaves
sliced tomatoes

1 In a saucepan of lightly salted boiling water, cook the macaroni for 8 to 10 minutes or until tender. Drain and rinse under cold running water and drain again. Transfer to a bowl. Pour the dressing over the macaroni and set aside.

2 In a bowl, combine the cheese, eggs, peas, celery and onion and mix.

3 In another bowl, combine the mayonnaise, mustard, horseradish, Worcestershire sauce and season with salt and pepper and blend. Add to the cheese mixture and stir well. Toss with the macaroni, cover and chill for up to 2 hours.

4 Serve on a platter lined with lettuce and garnished with sliced tomatoes.

1 quart (4 cups) broccoli florets
   (from 1 large bunch)
¼ pound small fresh mushrooms,
   stems trimmed, sliced
¾ cup sliced pitted ripe olives
1 cup halved cherry tomatoes
⅓ cup olive oil
1 tablespoon white wine vinegar
1 tablespoon lemon juice
2 tablespoons chopped parsley
1 green onion, minced
1 clove garlic, minced
salt and pepper

1 In a saucepan of lightly salted boiling water, blanch the broccoli florets for about 1 minute until bright green. Drain and transfer to a bowl.

2 Add the mushrooms, olives and tomatoes to the bowl and toss to mix.

3 In a small bowl, combine the oil, vinegar, lemon juice, parsley, onion and garlic and whisk. Season with salt and pepper and whisk again. Pour over the vegetables and toss lightly to coat. Cover and chill for at least 3 hours before serving.

MARINATED VEGETABLE SALAD

MAKES: *4 servings*

¾ cup chopped ripe olives
¾ cup chopped green olives
¾ cup diced cooked carrots
1 cup diced celery
½ cup chopped celery greens
1 cup cooked green peas
1 red onion, grated
Italian dressing
salt and pepper
mayonnaise for garnish
wheat crackers for garnish

1 In a large bowl, combine the olives, carrots, celery, celery greens, peas and onion and toss to mix. Add only enough dressing to coat lightly. Cover and chill for at least 2 hours.

2 Season with salt and pepper and serve in custard cups or decorative bowls garnished with a dab of mayonnaise and with crackers on the side.

MEDITERRANEAN SALAD

MAKES: *8 servings*

8 cooked turkey franks
1 can (16 ounces) kidney beans,
   drained
½ cup sliced sweet pickles
1 cup Kraft® French Dressing
1 small head butter lettuce, torn into
   pieces
1 red onion, thinly sliced

1 Slice the hot dogs into ½-inch slices and transfer to a bowl. Add the beans and pickles and toss to mix. Add ½ cup of the dressing and toss to coat. Cover and chill for at least 2 hours.

2 In a glass serving bowl, alternate layers of lettuce, salad mixture and onion slices. Drizzle with the remaining ½ cup of dressing and chill for about 1 hour before serving.

MISH-MASH SALAD

MAKES: *6 servings*

MOLDED APPLE SALAD

MAKES: *8 servings*

1 packet unflavored gelatin
1¾ cups apple juice
2 tablespoons lemon juice
2 red apples, diced
½ cup diced celery
¼ cup chopped walnuts
lettuce leaves
grapes for garnish
watercress for garnish
½ cup Kraft® blue cheese salad
   dressing

1 In a small saucepan, sprinkle the gelatin over ½ cup of apple juice and let soften for about 5 minutes. Heat over medium-low heat for 2 or 3 minutes, stirring, until dissolved. Add the remaining apple juice and the lemon juice and stir for 1 minute. Remove from the heat and chill for about 1 hour until thickened.

2 Add the apples, celery and walnuts and stir to incorporate. Pour into a lightly oiled 1-quart mold, cover and chill for at least 4 hours, or until firm.

3 Line a platter with lettuce leaves and unmold the salad onto the platter. If necessary, wrap the outside of the mold with a warm, damp towel to help the unmolding. Serve garnished with grapes and watercress and with the dressing on the side.

MOLDED GAZPACHO SALAD

MAKES: *16 servings*

2 packages (3 ounces) raspberry- or
   lemon-flavored gelatin
¾ cup boiling water
2 cans (16 ounces) stewed tomatoes
1 cup tomato juice
4 drops hot-pepper sauce
2 tablespoons red wine vinegar
1 cup diced celery
1 cup diced green bell pepper
½ cup diced red bell pepper
½ cup diced cucumber
½ cup sliced green onion
1 cup sour cream
2 tablespoons horseradish
½ teaspoon sugar
½ teaspoon salt
1 tablespoon lemon juice
1 cucumber, thinly sliced, for
   garnish
2 large hard-cooked eggs, sliced

1 In a small bowl, sprinkle the gelatin over the water and stir until dissolved.

2 In a bowl, mash the tomatoes until free of large lumps. Add the gelatin, tomato juice, pepper sauce, vinegar, celery, peppers, cucumber and onion and toss to mix. Transfer to a lightly oiled 2-quart mold, cover and chill for at least 4 hours or until firm.

3 In a bowl, combine the sour cream, horseradish, sugar, salt and lemon juice and stir until smooth. Cover and chill for at least 1 hour.

4 Invert the mold onto a serving platter. If necessary, wrap the outside of the mold with a warm, damp towel to help with the unmolding. Serve garnished with sliced cucumbers and eggs and with the dressing on the side.

MOLDED SALMON SALAD

MAKES: *6 to 8 servings*

1 packet unflavored gelatin
¼ cup cold water
1 cup mayonnaise
1 cup sour cream or plain yogurt
1 tablespoon minced white onion
¼ cup lemon juice
2 tablespoons minced parsley
1 can (16 ounces) salmon, drained, skin and bones removed
2 large hard-cooked eggs, chopped
½ cup chopped pimiento-stuffed green olives
½ cup chopped celery
salt and pepper
lettuce leaves
French or Italian salad dressing

1 In the top of a double boiler, sprinkle the gelatin over the water and set aside to soften for 5 minutes. Set over hot water and cook, stirring, over medium heat until the gelatin dissolves. Add the mayonnaise, sour cream, onion, lemon juice and parsley and stir. Remove from the heat and set aside.

2 In a large bowl, combine the salmon, eggs, olives and celery and toss to mix. Add the gelatin mixture, season with salt and pepper and spoon into a lightly oiled 1-quart ring mold. Chill for about 4 hours or until firm.

3 Line a platter with lettuce leaves and unmold onto the platter. If necessary, wrap the outside of the mold with a warm, damp towel to help with the unmolding. Serve with the dressing on the side.

MUNICH PINEAPPLE SALAD

MAKES: *4 servings*

½ large fresh pineapple
1 can (8 ounces) sauerkraut, drained
1 large red apple, diced
1½ cups 1-inch strips crisp bacon
3 tablespoons mayonnaise
2 tablespoons sour cream
2 tablespoons lemon juice
1 tablespoon chopped fresh dill or 1 teaspoon dried dill
¼ teaspoon dried rosemary
salt and pepper
butter lettuce leaves

1 Using a grapefruit knife, cut the flesh from the pineapple. Cut the flesh into chunks and transfer to a large bowl. Add the sauerkraut, apple and bacon and toss to mix. Cover and chill for at least 30 minutes.

2 In a small bowl, combine the mayonnaise, sour cream, lemon juice, dill and rosemary and season with salt and pepper. Cover and chill until ready to serve.

3 Line a serving bowl with lettuce leaves. Spoon the salad into the bowl and spoon the dressing over the salad. Serve with toothpicks.

ORANGE BEET SALAD

MAKES: *4 servings*

1 can (10.8 ounces) sliced beets, drained
½ cup sliced green onion
⅓ cup cider vinegar
¼ cup canola oil
2 to 3 tablespoons sugar
½ teaspoon curry powder
salt and pepper
2 large seedless oranges, peeled and sliced
chives for garnish
parsley for garnish

1 In a bowl, combine the beets and onion and toss gently.

2 In a small bowl, combine the vinegar, oil, sugar and curry powder and whisk until blended. Season with salt and pepper. Pour over the beet salad and toss to coat. Cover and chill for at least 2 hours. Serve garnished with oranges, chives and parsley.

PICKLE-AND-ONION MACARONI SALAD

MAKES: *4 servings*

4 ounces elbow macaroni, cooked
2 large hard-cooked eggs, sliced
¼ cup finely chopped green onion
2 large sweet pickles, chopped
¼ cup sliced green olives
½ cup mayonnaise
1 tablespoon prepared mustard
1 teaspoon crushed dried dill
2 tablespoons sweet pickle juice

1 In a large bowl, combine the macaroni, eggs, onions, pickles and olives.

2 In a small bowl, combine the mayonnaise, mustard, dill and pickle juice and stir well. Pour over the macaroni mixture and blend thoroughly. Cover and chill for at least 1 hour.

PINEAPPLE SALAD

MAKES: *8 servings*

2 cups crushed pineapple, drained
12 red maraschino cherries, quartered
12 green maraschino cherries, quartered
1½ cups miniature marshmallows
½ cup powdered sugar
2 packages (3 ounces each) cream cheese, at room temperature
½ cup mayonnaise or Kraft ® Salad Dressing
⅔ cup heavy cream, whipped
1 teaspoon vanilla extract
1 teaspoon almond extract
pineapple slices for garnish

1 In a bowl, combine the pineapple, cherries, marshmallows and sugar. Fold until the sugar is well blended and chill for about 30 minutes.

2 In a bowl, combine the cream cheese and mayonnaise and mash until smooth. Add to the fruit and toss until mixed. Add the cream and extracts and fold until incorporated. Pour into a 13-by-9-inch metal pan and freeze for about 4 hours or until just firm. Cut into squares serve garnished with pineapple slices.

1 small fresh pineapple
1 cup cooked cubed chicken
6 ounces ham, cut into strips
2 bananas, sliced
1 avocado, peeled and cut into chunks
2 stalks celery, sliced on the diagonal
¼ cup chopped walnuts
¼ cup quartered maraschino cherries
1 cup Yogurt Dressing (recipe follows)

1 Cut the pineapple in half lengthwise, cutting through the leaves and leaving them intact. Using a grapefruit knife, cut around the edge of the pineapple and through the center of the core without cutting into the outer shell. Scoop out the pineapple flesh and cut it into 1-inch cubes. Transfer the pineapple cubes to a bowl. Chill the shells until ready to use.

2 Add the chicken, ham, banana, avocado, celery, walnuts and cherries to the bowl and toss to mix. Cover and chill for at least 1 hour.

3 To serve, spoon the fruit mixture into the pineapple shells and serve with toothpicks and dressing on the side.

PINEAPPLE BOAT SALAD

MAKES: *4 servings*

YOGURT DRESSING

MAKES: *About 1 cup*

1 cup plain yogurt
1 teaspoon sugar
2 tablespoons catsup
¼ teaspoon dry mustard
¼ teaspoon paprika
salt and pepper

In a blender, combine the yogurt, sugar, catsup, mustard and paprika and process for 2 or 3 seconds until blended. Season with salt and pepper and blend for several seconds longer.

---

8 large peaches, cut in half and pits removed
1 package (8 ounces) cream cheese, at room temperature
1 cup mayonnaise or Kraft® Salad Dressing
1 cup heavy cream, whipped
1 cup chopped pecans
shredded lettuce

1 Place the peaches, hollow side up, in a 13-by-9-inch metal pan.

2 In a bowl, combine the cream cheese and mayonnaise and mash until smooth. Add the whipped cream and pecans and stir to mix. Pour over the peaches, cover and freeze until the cream mixture is just firm. Cut into squares and serve on a bed of lettuce.

P & P SALAD

MAKES: *8 servings*

POTATO-AND-HAM SALAD

MAKES: *4 servings*

4 large boiling potatoes, peeled and quartered
1 can (10 ounces) condensed consommé
1 clove garlic
1 cup diced cooked ham
¼ cup sliced green onion
3 tablespoons white wine vinegar
2 tablespoons olive oil
½ teaspoon prepared mustard
¼ teaspoon salt
½ cup grated Romano cheese
¼ cup chopped parsley

1 In a saucepan, combine the potatoes, consommé and garlic clove and bring to a boil over high heat. Reduce the heat to medium and cook for 20 to 25 minutes or until the potatoes are tender. Drain and cool.

2 Cut the potatoes and garlic into dice and transfer to a large bowl. Add the ham and onions and toss gently.

3 In a bowl, combine the vinegar, olive oil, mustard and salt and whisk to mix. Spoon the dressing over the potato salad and toss gently to coat. Sprinkle with cheese and parsley and serve.

SALAD BOAT

MAKES: *6 servings*

1 packages (3 ounces) sliced cooked ham
1 package (3 ounces) sliced cooked chicken
1 package (3 ounces) sliced cooked turkey
2 stalks celery, thinly sliced
¾ cup sweet pickle relish
¾ cup Blender Mayonnaise (see page 184)
1 loaf Vienna or white bread, unsliced
¼ cup butter or margarine, at room temperature
1 teaspoon prepared mustard
cherry tomatoes, halved
celery leaves

1 Reserve 5 slices of the cooked ham and then chop the remaining ham, the chicken and the turkey and transfer to a bowl. Add the celery, relish and mayonnaise. Cover and chill for about 1 hour.

2 Cut a thin horizontal slice from the top of the bread and scoop the soft bread from the center leaving a ¾-inch-thick shell. (Reserve the soft inside of the bread for another use.)

3 In a bowl, combine the butter and mustard and mash to mix. Spread in a thin layer over the inside of the bread shell. Line with the reserved ham slices and spoon the chilled meat mixture into the bread shell and spread to fill the shell evenly. Garnish with tomatoes and celery leaves. Slice and serve.

COOKING NOTE: This can be make with French or Italian bread, too. The soft inside of the bread can be used for croutons or bread crumbs. Depending on your preference, line the bread shell with slices of chicken or turkey instead of ham, or a combination of all three kinds of meat.

4 potatoes
¼ cup tarragon vinegar
2 tablespoons minced green onion
Tarragon Dressing (see page 66)
chopped parsley for garnish
paprika for garnish

1 Puncture the potatoes several times with the tines of a fork and put the potatoes in a saucepan. Add the vinegar and enough water to cover and bring to a boil over medium-high heat. Reduce the heat and simmer for 10 to 15 minutes or until the potatoes are fork-tender. Drain and return to the pan. Add enough cold water to cover the potatoes and set aside to cool for 2 or 3 minutes. Drain.

2 Slice the potatoes into ¼-inch-thick slices and transfer to a large bowl. Add the onions and toss to mix. Add enough dressing to coat the potatoes lightly. Sprinkle with parsley and paprika and serve.

POTATO SALAD WITH TARRAGON DRESSING

MAKES: *4 servings*

---

2 large hard-cooked eggs
1 cup Cottage Cheese Dressing
 (recipe follows)
¼ cup sour cream or plain yogurt
2 teaspoons cider vinegar
½ teaspoon Dijon mustard
pinch of dried oregano
pinch of fresh chervil
salt and pepper
3 potatoes, cooked, peeled and
 cubed
8 cherry tomatoes, quartered
8 strips crisp cooked bacon,
 crumbled
½ cup chopped green onion (green
 parts only)
lettuce leaves
ripe olives for garnish
carrot sticks for garnish
celery sticks for garnish

1 In a bowl, mash the eggs until smooth. Add the dressing, sour cream, vinegar, mustard, oregano and chervil and season with salt and pepper and toss to mix. Add potatoes, tomatoes, bacon and onions and toss again until coated.

2 Line a platter with lettuce and mound the salad on the lettuce. Serve garnished with olives, carrot sticks and celery sticks.

RICH POTATO SALAD

MAKES: *4 to 6 servings*

COTTAGE CHEESE DRESSING

MAKES: *About 2¾ cups*

1 carton (12 ounces) large-curd
 cottage cheese
½ cup mayonnaise
2 tablespoons snipped chives
2 tablespoons chopped green bell
 pepper
¼ teaspoon garlic powder

In a blender, combine the cottage cheese, mayonnaise, chives, pepper and garlic powder and process until smooth. Transfer to a bowl, cover and chill for at least 1 hour.

SOMETHING DIFFERENT SALAD

MAKES: *8 servings*

2 cups grated American cheese
8 dozen miniature marshmallows
1 jar (8 ounces) green maraschino cherries, chopped
1 can (6 ounces) crushed pineapple
1 cup Blue Cheese Mayonnaise (see page 24)
1 cup heavy cream, whipped
4 red bell pepper rings for garnish
4 green bell pepper rings for garnish
watercress for garnish

1 In a large bowl, combine the cheese, marshmallows, cherries, pineappple, mayonnaise and whipped cream and toss gently to mix. Spoon into 8 custard cups or dessert dishes and chill overnight or until firm.

2 Top each dish with a pepper ring and garnish with watercress.

SPINACH-AND-ROTELLE SALAD

MAKES: *4 to 6 servings*

1 pound fresh spinach or mustard leaves, washed and drained, tough stems trimmed
8 ounces fresh mushrooms, trimmed and sliced
1½ cups rotelle pasta, cooked, rinsed and drained
1 red onion, thinly sliced
6 to 8 strips crisp cooked bacon, crumbled
Extra-Rich Vinegar Mayonnaise, at room temperature (recipe follows)
variety breads

In a large bowl, combine the spinach, mushrooms, pasta, onion and bacon. Drizzle with mayonnaise and toss until well coated. Serve with bread.

COOKING NOTE: **Herbed croutons can be substituted for the bread.**

EXTRA-RICH VINEGAR MAYONNAISE

MAKES: *About 2⅓ cups*

1 cup mayonnaise
1 cup water
⅓ cup cider vinegar
1 tablespoon cornstarch
1 tablespoon sugar
salt and pepper

1 In a blender, combine the mayonnaise, water, vinegar, cornstarch and sugar and process until smooth. Season with salt and pepper and process for 1 or 2 seconds or longer until mixed.

2 Transfer to a saucepan and bring to a boil over medium heat. Cook for 1 minute, stirring. Remove from the heat and serve warm or at room temperature.

¾ pound fresh mushrooms, trimmed and thinly sliced
⅓ cup olive oil
¼ cup tarragon wine vinegar
1 jar (3 ounces) capers, drained
2 teaspoons chopped pimiento
pinch of cayenne
salt and pepper
1 pound fresh spinach leaves, washed and drained, tough stems trimmed
2 green bell pepper rings for garnish
2 red bell pepper rings for garnish
1 small hard-cooked egg, sliced, for garnish

1 Put the mushrooms in a bowl.

2 In a small bowl, combine the oil, vinegar, capers, pimiento and cayenne and whisk. Season with salt and pepper. Adjust the seasoning. Pour over the mushrooms, cover and chill for about 2 hours.

3 Put the spinach on 4 salad plates and top with the marinated mushrooms. Garnish each plate with a pepper ring and egg slices.

SPINACH SALAD WITH CAPERS

MAKES: *4 servings*

---

2 large avocados, halved, pits removed
6 tablespoons small-curd cottage cheese
2 tablespoons chopped almonds
2 tablespoons minced ripe olives
2 tablespoons snipped chives
lettuce leaves
Kraft® French Dressing

1 Carefully peel the avocado halves, leaving the avocado flesh intact.

2 In a bowl, combine the cottage cheese, nuts, olives and chives and mix well. Spoon the cottage cheese mixture into the avocado halves and wrap each in plastic wrap. Chill for 2 hours.

3 Unwrap the avocados and slice into ½-inch-thick slices. Serve with the dressing drizzled over the slices.

STUFFED AVOCADO SLICES

MAKES: *8 servings*

---

1 can (12½ ounces) pineapple tidbits, drained
1 can (11 ounces) mandarin orange segments, drained
1 cup miniature marshmallows
1 can (3½ ounces) flaked coconut
1 cup sour cream or plain yogurt, plus more for garnish
4 to 6 large lettuce leaves
chopped walnuts or pecans

1 In a large bowl, combine the pineapple, mandarin oranges, marshmallows, coconut and sour cream and stir well.

2 Press a lettuce leaf into a custard cup and spoon the salad mixture into each cup. Serve garnished with chopped nuts and a dab of sour cream.

HEAVENLY AMBROSIA SALAD

MAKES: *4 to 6 servings*

TOMATO-RICE SALAD

MAKES: *4 servings*

4 tomatoes
1 cup cooked jasmine rice, chilled
1 green onion, sliced
½ cup cooked peas
¼ cup finely chopped red bell
    pepper
⅓ cup mayonnaise
salt and pepper
ripe olive slices for garnish
lettuce leaves for garnish

1 Slice the top from each tomato and scoop out the pulp, leaving a shell. Turn the tomato slices upside down on paper towels to drain. Reserve the pulp for another use.

2 In a bowl, combine the rice, onion, peas, peppers and mayonnaise and mix well. Season with salt and pepper. Spoon the mixture into the tomato shells and top with olive slices. Arrange on a plate lined with lettuce leaves and chill until ready to serve.

TURKEY SALAD

MAKES: *4 to 6 servings*

2 cups diced cooked turkey breast
2 tart apples, cored and diced
⅓ cup thinly sliced celery
⅔ cup Blender Mayonnaise (see
    page 184)
2 tablespoons fresh lemon or lime
    juice
salt and pepper
½ cup chopped walnuts
crackers

1 In a bowl, combine the turkey, apples, celery, mayonnaise and lemon juice and toss to mix. Season with salt and pepper. Cover and chill for 1 hour.

2 Mound the salad on a platter, sprinkle with nuts and serve with crackers.

WATERCRESS-AND-PEAR SALAD

MAKES: *4 servings*

3 Bartlett pears, peeled and cored
1 bunch watercress, torn into pieces
⅓ cup Kraft® Italian Dressing
2 green onions, thinly sliced (white
    part only)
1 tablespoon lemon juice
¼ teaspoon crushed crystallized
    ginger
seasoned croutons for garnish

1 In a bowl, combine the pears and watercress. Cover and chill for about 1 hour.

2 In a small bowl, combine the dressing, onions, lemon juice and ginger and whisk well. Cover and chill until ready to use.

3 Pour the dressing over the salad and gently toss to coat. Serve with croutons on the side.

Chapter 5

MIDNIGHT RAID SANDWICHES

For years, sandwiches have been the food of choice for lunch and as between-meal snacks for grown-ups and kids (who doesn't cherish the sweet memory of peanut butter-and-jelly sandwiches?). This chapter is all about sandwiches—big, bold sandwiches and more modest fare, too, appropriate for munching before or after lunch and well into the wee hours. But if you are looking for dainty little things, look elsewhere—these are the real thing. Not finger food as much as two-handed affairs!

OPEN-FACED TURKEY SANDWICHES

MAKES: *10 servings*

10 slices Italian bread
Kraft® Thousand Island Dressing
10 lettuce leaves
3 packages (3 ounces each) sliced turkey
½ cup sliced pimiento-stuffed olives
¼ cup chopped pimiento
⅓ cup chopped white onions
10 sliced garlic dill pickles

Spread each slice of bread with dressing, spreading it to the very edge. Lay a lettuce leaf on each slice and lay 3 slices of turkey on the lettuce. Top with olives, pimientos, and onions. Lay pickle slices on top and serve.

CLUB SANDWICH

MAKES: *1 serving*

mayonnaise
2 slices white bread, toasted and buttered on 1 side
lettuce leaf
2 slices turkey
1 slice whole-wheat bread, toasted and buttered on both sides
¼ teaspoon chili sauce
½ teaspoon bacon bits
4 sweet pickle slices for garnish
4 radish slices for garnish

1 Spread mayonnaise over the buttered sides of the white bread. Top 1 slice with the lettuce leaf, a slice of turkey and then with a slice of whole-wheat bread.

2 Spread chili sauce and the bacon bits on the whole wheat bread and cover with the remaining slice of turkey. Top with the remaining slice of white bread, buttered side down.

3 Cut the sandwich in half diagonally into quarters. Separate on the plate and place a wooden toothpick in the center of each quarter. Skewer a slice of pickle and radish on each toothpick and serve.

BAKED DENVER SANDWICH

MAKES: *4 servings*

8 slices whole-wheat bread, buttered on one side and crusts trimmed
¼ cup shredded Cheddar or Colby cheese
1 cup finely chopped ham
¼ cup finely chopped green bell pepper
1 tablespoon chopped green onion
3 large eggs
2 cups milk
salt and pepper
avocado slices
paprika

1 Position the rack in the center of the oven and preheat to 375 degrees F.

2 In a shallow baking pan, lay 4 slices of the bread, buttered side down, and sprinkle with cheese, ham, peppers and onions. Top with the remaining slices of bread, buttered side up.

3 In a small bowl, combine the eggs and milk and whisk well. Season with salt and pepper. Pour over the sandwiches and using a pancake turner, press firmly on the sandwiches. Bake for 35 to 45 minutes, or until the sandwiches feel firm. Garnish with avocado slices and sprinkle with paprika.

3 cans (4.5 ounces each) chicken
   spread
¼ cup plus 3 tablespoons
   mayonnaise
1 loaf French bread, halved
   lengthwise
leaf lettuce
2 cucumbers, thinly sliced
2 tomatoes, thinly sliced
2 cups shredded Muenster or Swiss
   cheese
2 cans (4.5 ounces each) tiny
   deveined shrimp, rinsed and
   drained
grated romano cheese

1 In a bowl, combine the chicken spread and 2 tablespoons of mayonnaise and mix well. Spread over the bread halves. Top with lettuce, dabs of mayonnaise (about 2 tablespoons), cucumbers and tomatoes. Top with shredded cheese.

2 Combine the shrimp with the remaining mayonnaise (about 3 tablespoons) and spread over the cheese. Sprinkle with romano cheese, slice each bread half into 5 sandwiches.

SHRIMP-AND-CHICKEN SANDWICHES

MAKES: *10 servings*

---

11 large lettuce leaves
1 small cantaloupe, halved, seeded
   and cut into wedges
1 small honeydew melon, halved,
   seeded and cut into wedges
4 slices pimiento loaf
4 slices salami
4 slices bologna
4 slices turkey ham
1 package (3 ounces) sliced turkey
4 slices sharp Cheddar cheese
4 slices Tillamook cheese
4 slices Monterey Jack
1 cup small pimiento-stuffed olives
6 to 8 hard rolls
Tarragon Dressing (see page 66)
prepared mustard

Arrange the lettuce on a platter and set the melon wedges on it. Arrange the meats, cheeses and olives on the platter. Serve the rolls alongside the meat and cheese for making sandwiches, with the dressing and mustard on the side.

CHEESE-AND-MEAT COMBOS

MAKES: *6 to 8 servings*

---

1 tablespoon olive oil
½ pound extra-lean ground beef
salt and pepper
⅓ cup milk
1 tablespoon instant minced onion
6 large eggs, lightly beaten
1 cup shredded Cheddar cheese
4 pita pockets
sliced tomatoes
fresh alfalfa sprouts

1 In a skillet, heat the oil over medium heat and cook the beef for 3 or 4 minutes, stirring, until no longer pink. Pour off the fat. Season the meat with salt and pepper and set aside.

2 In a bowl, combine the milk, onion and eggs and whisk until blended. Add to the meat in the skillet and cook over medium heat, stirring, for 4 or 5 minutes or until the eggs begin to scramble. Add the cheese and cook, stirring gently, until the cheese melts. Remove from the heat.

3 Cut the top third off the pita pockets and fill each with the meat mixture. Top with tomatoes and sprouts.

BEEF-AND-EGG STUFFED POCKETS

MAKES: *4 servings*

BLUE CHEESE BURGERS

MAKES: *4 servings*

2 tablespoons butter or margarine, at
  room temperature
1 onion, finely chopped
1 large egg
⅓ cup whole-wheat bread crumbs
¼ teaspoon garlic powder
1 tablespoon Worcestershire sauce
1 pound lean ground beef
4 thin slices blue cheese
4 sesame-seeded hamburger buns
sliced tomatoes
lettuce
sweet pickles

1 In a large skillet, heat the butter over medium heat and sauté the onion for about 5 minutes until softened.

2 In a bowl, whisk the egg until foamy. Add the bread crumbs, garlic powder and Worcester-shire sauce and stir to mix. Add the reserved onions and the beef and mix until the ingredients are blended. Form the meat mixture into quarters and form each quarter into a flattened patty.

3 In the skillet, cook the patties over medium-high heat for 4 to 6 minutes on each side until browned and cooked through. After turning the patties, lay a slice of blue cheese on the top of each so that it softens while the patties complete cooking. Transfer each patty to a bun and top with tomatoes and lettuce. Serve garnished with pickles.

CHICKEN TACO POCKETS

MAKES: *8 servings*

1 small avocado, peeled, cored and
  thinly sliced
1½ teaspoons lemon juice
2 cups cubed cooked chicken
1 can (4 ounces) chopped green
  chiles, drained
1 white onion, thinly sliced and
  separated into rings
1 tablespoon canola oil
8 small pita pockets
2 cups shredded Monterey Jack or
  Wisconsin brick cheese
1 cup shredded lettuce
½ cup sour cream or plain yogurt
4 ounces prepared taco sauce

1 Brush the avocado slices with lemon juice and set aside.

2 In a microwave-safe casserole, combine the chicken, chiles, onion and oil and stir to mix. Cover with plastic wrap and microwave on high (100 percent) power for 4 or 5 minutes until the chicken is heated through. (If the microwave does not have a turntable, rotate the dish a half turn after about 2 minutes.)

3 Cut the top third off the pita pockets and fill with the chicken mixture. Top with the avocadoes, cheese and lettuce and serve with sour cream and taco sauce on the side.

8 slices whole-wheat bread, toasted
prepared mustard
¼ cup chopped walnuts
4 ounces sliced Gouda cheese
4 Romaine lettuce leaves, torn into
    pieces
½ cucumber, thinly sliced
¾ cup Herb Dressing (see page 304)

1 Spread 4 slices of the toast with mustard and sprinkle with nuts. Top with cheese.

2 In a small bowl, combine the lettuce and cucumber and toss with the dressing. Spread this mixture over the cheese and top with the remaining 4 slices of toast. Cut each sandwich into quarters and serve.

CHEESE-AND-WALNUT SANDWICHES

MAKES: *4 servings*

½ cup minced celery
½ cup chopped pecans
1 tablespoon snipped chives
2 cups shredded Monterey Jack or
    Muenster cheese
½ teaspoon curry powder
¼ teaspoon ground cumin
¼ cup mayonnaise or Kraft® Salad
    Dressing
4 pita pockets
2 tomatoes, diced

1 Position the rack in the center of the oven and preheat to 400 degrees F.

2 In a bowl, combine the celery, pecans, chives, cheese, curry, cumin and mayonnaise and toss to mix.

3 Cut the top third off the pita pockets and stuff with the cheese mixture. Wrap the sandwiches in aluminum foil and lay on a baking sheet. Bake for about 8 minutes until heated through. Unwrap and serve with a spoonful of tomatoes in each pocket. Serve hot.

CURRIED CHEESE-AND-PECAN SANDWICHES

MAKES: *4 servings*

---

1 can (7 ounces) tuna, drained and
    flaked
¼ cup chopped celery
2 tablespoons raisins
2 tablespoons thinly sliced green
    onion
¼ cup mayonnaise or Kraft® Salad
    Dressing
2 teaspoons lemon juice
½ teaspoon curry powder
2 English muffins, split
1 tablespoon butter or margarine
4 thin slices Cheddar cheese
celery leaves for garnish

1 Position the broiler rack 6 inches from the heat source and preheat the broiler.

2 In a bowl, combine the tuna, celery, raisins, and onion and stir.

3 In a cup, combine the mayonnaise, lemon juice and curry powder and mix well. Add to the tuna mixture and stir until well mixed.

4 Spread the muffin halves with butter and broil until golden brown. Spoon the tuna mixture on the muffins and top each with a slice of cheese. Broil for 2 or 3 minutes until the cheese melts. Cut into quarters and serve hot, garnished with celery leaves.

CURRIED TUNA MELTS

MAKES: *4 servings*

EGG-AND-TUNA SALAD SANDWICHES

MAKES: *8 servings*

EGG SALAD
6 large hard-cooked eggs
⅓ cup finely grated carrots
2 tablespoons chopped onion
⅓ cup mayonnaise or Kraft® Salad Dressing
salt and pepper

TUNA SALAD
1 can (7 ounces) white chunk tuna, drained and flaked
1 hard-cooked egg, chopped
¼ cup chopped celery
1 small apple, peeled, cored and chopped
2 tablespoons sweet pickle relish
¼ cup mayonnaise or Kraft® Salad Dressing
1 tablespoon lemon juice
16 slices whole-wheat bread, crusts trimmed
4 lettuce leaves
8 cherry tomatoes
potato chips
tortilla chips

1 To make the egg salad, in a bowl, mash the eggs with a fork and add the carrots and onions. Add the mayonnaise and stir until mixed. Season with salt and pepper, cover and chill for at least 1 hour.

2 To make the tuna salad, in a bowl, combine the tuna, egg, celery, apple, relish, mayonnaise and lemon juice and blend thoroughly. Cover and chill for at least 1 hour.

3 Spread the egg salad on 4 slices of the bread and the tuna salad on 4 slices. Lay a lettuce leaf on top of the tuna sandwiches. Top the sandwiches with the remaining slices of bread and cut each in half on the diagonal. Skewer each sandwich half with a toothpick and thread a cherry tomato on each. Serve with chips on the side.

FALAFELS

MAKES: *4 servings*

FALAFELS
1 can (15 ounces) garbanzo beans, drained
1 clove garlic, minced
¼ cup chopped parsley
½ teaspoon cumin
½ teaspoon turmeric
¼ teaspoon cayenne
2 tablespoons tahini
1 large egg
3 tablespoons wheat germ

SAUCE
⅓ cup tahini
1 cup plain yogurt or sour cream
1 large clove garlic, minced
3 tablespoons lemon or lime juice
1 tablespoon chopped parsley
1 tablespoon chopped green onion (green portions only)
pinch of cayenne
pinch of cumin
¼ to ½ cup canola oil
4 large pita pockets
1 cup shredded lettuce
2 tomatoes, chopped

1 To make the falafels, in a blender, combine the beans, garlic, parsley, cumin, turmeric,

cayenne, tahini, egg and wheat germ and process for 3 or 4 seconds until smooth. Transfer to a bowl, cover and chill for at least 1 hour.

2 To prepare the sauce, in a blender, combine the tahini, yogurt, garlic, lemon juice, parsley, onion, cayenne, and cumin and process on low for 4 to 6 seconds until thickened.

3 In a large skillet or deep-fat fryer, heat the oil until hot (375 degrees F. in a deep-fat fryer). Drop the falafel mixture by spoonfuls into the oil and fry for 3 or 4 minutes, turning, until browned on all sides. Drain the falafel balls on paper towels.

4 Cut the top third from the pitas and fill with the fried falafel balls. Top with lettuce and tomatoes and spoon the sauce over the vegetables and filling and serve.

1 package (8 ounces) cream cheese
1 tablespoon chopped green onion
1 teaspoon lemon juice or lime juice
1 teaspoon Worcestershire sauce
1 package (6 ounces) frozen snow crab, thawed
2 English muffins, split
1 tablespoon butter or margarine
4 tomato slices
½ cup shredded Edam cheese
½ avocado, cored, peeled and diced

1 Position the rack in the center of the oven and preheat to 350 degrees F.

2 In a bowl, mash the cream cheese until smooth. Add the onions, lemon juice, Worcestershire sauce and crabmeat and fold until incorporated.

3 Toast the muffin halves and spread with the butter. Top with the crab mixture and lay a tomato slice on each. Sprinkle with shredded cheese. Transfer to a baking sheet and bake for 12 to 15 minutes until the cheese melts.

4 While the cheese is still hot, sprinkle the avocado over the muffin halves and cut each into quarters. Serve hot.

HOT CRAB SANDWICHES

MAKES: *4 servings*

---

8 slices Swedish rye bread, crusts trimmed
4 slices Swiss or Muenster cheese
4 slices boiled ham
¼ cup butter or margarine
16 pimiento-stuffed olives for garnish

1 Using a rolling pin, roll each slice of bread so that it is about ¼ inch thick.

2 Lay 1 slice of cheese and 1 slice ham on each of 4 slices of bread. Top with the remaining 4 slices.

3 In a skillet, heat the butter over medium heat until it melts. Add the sandwiches and cook for 3 or 4 minutes or until browned and crisp on both sides. Cut into quarters and skewer each quarter with a toothpick. Thread an olive on each toothpick and serve.

HOT HAM-AND-CHEESE SANDWICHES

MAKES: *4 servings*

SLOPPY JOE SANDWICHES

MAKES: *4 servings*

¼ pound lean ground beef
1 onion, chopped
1 tablespoon all-purpose flour
1 teaspoon Worcestershire sauce
dash of hot-pepper sauce
½ cup water
½ cup chili sauce
1 can (16 ounces) pork-and-beans
4 hamburger buns, split
2 tomatoes, chopped
1 red onion, chopped

1 In a skillet, cook the ground beef over medium-high heat, stirring, for 6 to 8 minutes or until no longer pink. Discard the fat. Add the onion and cook, stirring, for about 5 minutes longer or until the onion softens.

2 Add the flour, Worcestershire sauce, hot pepper sauce, water, chili sauce and pork-and-beans and simmer, covered, for about 10 minutes until heated through.

3 Toast the hamburger buns. Spoon the sloppy joe mixture over the buns and serve garnished with tomatoes and red onions.

TUNA LIGHT SANDWICHES

MAKES: *4 servings*

1 can (6 ounces) chunk tuna, drained and flaked
¼ cup chopped tomatoes
¼ cup chopped green bell pepper
2 tablespoons chopped green onion
¼ cup mayonnaise or Kraft® Salad Dressing
1 tablespoon lemon juice or lime juice
¼ teaspoon crushed dried chervil
salt and pepper
2 large egg whites
3 tablespoons grated romano or Parmesan cheese
4 slices whole-wheat bread
1 tablespoon butter or margarine

1 Position the rack in the center of the oven and preheat to 450 degrees F.

2 In a bowl, combine the tuna, tomatoes, pepper, onion, mayonnaise, lemon juice and chervil, season with salt and pepper and mix well.

3 In another bowl, using an electric mixer on high speed, beat the egg whites until stiff but not dry peaks form. Fold the cheese into the whites and then scrape the whites into the tuna mixture. Fold gently to combine.

4 Toast the bread and butter on 1 side. Spread the tuna mixture on the unbuttered side and transfer to a baking sheet. Bake for 8 to 10 minutes or until the mixture is lightly browned. Cut in half and serve hot.

BROILED TURKEY SANDWICHES

MAKES: *6 servings*

2 cups chopped cooked turkey
½ cup chopped celery
¼ cup chopped green bell pepper
1 tablespoon chopped white onion
⅓ cup Kraft® Real Mayonnaise or other mayonnaise
2 teaspoons lemon juice
salt and pepper
6 slices honey whole-wheat bread
butter or margarine, at room temperature
1 cup shredded American or sharp Cheddar cheese

1 Position the broiler rack 4 inches from the heat source and preheat the broiler.

2 In a bowl, combine the turkey, celery, pepper, onion, mayonnaise and lemon juice and season with salt and pepper. Stir well.

3 Lay the bread on a pan and broil just until it is lightly toasted on 1 side. Butter the untoasted sides of the bread and spread the turkey mixture over the butter. Broil for about 3 minutes more, or until the turkey mixture is heated through. Sprinkle with cheese and broil for about 1 minute longer, or until the cheese melts. Serve hot.

MARINADE AND STEAK

¼ cup canola oil
¼ cup red wine vinegar
1 teaspoon dry mustard
1 large clove garlic, minced
1 teaspoon crushed dried chervil
salt and pepper
one 1½-pound flank steak, trimmed

RELISH

2 tomatoes, diced
1 large avocado, cored, peeled and diced
1 tablespoon lemon or lime juice
¼ cup chopped green onion
5 drops hot-pepper sauce

SANDWICH

4 large French rolls
salt and pepper
8 slices Monterey jack cheese

1 To make the marinade, in a shallow glass or ceramic dish, combine the oil, vinegar, mustard, garlic and chervil, season with salt and pepper and whisk well. Lay the steak in the dish

and turn to coat both sides with marinade. Cover and chill for at least 1 hour.

2 Meanwhile, to prepare the relish, in a bowl, combine the tomatoes, avocado, lemon juice, onion and hot-pepper sauce and stir well. Cover and set aside.

3 Prepare a charcoal or gas grill.

4 Grill the steak about 4 inches from the coals for 5 or 6 minutes on each side for medium-rare meat and 8 to 10 minutes on each side for well-done meat. Slice the steak on the diagonal into strips.

5 Cut the rolls in half horizontally but do not cut all the way through. Lay the rolls, cut side down, on the edge of the grill and toast lightly. Lay strips of steak on the bottom half of each roll and season with salt and pepper. Lay cheese on the meat and top with a spoonful of relish. Close the sandwiches and cut each into thirds. Serve immediately.

WESTERN-STYLE FLANK STEAK SANDWICHES

MAKES: *12 servings*

4 French rolls
Garlic Butter (see page 109)
1 small green bell pepper, sliced
1 small red onion, sliced
4 large radishes, sliced
4 cauliflower florets, chopped
2 tomatoes, sliced
1 small carrot, shredded
2 small dill pickles, shredded
Italian dressing
4 ounces Monterey Jack or Gouda cheese, thinly sliced
hot Italian-style pickled peppers for garnish

1 Cut the rolls in half horizontally but do not cut all the way through. Scoop out most of the soft insides to leave a shell. Brush

the shells with butter. Reserve the scooped-out soft insides for another use.

2 Divide the peppers, onions, radishes, cauliflower and tomatoes among the sandwiches, piling the vegetables into the scooped-out bottom shell of each roll. Top with carrots and pickles and drizzle with dressing. Lay the cheese over the top of each, close the sandwiches and cut each into thirds. Serve garnished with the pickled peppers.

COOKING NOTE: Use the scooped out bread to make bread crumbs or stuffing.

VEGETARIAN HERO SANDWICHES

MAKES: *12 servings*

CHEESE ROLLS WITH CHIVES

MAKES: *16 servings*

8 round hard rolls
1½ cups shredded mozzarella or Provolone cheese
⅓ cup Green Goddess® Salad Dressing
¼ cup butter or margarine, at room temperature
3½ tablespoons snipped chives

1 Position a broiler tray 6 inches from the heat source and preheat the broiler.

2 Cut the rolls in half.

3 In a bowl, combine the cheese, salad dressing, butter and chives and blend until smooth but still textured. Spread evenly on the rolls and place on the broiler tray. Broil for 3 to 5 minutes until the cheese bubbles and lightly browned. Serve hot.

CHEESY TOAST

MAKES: *6 servings*

¾ cup butter or margarine
1 cup shredded Cheddar cheese
½ cup shredded mozzarella cheese
½ cup grated Parmesan or romano cheese
½ teaspoon garlic powder
pepper
12 thin slices French bread

1 In a bowl, using an electric mixer on medium speed, beat the butter until light and fluffy. Add

the cheeses and garlic powder and season with pepper. Spread on both sides of the bread slices.

2 In a nonstick skillet, cook the bread over medium heat for 1 or 2 minutes until browned on the bottom. Turn over and cook the other side until browned. Serve immediately.

COLESLAW SANDWICHES

MAKES: *24 servings*

2½ to 3 cups shredded cabbage
1 can (6.5 ounces) tuna, drained and flaked
½ cup minced celery
¼ cup chopped green bell pepper
¼ cup chopped pecans or walnuts
¾ cup Tarragon Dressing (see page 66)
2 tablespoons minced white onions
1 tablespoon lime or lemon juice
salt and pepper
Herb Butter (see page 49)
24 slices sourdough bread, toasted
red or green bell peppers, cut into matchsticks, for garnish
ground pecans or walnuts for garnish

1 In a large bowl, combine the cabbage, tuna, celery, peppers and pecans and toss.

2 In a bowl, combine the dressing, onions and lime juice and season with salt and pepper and mix well. Pour over the vegetables and toss to blend.

3 Spread the butter over the toast, spreading it to the edges. Top with some coleslaw and garnish with the pepper matchsticks and ground nuts. Serve immediately.

2 cucumbers
apple cider vinegar
1 cup mayonnaise
½ cup sour cream
2 teaspoon Good Seasons® Blue
  Cheese Mix
1 teaspoon lemon juice
salt and pepper
Pepperidge Farm® cocktail bread

1 Using a fork, score the outside peel of the cucumbers and cut into thin slices. Transfer to a bowl and add enough vinegar just to cover. Cover and chill for at least 8 hours.

2 Drain the cucumbers and dry between paper towels.

3 In a bowl, combine the mayonnaise, sour cream, dressing mix and lemon juice and season with salt and pepper. Spread on the bread and top each with 2 cucumber slices.

CUCUMBER SANDWICHES

MAKES: *30 to 36 servings*

3 tablespoons Mushroom Butter (see
  page 155), at room temperature
3 slices whole-wheat bread, crusts
  trimmed
3 slices white bread, crusts trimmed
12 slices roast beef
24 strips crisp bacon
2 white onions, sliced

Spread the butter evenly on the bread, spreading it to the edges. Top each with 2 slices of beef, 4 strips of bacon and onion slices. Cut in half and serve immediately.

DANISH-STYLE BEEF-AND-BACON SANDWICHES

MAKES: *12 servings*

DANISH-STYLE CHEESE-AND-HAM SANDWICHES

MAKES: *6 servings*

3 tablespoons butter or margarine, at room temperature
1 teaspoon prepared mustard
6 slices honey whole-wheat bread, crusts trimmed
6 slices Swiss cheese
6 thin slices smoked ham
12 thin slices bread-and-butter pickles
3 cherry tomatoes, sliced thin.

In a cup, combine the butter and mustard and blend well. Spread on the bread and top with slices of cheese and ham. Garnish each with pickles and cherry tomatoes and serve immediately.

DANISH-STYLE CHICKEN SANDWICHES

MAKES: *6 servings*

3 tablespoons mayonnaise
6 slices white bread, crusts trimmed
12 thin slices cooked chicken
2 tomatoes, thinly sliced
1 cucumber, thinly sliced

Spread the mayonnaise on the bread. Top with chicken, tomatoes and cucumbers and serve immediately.

DANISH-STYLE CRAB SANDWICHES

MAKES: *8 servings*

3 tablespoons butter or margarine, at room temperature
6 slices Russian dark rye bread
1 can (12 ounces) crabmeat, drained and flaked
2 tablespoons finely chopped celery
3 tablespoons mayonnaise
¼ teaspoon lemon juice
chopped parsley

1 Spread the butter on the bread.
2 In a small bowl, combine the crabmeat, celery, mayonnaise and lemon juice and mix well. Spread on the bread, garnish with parsley and serve immediately.

3 tablespoons Anchovy Spread with
   Cheese (recipe follows)
6 slices whole-wheat bread
3 to 4 large hard-cooked eggs, thinly
   sliced
12 thin slices smoked salmon
lemon juice
snipped chives

Spread the spread on the bread
and arrange a ring of sliced eggs
around the edges. Top with 2
slices of salmon and a sprinkling
of lemon juice. Sprinkle with
chives and serve.

DANISH-STYLE EGG-AND-SALMON SANDWICHES

MAKES: *6 servings*

ANCHOVY SPREAD WITH CHEESE

MAKES: *About 1 cup*

¾ cup mashed anchovies
2 large hard-cooked eggs, mashed
2 tablespoons grated Parmesan
   cheese
dash of cayenne
heavy cream or evaporated milk

In a bowl, using an electric
mixer on medium speed, blend
the anchovies, eggs, cheese and
cayenne until smooth. Add
enough cream to bind. Cover
and chill for at least 1 hour.

¾ cup Egg-and-Sweetbread Filling
   (see page 170)
6 slices rye bread
sliced pimiento-stuffed olives

Spread the filling on the bread
and cut each slice in half. Garnish
with olives and serve.

DANISH-STYLE EGG SALAD SANDWICHES

MAKES: *12 servings*

---

6 slices whole-wheat bread, crusts
   trimmed
jellied consommé, thinly sliced
3 small lettuce leaves
½ pound cooked pork, fat trimmed
   and sliced
1 kosher pickle, thinly sliced

Top each slice of bread with several slices of consommé. Trim the
lettuce so that it fits over the consommé without overlapping. Top
with pork and several slices of
pickle. Serve immediately.

DANISH-STYLE JELLIED PORK SANDWICHES

MAKES: *6 servings*

DANISH-STYLE LIVERWURST SANDWICHES

MAKES: *6 servings*

3 tablespoons butter, at room temperature
1 can (4.5 ounces) liverwurst
1 teaspoon minced white onion
3 drops Tabasco sauce
6 slices cocktail rye bread
watercress for garnish

In a bowl, combine the butter, liverwurst, onion and Tabasco and blend until smooth. Spread on the bread, garnish with watercress and serve.

DANISH-STYLE SHRIMP SANDWICHES

MAKES: *6 servings*

3 tablespoons butter or margarine, at room temperature
6 slices rye bread
½ cup tiny deveined shrimp
¼ cup mayonnaise
1 tablespoon crushed fresh dill

1 Spread a thin layer of butter over 1 side of each slice of bread.

2 In a small bowl, combine the shrimp and mayonnaise and mix well. Spread on the bread and garnish with dill.

EVERYONE'S FAVORITE SANDWICH

MAKES: *8 to 10 servings*

1½ cups shredded Swiss cheese
1½ cups shredded carrots
½ cup chopped pecans
⅓ cup golden raisins
Ginger Dressing (see page 186)
12 slices honey whole-wheat bread

1 In a bowl, combine the cheese, carrots, pecans, raisins and enough dressing to moisten.

2 Spread more dressing on 6 slices of bread and then top with the cheese mixture. Top with the remaining bread, cut in half and serve.

COOKING NOTE: **The filling may be made ahead of time and refrigerated for up to 24 hours.**

8 slices honey whole-wheat bread, crusts trimmed
½ pound Swiss or Port Salut cheese, sliced
8 slices smoked ham, chopped
8 slices white bread, crusts trimmed
½ cup butter or margarine, melted
sliced sour pickles

1 Preheat a waffle iron according to the manufacturer's instructions.

2 Lay the whole-wheat bread on a work surface and top with cheese and ham. Put a slice of white bread on top of each sandwich and brush with butter. Turn the sandwich over and brush the whole-wheat bread with butter.

3 Cook the sandwiches, 1 or 2 at a time, in the waffle iron for about 2 minutes, or until browned. Cut into thirds and serve warm garnished with sliced pickles.

HOT HAM-AND-CHEESE SANDWICHES

MAKES: *8 serving*

1 cup shredded Monterey Jack or Tillamook cheese
2 tablespoons chopped carrot
1 tablespoon chopped shallot
1 tablespoon chopped red bell pepper
¼ cup Kraft® Real Mayonnaise or other mayonnaise
24 slices cocktail rye bread, toasted

1 Position the broiler rack 6 inches from the heat source and preheat the broiler

2 In a bowl, combine the cheese, carrot, shallot, red pepper and mayonnaise and blend well. Spread on the bread and transfer to an ungreased baking sheet and broil for 2 or 3 minutes until the cheese melts.

JACK BACKS

MAKES: *About 12 servings*

¼ cup Kraft® Real Mayonnaise or other mayonnaise
2 tablespoons butter or margarine, at room temperature
2 cup grated Wisconsin Brick or Tillamook cheese
2 tablespoons grated shallot
pinch of cayenne
8 strips crisp bacon, crumbled
4 Kaiser or hard rolls, halved

1 Position the rack in the center of the oven and preheat to 350 degrees F. Lightly grease a baking sheet.

2 In a bowl, combine the mayonnaise and butter and mash until blended. Add the cheese, shallot and cayenne and mix. Fold in the bacon.

3 Spread on the rolls and transfer to the baking sheet. Bake for 10 to 15 minutes or until the cheese melts and the edges of the rolls brown. Serve hot.

KAISER CHEESE DREAMS

MAKES: *8 servings*

LITTLE ONES

MAKES: *12 servings*

1 can (6 ounces) tomato paste
½ teaspoon garlic salt
¼ teaspoon oregano
12 melba toasts
2 ounces salami or pepperoni, diced
4 ounces shredded mozzarella or
   provolone cheese

1 Position the rack in the center
of the oven and preheat to 400
degrees F.

2 In a small bowl, combine the
tomato paste, garlic salt and
oregano and whisk. Spread a little of the mixture on the melba
toasts. Top each with salami and
cheese and transfer to a baking
sheet. Bake for 3 to 5 minutes or
until the cheese melts. Serve hot.

MINIATURE SMOKED HAM SANDWICHES

MAKES: *36 servings*

36 Miniature Chive Muffins (recipe
   follows)
6 tablespoons butter or margarine, at
   room temperature
2 packages (3 ounces each) cooked
   smoked ham, cut to fit the muffins
4 to 5 large hard-cooked eggs, thinly
   sliced
pepper

Slice the muffins in half crosswise and spread with butter. Lay
2 to 3 pieces of ham on the bottom half of each, top with a sliced
of egg and sprinkle with pepper.
Replace the top half of the muffin
and serve.

MINIATURE CHIVE MUFFINS

MAKES: *36 servings*

2 cups all-purpose flour
1 tablespoon baking powder
1 tablespoon sugar
1 tablespoon light-brown sugar
½ teaspoon salt
1 cup milk
¼ cup butter or margarine, melted
1 large egg
½ cup snipped chives

1 Position the rack in the center
of the oven and preheat to 400
degrees F. Lightly grease three
12-cup miniature muffin baking
pans.

2 In a bowl, combine the flour,
baking powder, sugars and salt
and whisk well. In another
bowl, combine the milk, butter
and egg and whisk until blended. Add the chives and stir.
Pour the wet ingredients into
the dry ingredients and stir just
until blended. Do not overmix.

3 Spoon the batter into the
muffin cups, filling each about
two-thirds full. Bake for 15 to 18
minutes, or until a golden
brown. Turn out onto a wire
rack to cool.

4 French rolls, sliced in half
  lengthwise
prepared mustard
crisp lettuce leaves
8 thin slices boiled ham
8 slices Kraft® American Cheese
2 large tomatoes, thinly sliced
2 large green bell peppers, sliced
  into rings

Spread both halves of the rolls with mustard. On the bottom half, layer the lettuce, ham, cheese, tomatoes and pepper rings. Top with the tops of the rolls, cut in half and secure with toothpicks.

COOKING NOTE: Substitute 1½- to 2-inch slices of French bread for the rolls.

NAPOLEANS

MAKES: *8 servings*

---

14 slices dark rye bread, toasted
prepared mustard
1 can (16 ounces) sauerkraut,
  drained
2 packages (3 ounces each) sliced
  corned beef, chopped
2 cups shredded Leyden or Swiss
  cheese
½ cup Extra-Rich Vinegar
  Mayonnaise (see page 198)

1 Position the rack in the center of the oven and preheat to 375 degrees F.

2 Spread the toast with mustard and transfer to an ungreased baking sheet.

3 Put the sauerkraut in a small bowl and use kitchen scissors or two sharp knives to cut any long pieces. Add the corned beef, cheese and mayonnaise and mix well.

4 Spread on the toast and bake for about 10 minutes, or until the cheese melts. Cut in half on the diagonal and serve hot.

OPEN-FACE REUBENS

MAKES: *28 servings*

1½ cups finely chopped cooked
  chicken
1 can (4 ounces) chopped drained
  green chilies
¾ cup shredded Cheddar or
  Wisconsin brick cheese
¼ cup finely chopped white onion
1 cup Kraft® Salad Dressing
36 slices rye or pumpernickel bread

1 Position the broiler rack 6 inches from the heat source and preheat the broiler.

2 In a large bowl, combine the chicken, chilies, cheese, onion and dressing and mix well. Spread on the bread and transfer to an ungreased baking sheet. Broil for about 5 minutes or until lightly browned. Serve hot.

PARTY SANDWICHES

MAKES: *36 servings*

SAUSAGE RYE ROUNDS

MAKES: *About 28 servings*

1 pound ground lean beef
1 pound ground pork
1 teaspoon garlic powder
1 pound Velveeta® cheese, cubed
cocktail rye bread

1 In a bowl, combine the beef, pork and garlic powder and mix well. Cover and chill for 24 hours.

2 Position the rack in the center of the oven and preheat to 400 degrees F.

3 In a skillet, cook the meat mixture over medium-high for about 15 minutes, stirring, until cooked through. Drain the fat, reduce the temperature, add the cheese and continue to cook, stirring, until melted.

4 Spoon on the bread and transfer to a baking sheet. Bake for about 5 minutes, or until heated through. Serve immediately.

SCANDINAVIAN-STYLE SMORGASBORD

MAKES: *36 servings*

36 slices cocktail rye bread, melba toast or crackers
mayonnaise or prepared mustard
36 small lettuce leaves, trimmed
1 can (6.5 ounces) tuna, drained and flaked
2 large hard-boiled eggs, sliced
¼ pound frozen cooked bay shrimp, thawed
½ cucumber, thinly sliced
36 asparagus tips, steamed
capers for garnish
plain yogurt for garnish
dill sprigs for garnish
pimiento strips for garnish
red or black caviar for garnish
sliced green onions for garnish

Arrange the bread on a large platter or tray and spread each slice with mayonnaise. Lay a lettuce leave on the bread so that it covers the entire slice of bread. Top with tuna, egg slices, shrimp, cucumber slices and asparagus tips. Garnish as desired with capers, yogurt, dill, pimiento strips, caviar or onions.

COOKING NOTE: **For variety, you can make different sandwiches, some with tuna, some with eggs and some with shrimp.**

SPAM SPREAD SANDWICHES

MAKES: *26 to 30 servings*

1 can (12 ounces) Spam® Luncheon Meat, grated
8 ounces sharp Cheddar cheese, grated
1 white onion, finely diced
2 large hard-cooked eggs,
Kraft® Real Mayonnaise or other mayonnaise
1 loaf Pepperidge Farm® cocktail party bread

1 Position the rack in the center of the oven and preheat to 350 degrees F.

2 In a small bowl, using an electric mixer on low speed, blend the meat, cheese, onion and eggs until smooth. Stir in enough mayonnaise to moisten. Spread evenly on the bread and transfer to a baking sheet. Bake for 18 to 20 minutes, or until the cheese melts. Serve immediately.

COOKING NOTE: **To increase the yield, slice the bread slices in half.**

½ a loaf of French bread
2 tablespoons Shrimp Butter (see page 168)
dark-green lettuce leaves, trimmed
1 cup shredded Muenster or Tilsit cheese
Extra-Rich Vinegar Mayonnaise (see page 198)
1 cucumber, very thinly sliced
1 tomato, very thinly sliced
1 can (4½ ounces) tiny deveined shrimp, rinsed and drained
3 tablespoons mayonnaise
grated Parmesan or romano cheese

1 Cut the bread in half lengthwise and lay the 2 halves next to each other on the work surface.

Spread both halves with the butter and top both with lettuce and cheese. Dab with mayonnaise and top with attractively arranged rows of cucumbers and tomatoes. Slice each half into thirds.

2 In a small bowl, combine the shrimp and mayonnaise and spoon over the sandwiches. Sprinkle with the cheese.

COOKING NOTE: **The secret to these sandwiches is to arrange the vegetables as attractively as possible on the bread before slicing it into 6 pieces.**

SHRIMP SANDWICH SLICES

MAKES: *6 servings*

1½ cups minced cooked veal
1 tablespoon chili sauce
½ teaspoon prepared horseradish
½ teaspoon apple cider vinegar
½ teaspoon prepared brown mustard
2 tablespoons butter or margarine, at room temperature
8 slices Russian rye bread
4 Bibb lettuce leaves

1 In a small bowl, combine the veal, chili sauce, horseradish, vinegar and mustard and mix well.

2 Spread the butter on the bread. Top 4 slices with the veal mixture and a lettuce leaf. Top with the remaining slices of bread, buttered side down, and cut into quarters on the diagonal.

TASTY VEAL SANDWICHES

MAKES: *4 Servings*

VEGETABLE BARS

MAKES: *12 to 16 servings*

1 package (10 ounces) Pillsbury®
   Crescent Dinner Rolls
3 packages (3 ounces each) cream
   cheese
½ cup mayonnaise or Kraft® Salad
   Dressing
1 package (1 ounce) Hidden Valley®
   Original Ranch Dressing mix
¾ cup chopped broccoli florets
¾ cup chopped cauliflower florets
¾ cup chopped green onion
¾ cup chopped green bell pepper
¾ cup chopped tomato
1½ cups shredded Swiss cheese

1 Position the rack in the center
of the oven and preheat to 350
degrees F. Lightly grease a 13-by-
9-inch baking pan.

2 Lay the rolls out flat in the baking pan and bake for 8 or 9 minutes or until lightly browned.

3 Meanwhile, in a bowl, using an
electric mixer on medium speed,
beat together the cream cheese,
mayonnaise and dressing mix
until smooth.

4 Cool the rolls slightly and
spread the cheese mixture on
them.

5 In another bowl, combine the
broccoli, cauliflower, onion, pepper and tomatoes and stir. Spread
over the cheese, pressing lightly
to adhere. Sprinkle with Swiss
cheese, cover and chill for at least
4 hours. Cut into squares and
serve.

VEGETABLE SANDWICHES

MAKES: *24*

2 cups shredded lettuce
2 cups shredded carrots
½ cup golden raisins
½ cup chopped unsalted peanuts
⅓ cup Garlic Dressing (recipe
   follows)
24 slices dark rye bread, toasted
Black Butter (see page 48)
bread-and-butter pickle slices for
   garnish

1 In a bowl, combine the lettuce,
carrots, raisins and peanuts and
toss gently. Add the dressing and
mix well.

2 Spread the bread generously
with the butter and top with the
vegetable mixture. Garnish with
pickles and serve.

COOKING NOTE: **Slice the bread
in half to increase the yield.**

GARLIC DRESSING

MAKES: *About 2 cups*

1⅓ cup canola oil
¾ cup cider vinegar
4 cloves garlic, sliced
1 teaspoon paprika
1 teaspoon salt
½ teaspoon dry mustard

In the container of a blender,
combine all the ingredients and
process for 2 or 3 seconds until
smooth. Use immediately or
cover and chill until ready to
use.

COOKING NOTE: **This dressing
is best made 24 hours before
using.**

Chapter 6

BEEF, LAMB AND PORK— ONE, TWO, THREE

Although meat, hot or cold, does not spring to mind when most people think of snack food, if you stop to think about it, many meat dishes qualify resoundingly. Without question, most can be served for supper, but they also hit the spot at other times of day. These are quick meat dishes—patties, meatballs, kabobs, ribs— all delicious, all falling into the snack-food category with a delightful blend of brashness and grace.

BROILED SHISH KABOBS

MAKES: *8 servings*

½ cup vegetable oil
¼ cup low-sodium soy sauce
½ cup red wine
2 small cloves of garlic, minced
1½ teaspoons curry powder
2 tablespoons catsup
¼ teaspoon pepper
¼ teaspoon Tabasco sauce
1 pound sirloin steak, cut into 1-inch-thick chunks
1 pound boneless leg of lamb, cut into 1-inch-thick chunks
1 pound pork tenderloin, cut into ½-inch-thick chunks
1 eggplant
3 tart, firm apples, cored, peeled and cut into 6 wedges
1 seeded green bell pepper, cut into 1½-inch squares
12 mushrooms, trimmed
½ pound thin-sliced bacon

1 In the container of a blender, combine the oil, soy sauce, wine, garlic, curry powder, catsup, pepper and Tabasco and blend on low until smooth.

2 Arrange the meats in a shallow glass dish, keeping each type separate from the other. Pour three-quarters of the soy sauce marinade over the meat, cover and chill for 24 hours. Cover and chill the remaining marinade.

3 Peel the eggplant and cut the flesh into ½-inch-thick slices. Cut the slices into 1½-inch squares. Transfer to a glass or ceramic bowl and add the apples, green pepper, and mushrooms. Sprinkle with the remaining marinade. Cover and set aside at room temperature for at least 3 hours.

4 Position the broiler rack 4 inches from the heat source and preheat the broiler.

5 Wrap a slice of bacon around each cube of lamb and thread on a long skewer. Add a cube of beef, a piece of eggplant, apple, green pepper, a mushroom and finally a cube of pork. Broil for 5 to 10 minutes on each side, or until the meat is cooked through and tender.

BEEF ROLLS

MAKES: *4 servings*

2 pounds top round or flank steak, cut into 4 pieces
¼ cup butter or margarine
4 large mushrooms, sliced
1 large clove garlic, minced
1 package (10 ounces) frozen chopped spinach, cooked and drained
½ teaspoon chopped fresh tarragon
1 tablespoon vegetable oil
½ cup beef broth
prepared béarnaise sauce, warmed

1 Position the rack in the center of the oven and preheat to 325 degrees F.

2 Using a meat mallet or small cast-iron skillet, pound the meat pieces to a thickness of ¼ inch and set aside.

3 In a large ovenproof skillet, melt 3 tablespoons of butter over medium heat and sauté the mushrooms and garlic for about 5 minutes until softened. Remove from the heat, add the spinach and tarragon and stir to mix.

4 Divide the mixture evenly among the meat and roll up as tightly as possible. Seal closed with a toothpick.

5 In the same skillet, melt the remaining tablespoon of butter and add the beef rolls. Brown for 4 to 5 minutes until browned on all sides. Add the broth, cover, and bake for about 1 hour, or until the meat is tender. Remove the toothpicks and transfer the rolls to a cutting board, seam-side down, and cut into ½-inch slices. Serve with the pan juices spooned over them.

¼ cup low-sodium soy sauce
1 clove garlic, minced
1½ teaspoons grated fresh ginger
1 to 1¼ pounds beef chuck steak, fat trimmed and cut across the grain into very thin strips.
¼ cup canola oil
1 green onion, green part only, chopped
1 large red bell pepper, cut into 1-inch squares
2 stalks celery, thinly sliced
1 tablespoon cornstarch
1 cup water
2 tomatoes, cut into wedges.

1 In a bowl, combine the soy sauce, garlic and ginger. Add the beef and stir gently to coat.

BEEF STRIPS WITH RED PEPPERS

MAKES: *6 to 8 servings*

2 In a large skillet, heat the oil over low heat. Raise the heat to medium-high, add the beef, and stir-fry for 3 to 4 minutes, or until no longer pink inside. Raise the heat to high, add the green onion, pepper and celery and stir-fry for 6 to 8 minutes until the vegetables are crisp-tender.

3 In a small bowl, combine the cornstarch and water and add to the pan, stirring until the pan liquid thickens. Add the tomatoes and remove from the heat and let sit for about 1 minute. Serve immediately.

---

2 tablespoons sugar
¼ cup low-sodium soy sauce
2 tablespoons peanut oil
2 teaspoons sesame seeds
¼ cup chopped green onion
½ teaspoon garlic powder
½ teaspoon black pepper
1 pound beef chuck steak, trimmed and cut into ¼-inch-wide slices
thin slices of green bell pepper for garnish
thin slices papaya for garnish.

1 In a bowl, combine the sugar, soy sauce, oil, sesame seeds, green onion, garlic powder and

KOREAN BULGOGI

MAKES: *6 to 8 servings*

pepper and stir to mix. Add the beef and stir gently to coat. Cover and chill for at least 2 hours. Let the meat and marinade come to room temperature before cooking.

2 Position the broiler rack 6 inches from the heat and preheat the broiler.

3 Lay the strips of meat on the boiler rack about 1 inch apart and cook for 1 minute on each side. Serve garnished with the green pepper and papaya slices.

---

1 package (12 ounces) refrigerated biscuits
1 pound lean ground beef
½ cup commercial barbecue sauce
1 tablespoon minced shallot
1½ tablespoons light-brown sugar
¾ cup shredded Cheddar or Tillamook cheese

1 Position the rack in the center of the oven and preheat to 400 degrees F. Lightly grease a 2½-inch 12-cup muffin pan.

BARBECUE BEEF CUPS

MAKES: *12 servings*

2 Open the package and separate the biscuits. On a work surface, flatten each biscuit to a thickness of ¼ inch and press into the muffin cups.

3 In a large nonstick skillet, cook the beef over medium-high heat for 7 to 8 minutes until browned. Drain the fat. Add the barbecue sauce, shallot, and brown sugar. Spoon into the biscuit cups and sprinkle with the cheese. Bake for about 10 to 12 minutes, or until the biscuit dough is golden brown.

BEEF-AND-BEAN-STUFFED EGG ROLLS

MAKES: *24 to 48 servings*

1 pound lean ground beef
½ cup chopped white onion
¼ cup chopped green bell pepper
1 can (15 ounces) Old El Paso®
 refried beans
½ cup shredded Cheddar cheese
2 tablespoons chili powder
2 packages egg roll wrappers
vegetable oil for frying
taco sauce

1 In a large nonstick skillet, cook the beef over medium heat, stirring, for 7 to 8 minutes until browned. Add the onion and peppers and cook for 3 to 4 minutes until the onions are translucent. Drain the fat. Add the beans, cheese, and chili powder and cook, stirring constantly, until the cheese melts.

2 On a work surface, lay out a few of the wrappers and spoon about a teaspoonful of the meat mixture onto the center of each. Starting at one side, roll up the wrappers, folding in the sides to make small squares. Dip your finger in water and moisten the edges to seal. Continue until all of the wrappers are used.

3 In a large deep skillet, pour in oil to a depth of 1½ to 2 inches and heat until hot (375 degrees F. on a deep-fat frying thermometer). Fry the egg rolls for 2 to 3 minutes on each side, or until golden brown. Serve warm with taco sauce.

BEEF-FILLED APPLES

MAKES: *4 servings*

SAUCE
1½ teaspoons butter or margarine
2 tablespoons cider vinegar
1½ tablespoons sugar
¼ cup water

APPLES
½ cup cracked bulgur
1 cup water
1 onion, chopped
2 teaspoons butter or margarine
½ pound lean ground beef
¼ teaspoon cinnamon
salt and pepper
4 large tart apples

1 In a small saucepan, combine the butter, vinegar, sugar and water and cook over medium-high heat until boiling, stirring. Set aside.

2 Position the rack in the center of the oven and preheat to 350 degrees F. Lightly grease a 13-by-9-inch baking dish.

3 In a small saucepan, combine the bulgur and water and bring to a boil over high heat. Reduce the heat and simmer for 15 minutes.

4 In a large skillet, melt the butter over medium heat. Add the onion, beef and cinnamon and cook, stirring, until the meat is browned. Drain off the fat. Stir in the bulgur and season to taste with salt and pepper.

5 Cut a thin slice from the stem end of each apple, reserving what you cut off. Using a spoon or a melon baller, hollow out each apple, leaving a ½-inch shell. Stuff with the bulgur filling and replace the reserved slices. Arrange in the baking dish and add boiling water to a depth of ½ inch. Bake for 20 minutes. Spoon some vinegar sauce over the apples and bake for about 20 minutes longer, or until the apples are fork-tender. Serve with the remaining sauce spooned over the apples.

16 ounces lean ground beef
1 small shallot, chopped
1 potato, finely chopped
1 can (8.5 ounces) mixed peas and
    carrots, drained
1 package (1 ounce) mushroom
    gravy mix
1 cup water
1 package (22 ounces) pie crust mix
paprika

1 In a nonstick skillet, combine the beef and shallot and cook for 7 to 8 minutes over medium heat, stirring, until the beef is browned. Drain the fat. Add the potato, peas and carrots, gravy mix and water and stir to blend. Raise the heat and bring to a boil. Reduce the heat and simmer for 2 to 4 minutes, or until the liquid is reduced by half.

2 Position the rack in the center of the oven and preheat to 400 degrees F.

3 Prepare the pie crust mix according to the package directions and roll out. Using a 3-inch biscuit cutter or upturned glass, stamp out about 18 rounds. Lay them on an ungreased baking sheet, leaving about 1 inch between them. Spoon a tablespoonful of the beef mixture over half of each round and then fold the pastry over the filling. Crimp the edges closed with the tines of a fork. Sprinkle with paprika and bake for 12 to 15 minutes or until the pastry is golden brown. Serve warm.

BEEF EMPANADAS

MAKES: *About 18 servings*

---

3 tablespoons low-sodium soy sauce
2 tablespoons honey
2 tablespoons sherry or white port
    wine
¼ teaspoon ground ginger
½ teaspoon garlic powder
1 pound boneless lean beef, cut into
    very thin slices
2 tablespoons peanut oil

1 In a bowl, combine the soy sauce, honey, sherry, ginger and garlic and stir to mix. Add the meat and stir gently to coat. Cover and chill for at least 2

hours. Let the meat and marinade come to room temperature before cooking.

2 Drain the marinade from the meat and set both aside.

3 In a skillet or wok, heat the oil over medium-high heat.

4 Add half the meat to the skillet and stir-fry for 2 to 3 minutes, or until browned. Transfer to a serving platter and repeat with the remaining meat.

5 Add the reserved marinade to the skillet and bring to a boil. Pour into a bowl and serve as a dipping sauce for the meat.

TERIYAKI STIR-FRIED BEEF

MAKES: *6 to 8 servings*

Beef Patties Chasseur

MAKES: *4 servings*

1¼ pounds lean ground beef
2 tablespoons butter or margarine
½ pound mushrooms, chopped
1 green onion, minced
¾ cup dry white wine
¼ cup canned beef consommé
1 teaspoon minced parsley
½ teaspoon dried chervil
½ teaspoon dried tarragon

1 Divide the beef into four equal parts, form each into a ball and flatten to a thickness of 1 inch. Arrange the patties in a large nonstick skillet and cook over medium heat for about 4 minutes on each side, or until cooked through. Transfer to a platter and cover to keep warm. Drain the fat from the pan.

2 Melt the butter in the skillet and add the mushrooms and onion. Sauté for 2 to 3 minutes until the softened. Add the wine and consommé, raise the heat, and cook, stirring, for 6 to 7 minutes longer until slightly thickened and the liquid is reduced by half. Add the parsley, chervil and tarragon and stir to mix. Pour over the patties and serve.

Beef Patties with Spinach

MAKES: *12 to 14 servings*

½ cup white bread crumbs
1 cup chopped fresh spinach
2 pounds lean ground beef
¼ cup finely chopped white onion
2 large eggs
pepper
1 large clove garlic, minced
all-purpose flour
olive oil, for frying

1 Place the bread crumbs in a small bowl and sprinkle with just enough water to moisten.

2 In a large nonstick skillet, cook the spinach over medium heat for 1 to 2 minutes until wilted. Cool slightly and squeeze dry.

3 In a large bowl, combine the spinach, beef, bread crumbs, onion, eggs, pepper, and garlic. Shape into 12 to 14 patties and sprinkle with flour. Shake off any excess.

4 In the skillet, heat the oil over medium heat. Cook the patties for 4 to 5 minutes on each side until crispy on the outside. Reduce the heat and cook for a few minutes longer until cooked through.

3 large eggs, beaten
2 cups soft bread crumbs
2 cups finely chopped apples
½ cup chopped white onion
¼ cup fresh snipped parsley
2 pounds lean ground beef
2 cans (11 ounces each) Cheddar
  cheese soup
1¼ cups milk
1½ teaspoons dried crushed dill

1 Position the rack in the center of the oven and preheat to 375 degrees F. Lightly grease a 13-by-9-inch baking dish.

2 In a bowl, combine the eggs, bread crumbs, apples, onion and parsley and mix. Add the beef

and mix well. Pinch off pieces and form into balls about the size of walnuts. Place the balls in the baking dish and bake for 20 to 25 minutes, or until cooked through. Drain on a double thickness of paper towels. Do not turn off the oven.

3 Place the meatballs in a 2½-quart casserole.

4 In a bowl, combine the soup, milk, and dill and stir to mix. Pour over the meatballs and bake for 25 to 30 minutes, or until thoroughly heated. Serve hot over hot cooked noodles.

CHEESE-FLAVORED SAVORY MEATBALLS

MAKES: *About 12 servings*

---

2 tablespoons hoisin sauce
1 tablespoon dry sherry
1 teaspoon brown sugar
½ teaspoon dark sesame oil
8 ounces boneless beef sirloin steak,
  cut into 1-inch cubes
3 green onions, cut into 2-inch
  pieces

1 In small microwave-safe bowl, combine the hoisin, sherry, sugar and oil and stir to mix. Microwave on high (100 percent) power for 10 to 15 seconds until hot.

2 In a glass or ceramic bowl, combine the beef and hoisin-sherry sauce, cover and set aside for 1 hour.

3 Thread the meat and onions on skewers. Lay the skewers over a microwave-safe dish and brush with the sauce. Cover with wax paper and cook on medium (50 percent) power for 3 minutes. Turn, brush with the remaining sauce, cover and microwave for 3 to 4 minutes longer, or until cooked through.

CHINESE BEEF KABOBS

MAKES: *About 8 kabobs*

COCKTAIL MEATBALLS

MAKES: *About 45 to 50 servings*

1 pound lean ground beef
½ pound pork sausage meat
⅓ cup fine dried pumpernickel bread crumbs
1 large egg, slightly beaten
2 tablespoons butter or margarine
⅓ cup chopped onion
⅓ cup chopped green bell pepper
1 teaspoon garlic powder
⅛ teaspoon crushed red pepper flakes
1 can (10 ounces) condensed mushroom soup
¼ cup water
1 teaspoon Worcestershire sauce

1 Position the broiler rack about 4 inches from the heat source and preheat the broiler.

2 In a large bowl, combine the beef, sausage, bread crumbs, and egg. Shape into balls about the size of large olives and arrange on a boiler tray. Broil for about 3 minutes. Turn and broil for 3 minutes longer, or until cooked through. Set aside.

3 In a large saucepan, melt the butter over medium heat. Add the onion, pepper, garlic and red pepper and sauté for 5 to 6 minutes until tender. Stir in the soup, water, and Worcestershire sauce and add the meatballs. Simmer for about 10 minutes until heated through. Transfer to a chafing dish and serve with toothpicks on the side.

DRIED BEEF BALLS

MAKES: *12 to 18 servings*

2 packages (3 ounces each) dried beef
8 green onions, trimmed and finely chopped
3 packages (8 ounces each) cream cheese, at room temperature
3 tablespoons Worcestershire sauce
salt and pepper
crackers for serving

1 Using a sharp knife or food processor, chop 1 package of dried beef until very fine. Chop the second package until coarsely chopped. Spread the coarsely chopped beef in a shallow dish.

2 In a bowl, combine the onions, cream cheese, Worcestershire sauce and the finely chopped dried beef. Season with salt and pepper. Form into a large ball and roll in the coarsely chopped beef. Wrap with wax paper and chill for 4 hours, or until firm.

3 Roll the ball in any leftover coarsely chopped beef and serve with crackers.

COOKING NOTE: **When seasoning, keep in mind that dried beef is salty.**

LEAF KABOBS

MAKES: *4 to 6 servings*

2 pounds top round beef, cut into long strips
3 tablespoons onion juice
3 tablespoons lemon juice
salt and pepper
4 to 6 wooden skewers soaked in water

1 Using a meat mallet, pound the beef strips as thin as possible.

2 In a bowl, combine the onion juice, lemon juice and salt and pepper. Add the meat, cover, and chill for at least 12 hours.

3 Preheat a stovetop grill or the broiler.

4 Thread the beef onto the skewers and grill for 10 to 15 minutes, or until browned. Turn frequently to assure even browning. Serve warm or at room temperature.

MEATBALLS

1 cup Kellogg® Rice Krispies cereal
⅔ cup nonfat dry milk
¼ cup finely chopped onion
2 tablespoons catsup
1 large egg
1 pound lean ground beef
salt and pepper

SAUCE

1 (15 ounces) can tomato sauce
½ cup catsup
¼ cup firmly packed brown sugar
¼ cup finely chopped onion
¼ cup sweet pickle relish
2 tablespoons Worcestershire sauce
1 tablespoon cider vinegar
¼ teaspoon pepper

1 Position the rack in the center of the oven and preheat to 400 degrees F. Line a 13-by-9-inch baking pan with aluminum foil.

2 In a large bowl, combine the cereal, dry milk, onion, catsup and egg and stir gently to blend. Add the beef and salt and pepper and use your hands to incorporate the cereal mixture with the meat. Pinch off pieces of the mixture and form into balls about the size of large olives. Put the balls in the baking pan and bake for 10 to 12 minutes, or until browned.

3 In a large saucepan, combine the tomato sauce, catsup, sugar, onion, relish, Worcestershire sauce, vinegar and pepper and simmer over low heat for about 15 minutes, stirring, until heated through. Add the meatballs and continue simmering for about 10 minutes until cooked through. Transfer to a chafing dish and serve with toothpicks on the side.

Holiday Meatballs

MAKES: *About 36 servings*

FILLING

1½ pounds lean ground beef
½ pound fresh ground lamb
½ cup all-purpose flour
1 large white onion, chopped
1 finely chopped green pepper
½ bunch parsley, finely chopped
1 can (14½ ounces) whole peeled
    tomatoes, drained and chopped
½ cup tomato sauce
¼ cup plus 2 tablespoons tomato
    paste
1 jar (3.5 ounces) diced pimientos,
    drained
3 large cloves garlic, minced
ground red pepper or cayenne
salt and pepper

CRUST

3 loaves (1 pound each) frozen bread
    dough, thawed
all-purpose flour

1 Position the rack in the center of the oven and preheat to 400 degrees F. Have 2 or 3 ungreased baking sheets ready.

2 To make the filling, in a large bowl, combine the ground meats and flour. Add the onion, pepper, parsley, tomatoes, tomato sauce, tomato paste, pimientos and garlic. Season with red pepper and salt and pepper.

3 Working with 1 pound of the dough at a time, on a lightly floured work surface, roll the dough into a large circle about ⅛-inch thick. Using a 2-inch cookie cutter or upturned glass, stamp out as many rounds as possible and lay the rounds on the baking sheets. Continue until all the dough is used.

4 Spread about 1 tablespoon of the meat mixture on each round. (Do not let excess liquid from the mixture saturate the rounds.) Bake for 15 to 20 minutes, or until the dough starts to brown. Serve hot or cold.

Lahmajoon

MAKES: *About 100 appetizers*

LIVERWURST PÂTÉ

MAKES: *12 to 14 servings*

1 pound liverwurst, mashed with a fork
2 cloves garlic, one crushed, one minced
½ teaspoon dried basil
3 tablespoons minced onion
1 package (8 ounces) cream cheese, at room temperature
⅛ teaspoon Tabasco® sauce
1 teaspoon mayonnaise
1 jar (3 ounces) black caviar
minced parsley or watercress for garnish
crackers or cocktail bread for serving

1 In a small bowl, combine the liverwurst, crushed garlic, basil and onion. Shape into a round or oval, cover loosely with wax paper and chill for at least 30 minutes.

2 In a bowl, combine the cream cheese, minced garlic, Tabasco® and mayonnaise and blend until smooth. Spread over the liver-wurst and top with caviar. Garnish with parsley or watercress. Cover again and chill for at least 8 hours. Serve with crackers or bread.

MEATBALLS OLÉ

MAKES: *About 20 servings*

⅓ cup taco sauce
⅓ cup chopped green chilies
½ pound lean ground beef
½ pound lean ground pork
salsa for serving

1 Position the rack in the center of the oven and preheat to 350 degrees F. Lightly grease a 15½-by-10½-inch jelly-roll pan.

2 In a bowl, combine the taco sauce, chilies, beef and pork and blend to mix. Pinch off pieces and form into balls about the size of walnuts. Place on the pan and bake for 18 to 20 minutes, or until browned. Drain on paper towels and serve with salsa.

MEATBALLS WITH JALAPEÑO DIP

MAKES: *7 to 9 dozen balls*

1½ pounds lean ground beef
½ pound lean ground pork
2 large eggs
⅔ cup dried whole-wheat bread crumbs
½ cup minced white onion
½ cup milk
¼ cup toasted sesame seeds
¼ cup chopped parsley
2 teaspoons Worcestershire sauce
1 teaspoon prepared horseradish
salt and pepper
Jalapeño Dip (see page 46)

1 Position the rack in the center of the oven and preheat to 400 degrees F.

2 In a large bowl, combine the beef, pork, eggs, bread crumbs, onion, milk, sesame seeds, parsley, Worcestershire sauce and horseradish and blend until well mixed. Season with salt and pepper.

3 Pinch off pieces and form into balls the size of walnuts. Place the meatballs in baking pans and bake for 18 to 20 minutes or until lightly browned. Serve with toothpicks and the dip on the side.

1 package (8 ounces) cream cheese,
   at room temperature
1 package (8 ounces) liverwurst
1 tablespoon minced shallot
½ teaspoon lemon or lime juice
1 teaspoon Worcestershire sauce
salt and pepper
cocktail rye or pumpernickel bread

In a bowl, and using an electric mixer on low speed, beat together the cheese and sausage until smooth. Beat in the remaining ingredients, cover and chill for 2 hours. Serve spread on the bread.

MOCK PÂTÉ

MAKES: *About 2 cups*

---

1 pound sirloin steak
8 green onions
⅓ cup sherry wine
¼ cup low-sodium soy sauce
2 teaspoons sugar
1 teaspoon ground ginger

1 Position the broiler rack 3 inches from the heat source and preheat the broiler.

2 Using a meat mallet, pound the meat to a thickness of about ⅛ inch. Cut into 4 strips and cut each strip in half. Lay an onion on each strip and, starting on the longest sides, roll the strips around the onions and secure with toothpicks.

3 In a small bowl, combine the sherry, soy sauce, sugar and ginger and whisk to mix. Lay the steak rolls on a broiler pan and brush with the sauce. Broil for about 3 minutes, turn over, brush again and broil for 2 to 3 minutes longer, or until cooked through. Remove the toothpicks and cut each roll into 1-inch-long pieces. Serve warm or at room temperature.

ORIENTAL STEAK ROLLS

MAKES: *About 24 servings*

PEARL BALLS

MAKES: *8 to 12 servings*

2 cups uncooked glutinous rice
1 pound lean ground beef
¼ pound new potatoes, boiled, mashed and cooled
2 large eggs
½ white onion, chopped
1 teaspoon sugar
2 teaspoon low-sodium soy sauce, plus more for serving
2 teaspoons ginger juice
prepared brown mustard

1 In a bowl, combine the rice with enough water to cover and set aside to soak for 8 hours or overnight.

2 In a bowl, combine the beef, potatoes, eggs and onion and blend to mix. Add the sugar, soy sauce and ginger juice and mix again. Pinch off small pieces and form into balls about the size of large olives.

3 Drain the rice and spread out on a platter. Roll the balls in the rice until coated. Put the balls in a damp cloth in a steamer and steam for 25 to 30 minutes, or until the filling is firm and the rice is tender. Serve with a brown mustard and soy sauce on the side.

COOKING NOTE: **Ginger juice and Asian-style glutinous (sticky) rice are available at Asian markets.**

PORCUPINE PATTIES

MAKES: *6 servings*

1 can (15 ounces) tomato sauce
½ pound lean ground beef
½ pound lean ground pork
½ cup uncooked brown rice
2 tablespoons chopped canned green chilies
¼ teaspoon garlic salt
¼ teaspoon crushed dried oregano
2 Herb Ox® beef or chicken flavored bouillon cubes
1 cup boiling water
1 cup shredded mozzarella or provolone cheese

1 Position the rack in the center of the oven and preheat to 350 degrees F.

2 Reserve 1 cup of tomato sauce. In a bowl, combine the remaining tomato sauce, beef, pork, rice, chilies, garlic salt and oregano and mix well.

3 Divide into 6 equal parts and form each into a ball. Place the balls in an ungreased 13-by-9-inch baking pan and flatten into ½-inch-thick patties. Bake for about 5 minutes, turning once. Drain off excess fat.

4 Dissolve the bouillon cubes in the water, add the reserved tomato sauce and stir. Pour over the patties, cover the pan with aluminum foil and bake for about 30 minutes. Spoon any pan juices over the patties, sprinkle with cheese and bake, uncovered, for about 5 minutes longer until the cheese melts.

1 cup uncooked brown rice
3 large eggs, lightly beaten
1 cup shredded Swiss or Gouda
  cheese
1 package (3 ounces) sliced smoked
  beef, chopped
½ teaspoon onion powder

1 Cook the rice according to the package directions and cool.

2 Preheat a greased skillet or griddle until hot.

3 In a large bowl, combine the rice, eggs, cheese, beef and onion powder. Drop by ¼ cupfuls onto the griddle and cook for about 3 minutes until the edges turn brown. Turn and cook for about 2 minutes until browned and cooked through.

RICE CAKES WITH BEEF

MAKES: *10 to 12 servings*

2 large eggs, lightly beaten
1 cup milk or light cream
½ cup dry bread crumbs
3 tablespoons butter or margarine
½ cup finely chopped white onion
1½ pounds lean ground beef
¾ teaspoon dried crushed dill
¼ teaspoon ground allspice
⅛ teaspoon ground nutmeg
salt and pepper
3 tablespoons all-purpose flour
1 Herb-Ox® beef bouillon cube
1 cup boiling water
½ cup light cream

1 In a large bowl, combine the eggs, milk and bread crumbs.

2 In a large skillet, melt 1 tablespoon of butter over medium heat and sauté the onions until softened. Add to the crumb mixture. Add the beef, ¼ teaspoon of dill, the allspice and nutmeg and season with salt and pepper. Cover and chill for at least 2 hours.

3 In a large skillet, heat the remaining 2 tablespoons of butter. Pinch off pieces of the mixture and shape into balls about the size of walnuts and cook for 3 to 5 minutes until browned on all sides. Remove the meatballs from the skillet and set aside.

4 Add the flour to the skillet and stir over medium heat until it forms a paste (roux). Add the remaining dill and stir.

5 In a cup, dissolve the bouillon cube in the water and add to the roux. Raise the temperature to high and bring to a boil, stirring, until thickened. Remove from the heat and add the cream and meatballs.

6 Return to the heat and simmer over low heat for about 30 minutes or until the meatballs are cooked through and the sauce is thickened. Transfer to a chafing dish and serve hot.

SWEDISH MEATBALLS

MAKES: *8 to 10 servings*

SWEET-AND-SOUR MEATBALLS

MAKES: *16 servings*

2 pounds lean ground beef
1½ cups finely chopped white onion
1 cup unsweetened applesauce
½ cup finely chopped green bell pepper
½ cup seedless raisins, chopped
½ cup diced fresh or canned and drained pineapple
3 large eggs, lightly beaten
2 slices day-old bread, crumbled
4 strips crisp cooked bacon, crumbled
3 tablespoons A1® steak sauce
3 tablespoons barbecue sauce
1 tablespoon Worcestershire sauce
salt and pepper
canola oil
Sweet-and-Sour Sauce (see page 105)

1 In a large bowl, combine the beef, onion, applesauce, pepper, raisins, pineapple, eggs, bread, bacon, steak sauce, barbecue sauce and Worcestershire sauce. Season with salt and pepper and stir well. Pinch off pieces and form into balls about the size of walnuts.

2 Add enough oil to a large skillet to cover the bottom of the pan and heat over medium heat. Add the meatballs and cook in batches for about 4 minutes on each side, or until evenly browned. Drain on paper towels. Serve with the sauce on the side.

TACO-FLAVORED BEEF BITES

MAKES: *About 36 servings*

1 pound lean ground beef
1 cup (4 ounces) shredded Cheddar cheese
1 cup (4 ounces) shredded Monterey Jack cheese
1 can (4 ounce) chopped canned green chilies, drained
½ cup bottled green taco sauce
2 large eggs, beaten

1 Position the rack in the center of the oven, and preheat to 350 degrees F.

2 In a large nonstick skillet, cook the beef over high heat for 4 to 5 minutes until no longer pink. Pour off the fat. Add the cheeses, chilies, taco sauce and eggs and stir well.

3 Spread evenly in an 8-inch-square baking pan and bake for 35 to 40 minutes, or until a knife inserted in the center comes out clean and the top is golden. Cool on a wire rack for about 15 minutes and serve.

1 pound lean ground beef
½ pound lean ground pork
⅔ cup soda cracker crumbs
⅓ cup minced shallot
1 large egg, lightly beaten
¼ teaspoon ground ginger
¼ cup milk
1 tablespoon vegetable shortening
2 tablespoons cornstarch
½ cup packed dark-brown sugar
1 can (13½ ounces) pineapple pieces, drained, juice reserve
⅓ cup rice vinegar
1 tablespoon low-sodium soy sauce
⅓ cup chopped green bell pepper

1 In a large bowl, combine the beef, pork, cracker crumbs, shallot, egg, ginger and milk. Pinch off pieces and form into balls the size of walnuts.

2 In a large skillet, heat the shortening over medium-high heat and cook the meatballs for 3 to 5 minutes until browned on all sides. Set aside and drain the fat from the pan.

3 Combine the cornstarch, sugar, reserved pineapple juice, vinegar, and soy sauce. Pour into the skillet and cook, stirring constantly until thickened. Add the meatballs, pineapple and green peppers and heat through before serving.

TAHITIAN-STYLE MEATBALLS

MAKES: *6 to 8 servings*

---

1 eggplant, 3 inches in diameter
salt
1 large egg
½ cup fresh rye bread crumbs
½ teaspoon dried oregano
½ cup chopped ripe olives
1 clove garlic, pressed
½ cup grated Parmesan or romano cheese
1½ pounds ground lamb
⅓ cup olive oil
1 large tomato, cut into 6 slices
1 cup shredded Cheshire cheese

1 Position the rack in the center of the oven and preheat to 450 degrees F.

2 Score the eggplant with a fork and cut into six ½-inch-thick slices. Lay the slices out between paper towels and sprinkle the salt on top of the paper towels. Set aside for 20 minutes.

3 In a bowl, combine the crumbs, oregano, olives, garlic and cheese. Add the lamb and blend thoroughly. Divide into 6 sections and form each into a patty about 4 inches in diameter.

4 In a skillet, heat the oil over medium-high heat. Remove the eggplant from between the paper towels and wipe dry with clean paper towels. Lay the slices in the skillet and cook for 1 to 2 minutes on each side until browned. Transfer to an ungreased 13-by-9-inch baking pan. Set a lamb patty on top of each slice and top with a tomato slice. Sprinkle with cheese and bake for 20 to 25 minutes, or until the patties and cheese are browned.

BAKED LAMB AND EGGPLANT PATTIES

MAKES: *6 servings*

BAKED LAMB PATTIES

MAKES: *8 servings*

2 pounds fresh ground lamb
4 large eggs
½ cup light cream
½ cup Quaker® old-fashioned rolled
   oats
1 cup minced white onion
½ cup finely chopped parsley
½ teaspoon dried rosemary
½ teaspoon dried basil
½ teaspoon dried oregano
salt and pepper
Mustard Sauce (recipe follows)

1 Position the rack in the center of the oven and preheat to 400 degrees F. Lightly butter a 15½-by-10½-inch baking pan.

2 In a bowl, combine the lamb, eggs, cream, oats, onion, and herbs. Season with salt and pepper and mix well. Divide into 8 equal pieces and shape each into a patty. Place the patties in the pan and bake for 18 to 20 minutes, or until cooked through. Serve with the sauce on the side.

MUSTARD SAUCE

MAKES: *About 1½ cups*

1 cup plain yogurt or sour cream
¼ cup vinegar
2 teaspoons prepared mustard
2 tablespoons minced white onion
2 tablespoons chopped parsley
salt and pepper

In a bowl, using an electric mixer on medium speed, combine the yogurt, vinegar, mustard, onion, parsley and salt and pepper to taste and beat until smooth. Use immediately or cover and chill for several days.

COSTOLLETTA AGNELLO SICILIAN

MAKES: *4 servings*

4 lamb shoulder chops
2 tablespoons lemon juice
1 teaspoon dried oregano
½ cup dry bread crumbs
2 tablespoons olive oil
1 small clove garlic, minced
¼ cup finely minced fresh cilantro
   (Chinese parsley)
salt and pepper
lemon slices for garnish
cilantro sprigs for garnish

1 Position the boiler rack about 6 inches from the heat source and preheat the broiler. Line a 13-by-9-inch baking pan with aluminum foil.

2 Brush the chops with lemon juice and sprinkle with oregano. Lay the chops in the pan. Broil for 8 to 10 minutes on each side, or until cooked through.

3 Combine the bread crumbs, oil, garlic and cilantro and season with salt and pepper. Transfer the chops to a heat-proof tray and sprinkle with the bread crumbs. Broil for 2 to 3 minutes until the crumbs brown. Garnish with lemon slices and cilantro sprigs.

3 tablespoons olive oil
1 pound ground lamb
¼ cup chopped shallots
2 cloves garlic, minced
¼ teaspoon ground coriander
¼ teaspoon ground cumin
¼ teaspoon pepper
¼ cup tomato paste
1½ teaspoons Harissa Sauce (recipe follows)
1 cup water
6 large eggs, lightly beaten
½ cup grated Gruyere or Edam cheese
¼ cup fine dry bread crumbs
lemon wedges for garnish

1 In a large skillet, heat the oil over medium heat and cook the lamb, shallots, garlic, coriander, cumin and pepper for about 2 minutes, stirring with a fork. Add the tomato paste and Harissa and stir for another 2 minutes. Reduce the heat to medium-low, add the water, and cook for about 15 minutes until most liquid is evaporated. Set aside.

2 Position the rack in the center of the oven and preheat to 350 degrees F. Lightly grease a 9-by-5-inch loaf pan.

3 In a bowl, combine the eggs, cheese and bread crumbs. Add the lamb mixture and blend well. Spread evenly into the pan and bake for 18 to 20 minutes, or until cooked through and lightly browned. Garnish with lemon wedges.

LAMB-AND-CHEESE LOAF

MAKES: *8 to 10 servings*

HARISSA SAUCE

MAKES: *About ⅔ cup*

8 to 10 hot red chilies, stemmed, seeded and chopped
1 tablespoon olive oil
4 large cloves garlic, minced
1 teaspoon ground coriander
1 teaspoon ground caraway
½ teaspoon salt
2 tablespoons water

1 Rinse the chilies under cold water and drain on paper towels.

2 In the container of a blender, combine the chilies, oil, garlic, coriander, caraway, salt and water and process for 2 to 3 seconds, or until smooth. If too thick, add water ½ teaspoon at a time. Serve immediately.

HERBED LAMB PATTIES

MAKES: *8 to 12 servings*

1½ pounds ground lamb
1 teaspoon grated lemon zest
1 tablespoon lemon juice
1 whole bay leaf, crushed
¼ teaspoon crushed dried rosemary
1 tablespoon chopped parsley
½ cup white port wine

1 In a bowl, combine the lamb, lemon zest, lemon juice, bay leaf, rosemary and parsley. Divide into 8 to 12 pieces and form each into a ball and then flatten into a patty.

2 In a large nonstick skillet, cook the patties over medium heat, a few at a time, turning occasionally until browned on both sides. Set the browned patties aside while browning the rest.

3 Put all the patties in the skillet, add the wine, reduce the heat to simmer and cook for about 20 minutes, or until cooked through.

LAMB BALLS WITH YOGURT SAUCE

MAKES: *4 servings*

1 pound ground lamb
1 teaspoon powdered turmeric
salt and pepper
2 teaspoons ground cumin
1 teaspoon ground coriander
½ teaspoon ground cloves
1 teaspoon ground cardamom
3 tablespoons canola oil
1 small onion, finely chopped
¾ cup hot water
1½ cups plain yogurt

1 In a bowl, sprinkle the lamb with turmeric, salt and pepper. Pinch off pieces and form into balls the size of walnuts.

2 In a cup, combine the cumin, coriander, cloves and cardamom and stir to mix.

3 In a large skillet, heat the oil. Add the onion and cook for about 5 minutes until softened. Add the mixed herbs and spices and stir for about a minute until fragrant.

4 Add the meatballs and cook for 5 to 7 minutes until browned on all sides. Add the water, bring to a boil, and then reduce and simmer 35 to 40 minutes, or until the water evaporates. Remove the pan from the heat and stir in the yogurt. Return to the heat and heat over very low heat just until heated through. Serve immediately.

1 large egg, beaten
2 tablespoons milk
1 cup fresh bread crumbs
2 tablespoons finely chopped white
  onion
½ teaspoon crushed dried tarragon
1 pound ground lamb
½ cup plain yogurt
¼ cup finely chopped cucumbers
1 tablespoon finely chopped parsley
salt and pepper

1 In a bowl, combine the egg, milk, bread crumbs, onion and tarragon and stir to mix. Add the meat and blend well. Pinch off pieces and form into balls about the size of walnuts.

2 Put about a third of the balls on a microwave-safe dish lined with paper towels and cover with a paper towel. Microwave on high (100 percent) power for 3 minutes. (If the microwave does not have a turntable, turn the dish once after 2 minutes of cooking.) Drain on paper towels and cover to keep warm while microwaving the remaining meatballs.

3 In a small bowl, combine the yogurt, cucumbers, and parsley and stir to mix. Season to taste with salt and pepper. Serve the meatballs with the yogurt on the side.

LAMB BITES

MAKES: *About 42 servings*

---

4 to 6 blade-bone lamb chops, each
  about ½-inch thick, trimmed
3 tablespoons lemon juice
white pepper
1 teaspoon crushed dried thyme
1½ tablespoons butter or margarine
½ tablespoon canola oil
lemon wedges for garnish

1 Put the chops in a 13-by-9-inch baking pan and drizzle with 2 tablespoons of lemon juice. Sprinkle with pepper and thyme, cover, and chill for at least 1 hour.

2 In a skillet, combine the butter and oil and heat over medium heat until the butter melts. Add the chops and cook for about 3 minutes on each side until browned and cooked through. Transfer to a plate and set aside. Drain the excess fat from the pan.

3 Add the remaining 1 tablespoon of lemon juice to the pan and stir over medium heat, scraping up the browned bits on the bottom of the pan. Drizzle over the chops and serve with lemon wedges.

LAMB CHOPS WITH LEMON

MAKES: *4 servings*

LAMB-FILLED ZUCCHINI

MAKES: *4 servings*

1 tablespoon olive oil
½ cup chopped white onion
1 large clove garlic, minced
¾ pound ground lamb
4 small zucchini (each about 6
    inches long), halved lengthwise
½ teaspoon crushed dried marjoram
¼ teaspoon pepper
½ cup grated Parmesan cheese
1 cup canned tomatoes, with juice

1 Position the rack in the center of the oven and preheat to 375 degrees F. Lightly grease a 13-by-9-inch baking pan.

2 In a large saucepan, heat the oil over medium heat and sauté the onion for about 5 minutes until softened. Add the garlic and cook for about 1 minute longer. Add the lamb and cook, stirring, for 5 to 8 minutes until no longer pink. Drain any excess fat during cooking.

3 In a steaming basket set over boiling water, steam the zucchini for about 5 minutes until barely tender. Cool slightly.

4 Scoop the centers from the zucchini and chop the flesh. Add the chopped zucchini flesh, marjoram and pepper to the meat and stir to mix.

5 Put the zucchini shells in the pan and fill each with meat mixture. Sprinkle the meat with cheese. Spoon any extra meat around the zucchini shells. Spoon the tomatoes and their juice around the zucchini and bake for 20 to 25 minutes, or until the tomatoes are bubbling and the meat is heated through.

LAMB PATTIES WITH CHEESE SAUCE

MAKES: *4 servings*

1 pound ground lamb
2 large eggs
¼ cup half-and-half
¼ cup Quaker® old-fashioned oats
½ cup minced white onion
¼ cup finely chopped parsley
¼ teaspoon dried rosemary
¼ teaspoon dried basil
¼ teaspoon dried oregano
¼ teaspoon pepper
Cheese Sauce (see page 20)
fresh oregano leaves for garnish

1 Position the rack in the center of the oven and preheat to 400 degrees F. Lightly grease a 13-by-9-inch baking pan.

2 In a large bowl, combine the lamb, eggs, half-and-half, oatmeal, onion, parsley, rosemary, basil, oregano and pepper and mix well. Divide into 4 equal sections and form each into a ball. Place the balls in the pan and flatten into patties.

3 Bake for 18 to 20 minutes or until cooked through. Spoon the sauce over the patties and garnish with fresh oregano.

1 can (8 ounces) pineapple chunks, drained, juice reserved
½ cup cider vinegar
¼ cup light corn syrup
¼ cup dark molasses
¼ cup soy sauce
¼ cup finely chopped mango chutney
2 teaspoons curry powder
3 pounds pork spareribs, trimmed and cut into individual ribs

1 In a small bowl, combine the reserved pineapple juice, vinegar, corn syrup, molasses, soy sauce, chutney and curry powder and mix well.

2 Place the ribs in a shallow glass or ceramic baking dish and pour the marinade over them. Turn the ribs several times to coat. Cover and chill for 24 hours. Turn the ribs several times during marinating.

3 Prepare a charcoal or gas grill and position the grilling rack about 6 inches from the coals.

4 Grill the ribs for about 45 minutes, turning several times, or until the meat is tender and nicely browned. Brush several times with the marinade during grilling. Serve with the pineapple chunks on the side.

COOKING NOTE: The marinade contains a lot of sugar from the pineapple juice, corn syrup and molasses and therefore will burn easily. Watch the ribs carefully during grilling.

CHUTNEY PORK RIBS

MAKES: *4 servings*

¼ cup bottled Kikkomen® Teriyaki Sauce
3 tablespoons unsweetened pineapple juice
2 tablespoons catsup
1½ tablespoons brown sugar
½ teaspoon ground ginger
1 large clove garlic, minced
2 pounds pork spareribs, trimmed and cut into individual ribs
4 slices fresh pineapple
4 tomato wedges

1 In a small bowl, combine the teriyaki sauce, pineapple juice, catsup, sugar, ginger and garlic and mix well.

2 Place the ribs in a shallow glass or ceramic baking dish and pour the marinade over them. Turn the ribs several times to coat. Cover and chill for 24 hours. Turn the ribs several times during marinating.

3 Prepare a charcoal or gas grill and position the grilling rack about 6 inches from the coals.

4 Grill the ribs for about 45 minutes, turning several times, or until the meat is tender and nicely browned. Brush several times with the marinade during grilling.

5 About 5 minutes before the ribs are done, brush the pineapple slices with marinade and lay on the grill. Grill, turning once, for about 5 minutes until heated through and lightly browned. Serve the ribs garnished with the pineapple slices and tomato wedges.

FIJI-STYLE SPARERIBS

MAKES: *4 servings*

GERMAN-STYLE HAM PATTIES

MAKES: *About 36 servings*

1 tablespoon vegetable oil
1 Bermuda onion, chopped
2 cups canned sauerkraut, well
   drained and chopped
1 pound ground ham
¼ cup all-purpose flour
5 large eggs
1 tablespoon prepared mustard
1 teaspoon Worcestershire sauce
¾ cup crumbled corn flakes
¼ cup butter or margarine

1 In a skillet, heat the oil over medium heat and cook the onions for about 5 minutes until softened. Transfer to a bowl.

2 Add the sauerkraut, ham, flour, 2 of the eggs, mustard and Worcestershire sauce to the bowl and mix well.

3 Spread the mixture in the skillet and cook over medium heat for about 10 minutes, stirring frequently, until cooked through. Remove from the heat and pinch off small pieces and form into small balls about the size of walnuts. Flatten each ball into ¼-inch-thick patties.

4 In a shallow bowl, lightly beat the remaining 3 eggs. Put the corn flakes in the another shallow bowl. Dip each patty in the eggs and then in the crumbs and coat on both sides.

5 Heat the butter in the skillet and cook the patties over medium heat for 4 or 5 minutes, or until well browned. Serve immediately.

GLAZED HAM BALLS

MAKES: *About 12 servings*

1½ pounds ground smoked ham
1 pound ground lean pork
2 large eggs
1 cup milk
2 cups saltine cracker crumbs
2 tablespoons Worcestershire sauce
1½ cups packed brown sugar
¾ cup water
⅓ cup vinegar
1 tablespoon dry mustard

1 Position the rack in the center of the oven and preheat to 350 degrees F. Lightly grease a 13-by-9-inch flameproof baking pan.

2 In a large bowl, combine the ham, pork, eggs, milk, cracker crumbs and Worcestershire sauce

and mix well. Pinch off small pieces and shape into balls about the size of walnuts. Transfer to the baking pan and arrange in a single layer. Bake for 10 to 12 minutes or until just cooked. Drain the fat.

3 In a saucepan, combine the sugar, water, vinegar and mustard and stir to mix. Heat over medium heat, stirring, until boiling. Pour over the ham balls and set the baking pan over medium heat. Cook for 18 to 20 minutes longer, spooning the sauce over the ham balls several times, until nicely glazed and thoroughly cooked. Serve with toothpicks.

1¼ cups all-purpose flour
¾ cup yellow cornmeal
3 tablespoons sugar
2½ teaspoons baking powder
½ cup buttermilk
2 large eggs, beaten
6 tablespoons butter or margarine, melted
1½ cups finely diced smoked ham
1 cup finely diced pears
canola oil

1 In a large bowl, combine the flour, cornmeal, sugar and baking powder and whisk to mix. Add the buttermilk, eggs and butter and stir until blended. Fold in the ham and pears and set aside.

2 In a large skillet, pour enough oil to reach a depth of about 2 inches and heat over high heat until hot. Drop the ham mixture by tablespoonfuls into the hot oil, taking care not to crowd the pan, and cook for 4 to 6 minutes until golden brown. Drain on paper towels and cook the remaining fritters.

Cooking note: Be sure to let the oil regain its temperature between batches of fritters. Serve these with a dipping sauce, if you desire.

Ham-and-Pear Fritters

Makes: *About 36 servings*

10 Pepperidge Farm® Party Rolls
½ cup butter or margarine, at room temperature
1 package (3 ounces) cream cheese, at room temperature
3 tablespoons poppy seeds
3 tablespoons brown mustard
1 teaspoon Worcestershire sauce
1 shallot, minced
8 ounces sliced Swiss cheese
¾ pound boiled ham, thinly sliced

1 Position the rack in the center of the oven and preheat to 400 degrees F.

2 Slice the party rolls in half crosswise and lay on a work surface.

3 In a small bowl, combine the butter, cream cheese, poppy seeds, mustard, Worcestershire sauce and shallot. Spread on the bottom half of each roll and top with cheese and ham. Replace the top of the rolls and transfer to an ungreased baking sheet. Bake for 18 to 20 minutes or until the rolls are golden brown and the cheese melts.

Ham Biscuits

Makes: *10 servings*

HAM LOGS WITH MUSTARD SAUCE

MAKES: *About 24 servings*

2 cups ground smoked ham
1 large egg, beaten
¼ teaspoon pepper
¼ cup seasoned bread crumbs
vegetable oil
pimiento strips for garnish
Mustard Sauce (see page 236)

1 In a bowl, combine the ham, egg and pepper and mix well. Pinch off small pieces and form into 1-inch-long rolls.

2 Spread the bread crumbs in a shallow bowl and roll the logs in the crumbs to coat. Transfer to a baking tray, cover and chill for at least 1 hour.

3 In a large skillet, pour the oil to a depth of about 2 inches and heat over high heat until hot. Fry the logs, taking care not to crowd the pan, for 2 to 3 minutes, or until golden brown. Drain on paper towels and continue cooking the remaining logs. Serve garnished with pimiento strips with the sauce on the side.

HAM SNACK ROLLS

MAKES: *20 servings*

1 can (8 ounces) refrigerated crescent dinner rolls
8 thin ham slices
4 teaspoons prepared mustard
1 cup shredded Swiss cheese
2 tablespoons sesame seeds

1 Position the rack in the center of the oven and preheat to 375 degrees F.

2 Unroll the dough into 4 long rectangles and press gently along the perforations to seal them. Place the ham slices on the dough. Spread the mustard on the ham and sprinkle with cheese. Starting at the shortest side, roll up each rectangle to form a log and press the edges to seal.

3 Spread the seeds on a plate and roll each log in the seeds. Cut each roll into 5 slices to make 20 slices in all. Transfer the rolls, cut side down, to an ungreased baking sheet and bake for 15 to 20 minutes or until golden brown. Serve hot.

HOT SAUSAGE BALLS

MAKES: *40 to 50 servings*

1 pound hot pork sausage
3 cups Bisquick® Baking Mix
1 cup grated extra-sharp Cheddar cheese
dash of cayenne pepper

1 Position the rack in the center of the oven and preheat to 350 degrees F. Lightly grease a baking sheet.

2 In a bowl, combine the sausage, Bisquick, cheese and cayenne and using your hands, mix well. Pinch off small pieces and form into balls about the size of walnuts. Put the balls on the baking sheet with about 1 inch between them. Bake for 15 to 20 minutes, or until a golden brown. Cool on a wire rack and serve at room temperature.

COOKING NOTE: **Serve these with a dipping sauce, if you desire.**

1 pound bulk Italian sausage
1 small red bell pepper, finely chopped
1 onion, finely chopped
1 tablespoon Italian seasoning
1 package (8 ounces) cream cheese, at room temperature
about ⅓ cup water
⅓ cup grated Parmesan cheese
1 loaf French bread, halved lengthwise and centers hollowed out
½ pound grated mozzarella or provolone cheese

1 In a nonstick skillet, cook the sausage over medium-high heat for 4 to 6 minutes, stirring, until browned. Drain. Add the onion, pepper and seasoning and con-tinue cooking, stirring, for about 5 minutes longer until the onion softens.

2 Remove from the heat and add the cream cheese. Stir until the cheese melts, adding enough water to make the mixture creamy. Add the Parmesan cheese and return to the heat, stirring, just until the mixture blends and is hot.

3 Spread the hot mixture in the bread halves and top with the mozzarella cheese. Cut each bread half into 4 slices and serve immediately.

ITALIAN SAUSAGE LOAF

MAKES: *8 to 10 servings*

---

2 spicy Italian sausages, casings removed
2 cups all-purpose flour
⅓ cup Romano cheese
1 tablespoon baking powder
½ teaspoon fresh chopped oregano leaves
salt and pepper
1 large egg
1 can (12 ounces) pizza sauce
2 tablespoons canola oil

1 Position the rack in the center of the oven and preheat to 400 degrees F. Lightly grease two 6-cup muffin pans.

2 In a nonstick skillet, cook the sausage over medium-high heat for 4 to 6 minutes, stirring, until browned. Drain and reserve the pan drippings (you will have about 1 tablespoon).

3 In a bowl, combine the flour, cheese, baking powder and oregano and stir to mix. Season with salt and pepper.

4 In a bowl, whisk the egg until foamy. Add the pizza sauce, oil and pan drippings and beat well. Add the sausage meat, cheese mixture and egg mixture and stir until moist. Spoon about 2 table-spoons into each muffin cup, pressing lightly to compact. Bake for 20 to 25 minutes or until firm and lightly browned. Cool on a wire rack for at least 30 minutes before serving.

ITALIAN SAUSAGE MUFFINS

MAKES: *12 servings*

LITTLE LINK WRAPS

MAKES: 24 *servings*

2 packages (8 ounces each)
   refrigerated crescent dinner rolls
24 small cooked smoked sausage
   links
catsup
prepared horseradish
prepared mustard

1 Position the rack in the center of the oven and preheat to 375 degrees F.

2 Separate the dough into 8 triangles and cut each lengthwise into thirds. Lay a sausage on the short end of each triangle.

3 Roll each triangle up to enclose the sausage and place, point side down, on an ungreased baking sheet. Bake for 12 to 15 minutes or until golden brown. Serve warm with catsup, horseradish and mustard on the side.

PIGS IN A BLANKET

MAKES: 30 *servings*

½ cup butter or margarine
1 cup all-purpose flour
½ cup small-curd cottage cheese
1 tablespoon Dijon mustard
six 5-inch links smoked Polish
   sausage
1 large egg
1 tablespoon milk

1 Position the rack in the center of the oven and preheat to 400 degrees F. Put the butter in the freezer for about 30 minutes until firm.

2 Cut the chilled butter into pieces and transfer to a bowl. Add the flour and using a pastry blender or two table knives, cut the butter into the flour until it resembles small crumbs. Add the cottage cheese and stir until the mixture forms a stiff dough. If

necessary, add 2 or 3 teaspoons of ice water to make the dough cohesive. Divide the dough into 6 equal parts.

3 On a lightly floured surface, roll each piece of dough into a rectangle approximately 6-by-3 inches. Spread each rectangle with mustard and top with a sausage link. Fold the dough around the sausage. Brush the edges with cold water and press to seal. Transfer the rolls, seam-side down, to an ungreased baking sheet and prick with a fork.

4 In a small bowl, combine the egg and milk and whisk to mix. Brush the rolls with the egg wash and bake for 20 to 25 minutes, or until lightly browned. Slice into 1-inch pieces and serve hot.

2 tablespoons minced white onion
¼ cup light soy sauce
¼ cup packed dark-brown sugar
¼ cup lemon or lime juice
½ teaspoon garlic powder
¾ teaspoon ground coriander
⅛ teaspoon ground cayenne
2 pounds pork tenderloin, cut into 1-inch pieces
2 pounds boneless turkey roast, cut into 1-inch cubes

1 In container of a blender, combine the onion, soy sauce, sugar, lemon juice, garlic powder, coriander and cayenne and process until smooth.

2 In a glass or ceramic bowl, combine the pork and turkey, pour the marinade over the meat and toss to coat. Cover and chill for at least 4 hours.

3 Position the broiler rack about 5 inches from the heat source and preheat the broiler.

4 Thread the meat on wooden or metal skewers and lay on a broiling pan. Broil for about 8 minutes, turn and continue broiling for about 8 minutes longer or until browned. Turn again and broil for about 5 more minutes until cooked through. Serve immediately.

COOKING NOTE: If using wooden skewers, soak them in cold water for about 20 minutes to prevent scorching during cooking.

PORK-AND-TURKEY KABOBS

MAKES: *12 to 16 servings*

---

1 pound ground pork
1 can (8 ounces) water chestnuts, drained and finely chopped
¼ cup minced green onion
1 large clove garlic, minced
1 large egg
2 tablespoons soy sauce
⅓ cup plus 1 tablespoon cornstarch
1 tablespoon vegetable oil
1 can (20 ounces) chunk pineapple, with juice
1 tablespoon grated fresh ginger
½ green bell pepper, cut into thin strips

1 In a large bowl, combine the pork, water chestnuts, onion, garlic, egg, 1 tablespoon of soy sauce and 1 teaspoon of cornstarch. Pinch off small pieces and form them into balls about the size of walnuts.

2 Spread all but 1 tablespoon of the cornstarch in a shallow bowl and roll each ball in it to coat.

3 In a skillet, heat the oil over high heat and sauté the balls for about 10 minutes until browned on all sides. Drain on paper towels.

4 In a large saucepan, combine the juice from the pineapple, ginger, remaining tablespoon of cornstarch and remaining tablespoon of soy sauce and bring to a boil over medium-high heat, stirring, until thickened and clear. Add the pineapple and pepper and mix well. Add the meatballs and stir gently until coated with sauce and heated through. Serve immediately or keep warm in a chafing dish.

PORK BALLS WITH WATER CHESTNUTS

MAKES: *About 48 servings*

SAUSAGE-AND-CHEESE TARTS

MAKES: *18 servings*

1 package (14 ounces) pie crust mix
8 ounces ground pork
1⅓ cups shredded Swiss or Gouda cheese
6 green onions, sliced (green portions only)
4 large eggs
1⅓ cups sour cream or plain yogurt
1 teaspoon Worcestershire sauce
salt and pepper
paprika

1 Position the rack in the center of the oven and preheat to 375 degrees F.

2 Prepare the pie crust according to the package directions and divide into 2 equal parts. On a lightly floured surface, roll out 1 piece of dough so that it is very thin and stamp out nine 4-inch rounds. Repeat with the remaining half of the dough. Press the rounds into 2½-inch muffin pans, taking care not to tear them, to make cups.

3 In a skillet, sauté the pork for 6 or 7 minutes over medium-high heat or until no longer pink. Drain and transfer the meat to a bowl. Add the cheese and onions and mix well. Spoon into the muffin cups, filling each about half full.

4 In another bowl, using an electric mixer on medium speed, beat the eggs until foamy. Add the sour cream and Worcestershire sauce and season with salt and pepper. Spoon approximately 2 tablespoons of the egg mixture over the meat mixture and sprinkle with paprika. Bake for 25 to 30 minutes, or until the crust is golden brown. Serve warm.

SAUSAGE MUFFINS

MAKES: *12 muffins*

½ pound pork sausage
butter or margarine, melted
2 cups all-purpose flour
2 tablespoons sugar
1 tablespoon baking powder
½ teaspoon salt
1 large egg
1 cup milk
½ cup shredded American or Cheddar cheese

1 Position the rack in the center of the oven and preheat to 375 degrees F. Lightly grease 12 muffin cups or line them with paper liners.

2 In a saucepan, cook the sausage over medium heat, stirring with a fork, for 7 or 8 minutes or until browned. Drain, reserving the drippings. Add enough melted butter to the drippings to measure ¼ cup.

3 In a bowl, combine the flour, sugar, baking powder and salt and whisk to mix.

4 In another bowl, using an electric mixer on medium speed, beat the egg until foamy. Add the milk and the drippings and beat well. Add the flour mixture and stir just until moistened. Add the cheese and sausage and mix well.

5 Spoon the mixture into the muffin cups and bake for 15 to 18 minutes or until a toothpick inserted in the center of a cup comes out clean. Cool on wire racks.

1 tablespoon cornmeal
¾ pound bulk Italian sausage
1 clove garlic, minced
¼ cup chopped shallot
1 cup chopped fresh spinach
¾ cup shredded mozzarella cheese
¼ cup chopped fresh mushrooms
2 tablespoons grated Parmesan cheese
2 packages (8 ounces) refrigerated crescent dinner rolls
1 large egg
1 tablespoon water

1 Position the rack in the center of the oven and preheat to 350 degrees F. Lightly grease a baking sheet and sprinkle it with cornmeal.

2 In a saucepan, cook the sausage over medium heat, stirring with a fork, for 7 or 8 minutes or until browned. Add the garlic, shallot and spinach and cook for about 5 minutes longer or until tender. Add the mozzarella cheese, mushrooms and Parmesan cheese and stir until the cheese begins to melt. Remove from the heat.

3 Separate the rolls into 8 rectangles and smooth along the perforations to seal. Spread about ½ cup of the sausage mixture on one half of each rectangle, leaving a ½-inch border.

4 In a small bowl, whisk the egg and water until foamy. Using a pastry brush, brush the borders and top of each triangle and fold the empty half over the filling, pressing to secure. Transfer to the baking sheet and bake for 15 to 20 minutes or until golden brown. Cool slightly on wire racks and serve warm.

SAUSAGE POCKETS

MAKES: *8 servings*

6 Brazil nuts, finely chopped
1 cup minced white onion
2 large cloves garlic, minced
2 tablespoons ground coriander
2 tablespoons brown sugar
¼ cup lemon juice
¼ cup soy sauce
¼ cup olive oil
4 pequin chiles or other hot chiles, crushed
2 pounds pork tenderloin, cut crosswise into 1-inch cubes
slice candied kumquats
orange or lemon leaves for garnish

1 In a large glass or ceramic bowl, combine the nuts, onion, garlic, coriander, sugar, lemon juice, soy sauce, oil and chiles and stir to mix. Add the pork and stir to coat. Cover and set aside to marinate for at least 10 minutes.

2 Preheat a stovetop grill or prepare a charcoal or gas grill until very hot.

3 Thread the pork on 4 skewers and grill for 10 to 15 minutes, turning and brushing with marinade until cooked through. Serve garnished with kumquats and orange leaves.

COOKING NOTE: If using wooden skewers, soak them in cold water for about 20 minutes to prevent scorching during cooking. If you plan to marinate the meat for longer than 10 minutes, put it in the refrigerator.

SOUTHEAST-ASIAN PORK TENDERLOIN

MAKES: *4 servings*

PORK SAUSAGE FRITTATA

MAKES: *12 servings*

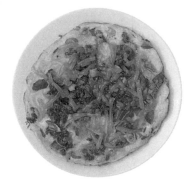

2 tablespoons canola oil
½ pound pork sausage meat
3 green onions, greens parts only, sliced
8 large eggs
¼ cup milk
black pepper
¼ cup butter or margarine, at room temperature
1 tomato, chopped
1 cup shredded sharp Cheddar or Wisconsin brick cheese

1 In a large skillet, heat the oil over medium-high heat and sauté the sausage and onions for 3 to 4 minutes or until the meat is no longer pink. Pour off the excess fat and set the meat aside.

2 In a medium bowl, using an electric mixer or wire whisk, beat the eggs until thick and light colored. Beat in the milk and season with pepper.

3 In an omelette pan, melt 1 tablespoon of butter and heat until no longer foamy. Pour a quarter of the egg mixture into the pan and cook until the eggs start to set around the edge. Sprinkle a quarter of the sausage mixture over the eggs and top with a quarter of the tomatoes and a quarter of the cheese. Continue to cook until the eggs are set and the cheese is melted but not runny. Slide from the skillet to a serving platter, fold in half and cut into 3 wedges. Cover and set aside to keep warm. Repeat with the remaining egg and sausage to make 4 frittata and 12 wedges.

BEANS AND SAUSAGE

MAKES: *8 servings*

2 cups dry navy beans
4 cups water
1 bay leaf
1 tablespoon butter or margarine
5 links Italian sausages, cut diagonally into ½-inch slices
1 small clove garlic, minced
1 small red onion, minced
1 can (8 ounces) tomato sauce
½ teaspoon dried sage leaves
1 teaspoon Worcestershire sauce
2 tablespoons chopped parsley
salt and black pepper
Ritz® crackers

1 Thoroughly wash and pick over the beans. In a large saucepan, combine the beans, water and bay leaf and bring to a boil over high heat. Cook for about 2 minutes and then remove from the heat. Cover and set aside to soften for 1 hour. Drain.

2 Add enough fresh cold water to the beans to cover by about 2 inches and bring to a boil over high heat. Reduce the heat and simmer over medium heat for about 1 hour or until the beans are just tender. (They should be firm in the center.) Do not overcook. Drain and reserve 1 cup of the cooking liquid. Return to the beans to the saucepan.

3 In a skillet, melt the butter over medium-high heat and sauté the sausage for 3 to 4 minutes on each side until browned. Add the garlic and onions and cook for about 5 minutes longer until the vegetables are tender. Add the sausage mixture and the reserved cup of cooking liquid to the beans. Add the tomato sauce, sage, Worcestershire sauce and parsley and stir to mix. Season to taste with salt and pepper.

4 Cover and simmer over medium-high heat for 20 to 25 minutes, or until the beans are tender and cooked through. Adjust the consistency by adding more water as desired. Ladle into a serving bowl and serve with crackers.

1 recipe Pizza Crust (recipe follows)
½ pound hot Italian sausage, crumbled
1 can (16 ounces) pork and beans with tomato sauce
¼ teaspoon oregano leaves, crumbled
1 large tomato, thinly sliced
3 ounces Mozzarella cheese, thinly sliced
3 ounces Provolone cheese, thinly sliced

1 Position the rack in the center of the oven and preheat to 425 degrees F. Lightly grease a 12-inch pizza pan or a 9-by-13-inch baking pan.

2 Press the pizza dough into the pan.

3 In a skillet, cook the sausage meat over medium heat, stirring frequently, for 4 to 5 minutes, or until browned. Drain off excess fat and transfer the meat to a small bowl. Add the pork and beans and oregano and toss to mix.

4 Spread the mixture over the pizza dough and bake for about 10 minutes. Arrange the tomato and cheese slices over the meat and bake for an additional 10 minutes, or until the cheese is completely melted. Cut into wedges or small squares and serve.

COOKING NOTE: A pizza baked in a rectangular baking pan is easier to cut into evenly sized pieces.

SAUSAGE PIZZA WITH BEANS

MAKES: *8 servings*

PIZZA CRUST

MAKES: *one 12-inch pizza crust*

⅔ cups warm water (105 to 115 degrees F)
1 package (¼ ounce) dry yeast
1 tablespoon sugar
1½ cup all-purpose flour
¾ teaspoon salt

1 In a small bowl, combine the water, yeast and sugar and set aside for about 5 minutes until the mixture bubbles and foams.

2 In a large bowl, combine the flour and salt and whisk to mix. Add the yeast mixture and stir with a wooden spoon until a soft dough forms.

3 On a lightly floured work surface, knead the dough for about 5 minutes or until smooth and elastic. Cover and set aside in a warm place until doubled in bulk.

4 Turn out onto a lightly floured work surface and knead again for 3 to 4 minutes. Roll out or stretch to fit a 12-inch pizza pan or rectangular baking pan.

COOKING NOTE: To make whole-wheat pizza crust, use 1 cup of all-purpose flour and ½ cup of whole-wheat flour.

STEAMED PORK BALLS

MAKES: *4 servings*

1 pound uncooked glutinous rice
1 pound lean ground pork
1 large egg white
4 tablespoons chopped leeks
1 tablespoon soy sauce plus more for serving
1 tablespoon sherry or white port wine

1 In a saucepan, combine the rice with enough cold water to cover and set aside to soak for 3 hour.

2 In a bowl, combine the pork, egg white, leeks, soy sauce and sherry and use your hands to mix well. Form into 4 portions and roll each into a ball.

3 Drain the rice and spread it on a platter. Roll each ball in the rice until thickly coated. Transfer to a plate and flatten each into a ½-inch-thick patty.

4 In a steaming basket set over boiling water, steam the patties for 35 to 40 minutes or until cooked through. Serve with soy sauce.

COOKING NOTE: **Asian-style glutinous (sticky) rice is available at Asian markets.**

STEAMED PORK BUNS

MAKES: *About 40 servings*

8 ounces ground pork
⅔ cup Wish-Bone® Russian Dressing
1 tablespoon soy sauce
1 can (8.5 ounces) water chestnuts, drained and finely chopped
½ cup shredded cabbage
2 tablespoons finely chopped shallots
2 packages (8 ounces each) Pillsbury® refrigerated buttermilk biscuits

1 Position the rack in the center of the oven and preheat to 400 degrees F.

2 In a skillet, cook the pork over a medium heat for 7 or 8 minutes, stirring, until no longer pink. Drain and discard the fat. Add ½ cup of the dressing, the

soy sauce, water chestnuts, cabbage and shallots. Cook, stirring constantly, for about 5 minutes longer or until heated through.

3 Flatten the biscuits into 2-inch-diameter circles and place about 1 teaspoon of the meat mixture on each. Gather the edges over the top of the filling and twist to seal. Transfer, twisted side down, to a rack set over a shallow roasting pan. Add enough water to the pan to cover the bottom by about ½ inch. Cover loosely with foil and seal the edges. Bake for 18 to 20 minutes or until the tops of the buns are shiny. Brush with the remaining dressing and serve warm.

PORK BALLS

1½ pounds ground lean pork
1¼ pounds ground lean beef
2 cups crushed corn flakes
2 large eggs, beaten
1 cup milk
3 tablespoons prepared horseradish
3 tablespoons Worcestershire sauce
2 teaspoons dry mustard
salt and pepper

SAUCE

1 cup catsup
½ cup firmly packed brown sugar
½ cup water
⅓ cup soy sauce
2 tablespoons honey
2 tablespoons cider vinegar
1 teaspoon dry mustard
1 can (8 ounces) crushed pineapple, drained

1 Position the rack in the center of the oven and preheat to 450 degrees F.

2 To make the pork balls, in a large bowl, combine the pork, beef, corn flakes, eggs, milk, horseradish, Worcestershire sauce and mustard and season to taste with salt and pepper. Pinch off pieces and shape into balls about the size of walnuts. Transfer the balls to a rack set in a shallow roasting pan and bake for 12 to 15 minutes, or until brown. Remove from the oven and set aside.

3 To make the sauce, in a saucepan, combine the catsup, sugar, water, soy sauce, honey, vinegar and mustard and bring to a boil over high heat. Reduce the heat and simmer for about 10 minutes, stirring occasionally. Add the pineapple and stir to mix.

4 Add the meatballs to the sauce and stir gently to coat. Cook for 10 to 15 minutes or until the meatballs are heated through. Transfer to a chafing dish and serve hot.

TROPICAL PORK BALLS

MAKES: *About 75 servings*

---

2 tablespoons butter or margarine
½ cup finely chopped white onion
3 cups dry white bread crumbs
2 apples, peeled and cored
½ cup water
salt and pepper
4 large veal cutlets
½ cup unsweetened apple juice
1 tablespoon cornstarch
½ cup sliced celery
lemon juice

1 In a skillet, heat 1 tablespoon of butter over medium heat and cook the onion for about 5 minutes or until lightly browned. Add the bread crumbs and stir until the butter is absorbed.

2 Dice 1 of the apples and add to the skillet with ¼ cup of the water. Season to taste with salt and pepper and stir well.

3 Lay the cutlets on a work surface and spoon filling on top of each. Roll each into a cylinder.

4 Heat the remaining 1 tablespoon of butter over medium-high heat and add the veal rolls, seam-side down, to the skillet. Cook, turning, for about 5 minutes until browned on all sides. Add the apple juice, reduce the heat, cover and simmer for 15 to 20 minutes, or until the meat is tender. Lift the veal rolls from the pan and set aside, covered, to keep warm.

5 In a cup, combine the remaining ¼ cup of water and the cornstarch and whisk until smooth. Add to the pan juices with the celery and stir until the sauce thickens. Spoon over the rolls.

6 Slice the remaining apple into slices, brush with lemon juice to prevent discoloring, and use to garnish the veal rolls.

APPLE VEAL ROLLS

MAKES: *4 to 8 Servings*

BREADED VEAL CUTLETS

MAKES: *4 servings*

2 tablespoons all-purpose flour
¼ teaspoon ground cloves
⅛ teaspoon white pepper
2 teaspoons Worcestershire sauce
1 large egg, beaten
½ cup dry whole-wheat bread crumbs
4 veal cutlets
3 tablespoons canola oil

1 In a small shallow dish, combine the flour, cloves and pepper and whisk to mix.

2 In another small shallow dish, combine the Worcestershire sauce and egg and whisk to mix. Spread the bread crumbs in another small shallow bowl.

3 Dredge the cutlets first in the flour mixture, next in the egg mixture and finally in the bread crumbs.

4 In a skillet, heat the oil over medium-low heat and cook the cutlets for 2 or 3 minutes on each side until browned. Continue cooking for 5 to 7 minutes or until cooked through. Serve immediately.

TENDER VEAL MACARONI

MAKES: *4 to 6 Servings*

1 cup fine dry bread crumbs
1½ pounds boneless veal, cut into 1-inch cubes
canola oil for frying
1 cup water
3 cans (10¾ ounces each) cream of mushroom soup
2 cans (12 ounces each) evaporated milk
2 cups cooked small shell macaroni

1 Spread the crumbs in a shallow dish and roll the cubes in the crumbs to coat on all sides.

2 In a large skillet, pour in enough oil to cover the bottom of the pan and heat over medium-high heat. Sauté the veal for 4 or 5 minutes, turning, until browned. Drain off any oil and add the water. Cover and simmer over low heat for 35 to 40 minutes, or until the meat is tender. Lift the meat from the pan and set aside, covered, to keep warm.

3 Raise the heat to medium-high and cook, uncovered, for about 5 minutes or until the pan liquid is reduced by about half. Add the soup and milk and stir to blend. Add the shells and cook for about 5 minutes, or until heated through. Spoon over the veal and serve at once.

2 tablespoons butter or margarine
2 pounds boneless veal, cut into 1-inch cubes
2 tablespoons all-purpose flour
salt and pepper
two 1-inch-wide strips of lemon or orange zest (about 2 inches long)
1 cup boiling water
1 cup heavy cream
2½ to 3 cups hot cooked egg noodles

1 In a large skillet, heat the butter over medium-high heat and cook the veal, stirring, for 5 or 6 minutes or until browned. Sprinkle with flour and add the lemon zest and water and stir gently. Cover and simmer for about 1 hour or until the meat is very tender.

2 Remove the zest and add the cream. Cook over medium heat, stirring, until heated through. Serve over the noodles.

VEAL BITES

MAKES: *6 Servings*

6 veal cutlets
3 tablespoons all-purpose flour
3 tablespoons canola oil
1 small shallot, finely chopped
2 cloves garlic, minced
2 Herb-Ox® chicken bouillon cubes
1 cup dry white wine
1 cup water
2 teaspoons chopped fresh oregano

1 Using a meat mallet, pound the veal several times on both sides to flatten. Rub on both sides with flour.

2 In a large skillet, heat the oil over medium heat and cook the veal for 2 or 3 minutes on each side or until lightly browned. Transfer to a warm platter and cover to keep warm.

3 Add the onions and garlic to the pan and cook for 1 or 2 minutes until the onions begin to soften. Add the bouillon, wine, water and oregano and stir to mix. Return the veal to the pan, cover and simmer over medium-low heat for about 1 hour. Cool in the pan, cover and chill for at least 8 hours.

4 Set the pan with the veal and other ingredients over medium heat and add a little more wine. Heat gently and serve when hot.

VEAL IN WINE SAUCE

MAKES: *6 Servings*

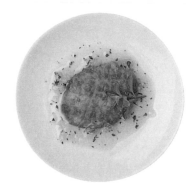

VEAL WITH ROQUEFORT

MAKES: *4 servings*

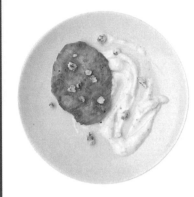

1 pound thin-sliced veal, cut into 4
  pieces
2 tablespoons all-purpose flour
2 tablespoons butter or margarine
½ cup heavy cream
2 ounces Roquefort cheese,
  crumbled

1 Using a meat mallet, pound
the veal on both sides to flatten.
Rub with flour.

2 In a large skillet, heat the butter over medium heat and cook
the veal for 2 or 3 minutes on

each side until lightly browned.
Continue cooking for 5 to 7 minutes longer or until the meat is
tender and cooked through.
Remove from the pan and set
aside, covered, to keep warm.

3 Add the cream and cheese to
the skillet and cook, stirring, for
several minutes or until the
cheese melts. Spoon over the veal
and serve.

Chapter 7

CHICKEN AND TURKEY ON THE RUN

Surely the name of this chapter says it all. These recipes for chicken and turkey are quick and easy to prepare—and even easier to eat! Many chicken dishes qualify as snack foods—who has not toted chicken legs (the kids call them drumsticks) along on a picnic or served a platter piled high with spicy chicken wings to a crowd? Here you'll discover all manner of yummy, finger-licking chicken and turkey recipes. It's interesting to note that the popularity of chicken wings as snack food is relatively recent. Time was when they were considered "throw-away" chicken parts. But those days thankfully are over, as many of the following recipes demonstrate.

CALCUTTA CHICKEN SALAD

MAKES: *8 servings*

6 cups cubed cooked chicken
2 cans (11 ounces each) mandarin orange segments, drained
1 can (8 ounces) sliced water chestnuts, drained
1 cup sliced pea pods
1 package (8 ounces) cream cheese, at room temperature
⅓ cup lime or orange juice
2 teaspoons grated lime or orange zest
1 teaspoon curry powder
1 can (5 ounces) chow mein noodles

1 In a bowl, combine the chicken, orange segments, water chestnuts and pea pods and toss to mix.

2 In a blender, combine the cream cheese, lime juice, lime zest and curry powder and process for 2 or 3 seconds until smooth. Pour over the chicken mixture and toss to coat.

3 Press into a lightly oiled 1-quart ring mold, cover and chill for at least 1 hour. Unmold onto a serving platter and serve garnished with chow mein noodles.

CHICKEN AND MANDARIN SEGMENTS WITH ALMONDS

MAKES: *6 to 8 servings*

½ cup sliced almonds
3 tablespoons sugar
4 heads Bibb lettuce, torn into bite-size pieces (about 6 cups)
3 cups cubed cooked chicken
1 cup chopped celery
2 green onions, thinly sliced
1 can (11 ounces) mandarin orange segments, drained
2 tablespoons canola or peanut oil
1 tablespoon white wine or cider vinegar
salt and pepper

1 In a saucepan, combine the almonds and sugar and cook over low heat for 2 or 3 minutes, stirring constantly, until the sugar melts and coats the almonds. Transfer the nuts to a plate or baking sheet and let cool. When cool, break into pieces and store in a tightly lidded container at room temperature for up to 24 hours.

2 In a bowl, combine the lettuce, chicken, celery, onions and orange segments and toss to mix.

3 In small bowl or cup, whisk together the oil and vinegar and season with salt and pepper. Pour over the chicken salad and toss until coated. Add the almonds and toss again. Serve immediately.

⅔ cup mayonnaise
⅓ cup prepared salsa
1½ pounds boneless, skinless chicken breasts, cut into 3-by-1-inch strips
2 tablespoons canola oil

1 In a bowl, combine the mayonnaise and salsa and whisk until thoroughly mixed. Reserve ¼ cup.

2 Add the chicken to the bowl and stir gently to coat. Cover and chill for about 1 hour. Remove from the refrigerator and let sit at room temperature for no longer than 15 minutes to come to room temperature.

3 In a skillet, heat the oil over medium-high heat. Add the chicken and sauté for 4 or 5 minutes or until cooked through and lightly browned. Serve with the reserved sauce.

CHICKEN FINGERS, SOUTHERN-STYLE

MAKES: *8 servings*

½ cup soy sauce
¼ cup honey
½ teaspoon garlic powder
1½ teaspoons ground ginger
1½ pounds boneless, skinless chicken, cut into bite-sized pieces
2 tablespoons peanut oil

1 In a bowl, combine the soy sauce, honey, garlic powder and ginger and whisk until smooth. Add the chicken, toss to coat, cover and chill for at least 8 hours.

2 In a large skillet, heat the oil over medium-high heat until very hot and beginning to smoke. Lift the chicken from the marinade, reserving the marinade, and cook the chicken for 4 or 5 minutes or until cooked through. Set aside, covered, to keep warm.

3 Transfer the reserved marinade to a small saucepan and heat over medium heat until boiling. Cook, stirring, for about 1 minute. Brush some of the marinade over the chicken and serve the remaining on the side.

CHICKEN TERIYAKI

MAKES: *8 servings*

CHICKEN TACOS OLÉ

MAKES: 10 servings

1 package (8 ounces) cream cheese
⅓ cup heavy cream
1½ cups cooked chopped chicken
1 (4 ounces) can chopped green
   chilies, drained
½ teaspoon salt
¼ teaspoon chili powder
1 package (10 shells) Old El Paso®
   Taco Shells
shredded lettuce
chopped tomatoes

1 In a saucepan, combine the cream cheese and cream and cook over medium heat, stirring, until smooth. Add the chicken, chilies, salt and chili powder and cook for 5 or 6 minutes, stirring, until blended and heated through.

2 Fill the taco shells with the mixture and top with lettuce and tomatoes.

CHICKEN WINGS WITH MUSTARD SAUCE

MAKES: 8 servings

16 chicken wings (about 2½ pounds)
1 large lemon, cut into 14 thin slices
1 cup Mustard Sauce (see page 236)

1 Thoroughly wash the chicken wings under running water and cut off the tips and discard.

2 In a microwave-safe dish, arrange the wings and lemon slices in a single layer. Brush ¼ cup of the sauce over the wings; reserve the remaining sauce. Cover tightly with plastic wrap and microwave on high (100 percent) power for 12 to 15 minutes or until the chicken is cooked through. (If the microwave does not have a turntable, rotate the dish a half turn after about 7 minutes.)

3 Lift the chicken wings from the dish and transfer to a platter. Brush with some of the reserved sauce and serve hot, with the remaining sauce on the side.

CRISPY CHICKEN WINGS

MAKES: 8 servings

12 chicken wings (about 2 pounds)
1 large egg
2 teaspoons canola oil
2 teaspoons soy sauce
1 teaspoon sugar
½ teaspoon five-spice powder
salt and pepper
¼ cup sherry
½ cup all-purpose flour
¼ cup cornstarch
½ teaspoon baking soda
vegetable oil

1 Thoroughly wash the chicken wings under running water and cut off the tips and discard. Cut the wings at the joints.

2 In a large bowl, combine the egg, canola oil, soy sauce, sugar and spice powder and season with salt and pepper. Add the chicken wings, toss to coat, cover and chill for at least 1 hour.

3 In a small bowl, combine the sherry, flour, cornstarch and baking soda and whisk well. Pour over the chicken and stir gently.

4 In a large skillet or deep-fat fryer, pour oil to a depth of ½ inch and heat until hot (350 degrees F. in a deep-fat fryer).

5 Fry the chicken wings, 5 or 6 at a time, for about 5 minutes, turning several times, until the nicely browned. Drain on paper towels and fry the remaining wings. Serve hot.

½ cup water
⅓ cup butter or margarine
⅔ cup all-purpose flour
salt
2 large eggs
1 package (8 ounces) cream cheese, softened
¼ cup milk
dash of curry powder
pepper
1½ cups chopped cooked chicken
⅓ cup slivered almonds
2 tablespoons sliced green onion

1 Position the rack in the center of the oven and preheat to 400 degrees F.

2 In a saucepan, combine the water and butter and bring to a boil over medium-high heat. Reduce the heat to low and add the flour and a pinch of salt. Stir vigorously until the mixture forms a ball.

3 Remove from the heat and add the eggs, one at a time, beating after each addition until smooth. Drop the batter by level tablespoons onto an ungreased baking sheet and bake for about 25 minutes or until golden brown. Cool on a wire rack. Reduce the oven temperature to 300 degrees F.

4 In a bowl, combine the cream cheese, milk, and curry powder and season with salt and pepper and whisk until smooth. Add the chicken, almonds and onion and toss until coated.

5 Cut the tops off the puffs and fill with the chicken mixture. Replace the tops and transfer to the baking sheet. Warm the puffs in the oven for about 5 minutes or until warmed through.

CURRIED CHICKEN PUFFS

MAKES: *16 servings*

20 chicken wings (about 3 pounds)
2 tablespoons canola oil
1 can (10 ounces) Franco-American® brown gravy with onions
¼ cup catsup
1½ teaspoons hot-pepper sauce
1 teaspoon brown sugar
½ teaspoon cider vinegar

1 Position the broiler rack 6 inches from the heat and preheat the broiler.

2 Thoroughly wash the chicken wings under running water and cut off the tips and discard. Arrange the wings on a broiling pan and brush with oil.

3 In a small bowl, combine the gravy, catsup, hot-pepper sauce, sugar and vinegar and whisk well.

4 Broil the chicken wings for about 15 minutes, or until cooked through, turning and brushing several times with the sauce. Serve hot.

HOT-AND-SPICY CHICKEN WINGS

MAKES: *10 to 12 servings*

LA BAMBA CHICKEN

MAKES: *18 to 20 servings*

1¼ cup crushed plain tortilla chips
1 package (1.25 ounces) Lawry's®
   taco seasoning mix
18 to 20 chicken legs
salsa for dipping

1 Position the rack in the center of the oven and preheat to 350 degrees F. Lightly grease a 13-by-9 inch baking pan.

2 In a large heavy plastic or paper bag, combine the chips and taco mix. Brush a few legs with water and drop in the bag. Shake to coat and transfer the legs to the baking pan. Continue with the remaining legs. Bake for 25 to 30 minutes, or until golden brown and crispy and chicken is cooked through. Serve with salsa on the side.

LIME-AND-GINGER CHICKEN

MAKES: *6 servings*

1 can (14 ounces) chicken broth
2 tablespoons lime juice
2 tablespoons canola oil
2 tablespoons light soy sauce
1 tablespoon brown sugar
¼ teaspoon ground ginger
¼ teaspoon crushed red pepper
   flakes
2 cloves garlic, minced
2 pounds boneless, skinless chicken
   breasts, cut into 1-inch pieces
2 tablespoons cornstarch

1 In a saucepan, combine the broth, lime juice, oil, soy sauce, sugar, ginger, pepper flakes and garlic and cook over low heat, stirring, until blended. Pour into a 13-by-9-inch baking pan.

2 Thread about 5 pieces of chicken on each of 6 skewers and lay them in the marinade. Cover and chill for about 1 hour.

3 Position the broiler rack about 4 inches from the heat and preheat the broiler.

4 Remove the kabobs from the marinade and set on a rack in a broiling pan. Reserve the marinade.

5 Transfer the marinade to a saucepan, add the cornstarch and bring to a boil over medium heat. Cook, stirring, for 4 or 5 minutes until the sauce thickens.

6 Broil the chicken for 10 to 12 minutes, brushing with the sauce, until cooked through.

7 Heat the remaining sauce over medium-high heat until boiling and serve with the chicken.

COOKING NOTE: **If using wooden skewers, soak them in water for 30 minutes before threading with chicken.**

10 chicken wings (about 1¾ pounds)
¾ cup Bisquick® baking mix
2 tablespoons cornmeal
1 tablespoon chili powder
¼ teaspoon pepper
¼ teaspoon salt
½ cup buttermilk
¼ cup butter or margarine, melted

1 Position the rack in the center of the oven and preheat to 425 degrees F.

2 Thoroughly wash the chicken wings under running water and cut off the tips and discard. Cut the wings at the joints.

3 In a bowl, combine the baking mix, cornmeal, chili powder, pepper and salt. Dip the chicken wings in buttermilk and then coat them with the dry ingredients. Place in an ungreased 13-by-9-by-2-inch baking pan and drizzle with butter. Bake for 35 to 40 minutes or until lightly browned.

MEXICAN CHICKEN WINGS

MAKES: *4 to 6 servings*

¼ cup lime juice
¼ cup canola oil
½ teaspoon crushed red pepper flakes
10 chicken wings (about 1¾ pounds)
½ cup yellow cornmeal
2 tablespoons all-purpose flour
½ teaspoon ground cumin
salt and pepper
2 tablespoons butter or margarine, melted
Chili Dip (see page 32)

1 In a bowl, combine the lime juice, oil and pepper flakes.

2 Thoroughly wash the chicken wings under running water and cut off the tips and discard. Cut the wings at the joints and put in the bowl. Stir to coat with the oil, cover and chill for at least 3 hours. Stir several times during marinating.

3 Position the rack in the center of the oven and preheat to 425 degrees F. Lightly grease a 13-by-9-inch baking pan.

4 In a shallow bowl, combine the cornmeal, flour and cumin and season with salt and pepper. Coat the chicken with the dry ingredients and arrange in the pan. Drizzle with butter and bake for 20 minutes. Turn the chicken and cook for 20 to 25 minutes longer or until cooked through and golden brown. Serve with the dip on the side.

SOUTHERN-STYLE CHICKEN WINGS

MAKES: *4 to 6 servings*

BARBECUED CHICKEN

MAKES: *6 servings*

¾ cup tomato juice
1 small onion, finely chopped
3 tablespoons lemon juice
2 tablespoons butter or margarine
1½ teaspoons Worcestershire sauce
1½ teaspoons paprika
½ teaspoon sugar
salt and pepper
1 2½-pound chicken, cut up

1 Prepare a charcoal or gas grill and position the grilling rack at least 6 inches from the heat source.

2 In a saucepan, combine the tomato juice, onion, lemon juice, butter, Worcestershire sauce, paprika and sugar and cook over medium heat until hot. Season with salt and pepper and continue cooking until almost boiling. Remove from the heat and brush over the chicken pieces.

3 Grill the chicken over medium-hot coals for 20 to 30 minutes, turning often and brushing the chicken with the sauce as it cooks. Serve hot.

BARBECUED CHICKEN, PAKISTANI-STYLE

MAKES: *4 to 6 servings*

1½ teaspoons honey
4 small cloves garlic
fresh ginger, about 1 inch long, peeled and chopped
¼ teaspoon powdered cumin
5 mint leaves
¼ teaspoon cayenne pepper
⅛ teaspoon ground nutmeg
1 pound chicken thighs

1 In the container of a blender, combine the honey, garlic, ginger, cumin, mint, cayenne and nutmeg and process until smooth. Transfer to a small bowl and set aside.

2 Peel the skin from the chicken to the first joint without disconnecting it. Spread a little of the garlic-honey paste on the meat and pull the skin over it. Transfer to a platter, cover and chill for at least 4 hours.

3 Position the rack in the center of the oven and preheat to 375 degrees F.

4 Arrange the chicken on a rack set in a shallow roasting pan and bake for 30 to 35 minutes or until tender. Peel and discard the skin before serving the chicken thighs hot.

BARBECUED CHICKEN WINGS

MAKES: *18 servings*

1 can (8 ounces) jellied cranberry sauce
1½ teaspoons packed light-brown sugar
1 teaspoon prepared mustard
1 teaspoon Worcestershire sauce
18 chicken wings

1 In a saucepan, combine the cranberry sauce, sugar, mustard and Worcestershire sauce and heat, stirring, over low heat until very hot and smooth.

2 Arrange the chicken wings in a shallow glass or ceramic dish and pour the marinade over them. Cover and chill for at least 2 hours.

3 Prepare a charcoal or gas grill and position the grilling rack at least 6 inches from the heat source.

4 Grill the wings for 25 to 35 minutes, brushing with the marinade and turning several times until cooked through.

1 cup plain yogurt
2 tablespoons mayonnaise or Kraft®
  Salad Dressing
2 tablespoons Kraft® crumbled blue
  cheese
½ teaspoon celery seed
1 tablespoon canola oil
1 tablespoon cider vinegar
2 drops hot-pepper sauce
12 chicken legs

1 In a small bowl, combine the yogurt, mayonnaise, blue cheese and celery seed and blend. Cover and chill for at least 1 hour.

2 In a heavy plastic bag, combine the oil, vinegar and pepper sauce. Add the chicken legs and shake until well coated. Chill the chicken in the bag for at least 1 hour.

3 Position the broiler rack so that it is about 6 inches from the heat source and preheat the broiler. Place the legs on the rack and cook for 35 to 40 minutes, turning several times. Serve hot with the sauce.

BROILED DRUMSTICKS
MAKES: *6 servings*

¼ cup plus 2 tablespoons sesame oil
2 slices fresh ginger
1 small leek, diced (white portion
  only)
2 chicken breasts, cut into 1½-inch
  pieces (including bone)
¼ cup plus 2 tablespoons soy sauce
2 tablespoons sherry
2 cups water
1 tablespoon sugar
1 pound fresh chestnuts, shelled,
  boiled, peeled and halved

1 In a large skillet or wok, heat the oil over medium-high heat and stir-fry the ginger and leeks for 3 or 4 minutes until tender. Add the chicken and cook for about 5 minutes or until the chicken changes color.

2 Add the soy sauce, sherry and water, cover, reduce the heat and simmer for about 40 minutes, stirring occasionally, until the chicken is cooked through. Add the sugar and chestnuts, simmer for 15 minutes longer or until heated through. Serve hot.

COOKING NOTE: **To prepare the chestnuts, cut off the outer shell and cook the chestnuts in boiling water for 11 or 12 minutes. Remove the pan from the heat and, one at a time, lift the chestnuts from the water and peel the outer skin with a sharp knife. (Keeping the chestnuts wet facilitates peeling.) Cut the nuts in half once peeled.**

CHESTNUT CHICKEN
MAKES: *4 to 6 servings*

CHICKEN-AND-CHEESE SANDWICHES

MAKES: *6 servings*

½ cup shredded mild Cheddar cheese

½ cup shredded Swiss cheese

1 can (5 ounces) chunk chicken, drained

1 can (4 ounces) chopped green chilies, drained

1 package (3 ounces) cream cheese, at room temperature

6 plain bagels, halved

1 In a bowl, using an electric mixer on low speed, beat the Cheddar and Swiss cheeses, chicken, chilies and cream cheese until as smooth as possible.

2 Spread on the bagel halves. Place 2 or 3 bagel halves on a double thickness of paper towels and microwave on high (100 percent) power for 30 to 40 seconds or until hot. Repeat with the remaining bagels and serve at once.

CHICKEN-CHEESE LOG

MAKES: *10 to 12 servings*

3 packages (8 ounces each) cream cheese

¼ cup Kraft® Real Mayonnaise

2 tablespoons lemon juice

¼ teaspoon ground ginger

4 drops hot-pepper sauce

salt and pepper

2 cups finely diced cooked chicken

1 large hard-cooked egg, chopped

¼ cup sliced green onion

3 green or red bell pepper rings for garnish

1 tablespoon toasted sesame seeds for garnish

3 tablespoons chopped green bell pepper for garnish

3 tablespoons chopped pitted ripe olives for garnish

1 jar (3 ounces) chopped pimientos for garnish

crackers

1 In a large bowl, and using an electric mixer on low speed, beat together the cream cheese, mayonnaise, lemon juice, ginger and hot-pepper sauce. Season with salt and pepper. Add the chicken, egg and onion and stir gently to mix.

2 Shape the mixture into a log about 8 inches long and 2 inches in diameter. Wrap in plastic wrap and chill for 4 hours or until firm.

3 Place the log on a serving platter and lay the pepper rings across the log. Sprinkle the sesame seeds on a quarter of the log, the green peppers on a quarter, the olives on a quarter and the pimientos on another. Serve with crackers.

COOKING NOTE: **The garnish can be varied using any vegetable, nut, or grain that can be finely chopped.**

1 tablespoon butter or margarine
4 small stalks celery, finely chopped
1 small shallot, finely chopped
½ cup diced cooked chicken
1 package (8 ounces) cream cheese,
   at room temperature
1 can (4 ounces) sliced mushrooms,
   drained
4 tubes (8 ounces each) refrigerated
   crescent dinner rolls
melted butter
crushed corn flakes

1 Position the rack in the center of the oven and preheat to 350 degrees F. Lightly grease 2 baking sheets.

2 In a small nonstick skillet, heat the butter over medium heat and sauté the celery and shallot for 3 or 4 minutes or until tender. Transfer to a bowl, add the chicken, cream cheese and mushrooms and stir with until blended.

3 Separate the dough into triangles and spoon about 1 tablespoon of the chicken mixture in the center of the large end of each. Roll up.

4 Pour the butter in a shallow bowl and spread the corn flakes in another shallow bowl. Dip each roll first in the butter and then in the corn flakes and place on the baking sheets. Bake according to the package directions and serve warm.

CHICKEN-FILLED CRESCENTS

MAKES: *40 servings*

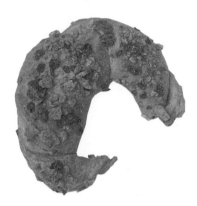

---

1 onion, chopped
⅓ cup chopped celery
2 tablespoons butter or margarine
2 cups diced cooked chicken
1½ cups uncooked instant rice
1½ cups hot water
1 package (8 ounces) mixed dried
   fruit, chopped
2 tablespoons raisins
2 Herb Ox® chicken bouillon cubes
¼ teaspoon crushed dried thyme
¼ teaspoon ground cinnamon
salt and pepper
¼ cup chopped pecans

1 In a 2-quart microwave-safe dish, combine the onion, celery and butter and cover the dish with a paper towel. Microwave on high (100 percent) power for 2 to 3 minutes, or until the onion is soft.

2 Add the chicken, rice, water, fruit, raisins, bouillon, thyme and cinnamon and stir to mix. Cover and microwave on high (100 percent) power for 10 to 12 minutes, or until most of the water has been absorbed. Season to taste with salt and pepper and stir in the nuts.

CHICKEN-FRUIT PILAF

MAKES: *6 servings*

CHICKEN GOLD

MAKES: *About 36 servings*

½ cup cornmeal
1 tablespoon chili powder
2 teaspoons ground cumin
4 boneless, skinless, chicken breasts, cut into 1-inch cubes
3 tablespoons canola oil

1 In a large bowl, combine the cornmeal, chili powder and cumin and stir to mix Add the chicken cubes and toss to coat.

2 In a large skillet, heat the oil over medium-high heat until hot. Add the chicken and cook for 5 or 6 minutes, stirring, until the browned and cooked through. Serve immediately.

COOKING NOTE: **This chicken is good served with a hot spicy sauce.**

CHICKEN LIVER PATE

MAKES: *About 12 servings*

6 ounces chicken livers
2 ounces chicken gizzards
½ cup rendered chicken fat
¼ teaspoon ground nutmeg
1 teaspoon dry mustard
⅛ teaspoon ground cloves
⅛ teaspoon cayenne
2 tablespoons finely minced shallot
crackers or bread

1 In a small saucepan, combine the livers and gizzards and add enough cold water to cover. Bring to a boil over high heat.

Reduce the heat and simmer for 15 to 20 minutes or until tender. Drain.

2 Transfer to food processor and process until smooth and paste-like. Add the chicken fat, nutmeg, mustard, cloves and cayenne and process until smooth. Add the shallots and process just until blended. Spoon into a crock, bowl or small loaf pound and press to compress. Cover and chill for at least 8 hours. Serve with crackers or bread.

CHICKEN MAKAPŪNO

MAKES: *24 servings*

1 cup Wish-Bone® Sweet n Spicy French Dressing
1 tablespoon plus 1½ teaspoons soy sauce
2 teaspoons ground ginger
12 chicken wings
shredded coconut

1 Position the rack in the center of the oven and preheat to 400 degrees F. Line a 13-by-9-inch baking pan with aluminum foil.

2 In bowl, combine the dressing, soy sauce and ginger and whisk well. Remove about ⅓ cup of the sauce, cover and chill until ready to use.

3 Cut the chicken wings at their joints and cut off and discard the tips. Transfer to the bowl and stir to coat. Lift the chicken wings from the sauce, lay on the pan and bake for 25 to 30 minutes or until the chicken is done.

4 Dip the hot chicken wings in the reserved sauce and sprinkle with coconut. Serve immediately.

1 pound boneless, skinless chicken breasts
1 teaspoon coarse sea salt
¼ cup rice wine vinegar
2½ tablespoons soy sauce
2 tablespoons sake (rice wine)
1 tablespoon sugar
1½ teaspoons prepared mustard
assorted thin crackers and wafers

1 Sprinkle the chicken with salt and place the chicken in a steaming basket set over boiling water and steam, covered, for 18 to 20 minutes or until tender. Set aside to cool completely.

2 Cut the chicken into 1½-inch cubes and spear each with a toothpick.

3 In a the top of a double boiler, combine the vinegar, soy sauce, sake, sugar and mustard and heat over boiling water, stirring, until smooth and heated through. Serve the chicken with the sauce and crackers.

CHICKEN NIBBLES

MAKES: *About 24 servings*

1 large egg
⅓ cup water
⅓ cup all-purpose flour
2 teaspoons sesame seeds
4 boneless, skinless chicken breast halves, cut into 1-inch cubes
vegetable oil
1 red onion, sliced into rings for garnish
soy sauce for dipping

1 In a large bowl, combine the egg and water and whisk until foamy. Add the flour and sesame seeds and whisk to make a batter. Add the chicken cubes and stir gently to coat.

2 In a deep skillet or saucepan, pour oil to a depth of 3 inches and heat until very hot. Lift the chicken from the batter and let any excess batter drip back into the bowl. Cook the chicken, a few pieces at a time, for about 4 minutes, turning until golden brown on all sides. Serve garnished with the onions and with soy sauce for dipping.

COOKING NOTE: **Serve with your choice of dipping sauce rather than soy sauce if you desire.**

CHICKEN NUGGETS

MAKES: *About 8 servings*

1 package (8 ounces) cream cheese, at room temperature
2 tablespoons finely chopped pecans
12 slices cooked chicken
1 can (8 ounces) sliced peaches, drained

1 In a small bowl, combine the cream cheese and pecans and mix to blend.

2 Lay 9 slices of chicken on a baking tray and spread with the cheese mixture. Stack to make 3 stacks and top with the remaining slices of chicken. Wrap in plastic wrap and chill for at least 2 hours or until the cheese filling is firm.

3 Cut each stack into wedges and secure a peach slice on top of each wedge with a toothpick. Serve chilled.

COOKING NOTE: **In place of the peaches, garnish the stacks with another sliced fruit or with pickles, green peppers, pimientos or olives.**

CHICKEN STACKS

MAKES: *About 10 servings*

CHICKEN PIZZA

MAKES: *About 8 servings*

1 package (8 ounces) refrigerated crescent dinner rolls
¼ cup canola oil
4 boneless, skinless chicken breasts, cut into 1-inch cubes
1 large onion, sliced into rings
1 large green bell pepper, sliced into rings
½ pound fresh mushrooms, sliced
½ cup pitted sliced ripe olives
1 can (10½ ounces) pizza sauce with cheese
¼ cup grated Parmesan or romano cheese
1 teaspoon garlic salt
1 teaspoon dried oregano
2 cups shredded mozzarella or provolone cheese

1 Position the rack in the center of the oven and preheat to 425 degrees F. Lightly grease a 12-inch pizza pan.

2 Separate the rolls into 8 triangles. Press the triangles into the pizza pan, smoothing the edges together to seal and make an unbroken shell.

3 In a large, deep skillet, heat the oil over medium-high heat until hot and cook the chicken, onion, pepper, mushrooms and olives, stirring, for about 5 minutes or until the chicken is cooked through.

4 Spread the sauce over the dough and spoon the chicken mixture evenly over the sauce. Sprinkle with the garlic salt, oregano and Parmesan. Top with the mozzarella and bake for 18 to 20 minutes or until the crust is golden brown and the cheese melts.

CHICKEN PUFFS

MAKES: *45 to 50 servings*

PUFFS
1 cup water
½ cup butter or margarine
⅛ teaspoon salt
1 cup all-purpose flour, sifted
4 large eggs

FILLING
2 tablespoons butter or margarine
¼ cup finely chopped green bell pepper
¼ cup finely chopped onion
1 clove garlic, minced
1 teaspoon curry powder
1 can (10 ounces) condensed cream of mushroom soup
1½ cups finely chopped cooked chicken
⅓ cup chopped water chestnuts
2 tablespoons chopped chutney

1 Position the rack in the center of the oven and preheat to 400 degrees F.

2 To make the puffs, in a saucepan, combine the water, butter and salt and cook over high heat until boiling. Add the flour all at once and stir vigor-ously until the mixture forms a ball and pulls away from the sides of the pan. Remove from the heat and add the eggs, 1 at a time, stirring until smooth after each addition. Drop by teaspoon-fuls onto an ungreased baking sheet and bake for 25 to 30 min-utes, or until puffed and golden brown. Cool on wire racks. Do not turn off the oven.

3 To prepare the filling, in a small saucepan, melt the butter over medium heat. Add the pep-per, onion and garlic and cook for about 5 minutes until the veg-etables are just tender. Stir in the curry powder and remove from the heat. Add the soup, chicken, water chestnuts and chutney and mix well.

4 Cut the puffs in half and fill the bottom of each with filling. Replace the tops and return to the baking sheets. Bake for 8 to 10 minutes or until heated through.

15 chicken wings (about 2½ pounds)
salt and pepper
2 tablespoons peanut or olive oil
1 small shallot, minced
1 can (8 ounces) crushed pineapple
  with juice
⅔ cup plum jam
¼ cup port wine
1 tablespoon soy sauce
1½ teaspoon lemon juice
1½ teaspoons Dijon mustard

1 Thoroughly wash the chicken wings under running water and cut off the tips and discard. Cut the wings at the joints. Season lightly with salt and pepper.

2 In a wok or heavy skillet, heat the oil over high heat until very hot and stir-fry the chicken wings for 18 to 25 minutes or until golden brown.

3 Drain the pan drippings, add the shallots and stir-fry for about 5 minutes until tender. Add the pineapple and its juice, jam, port, soy sauce, lemon juice and mustard, bring to a boil and cook for about 5 minutes, or until the sauce reduces by about half and coats the chicken with a pleasing glaze. Serve warm.

CHICKEN WINGS IN PLUM SAUCE

MAKES: *15 servings*

---

1 package (3 ounces) cream cheese,
  at room temperature
2 tablespoons mayonnaise or Kraft®
  Salad Dressing
1 cup ground cooked chicken
1 cup finely ground almonds
1 tablespoon chopped chutney
1 tablespoon curry powder
½ cup shredded coconut

1 In a large bowl, using an electric mixer on medium speed, blend together the cream cheese and mayonnaise. Add the chicken, almonds, chutney and curry powder and mix well. Pinch off small pieces and shape into balls about the size of walnuts.

2 Spread the coconut in a shallow bowl and roll each ball in the coconut to coat. Transfer to a tray or platter and chill for at least 1 hour before serving.

COCONUT CHICKEN BALLS

MAKES: *36 to 40 servings*

COLD CHICKEN LIVERS WITH GIBLETS

MAKES: *6 to 8 serving*

1 pound fresh chicken livers
1 pound fresh chicken giblets
6 slices fresh ginger
½ leek, diced
2 tablespoons sugar
2 whole star anise
1 teaspoon pepper
1 cup soy sauce
½ cup sherry or white port wine

1 Thoroughly wash the livers and giblets and transfer to a saucepan. Add enough cold water to cover and bring to a boil over high heat. Remove from the heat, drain and discard the water.

2 Add the ginger, leek, sugar, star anise, pepper, soy sauce and wine and stir gently. Bring to a boil and cook for no longer than 10 minutes until the livers are cooked through. Lift the livers from the pan and set aside to cool.

3 Continue to boil the giblets for 25 to 40 minutes longer, or until cooked through. Remove from the heat and lift the giblets from the pan to cool. When cool, slice the livers and giblets. Strain the pan juices and serve with the giblets and livers.

CORNMEAL-COATED CHICKEN WINGS

MAKES: *20 servings*

¼ cup lime juice
¼ cup vegetable oil
½ teaspoon crushed red pepper flakes
10 chicken wings (about 1¾ pounds)
2 tablespoons butter or margarine
½ cup yellow cornmeal
2 tablespoons all-purpose flour
½ teaspoon ground cumin
⅛ teaspoon pepper

1 In a small bowl, combine the lime juice, oil and pepper flakes and mix well.

2 Thoroughly wash the chicken wings under running water and cut off the tips and discard. Cut the wings at the joints. Transfer to a bowl and pour the oil mixture over the wings. Stir gently to coat, cover and chill for at least 3 hours.

3 Position the rack in the center of the oven and preheat to 425 degrees F.

4 In a 13-by-9-inch baking pan, melt the butter in the oven. Tilt the pan to coat the bottom of the pan.

5 In a heavy-duty plastic bag, combine the cornmeal, flour, cumin and pepper. Lift the chicken from the marinade and drop into the bag, shaking to coat.

6 Lay the chicken in the pan and bake for 40 to 50 minutes, turning the chicken occasionally, until golden brown and thoroughly cooked.

1 pound chicken livers, washed, trimmed and cut into thirds
½ cup all-purpose flour
salt and pepper
½ cup butter or margarine

1 In a heavy-duty plastic bag, combine the livers, flour and salt and pepper and shake to mix.

2 In a large skillet, heat the butter over medium heat. Lift the livers from the plastic bag, shake off excess flour and sauté the for 3 to 5 minutes, or until cooked through. Serve hot.

COOKING NOTE: **Serve this with a sweet-and-sour dipping sauce, if you desire.**

CRISP CHICKEN LIVERS

MAKES: *25 to 30 servings*

---

1 cup red wine vinegar
4 small cloves garlic
½ teaspoon crushed black peppercorns
skin from 4 chickens
vegetable oil
salt

1 In the container of a blender, combine the vinegar, garlic and peppercorns and process on low speed until the garlic is puréed. Transfer to a bowl and add the skins. Stir gently to coat, cover and chill for at least 8 hours.

2 Lift the skins from the marinade and pat dry with paper towels.

3 In a large skillet or wok, pour oil to a depth of ¼ inch and heat over medium-high heat until hot. In batches, cook the skins for about 5 minutes until crisp. Lift from the oil and drain on paper towels. Sprinkle with salt and serve hot.

COOKING NOTE: **Cut the skin from the chicken in good sized strips using a sharp knife. Do not worry if the chicken skins are of varying sizes. Use the skinned chickens in other recipes. They can be frozen, well wrapped, for up to 1 month.**

CRISP CHICKEN SKINS

MAKES: *12 servings*

EMPANADILLOS DE POLLO

MAKES: *32 servings*

1½ cups finely chopped cooked chicken
¼ cup Wish-Bone® Russian Dressing
¼ cup chopped toasted hazelnuts or almonds
¼ teaspoon crushed red pepper flakes
2 packages (8 ounces each) refrigerated crescent dinner rolls

1 Position the rack in the center of the oven and preheat 375 degrees F.

2 In small bowl, combine the chicken, dressing, hazelnuts and pepper flakes and stir well.

3 Separate the dough into triangles and lay on a work surface. Cut each triangle in half and use your hand to flatten slightly. Top each triangle with about ½ tablespoon of the chicken mixture and fold the dough around the filling, sealing the edges securely. Transfer to ungreased baking sheets and bake for 12 to 15 minutes, or until golden brown.

GRILLED CHICKEN SANDWICHES

MAKES: *4 sandwiches*

½ cup dry white wine
2 tablespoons finely chopped parsley
1 teaspoon minced white onion
1 teaspoon fresh chopped thyme
4 boneless, skinless chicken breast halves
3 tablespoons mayonnaise or Kraft® Salad Dressing
1 teaspoon prepared mustard
8 slices white or whole-wheat sandwich bread
lettuce
1 large tomato, thinly sliced

1 Prepare a charcoal or gas grill and position the grilling rack about 6 inches from the heat.

2 In a small bowl, combine the wine, 1 tablespoon of parsley, onion and ½ teaspoon thyme and stir to mix.

3 Grill the chicken for about 15 minutes, brushing several times with the wine sauce. Turn the chicken and grill for about 10 minutes longer, brushing with the sauce several times, until cooked through. Set aside.

4 In a small bowl, combine the mayonnaise, mustard, remaining parsley and remaining thyme and mix well. Spread on 4 slices of the bread and top each with lettuce, a chicken breast half and 2 slices of tomato. Top with the remaining bread and cut the sandwiches in half on the diagonal to serve.

HUEVOS A LA ESPAÑOLA

MAKES: *About 25 servings*

¼ cup Wish-Bone® Italian Dressing
1 can (16 ounces) whole tomatoes, drained and chopped
½ cup finely chopped green bell pepper
½ cup finely chopped Bermuda onion
8 large eggs
2 tablespoons finely chopped cilantro (Chinese parsley)
¼ pound chorizo or pepperoni, cut into ¼-inch-thick slices
salsa

1 Position the rack in the center of the oven and preheat to 400 degrees F. Lightly grease a jelly roll pan.

2 In a bowl, combine 2 tablespoons of the dressing, tomatoes, pepper and onion and spread evenly in the pan. Bake for 15 minutes and immediately remove from the oven.

3 In the same bowl, using an electric mixer on high speed, beat the eggs until thick and light colored. Add the remaining dressing and cilantro. Spread over the ingredients in the pan and scatter the sausage over the top. Bake for 8 to 10 minutes or until firmly set. Cut into 2-inch squares and serve with salsa.

3 tablespoons vegetable shortening
3 tablespoons butter or margarine
⅓ cup all-purpose flour
1 teaspoon ground ginger
salt and pepper
3 pounds chicken legs with thighs
⅓ cup honey
⅓ cup chili sauce
⅓ cup soy sauce

1 Position the rack in the center of the oven and preheat to 425 degrees F.

2 In a 13-by-9-inch baking pan, melt the butter in the oven. Tilt the pan to coat the bottom of the pan.

3 In a heavy-duty plastic bag, combine the flour and ½ teaspoon of the ginger and season with salt and pepper. Add the chicken and toss to coat. Arrange the chicken in the pan and bake for 40 to 45 minutes, turning occasionally. Lift the chicken from the pan and set aside.

4 Drain the fat from the pan and line it with aluminum foil. Return the chicken to the pan.

5 In a bowl, combine the honey, chili sauce, soy sauce and remaining ½ teaspoon of ginger and stir. Drizzle over the chicken and bake for about 15 minutes longer, basting, until cooked through and golden brown. Serve immediately.

HONEY-GINGERED CHICKEN

MAKES: *6 servings*

---

2 tubes (8 ounces) refrigerated crescent dinner rolls
4 cups chopped cooked chicken
2 cups chopped cooked fresh broccoli
1½ cups shredded Swiss cheese
¼ cup chopped shallot
2 tablespoons Dijon mustard
salt and pepper
1 large egg, lightly beaten

1 Position the rack in the center of the oven and preheat to 375 degrees F.

2 Separate the dough from 1 can of dinner rolls to make 2 long rectangles. Press perforations with your fingertips to seal. Transfer the rectangles to a jelly-roll pan to cover the pan as a single rectangle. Press along the seams to seal and work the dough about ¼ inch up the sides of the pan. Bake for 6 to 8 minutes, or until lightly browned.

3 In a bowl, combine the chicken, broccoli, cheese, shallot and mustard and mix well. Season with salt and pepper and spread on the pastry crust.

4 Separate the dough from the remaining can of dinner rolls to make 2 long triangles. Cut each lengthwise into 5 strips. Lay 6 strips lengthwise over the chicken.

5 Cut the remaining 4 strips in half crosswise and lay them over the 6 strips to make a criss-cross pattern. Brush the pastry strips with the egg and bake for 18 to 24 minutes, or until golden brown. Cut into rectangles to serve

OPEN-FACE CHICKEN PIE

MAKES: *About 8 servings*

PAPER-WRAPPED FRIED CHICKEN

MAKES: *30 servings*

½ pound chicken fillets, cut into 60 pieces
30 thin slices fresh ginger
30 snow peas
30 thin slices shallot
2 tablespoons sherry or white port wine
2 tablespoons soy sauce
¼ cup sesame oil
peanut oil

1 In a bowl, combine the chicken, ginger, snow peas, shallot, sherry and soy sauce. Toss thoroughly.

2 Cut out thirty 6-inch squares of parchment paper and rub a little sesame oil in the center of each.

Top with 2 pieces of chicken, 1 slice of ginger, 1 snow pea and 1 slice of shallot. Fold the paper up and over the ingredients to create a triangle. Fold the sides in and tuck the top down into the side folds.

3 In a large skillet, pour peanut oil to a depth of 1 inch and heat over high heat until very hot. Fry the wrapped chicken, flap side down, for about 6 to 8 minutes, or until the paper is light brown. Remove from the oil, cool briefly and unwrap the paper. Serve the chicken hot.

SESAME CHICKEN BITES

MAKES: *24 servings*

⅓ cup dry sherry or white port wine
⅓ cup sesame oil
¼ cup soy sauce
½ teaspoon ground ginger
¼ teaspoon garlic powder
4 boneless, skinless chicken breast halves, each cut into 6 pieces (24 pieces total)
⅓ cup toasted sesame seeds

1 In a bowl, combine the sherry, oil, soy sauce, ginger and garlic powder and whisk well. Add the chicken, toss, cover and chill for at least 4 hours.

2 Position the broiler rack about 6 inches from the heat source and preheat the broiler.

3 Shake the excess marinade from the chicken and broil for 6 to 8 minutes on each side. Sprinkle liberally with sesame seeds and serve with toothpicks.

20 chicken wings (about 3 pounds)
¼ cup plus 2 tablespoons butter or
   margarine, melted
1½ cups Bisquick® Baking Mix
½ cup sesame seeds
2 teaspoons paprika
1½ teaspoons dry mustard
2 large eggs
2 tablespoons milk

1 Position the rack in the center of the oven and preheat to 425 degrees F. Spread a 13-by-9-inch baking pan with 1 tablespoon of the butter.

2 Cut the wings at the joints and cut and discard the tips. Toss the chicken wings with 2 tablespoons of butter.

3 In a bowl, combine the Bisquick, sesame seeds, paprika and mustard and stir.

4 In a small bowl, whisk the eggs and milk until foamy. Dip the chicken wings in the egg mixture and roll in the sesame seed mixture. Lay the wings on the pan and drizzle with the remaining ¼ cup of butter. Bake for 35 to 40 minutes, or until crisp and brown and cooked through.

Sesame Chicken Wings

MAKES: *40 servings*

2½ teaspoons cornmeal
2¼ cups diced cooked chicken
1 cup shredded Cheddar cheese
½ cup sour cream, plus more for
   serving
½ cup sliced pitted ripe olives
½ cup chopped Bermuda onion
1 can (4 ounces) Old El Paso®
   chopped green chilies, drained
2 tubes (8 ounces) refrigerated
   crescent dinner rolls
1 large egg white
1 tablespoon water
1 jar (12 ounces) green chile salsa

1 Position the rack in the center of the oven and preheat to 375 degrees F. Lightly grease a baking sheet and dust with about 1½ teaspoons of cornmeal.

2 In a large bowl, combine the chicken, cheese, sour cream, olives, onion and chilies.

3 Separate the dough into 8 rectangles and press along the perforations to seal. Spoon about ½ cup of the chicken mixture on each rectangle, spreading to leave a 1-inch border. Starting at the longest side, roll into 8 logs, pinching the ends to seal. Place seam-side down on the baking sheet.

4 In a small bowl, whisk together the egg white and water and brush over each log. Sprinkle with the remaining cornmeal. Bake for 20 to 25 minutes, or until golden brown. Serve with the salsa spooned over the logs and sour cream on the side.

South Of The Border Roll-Ups

MAKES: *8 servings*

SWEET-AND-SOUR CHICKEN WINGS

MAKES: *12 servings*

1 to 2 tablespoons canola oil
12 chicken wings (about 1¾ pounds)
½ cup cider vinegar
½ cup water
½ cup catsup
½ cup sugar
1 teaspoon soy sauce
salt
1 tablespoon cornstarch mixed with
    2 tablespoons water

1 In a heavy skillet, heat the oil over medium-high heat and cook the chicken wings for 15 to 20 minutes, turning, until golden brown and cooked through. (Use as little oil as possible.) Drain on paper towels.

2 In a small saucepan, combine the vinegar, water, catsup, sugar, soy sauce and salt to taste and cook over medium heat, stirring, until hot. Stir the cornstarch mixture into the sauce and stir until thickened. Serve with the chicken wings.

BACON-TURKEY BURGERS

MAKES: *4 servings*

4 strips bacon, cut into ½-inch
    pieces
½ cup chopped green bell pepper
1 pound ground turkey
¼ teaspoon onion powder
⅛ teaspoon cayenne
½ teaspoon Worcestershire sauce
¼ cup shredded mozzarella cheese
¼ cup shredded mild Cheddar
    cheese
4 Kaiser sandwich buns

1 Position the broiling pan about 6 inches from the heat source and preheat the broiler.

2 In a skillet, cook the bacon over medium-high heat until crisp. Drain, leaving 1 tablespoon of the drippings in the pan. Add the pepper and cook over medium heat for about 5 minutes until tender.

3 In a bowl, combine the turkey, onion powder, cayenne and Worcestershire sauce. Divide into 4 portions and form each into a ball. Flatten the balls to make ½-inch-thick patties.

4 Broil for 8 to 10 minutes, turning once, until cooked through. Top each patty with bacon and peppers and sprinkle with the cheeses. Broil for 1 or 2 minutes longer, or until the cheese melts. Serve on Kaiser buns.

TURKEY-CHEESE BALLS

MAKES: *12 servings*

1 cup finely ground smoked turkey
1 package (8 ounces) cream cheese
3 tablespoons Miracle Whip®
    Dressing
½ cup chopped pecans or walnuts
crackers or cocktail bread

1 In a bowl, combine the turkey, cream cheese and Miracle Whip and mix well. Cover and chill for at least 2 hours or until firm.

2 Divide in half and form each portion into a ball.

3 Spread the pecans in a shallow dish and roll the balls in the nuts to coat. Wrap each in wax paper and chill for at least 1 hour. Serve with crackers or bread.

TURKEY PASTRY
MAKES: *8 servings*

¼ cup grated Parmesan cheese
1 package (14 ounces) pie crust mix
¼ cup plus 2 tablespoons butter or margarine, at room temperature
½ cup minced onion
½ cup coarsely chopped celery
½ cup chopped pecans
3 cups coarsely chopped, cooked turkey
1½ teaspoons caraway seeds
¼ teaspoon salt
¼ pound fresh mushrooms, chopped
1 cup Cheese Whiz® Spread
¼ cup sliced pimientos

1 In a bowl, combine the cheese and pie crust mix and stir. Prepare the mix according to the package directions for 1 single crust. Form into a ball, wrap in wax paper and chill for about 2 hours.

2 Position the rack in the center of the oven and preheat to 425 degrees F. Lightly grease a baking sheet.

3 In a skillet, heat ¼ cup of butter over medium heat and sauté the onions, celery and pecans for 8 to 10 minutes, or until golden brown. Add the turkey, caraway seeds and salt. Mix well and remove from the heat. Set aside to cool slightly.

4 On a lightly floured work surface, roll the pastry into a 13-inch square and transfer to the baking sheet. Spoon the filling on the pastry so that it covers only the center of the pastry. Gather the corners of the dough over the filling and pinch together. Seal and pinch all loose edges to make a closed package. Bake for 25 to 30 minutes, or until golden brown.

5 In a small saucepan, heat the remaining 2 tablespoons of butter over medium heat and sauté the mushrooms for about 5 minutes or until soft. Add the cheese spread and pimientos and stir until blended.

6 Serve the pastry packet with the mushroom-cheese sauce spooned over the top.

TURKEY WITH FRESH MELON
MAKES: *About 4 servings*

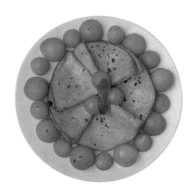

1 pound turkey, thinly sliced
1 large cantaloupe
½ honeydew melon
1 head Boston or red leaf lettuce
12 cherry tomatoes
Tarragon Dressing (see page 66)
mint leaves for garnish

1 Tightly roll the turkey slices and put them in a shallow pan small enough to hold them snugly. Cover and chill for about 2 hours.

2 Quarter the cantaloupe and discard the seeds (do not peel). Peel the honeydew melon, discard the seeds and slice into thin slices. Arrange the melon on a platter, cover and chill for about 2 hours.

3 Spread the lettuce on a platter and beginning in the center of the platter, arrange the turkey rolls in a sunburst. Continue by arranging the cantaloupe, melon and tomatoes artfully on the platter. Drizzle the dressing over the turkey and garnish with mint leaves.

Chapter 8

FISH AND SEAFOOD IN A HURRY

Snacks made of food from the sea are exquisite creations made with lightly cooked or impeccably fresh raw seafood and preferred by the most discriminating palates. These recipes are no exception, although many are made with canned products, which makes them easier and more efficient to prepare. Fresh fish and seafood of course must be well refrigerated, and all preparations should be kept chilled until serving or served immediately after cooking.

LOBSTER-AND-SHRIMP TROPICAL SALAD

MAKES: *4 servings*

1 package (10 ounces) frozen lobster tail, thawed
8 large raw shrimp, in the shell
1 fresh sliced lemon
2 quarts water
2 fresh ripe papayas
2 green onions, minced
2 tablespoons olive oil
1 tablespoon lime juice
salt and pepper
1 large avocado, peeled, pitted and sliced in ¼ inch slices
1 head Romaine lettuce
1 cup Banana Dressing (see page 187)

1 In a large saucepan, combine the lobster, shrimp, lemon and water, bring to a boil over medium heat and cook for about 5 minutes until the shrimp turn pink. Remove the shrimp, rinse under cold running water and peel the shells. Set the shrimp aside.

2 Continue cooking the lobster until cooked through, according to the package directions. Drain and immerse in cold water until cool enough to handle. Remove the lobster meat from the shell and cut into ¾-inch-thick pieces. Add to the shrimp.

3 Peel the papaya, cut in half, remove the seeds and dice the meat into ¾-inch cubes. Add the papaya and onions to the shrimp and lobster.

4 In a small cup, combine the oil and lime juice and season with salt and pepper. Drizzle over the seafood, toss, cover and chill for at least 4 hours.

5 Toss with the avocado and serve piled on top of the lettuce with the dressing on the side.

OYSTER CREOLE

MAKES: *4 servings*

3 tablespoons butter or margarine
½ cup minced celery
½ cup minced red or green bell pepper
1 pint shucked oysters
1 cup chili sauce
pinch of cayenne
dash of Worcestershire sauce
dash of hot red-pepper sauce
3 tablespoons oyster cracker crumbs
½ teaspoon fresh tarragon leaves
grated lemon zest for garnish

1 Position the rack in the center of the oven and preheat to 375 degrees F. Lightly butter a 9-inch-square baking dish.

2 In a skillet, melt 1 tablespoon of the butter over medium heat and sauté the celery and peppers for about 5 minutes or until they begin to soften. Remove the vegetables from the skillet, add the oysters and cook for 2 or 3 minutes or until the edges curl. Return the vegetables to the pan and stir just to mix. Transfer to the baking dish.

4 In a small bowl, combine the chili sauce, cayenne, Worcestershire sauce and pepper sauce and stir to mix. Spoon over the oysters and sprinkle them with cracker crumbs and tarragon. Dot with the remaining butter and bake for 20 to 25 minutes, or until heated through. Serve garnished with lemon zest and toothpicks on the side.

1 can (15 ounces) salmon, drained and flaked
4 green onions, thinly sliced
1 egg, lightly beaten
½ cup fresh white bread crumbs
white pepper
12 French-Style Crêpes (recipe follows)
¾ cup Tarragon Dressing (see page 66)
2 cups shredded Monterey Jack or Colby cheese
2 tablespoons finely chopped pitted ripe olives

1 Position the rack in the center of the oven and preheat to 400 degrees F. Lightly grease a 13-by-9-inch baking dish.

2 In a bowl, combine the salmon, onions, egg and bread crumbs and season with pepper. Spoon about 2 tablespoons of the mixture along 1 side of each crêpe, fold the nearest edge over the filling and roll into a cylinder. Transfer to the baking dish and continue filling the crêpes. Arrange them so that they fit snugly in the dish.

3 Pour the dressing over the crêpes and sprinkle with cheese and olives. Bake for 20 to 25 minutes or until lightly browned. Serve slightly cooled.

SALMON CRÊPES WITH TARRAGON DRESSING

MAKES: *8 servings*

FRENCH-STYLE CRÊPES

MAKES: *7 to 12 crepes*

1 cup all-purpose flour
¾ cup water
⅔ cup milk
3 large eggs
2 tablespoons canola oil
¼ teaspoon salt
butter

1 In the container of a blender, combine the flour, water, milk, eggs, oil and salt and process for 3 or 4 seconds until smooth. Transfer to a bowl, cover and chill for at least 1 hour. Stir before using.

2 In a crêpe pan or skillet, melt about 2 teaspoons of butter over medium-low heat. Pour 3 or 4 tablespoons of batter into the pan and tilt the pan so that the batter flows from the center to the sides to create a large circle. As soon as the surface appears dry, turn the crêpe over and cook for 1 or 2 minutes longer until lightly browned on the bottom. Transfer to a plate and continue making crêpes, using the remaining batter and more butter, as needed. Stack the crêpes with pieces of wax paper between them. Use warm or at room temperature.

COOKING NOTE: **The crêpes can be made ahead of time, covered and stored in the refrigerator for up to 24 hours. Let them reach room temperature before using.**

PEEK-A-BOO FISH

MAKES: *4 servings*

2 pounds halibut fillets
½ cup all-purpose flour
½ teaspoon salt
½ teaspoon cumin
½ cup beer or ale
1 large egg, beaten
canola oil
4 pita pockets
1 cucumber, very thinly sliced
1 chopped green onion (scallion),
　green portions only
1 tomato, chopped
½ cup sour cream or plain yogurt
1 cup crumbled feta cheese
salt and pepper

1 Cut the fish into 2-inch-wide strips and the cut the strips into 2-inch-long pieces.

2 In a bowl, combine the flour, salt, cumin, beer and egg and whisk well. Dip the fish in the batter, turning until well coated.

3 In a deep skillet, pour the oil to a depth of about 3 inches and heat over medium-high heat until hot. Fry the fish, a few pieces at a time, for 3 or 4 minutes, turning, until golden brown. Drain on a paper towels and cover to keep warm while frying the rest of the fish.

4 Cut the top third off the pita pockets and fill each with fish, cucumber, onions and tomatoes. Top with yogurt and cheese and sprinkle with salt and pepper.

COOKING NOTE: **You may substitute milk for the beer or ale. If using beer or ale, it can be flat, but does not have to be.**

SALMON CROQUETTES

MAKES: *About 24 servings*

canola oil
1 can (15 ounces) salmon
1 large egg
¼ cup all-purpose flour
¼ cup dried potato flakes
1 small white onion, grated
pepper
1 teaspoon baking powder
lemon wedges for garnish
small cherry tomatoes for garnish

1 In a large skillet or deep-fat fryer, pour oil to a depth of about 3 inches and heat over medium-high heat until hot. (In a deep-fat fryer, heat to 375 degrees F.)

2 Drain the salmon, reserving ¼ cup of the liquid. Remove any skin or bones and transfer the salmon to a bowl. Flake the salmon with a fork and then add the egg and blend well. Add the flour, potato flakes and onions and season with pepper.

3 In a small bowl or cup, whisk the baking powder with the reserved salmon liquid and add this to the salmon mixture, stirring well.

4 Drop spoonfuls of the mixture into the hot oil and cook for 4 to 6 minutes, or until golden brown. Drain on paper towels and cover to keep warm while cooking the rest of the croquettes. Serve hot, garnished with lemon wedges and tomatoes.

1 can (15 ounces) salmon, drained, cleaned, boned and flaked
4 green onions, sliced
one 9-inch prebaked pastry shell
3 large eggs
1½ cups light cream
2 tablespoons crushed fresh dill
salt and pepper

1 Position the rack in the center of the oven and preheat to 375 degrees F.

2 In a bowl, combine the salmon and onions and mix well. Spread over the pastry shell and set aside.

3 In the same bowl, using an electric mixer on high speed, beat the eggs until thick and light colored. Add the cream and mix well. Add the dill and season with salt and pepper and mix just to blend. Pour over the salmon and bake for 30 to 35 minutes, or until set and a toothpick inserted in the center comes out clean. Cool slightly on a wire rack and serve cut into wedges.

SALMON QUICHE

MAKES: *6 to 8 servings*

---

2 tablespoons butter or margarine
2 large tomatoes, peeled and sliced (slice 1 very thin; the other into 8 slices)
¼ teaspoon crumbled fresh oregano leaves
salt and pepper
5 large eggs
2 tablespoons water
1 can (3 ounces) sardines, drained
½ cup shredded Tillamook or Wisconsin brick cheese
4 English muffins, halved and toasted
green bell pepper, cut into matchsticks, for garnish

1 In a large skillet, melt the butter over a medium heat and arrange the thickest slices of tomato in the pan (reserve at least 8 slices for garnish). Sprinkle with oregano and salt and pepper and cook gently for 1 or 2 minutes.

2 In a bowl, using an electric mixer on high speed, beat the eggs until thick and light colored. Beat in the water and pour over the tomatoes in the skillet. Cover and cook over medium-low heat for about 3 minutes, until the eggs begin to set around the edges. Lay the sardines over the eggs, sprinkle with cheese and cook, covered, for about 4 minutes longer until the eggs are firm. Remove from the heat.

3 Cut the omelet into 8 squares and put 1 on each English muffin half. Garnish with peppers and the remaining thin slices of tomato.

SARDINE-TOMATO OMELET

MAKES: *8 servings*

---

1 pound cooked medium, shelled shrimp
2 cans (14 ounces each) water-packed artichoke hearts, drained and halved
¾ cup Wish-Bone® Italian Dressing
¼ cup finely chopped cilantro

1 In a bowl, combine the shrimp, artichoke hearts, dressing and cilantro and stir gently to mix. Cover and chill for at least 8 hours, stirring occasionally.

2 Thread the shrimp and artichokes, alternating each, onto 4-inch toothpicks.

BAÑDERILLAS

MAKES: *About 20 servings*

SCALLOPS IN WHITE WINE SAUCE

MAKES: *4 servings*

2 tablespoons butter
2 tablespoons all-purpose flour
1 bottle (8 ounces) clam juice
¾ cup white wine
salt and pepper
3 tablespoons fresh chopped dill
1 tablespoon lemon juice
1 pound scallops
6 ounces frozen baby shrimp
½ cup whipping cream

1 In a large saucepan, melt the butter over medium-low heat. Add the flour and stir to mix. Raise the heat and cook, stirring constantly, until the mixture thickens a little. Stir in the clam juice and wine. Adjust the seasoning. Raise the heat to medium and whisk gently until the mixture starts to boil. Continue to cook for about 3 minutes and then reduce the heat to low and cook for 5 minutes longer, or until quite thick.

2 Add the dill, lemon juice, scallops and shrimp and toss gently. Raise the heat and bring to a boil. Reduce the heat and simmer for about 3 minutes or until heated through. Remove from the heat and add the cream, stirring gently to mix. Serve in small bowls or ramekins.

SHRIMP COCKTAIL

MAKES: *4 servings*

1 pound cooked shrimp, shelled and deveined
½ cup sour cream or plain yogurt
1 cup mayonnaise
½ tablespoon lemon juice
2 tablespoons chili sauce
pinch of sugar
pinch of paprika
salt and pepper
1 red bell pepper, finely chopped
pumpernickel cocktail bread

1 Put the shrimp in a glass or ceramic bowl, cover and chill for at least 2 hours.

2 In the container of a blender, combine the sour cream, mayonnaise, lemon juice, chili sauce, sugar and paprika and process on low until smooth. Season with salt and pepper. Add half of the pepper and process just until blended. Transfer to a small bowl, cover and chill for at least 2 hours.

3 Set the bowl of shrimp in a larger bowl filled with shaved ice and pour the sauce over the shrimp. Garnish with the remaining pepper and serve with the bread.

1 cup dry bread crumbs
2 cans (7 ounces each) salmon, drained and flaked
1 tablespoon lemon juice
2 tablespoons grated onion
½ cup mashed unseasoned potatoes
1 large egg, lightly beaten
salt and pepper
vegetable oil for frying

1 In a large bowl, combine the bread crumbs, salmon, lemon juice, onions, potatoes and egg and blend well. Season to taste with salt and pepper. Cover and chill for at least 1 hour.

2 In a deep skillet or deep-fat fryer, pour oil to a depth of about 2 inches and heat until hot (375 degrees F. in a deep-fat fryer).

3 On a lightly floured work surface, pat the salmon mixture so that it is about ½ inch thick. Using a doughnut or round 2- to 3-inch cookie cutter, cut as many rounds as you can. Gather the scraps and pat until flattened. Continue cutting out doughnuts or rounds until all the mixture is used.

4 Carefully drop the doughnuts into the hot oil and cook for 2 to 3 minutes, turning once or twice until golden brown. Drain on paper towels and serve hot.

ALASKA SALMON DOUGHNUTS

MAKES: *12 to 15 doughnuts*

---

6 chopped hard-cooked eggs
1 tablespoon minced onion
½ cup minced canned clams, drained
¼ cup mayonnaise or Kraft® Salad Dressing
salt and pepper
⅔ cup chopped walnuts

1 In a bowl, combine the eggs, onion, clams and mayonnaise and mix well. Season with salt

and pepper. Pinch off pieces of the mixture and form into balls about the size of large olives.

2 Spread the nuts in a shallow bowl and roll the balls in them to coat. Transfer to a platter, cover and chill for at least 1 hour.

COOKING NOTE: Substitute pumpernickel bread crumbs for the walnuts.

CLAM BALLS

MAKES: *About 40 servings*

---

1 cup chunk-style tuna, drained and flaked
½ cup mayonnaise or Kraft® Salad Dressing
½ teaspoon curry powder
salt
butter or margarine, at room temperature
14 thin slices bread, crusts trimmed
paprika

1 In a bowl, combine the tuna, mayonnaise and curry powder and blend with a fork. Season with salt.

2 Lightly butter the bread, top with the tuna mixture and sprinkle with paprika. Roll each slice into a tight roll, wrap each in plastic and chill for at least 2 hours.

3 Cut each roll into thirds, secure with toothpicks and serve.

CURRIED TUNA ROLLS

MAKES: *About 42 servings*

CLAM PIE

MAKES: *12 servings*

2 cans (6½ ounces each) minced clams, undrained
2 tablespoons lemon juice
2 tablespoons water
1 shallot, diced
1 clove garlic, diced
1 small green onion, diced
¼ cup chopped fresh parsley
1 tablespoon chopped fresh oregano
½ cup butter or margarine
¾ cup dry sourdough bread crumbs or other white bread crumbs
grated Romano cheese
crackers

1 Position the rack in the center of the oven and preheat to 350 degrees F. Lightly grease a 9-inch-square baking pan.

2 In a skillet, combine the clams and lemon juice and cook over low heat, stirring, for 10 to 12 minutes, or until cooked through. Set aside

3 In the container of a blender, combine the water, shallot, garlic, onion, parsley and oregano and process for 30 to 35 seconds or just until blended.

4 In a large skillet, melt the butter over medium heat. Add the contents of the blender and cook for 3 or 4 minutes. Add the clam mixture and bread crumbs and stir well. Spread in the pan and sprinkle with cheese. Bake for 12 to 15 minutes until lightly browned and crusty. Serve with crackers.

CRAB-AND-CHEESE BITES

MAKES: *12 servings*

1 large can (7.5 ounces) crabmeat, drained and flaked
1 tablespoon chopped green onion, green portions only
4 ounces shredded Swiss cheese
½ cup Kraft® Real Mayonnaise
1 tablespoon oyster sauce
¼ teaspoon curry powder
1 package (8 ounces) flaky refrigerated biscuits
1 can (6.8 ounces) chopped water chestnuts, drained

1 Position the rack in the center of the oven and preheat to 400 degrees F. Lightly grease a baking sheet.

2 In a bowl, combine the crabmeat, onion, cheese, mayonnaise, oyster sauce and curry powder and mix well.

3 Separate the biscuits into 3 layers and place on the baking sheet. Spoon the crabmeat mixture on the biscuits and top with a few slices of water chestnuts. Bake for 10 to 12 minutes, or until the biscuits are golden brown.

1½ cups all-purpose flour
1 cup yellow cornmeal
1 tablespoon plus 2 teaspoons
   baking powder
1½ cups milk
2 large eggs, beaten
⅓ cup vegetable oil
2 cans (6 ounces each) crabmeat,
   drained and flaked
sour cream

1 Preheat a nonstick griddle or large skillet until hot (400 degrees F. for an electric griddle).

2 In a bowl, combine the flour, cornmeal and baking powder. Add the milk, eggs, oil and crabmeat and stir to mix.

3 Drop by ¼-cupfuls onto the griddle and cook for 1 to 2 minutes on each side until browned. Serve hot with the sour cream.

CRAB CAKES
MAKES: *About 18 servings*

---

3 packages (3 ounces each) cream
   cheese, at room temperature
2 teaspoons Worcestershire sauce
1 teaspoon lemon juice
2 tablespoons mayonnaise or Kraft®
   Salad Dressing
1 small shallot, chopped
2 tablespoons Heinz® chili sauce
1 can (6 ounces) crabmeat, drained
   and flaked
finely chopped fresh parsley for
   garnish
crackers

1 Lightly grease a 6-by-3½-by-2-inch loaf pan.

2 In a bowl, using an electric mixer on medium speed, beat together the cheese, Worcestershire sauce, lemon juice, mayonnaise, shallot, chili sauce and crabmeat until quite smooth. Transfer to the pan and smooth the top. Lay a piece of wax paper on top and weight with cans or a second loaf pan filled with beans or flour. Chill for at least 24 hours.

3 Garnish with parsley and serve with crackers.

CRAB PÂTÉ
MAKES: *6 to 8 servings*

---

1 tablespoon butter or margarine
1 cup chopped celery
1 can (10.75 ounces) Campbell's®
   Cream of Shrimp Soup
2 large cans (7.5 ounces each)
   crabmeat, drained and flaked
½ cup sour cream or plain yogurt
1 tablespoon grated lemon or lime
   zest
dash of Angostura bitters
4 English muffins, split and toasted
sweet Hungarian paprika

1 In a medium skillet, melt the butter over medium-high heat and sauté the celery for about 5 minutes until softened. Add the soup, crabmeat, sour cream, lemon zest and bitters. Stir and heat just to boiling.

2 Spoon over the muffins and serve sprinkled with paprika.

CRABBY MUFFINS
MAKES: *8 servings*

FISH COCKTAIL

MAKES: *About 6 servings*

1 small white onion, sliced
2 carrots, sliced
2 cups water
salt and pepper
¾ pound white fish fillets, such as cod, flounder, halibut or hake
2 tablespoons diced pickles
1 tablespoon capers
½ cup mayonnaise or Kraft® Salad Dressing
3 tablespoons brandy
2 tablespoons lemon juice
½ cup catsup
1 lemon, thinly sliced

1 In a large skillet, combine the onions, carrots and water and simmer over medium heat for about 5 minutes. Season with salt and pepper, add the fish and continue simmering gently for 12 to 15 minutes or until the fish is opaque and flakes. Lift the fish from the pan and set aside to cool. Discard the vegetables and water.

2 Cut the fish into ½ inch squares and transfer to a bowl. Add the pickles and capers, toss and set aside.

3 In a small bowl, combine the mayonnaise, brandy, lemon juice and catsup. Spoon the fish onto plates and top with dressing. Serve garnished with lemon slices.

FISH REUBENS

MAKES: *6 to 12 servings*

1 package (15 ounces) frozen fish sticks
1 can (16 ounces) sauerkraut
prepared tartar sauce
6 slices rye bread
1 cup shredded Swiss cheese
sliced pickled beets

1 Bake the fish sticks according to the package directions and set aside.

2 Position the rack in the center of the oven and preheat to 425 degrees F.

3 Using two knives or kitchen scissors, shred the sauerkraut. Transfer to a saucepan with its juices and bring to a boil over medium heat. Drain and set aside.

4 Spread the tartar sauce on the bread and arrange the bread on an ungreased baking sheet. Place 3 or 4 fish sticks on each slice and spread with tartar sauce. Top with sauerkraut and cheese and bake for 3 to 5 minutes or until cheese melts. Serve garnished with pickled beets.

FRIED FISH FILLETS

MAKES: *6 to 8 servings*

½ pound white fish fillets, such as cod, flounder, halibut or hake, cut into pieces 1½ inches long and ½ inch wide
2 tablespoons sherry or white port wine
dash of white pepper
2 tablespoons cornstarch
1 large egg white
peanut oil for frying

1 In a bowl, combine the fish and sherry and sprinkle with pepper and 1 tablespoon of cornstarch and toss to coat.

2 In a bowl, using an electric mixer on high speed, beat the egg white and remaining 1 tablespoon of cornstarch until it forms stiff but not dry peaks.

3 In a heavy saucepan or a deep-fat fryer, pour oil to a depth of about 2 inches and heat until hot (375 degrees F. in a deep-fat fryer).

4 Dip the fish in the egg whites and fry for 3 to 5 minutes, turning, until cooked through. (Do not let the fish brown.) Drain on paper towels and serve hot.

1 package (8 ounces) cream cheese,
at room temperature
1 large clove garlic, minced
½ cup finely chopped celery
½ teaspoon lemon juice
½ teaspoon crushed dried basil
⅛ teaspoon crushed dried oregano
⅛ teaspoon crushed dried thyme
1 package (6 ounce) frozen cooked
shrimp, thawed and rinsed
2 packages (8 ounces each)
refrigerated crescent dinner rolls

1 Position the rack in the center
of the oven and preheat to 375
degrees F.

2 In a bowl, using an electric
mixer on medium speed, beat the
cream cheese, garlic, celery,
lemon juice, basil, oregano and
thyme until smooth. Using a
fork, fold in the shrimp.

3 Separate the dough into 8 rectangles and press the perforations to seal. Spread the filling
over each, leaving a ¼-inch border. Starting with a long side, roll
them into tight rolls and press
along the seam to seal. Cut each
roll into quarters and transfer,
seam-side down, to an ungreased
baking sheet. Bake for 15 to 20
minutes or until golden brown.
Serve hot.

ITALIAN-FLAVORED SHRIMP PUFFS

MAKES: *32 servings*

---

2 pounds halibut fillets, cut on the
diagonal into paper-thin slices
2 teaspoons grated lemon zest
1½ cups lemon juice
1 cup finely chopped onions
2 tomatoes, peeled, seeded, finely
chopped
salt and pepper
bottled taco sauce
tortilla chips

1 In a shallow baking dish, combine the fish and lemon zest and
toss gently. Slowly pour the
lemon juice into the mixture, stirring until the juice is nearly evaporated. Set aside for 15 to 20 minutes. The fish will turn opaque.

2 Add the onions and tomatoes
and season with salt and pepper.
Sprinkle with the taco sauce.
Cover and chill for at least 2
hours. Drain off excess liquid and
serve with tortilla chips.

COOKING NOTE: **Cut the fish so
thin that it appears to be grated.
Two pounds will yield approximately 4 cups.**

PESCE MESSICANO

MAKES: *About 12 servings*

SALMON CAKES

MAKES: *4 servings*

3 large eggs
2 tablespoons all-purpose flour
2 teaspoons lemon or lime juice
2 drops hot-pepper sauce
salt and pepper
1 can (12 ounces) whole-kernel corn, drained
1 can (7 ounces) salmon, drained and flaked
Pimiento Sauce (see page 47)

1 Lightly grease a griddle or skillet and heat until hot.

2 In a bowl, using an electric mixer on high speed, beat the eggs until thick and light. Add the flour, lemon juice and hot sauce and season with salt and pepper. Stir in the corn and salmon.

3 Drop the mixture by ½ cupfuls onto the griddle and flatten into a patty. Cook for about 3 minutes on each side until golden brown. Serve warm with the sauce.

SALMON CHEESE BALLS

MAKES: *20 to 24 servings*

1 package (8 ounces) cream cheese, at room temperature
1 cup shredded Cheddar or Wisconsin brick cheese
¼ cup Wish-Bone® California Onion Dressing
1 can (7 ounces) salmon, drained and flaked
½ teaspoon crushed fresh dill
¼ teaspoon garlic powder
¼ cup finely chopped celery leaves
crackers

1 In a bowl, combine the cream cheese and Cheddar and mash with a fork until blended. Add the dressing, salmon, dill and garlic powder and blend until smooth. Form into a ball, cover and chill for at least 4 hours or until firm.

2 Roll the ball in celery leaves and transfer to a serving plate. Press lightly to flatten the ball slightly. Serve with crackers.

SALMON PÂTÉ

MAKES: *6 to 8 servings*

1 can (3.75 ounces) salmon, drained and flaked
1 package (8 ounces) cream cheese
¼ teaspoon liquid smoke (optional)
2 tablespoons finely chopped green onion
1 tablespoon prepared horseradish
1 tablespoon lemon juice
½ cup finely chopped pecans
parsley for garnish
crackers

1 In a bowl, using an electric mixer on medium speed, beat the salmon, cream cheese, liquid smoke, onions, horseradish and lemon juice until smooth. Form into a log 1½-inches in diameter, wrap in plastic wrap and chill for at least 4 hours or until firm.

2 Unwrap the log and roll it in the pecans to coat. Garnish with parsley and serve with crackers.

½ cup olive oil
¼ cup chopped onions
1 can (4.5 ounces) boneless skinless sardines, drained and mashed
1 large egg, slightly beaten
2 tablespoons grated Parmesan or romano cheese
1 tablespoon catsup
2 tablespoons lemon juice
¼ teaspoon cayenne
¼ teaspoon crushed dried thyme
pinch of pepper
1 cup cooked rice
1 large egg white, beaten
2 tablespoons water
½ cup dry bread crumbs

1 In a skillet, heat 1 tablespoon of oil over medium heat and cook the onions for about 5 minutes until softened. Set aside to cool.

2 In a large bowl, combine the sardines, egg, cheese, catsup, lemon juice, cayenne, thyme, pepper, rice and cooled onions. Cover and chill for at least 1 hour.

3 In a small bowl, combine the egg white and water and whisk to mix. Pinch off pieces of the mixture and shape into balls about the size of walnuts. Dip each ball in the egg wash and roll in the bread crumbs to coat. Transfer to a platter, cover and freeze for no longer than 30 minutes until very firm.

4 In a large skillet, heat the remaining oil over medium heat until hot. Add the balls, a few at a time, and cook for 2 or 3 minutes, turning, until browned. Drain on paper towels and serve with toothpicks. Add more oil if necessary during cooking.

Cooking note: Flaked tuna or crabmeat can be substituted for sardines.

SARDINE RICE PUFFS

Makes: *About 30 servings*

½ pound mushrooms, stemmed
1 package (8 ounces) frozen cooked shrimp, thawed
1 package (8 ounces) frozen breaded shrimp, thawed
1 can (8.5 ounces) water-packed artichoke hearts, drained and quartered
1 green bell pepper, cut into 1-inch pieces
2 lemons or limes, cut into eighths
3 to 4 cups hot cooked Jasmine rice or other long-grain white rice
sweet Hungarian paprika
Anchovy Sauce (recipe follows)

1 Position the broiler rack about 4 inches from the heat source and preheat the broiler. Lightly grease a broiling pan.

2 Thread the mushrooms, shrimp, artichoke hearts, peppers and lemon wedges on skewers, alternating pieces and lay on the broiling pan. Broil for 8 to 10 minutes, or until the vegetables are tender and the shrimp are heated through.

3 Serve on the rice, sprinkled with paprika and the sauce on the side.

SEAFOOD KABOBS

Makes: *6 servings*

ANCHOVY SAUCE

Makes: *½ cup*

½ cup butter or margarine, at room temperature
1½ teaspoons anchovy paste
1 teaspoon lemon juice
¾ teaspoon oyster or clam juice
½ teaspoon onion juice

In a saucepan, combine the butter, anchovy paste, lemon juice, oyster juice and onion juice and cook over medium heat, stirring, until smooth and nearly boiling. Serve warm.

SEAFOOD SQUARES

MAKES: *60 servings*

2 cans (8 ounces each) refrigerated
   crescent dinner rolls
1 cup shredded sharp Cheddar
   cheese
1 cup shredded Swiss cheese
1 package (8 ounces) frozen cooked
   shrimp, thawed
1 can (6 ounces) crabmeat, drained
   flaked
1¾ cups half-and-half
6 large eggs, beaten
1 teaspoon dry mustard
½ teaspoon Worcestershire sauce
⅛ teaspoon hot-pepper sauce
finely chopped fresh parsley

1 Position the rack in the center
of the oven and preheat to 400
degrees F.

2 Separate the rolls into 4 long
rectangles. Transfer to a jelly-roll
pan and smooth over the bottom

and about 1 inch up the side to
form a crust. Press along the perforations to seal the seams and
bake for about 5 minutes until
lightly browned.

3 Sprinkle with the cheeses,
shrimp and crabmeat.

4 In a bowl, combine the half-
and-half, eggs, mustard, Worcestershire sauce and pepper sauce
and whisk. Pour over the crust,
sprinkle with parsley and bake
for 20 to 25 minutes longer or
until a knife inserted in the center
comes out clean and the edges
are golden brown. Cool on a wire
rack for about 5 minutes before
cutting into squares for serving.

SEAFOOD TARTLETS

MAKES: *4 servings*

thin-sliced white bread
⅓ cup butter or margarine, melted
1 can (4½ ounces) tiny deveined
   shrimp, drained
¾ cup mayonnaise or Kraft® Salad
   Dressing
⅓ cup grated Parmesan or romano
   cheese
⅓ cup grated Swiss cheese
¼ teaspoon Worcestershire sauce
⅛ teaspoon hot-pepper sauce
paprika
parsley or watercress sprigs for
   garnish

1 Position the rack in the center
of the oven and preheat to 400
degrees F. Lightly grease a 2-inch
muffin-cup pan.

2 Using a 2½- or 3-inch daisy
cookie cutter, cut out 4 or 5 flow-
ers. Brush each side with butter
and press into the muffin cups.
Bake for 8 to 10 minutes, or until
toasted.

3 Put the shrimp in a bowl and
cover with ice water.

4 In a bowl, combine the mayonnaise, Parmesan and Swiss
cheese, Worcestershire sauce and
hot sauce and stir to mix. Drain
the shrimp and pat dry with
paper towels. Add to the cheese
mixture and fold gently. Spoon
into the daisies and sprinkle with
paprika. Bake for 8 to 10 minutes
or until the cheese melts. Garnish
with parsley or watercress sprigs.

1½ pounds shrimp, shelled, deveined and finely chopped
½ teaspoon minced fresh ginger
1 large egg white
1 tablespoon sherry or white port wine
1 tablespoon cornstarch
peanut oil
3 cups Chicken Stock (recipe follows)
1 tablespoon cornstarch

1 In a bowl, combine the shrimp, ginger, egg white, sherry and cornstarch and whisk well. Drop by spoonfuls onto wax paper and flatten into small cakes.

2 In a large skillet, pour oil to a depth of ½ inch and heat over medium heat. Using a pancake turner, transfer the cakes to the hot oil and cook for 2 or 3 minutes on each sides, or until a golden brown and cooked through. Drain on paper towels.

3 In a saucepan, bring the stock to a boil over medium-high heat. Add the shrimp cakes, reduce the heat and simmer for about 5 minutes. Lift the cakes from the broth and set aside on a platter. Return the stock to a boil. Whisk the cornstarch and water together and add to the stock, stirring until the stock thickens slightly. Pour over the shrimp cakes and serve hot.

SHRIMP CAKES

MAKES: *14 to 18 servings*

CHICKEN STOCK

MAKES: *1½ to 2 quarts*

2 quarts water
6 pounds chicken, cut into pieces
1 large onion, chopped
1 large carrot, chopped
1 leek, chopped
1 stalk celery, chopped
2 sprigs fresh parsley
1 bay leaf, crushed
salt and pepper

1 In a stockpot, combine the water and chicken and bring to a boil over medium-high heat. Reduce the heat and simmer for about 20 minutes, skimming any foam that rises to the surface.

2 Add the onions, carrots, leeks, celery, parsley and bay leaf, partially cover and simmer on low heat for 1½ to 2 hours. Strain the stock and season with salt and pepper. Cool to room temperature and skim the fat that rises to the surface. Chill until ready to use.

COOKING NOTE: **This is a great stock for making aspic.**

¼ cup sherry
¼ cup soy sauce
1 tablespoon corn oil or peanut oil
1 teaspoon ground ginger
1 clove garlic, minced
24 fresh shrimp, peeled and deveined
2 tablespoons canola oil

1 In a bowl, combine the sherry, soy sauce, corn, oil, ginger and garlic and whisk well. Add the shrimp, toss and cover and chill for no longer than 1 hour.

2 In a skillet, heat the canola oil over medium heat until hot. Lift the shrimp from the marinade and cook, stirring, for about 5 minutes or until they turn pink. Serve with toothpicks.

SHRIMP IN SHERRY

MAKES: *8 servings*

SHRIMP ON A MUFFIN

MAKES: *12 servings*

1 can (8 ounces) cooked and
  deveined baby shrimp
1 jar (6 ounces) processed American
  cheese spread
½ teaspoon garlic powder
12 English muffin halves, quartered

1 Position the broiler rack about
4 inches from the heat and preheat the broiler.

2 In a small bowl, combine the
shrimp, cheese and garlic powder and stir until well mixed.
Spread on the muffin quarters
and transfer to a broiling pan.
Broil for 2 or 3 minutes or until
the cheese melts. Serve
immediately.

SMOKED HADDOCK PÂTÉ

MAKES: *8 to 10 servings; about 1½ cups*

½ pound smoked haddock
2 tablespoons lemon juice
½ teaspoon crushed dried thyme
½ cup butter or margarine, melted
⅓ cup whipping cream
pepper
chopped parsley for garnish
sliced ripe olives for garnish
French bread slices, toasted

1 In a small saucepan, combine
the haddock with enough cold
water to cover by about 1 inch.
Bring to a boil over medium-high
heat, reduce the heat and simmer
for 15 to 20 minutes until the fish
flakes. Remove from the heat and
let cool in the cooking liquid. Lift
from the cooking liquid and
remove the bones.

2 In the container of a blender,
combine the haddock, lemon
juice and thyme and process on
medium speed until smooth.
With the blender running, add
the butter in a slow, steady
stream until incorporated. Transfer to a bowl.

3 In another bowl, using an electric mixer on medium speed, beat
the cream until stiff peaks form.
Fold into the haddock mixture
and season with pepper. Cover
and chill for at least 3 hours.

4 About 30 minutes before serving, remove from the refrigerator.
Serve garnished with parsley and
olives with French bread on the
side.

1 can (12 ounces) crabmeat, drained and flaked
1 package (8 ounces) cream cheese, at room temperature
2 tablespoons grated romano cheese
¼ teaspoon Worcestershire sauce
¼ teaspoon garlic powder
1 package egg roll wrappers
vegetable oil

1 In a bowl, using an electric mixer on low speed, beat together the crabmeat, cream cheese, romano cheese, Worcestershire sauce and garlic powder until smooth.

2 Lay about 10 wrappers on a work surface and spoon teaspoonfuls of filling into the center of each. Fold into a bundles, tucking in the sides and moistening the edges with cold water to seal. Set aside under a damp, well-wrung dishtowel while making the remaining crab rolls.

3 In a large-skillet or deep-fat fryer, pour oil to a depth of 2 inches and heat until hot (350 degrees F. in a deep-fat fryer).

4 Fry the crab rolls in batches for 3 or 4 minutes on each side until golden brown. Drain on paper towels and set aside, covered, to keep warm while frying the rest of the rolls. Serve immediately.

SOUTHEAST ASIA CRAB ROLLS

MAKES: *About 35 servings*

---

2 tablespoons butter or margarine
⅓ cup finely chopped celery
¼ cup finely chopped onions
1 large clove garlic, minced
1 teaspoon crushed dried oregano
1 can (10.75 ounce) condensed Manhattan-style clam chowder
¼ cup chopped parsley
2 strips crisp-cooked bacon, crumbled
⅛ teaspoon hot-pepper sauce
1 cup packaged herb-seasoned stuffing mix
1½ pounds medium shrimp, shelled, deveined, tails intact
lemon juice

1 Position the broiler rack about 4-inches from the heat source and preheat the broiler.

2 In a saucepan, melt the butter over medium heat and sauté the celery, onions, garlic and oregano for about 5 minutes until the vegetables soften. Add the soup, parsley, bacon and pepper sauce, stir well and cook until heated through. Add the stuffing mix and mix well. Remove from the heat, cover and let stand for about 5 minutes.

3 Cut each shrimp along the vein line, splitting almost in half, and flatten. Arrange on a broiling pan, brush with lemon juice and broil for about 5 minutes. Spoon 1 tablespoon of the stuffing on each shrimp, brush with more lemon juice and broil for about 5 minutes longer or until cooked through.

STUFFED SHRIMP

MAKES: *45 to 50 servings*

TOASTED TUNA AND CHEESE SANDWICH

MAKES: *6 servings*

3 rolls or buns (3 inches in diameter), split and buttered
1 can (9.25 ounces) tuna, drained and flaked
1 package (3 ounces) cream cheese, at room temperature
2 tablespoons Kraft® Real Mayonnaise
2 teaspoons lime juice
1½ teaspoons minced shallots
1 teaspoon prepared horseradish
1 can (16 ounces) cut green beans, drained
1 cup shredded processed American cheese

1 Position the broiler rack about 4 inches from the heat source and preheat the broiler. Preheat the oven to 350 degrees F. (See note.)

2 Broil the roll halves for about 2 minutes until lightly toasted. Set aside.

3 In a bowl, combine the tuna, cream cheese, mayonnaise, lime juice, shallots and horseradish and mix until smooth. Add the beans, stir to mix and then spoon on the rolls. Sprinkle with cheese and bake for about 10 minutes, or until the cheese melts. Serve immediately.

COOKING NOTE: **If the broiler and oven occupy the same unit, turn off the broiler and let the oven preheat before baking the rolls.**

TUNA FRITTERS

MAKES: *About 30 servings*

vegetable oil
1 cup all-purpose flour
1 tablespoon baking powder
1 cup flaked canned chunk-style tuna
½ cup milk or light cream
2 tablespoons canola oil
1 large egg, lightly beaten
grated romano cheese

1 In a deep skillet or deep-fat fryer, pour the vegetable oil to a depth of about 2 inches and heat until hot (370 degrees F. in a deep-fat fryer).

2 In a bowl, combine the flour and baking powder and whisk. Add the tuna, milk, canola oil and egg and stir until well mixed.

3 Drop by teaspoonfuls into the oil and cook for about 2 minutes on each side until lightly browned. Drain on paper towels.

4 Spread the romano cheese in a shallow dish and roll the fritters, while still quite warm, in the cheese. Serve immediately.

TUNA PINWHEELS

MAKES: *About 60 servings*

1 can (6 ounces) tuna, drained and flaked
½ cup Kraft® Real Mayonnaise
½ cup finely chopped celery
2 tablespoons chopped pickles
1 teaspoon prepared mustard
¼ cup butter or margarine, softened
¼ cup butter or margarine, melted
20 slices white bread, crusts trimmed
paprika

1 Position the broiler rack about 4 inches from the heat source and preheat the broiler.

2 In a bowl, combine the tuna, mayonnaise, celery, pickles and mustard and stir until mixed.

3 Spread a thin layer of butter on the bread and top with the tuna mixture. Roll each slice into a cylinder and cut each into 3 slices. Secure with toothpicks and transfer to a broiling tray. Brush with melted butter and sprinkle with paprika. Broil for 2 or 3 minutes or until lightly browned. Serve immediately.

⅓ cup shredded carrots
⅓ cup sliced green onions
3 tablespoons mayonnaise
1 tablespoon picante sauce
1 can (6 ounces) tuna, drained and flaked
4 (7-inch) flour tortillas
½ cup alfalfa sprouts

1 In a bowl, combine the carrots, onions, mayonnaise, picante sauce and tuna and mix well.

2 Spread about ⅓ cup of the mixture down the center of each tortilla and top with alfalfa sprouts. Roll up tightly and serve immediately.

COOKING NOTE: These can be assembled and chilled for up to 4 hours before serving.

TUNA ROLL-UPS

MAKES: *4 servings*

2 cups uncooked elbow macaroni
1 jar (8 ounces) processed pimiento cheese spread
1 jar (2 ounces) pimiento-stuffed olives, drained and chopped
2 cans (6.5 ounces each) tuna, drained and broken into chunks
1 cup sliced celery
½ cup Kraft® Real Mayonnaise
2 teaspoons lemon or lime juice
salt and pepper
chopped parsley
Corn Flake Biscuits (recipe follows)

1 Cook the macaroni according to the package directions. Drain and while still warm, transfer to a bowl. Add the cheese and stir until melted.

2 Add the olives, tuna, celery, mayonnaise and lemon juice and season with salt and pepper. Cover and chill for at least 2 hours.

3 Serve garnished with parsley and with the biscuits on the side.

TUNA SALAD WITH CORN FLAKE BISCUITS

MAKES: *6 servings*

CORN FLAKE BISCUITS

MAKES: *7 to 12 biscuits*

½ cup butter or margarine, melted
1 cup crushed corn flakes
2 cups Bisquick® Baking Mix
½ cup cold water

1 Position the rack in the center of the oven and preheat to 425 degrees F. Pour ¼ cup of the butter into a 9-inch square baking pan and tilt to coat the pan. Sprinkle about ½ cup of the corn flakes over the bottom of the pan.

2 In a bowl, combine the baking mix and the water and stir until a soft, smooth dough forms. Drop the dough by tablespoons into the pan. Drizzle each mound of dough with some of the remaining butter and press the remaining corn flakes into the top of each. Bake for 12 to 15 minutes, or until lightly browned.

COOKING NOTE: Make the biscuits slightly smaller for a greater yield.

Chapter 9

VEGETABLE NIBBLES

When vegetables are eaten as snacks they take on a dimension slightly but firmly removed from their more traditional role as "side dishes." Beyond raw carrot and celery sticks, broccoli and cauliflower florets and sliced raw mushrooms, vegetables can be cooked into full-bodied and flavorful light dishes that fit nicely into the category of snack foods. Buy vegetables in season, if possible, and from local farmers for the best and fullest flavor. And don't worry if they are not picture perfect, just make sure they are ripe and ready for preparation. When necessary, canned and frozen veggies are more than acceptable and often easier to prepare than fresh.

ASPARAGUS CUSTARD

MAKES: *4 to 6 servings*

1 pound fresh asparagus, cut into
  1-inch pieces
6 large eggs
¾ cup milk
2 tablespoons Dijon mustard
1 teaspoon dry mustard
¼ cup chopped white onion
2 cups diced cooked ham
2 cups grated Swiss or firm goat
  cheese
asparagus tips for garnish
ham, cut into matchsticks, for
  garnish

1 Position the rack in the center
of the oven and preheat to 400
degrees F. Lightly grease a 9-
inch-square baking pan.

2 In a steaming basket set over
boiling water, steam the asparagus for 5 to 7 minutes until fork-
tender. Drain and set aside.

3 In a bowl, whisk the eggs until
foamy and light colored. Add the
milk and both mustards and
whisk until smooth. Add the
onion, diced ham and cheese and
mix. Add the steamed asparagus
and stir gently.

4 Pour into the pan and garnish
with asparagus tips and ham
matchsticks. Bake for 30 to 35
minutes or until a knife inserted
in the center comes out clean.
Cool slightly and then cut into
squares for serving.

BEAN-RICE BURGERS

MAKES: *4 serving*

1 cup sunflower seeds
2 tablespoons butter or margarine
2 tablespoons sliced green onions
¼ cup finely minced celery
1 cup chopped cooked soy beans
1 cup cooked brown or wild rice
½ cup shredded Cheddar cheese
¼ cup whole-wheat flour
2 teaspoons sweet pickle relish
2 tablespoons catsup
2 teaspoons soy sauce
½ teaspoon crumbled fresh basil
  leaves
2 large eggs, lightly beaten
salt and pepper
sliced onion rings for garnish
pickle slices for garnish
Black Bean Dip (see page 25)

1 In the container of a blender,
process the sunflower seeds on
high until finely ground.

2 In a large skillet, melt the butter over medium-low heat and
cook the onions and celery for 2
or 3 minutes until the onions
begin to soften. Add the beans,
rice, ground sunflower seeds,
cheese, flour, relish, catsup, soy
sauce, basil and eggs and season
with salt and pepper. Stir well
and cook for 2 or 3 minutes until
heated through. Transfer to a
bowl or plate.

3 Using a small melon baller or
ice-cream scoop, drop small balls
of the mixture into the skillet,
flattening with a pancake turner
to a thickness of ¼ inch. Cook,
turning once, for 5 or 6 minutes,
or until well browned. Transfer
to a platter, garnish with the
onion rings and pickles and serve
with the dip.

2 large eggs
2 tablespoons water
¼ teaspoon salt
pinch of white pepper
pinch of cayenne
fine dry white bread crumbs
2 cans (16 ounces each) whole new
   potatoes, drained

1 Preheat the oven to 350 degrees F. Lightly grease a 13-by-9-inch baking dish.

2 In a bowl, combine the eggs, water, salt, pepper and cayenne and whisk well.

3 Spread the bread crumbs in a shallow dish. Dip the potatoes in the egg mixture and then roll them in the crumbs to coat. Transfer to the pan and bake for about 30 minutes, turning several times, until tender.

BREADED POTATO BAKE
MAKES: *6 to 8 servings*

1½ pounds broccoli florets
1½ cups water
1 teaspoon sugar
2 tablespoons butter or margarine, at
   room temperature
2 tablespoons all-purpose flour
1 cup milk
salt and pepper
¼ teaspoon ground nutmeg
2 tablespoons butter or margarine,
   melted
2 tablespoons fine dry bread crumbs

1 Position the rack in the center of the oven and preheat to 350 degrees F. Lightly grease an ovenproof baking dish.

2 In a saucepan, combine the broccoli, water and sugar and bring to a boil over high heat. Reduce the heat, cover and cook for 5 to 8 minutes, or until the broccoli turns bright green and is fork-tender. Drain.

3 In a saucepan, combine the room temperature butter and the flour and stir until blended. Add the milk and bring to a boil. Cook, stirring, for 2 or 3 minutes until thickened. Season with salt and pepper and the nutmeg. Remove from the heat and set aside.

4 In a small bowl, combine the melted butter and bread crumbs.

5 Arrange the broccoli in the dish and pour the sauce over the top. Sprinkle the bread crumb mixture over the sauce and bake for 25 to 30 minutes, or until bubbling and lightly browned.

BROCCOLI AU GRATIN
MAKES: *4 servings*

BROCCOLI TART

MAKES: *6 to 8 serving*

Pastry Crust (recipe follows)
2 teaspoons Mustard Butter (see page 154)
1 package (10 ounces) frozen broccoli florets
1 cup heavy cream
4 large eggs
pinch of cayenne
¼ teaspoon ground nutmeg
salt and pepper
1½ cups grated Swiss or Monterey Jack cheese
¼ cup sunflower seeds for garnish
Herb Dressing (recipe follows)

1 Position the rack in the center of the oven and preheat to 375 degrees F.

2 Press the dough in a 9-inch pie plate and brush with mustard butter.

3 In a saucepan, cook the broccoli according to the package directions. Drain and add the cream, eggs, cayenne and nutmeg, season with salt an pepper and stir to mix. Add the cheese and heat, stirring, until the cheese begins to melt. Pour into the prepared crust and sprinkle the sunflower seeds over the top. Bake for 30 to 35 minutes or until firm. Cool slightly and cut into wedges to serve. Pass the dressing on the side.

PASTRY CRUST

MAKES: *one 9-inch pie crust*

1½ cups all-purpose flour
½ teaspoon salt
½ cup butter or margarine, chilled
1 large egg, lightly beaten
2 tablespoons ice water

1 In a large bowl, combine the flour and salt. Using a pastry blender, a fork or two knives, cut the butter into the flour until the mixture resembles coarse crumbs. Add the egg and water and stir until the mixture holds together and forms a smooth ball. Cover and chill for at least 2 hours.

2 On a lightly floured surface, roll out the dough to the desired thickness.

HERB DRESSING

MAKES: *About ½ cup*

6 tablespoons canola oil
½ teaspoon crushed dried oregano
½ teaspoon crushed dried basil leaves
¼ teaspoon crushed dried chervil
¼ teaspoon dry mustard
¼ teaspoon pepper
¼ teaspoon Worcestershire sauce
1 small clove garlic, minced
2 tablespoons wine vinegar
1 tablespoon lemon juice

In a small bowl, combine all of the ingredients and whisk well. Use immediately or cover and chill for up to 24 hours.

4 large baking potatoes
¼ cup butter or margarine, melted
¼ cup canola oil
2 cloves garlic, minced
½ teaspoon dried thyme leaves
salt and pepper
watercress sprigs
Pimiento Sauce (see page 47)

1 Position the rack in the center of the oven and preheat to 400 degrees F. Lightly grease a baking dish.

2 Cut the potatoes into ¼-inch-thick slices and lay in an overlapping pattern in the baking dish.

3 In a bowl, whisk together the butter and oil and brush the mixture on the potatoes. Sprinkle with the garlic and thyme and season with salt and pepper. Bake for 25 to 30 minutes or until the potatoes are fork-tender. Garnish with watercress and serve with the sauce for dipping.

BAKED SLICED POTATOES

MAKES: *4 serving*

---

1 prepared unbaked pastry shell
1 large carrot, shredded
4 sliced green onions (green portion only)
2 cups half-and-half
2 teaspoons dried dill
4 large eggs
¼ cup grated Cheddar or Wisconsin brick cheese
Drawn Butter Sauce (see page 16)

1 Position the rack in the center of the oven and preheat to 425 degrees F.

2 Press the pastry into a 9-inch fluted quiche pan, prick the bottom of the pastry and bake for about 10 minutes, or until the shell starts to harden. Do not let it brown.

3 In a saucepan, combine the carrots, onions, half-and-half and dill and bring to a boil over medium heat. Remove from the heat and cool slightly.

4 Add the eggs 1 at a time, whisking after each addition, and pour the mixture into the pastry shell. Sprinkle the cheese over the top and bake for 25 to 30 minutes or until firm and lightly browned. Cool on a wire rack for about 5 minutes before cutting into wedges and serving with the sauce.

CARROT-AND-DILL QUICHE

MAKES: *4 to 6 servings*

CORN-STUFFED PEPPERS

MAKES: *4 servings*

4 strips crisp cooked bacon, chopped
2 tablespoons bacon drippings
1 cup diced cooked chicken
4 green onions, chopped (green portions only)
2 cups frozen whole-kernel corn
1 teaspoon paprika
salt and pepper
4 large green bell peppers
1 cup soft whole-wheat bread crumbs
2 tablespoons butter or margarine, at room temperature

1 Position the rack in the center of the oven and preheat to 350 degrees F. Lightly grease an 8-inch-square baking pan.

2 In a skillet, heat the bacon drippings and sauté the chicken for 2 or 3 minutes. Add the onions, corn and paprika and season with salt and pepper. Cover and cook over low heat for about 5 minutes.

3 Slice the tops off the peppers and scoop out the seeds and membranes. Fill each with the chicken mixture and put in the pan.

4 In a small bowl, combine the crumbs and butter and stir to blend. Sprinkle over the top of the peppers and bake for 25 to 30 minutes, or until the peppers are tender but still firm. Serve immediately.

COOKING NOTE: **Use smaller peppers for a greater yield.**

MEDITERRANEAN-STYLE STUFFED EGGPLANT

MAKES: *4 servings*

1 large eggplant
2 tablespoons oil
½ cup chopped white onion
1 clove garlic, minced
2 tablespoons butter or margarine, at room temperature
2 tablespoons all-purpose flour
1 can (24 ounces) tomatoes, drained and diced, juice reserved
¼ teaspoon dried oregano
¼ teaspoon dried marjoram
¼ teaspoon pepper
½ cup cottage cheese
Swiss cheese strips for garnish

1 Position the rack in the center of the oven and preheat to 350 degrees F.

2 Cut the eggplant in half lengthwise and scoop out the pulp to leave a ½-inch-thick shell. Chop the pulp into ½-inch cubes.

3 In a skillet, heat the oil over medium heat and sauté the eggplant pulp, onion and garlic for about 5 minutes until tender.

4 In a small saucepan, combine the butter and flour and stir until blended. Cook over medium heat until heated through and smooth.

5 Combine the reserved tomato juice with enough water to fill the 24-ounce can and slowly add this to the flour mixture, stirring until the liquid is absorbed and the sauce thickens. Add to the eggplant mixture. Add the tomatoes, oregano, marjoram and pepper and stir well. Spoon into the eggplant shells and dot with dollops of cottage cheese. Put the shells on a baking sheet and cover with tented aluminum foil. Bake for 30 to 35 minutes or until the shells are tender. Serve immediately garnished with cheese strips.

1 prepared unbaked pastry shell
¼ cup butter or margarine
5 Bermuda onions, thinly sliced
4 thick strips cooked bacon, cut into
   1-inch squares
3 large eggs, lightly beaten
½ cup heavy cream
½ teaspoon salt
½ teaspoon caraway seeds
chopped parsley for garnish

1 Position the rack in the center of the oven and preheat to 450 degrees F. Press the pastry into a 9-inch fluted quiche pan, prick the bottom of the pastry and bake for about 10 minutes, or until the shell starts to harden. Do not let it brown.

2 In a large frying pan, melt the butter over medium heat and cook the onions, stirring, for about 10 minutes or until softened and lightly browned. Remove from the heat and stir in the bacon, eggs, cream and salt.

3 Pour the egg mixture into the prepared pastry shell and sprinkle with caraway seeds. Bake for 12 to 15 minutes, or until firm. Let cool slightly, garnish with parsley and serve cut into wedges.

ONION-AND-BACON QUICHE

MAKES: *4 to 6 servings*

---

2 tablespoons butter or margarine
1 onion, thinly sliced
2 pears, peeled, cored and thinly
   sliced
pepper
chopped parsley
lemon juice

1 In a skillet, melt 1 tablespoon of butter over medium heat and sauté the onions for 6 to 8 minutes or until golden brown. Drain on paper towels.

2 Melt the remaining butter and sauté the pears for about 10 minutes or until golden brown but still firm. Return the onions to the skillet, sprinkle with pepper and heat for about 1 minute. Serve garnished with parsley and sprinkled with lemon juice.

SAUTÉED ONIONS AND PEARS

MAKES: *4 servings*

SPINACH QUICHE

MAKES: *4 to 6 servings*

1 prepared unbaked pastry shell
1 tablespoon Herb Butter (see page 49)
3 tablespoons butter or margarine
2 tablespoons minced green onion, white portion only
1 package (10 ounces) frozen chopped spinach, cooked and drained
1 cup ricotta or cottage cheese
pinch of ground nutmeg
salt and pepper
3 large eggs, lightly beaten
½ cup heavy cream
¼ cup shredded Swiss or Gouda cheese

1 Position the rack to the center of the oven and preheat to 450 degrees F. Press the pastry into a 9-inch fluted quiche pan, prick the bottom of the pastry and bake for about 10 minutes, or until the shell starts to harden. Do not let it brown. Reduce the oven temperature to 375 degrees F.

2 Brush the pastry shell with the Herb Butter and set aside.

3 In a skillet, melt 2 tablespoons of the butter over medium heat and sauté the onions for about 5 minutes until golden brown. Add the spinach and cook for about 1 minute. Add the ricotta cheese and nutmeg, season with salt and pepper and stir. Add the eggs and cream and mix well. Pour into the pastry shell, sprinkle with Swiss cheese and dot with the remaining 1 tablespoon of butter. Bake for 25 to 30 minutes or until set firm.

SQUASH-AND-ONION KEBOBS

MAKES: *4 servings*

4 summer squash, halved lengthwise
four ½-inch onion slices
1 tablespoons plus 1½ teaspoons butter or margarine, melted
½ teaspoon dried oregano
½ teaspoon dried chervil
½ teaspoon dried basil
salt and pepper
cherry tomatoes for garnish

1 Position the rack in the center of the oven and preheat to 350 degrees F.

2 Lay an onion slice between the halves of each squash and spear with skewers. Lay each kebob on a large sheet of heavy-duty foil.

3 Drizzle the kebobs with butter and sprinkle with oregano, chevil, basil and salt and pepper. Fold the foil tightly over the kebobs and transfer to a baking dish. Bake for 40 to 45 minutes until the squash is tender. Unwrap and serve hot, garnished with cherry tomatoes.

½ pound summer squash, quartered
salt
3 tablespoons butter or margarine
1 Bermuda onion, thinly sliced
1 can (7 ounces) green chiles, sliced
4 large eggs
pepper
chopped parsley
Cheese Sauce (see page 20)

1 In a large saucepan, combine the squash with enough water to cover by about 1 inch, salt lightly and bring to boil over high heat. Reduce the heat and simmer for 8 to 10 minutes our until fork-tender. Drain.

2 Position the broiler rack about 6 inches from the heat source and preheat the broiler. Lightly grease a 13-by-9-inch baking pan.

3 In a large skillet, melt the butter over medium heat and sauté the onion for about 5 minutes or until lightly browned and soft. Add the squash and chiles, stir well and remove from the heat.

4 In a bowl, using an electric mixer on high speed, beat the eggs until light colored. Pour over the squash and season with salt and pepper. Transfer to the baking pan and broil for 4 to 6 minutes, or until firm and golden brown. Sprinkle with parsley and cut into squares. Serve with the sauce on the side.

SQUASH FRITTATA
MAKES: *4 servings*

---

1 prepared unbaked pastry shell
1 package (10 ounces) frozen kernel corn, thawed
1 package (10 ounces) frozen baby lima beans, thawed
1 cup grated Cheddar or Colby cheese
3 chopped green onions (green portions only)
3 large eggs
1¼ cups light cream or half-and-half
½ teaspoon crushed dried basil leaves
½ teaspoon crushed dried thyme
¼ teaspoon crushed dried chervil
salt and pepper

1 Position the rack in the center of the oven and preheat to 450 degrees F. Press the pastry into a 9-inch pie pan, prick the bottom of the pastry and bake for about 10 minutes, or until the shell starts to harden. Do not let it brown. Reduce the oven temperature to 350 degrees F.

2 In a bowl, combine the corn, lima beans, cheese and onion and toss to mix.

3 In another bowl, using an electric mixer on high speed, beat the eggs until light colored. Add the cream and herbs, season with salt and pepper and beat until foamy. Pour over the vegetables, stir gently and transfer to the pastry shell. Bake for 30 to 35 minutes, or until firm and lightly browned. Cool slightly and cut into wedges to serve.

SUCCOTASH PIE
MAKES: *6 to 8 serving*

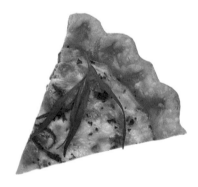

TOMATO CORN PIE

MAKES: *4 to 6 servings*

1 prepared unbaked pastry shell
4 large eggs
½ cup heavy cream
½ teaspoon crumbled dried chervil
1 cup shredded Wisconsin cheese
1 can (8 ounces) cream-style corn
1 large tomato, diced
tomato slices for garnish

1 Position the rack in the center of the oven and preheat to 450 degrees F. Press the pastry into a 9-inch pie pan, prick the bottom of the pastry and bake for about 10 minutes, or until the shell starts to harden. Do not let it brown. Reduce the oven temperature to 425 degrees F.

2 In a bowl, using an electric mixer, beat the eggs until light colored. Add the cream and chervil and beat to mix. Stir in the cheese, corn and diced tomato and transfer to the pastry shell. Bake for about 10 minutes, reduce the heat to 350 degrees F. and bake for 30 minutes longer, or until a knife inserted in the center comes out clean. Cool slightly and top with sliced tomatoes. Cut into wedges to serve.

YAM-AND-ORANGE FRY

MAKES: *4 servings*

¼ cup packed light-brown sugar
2 tablespoons unsalted butter
2 tablespoons orange marmalade
1 can (18 ounces) sweet potato pieces, cubed
1 can (11 ounces) mandarin orange segments, drained

In a skillet, combine the sugar and butter and heat over medium heat, stirring, until the sugar dissolves. Add the marmalade and potatoes and stir, making sure to spoon the pan juices over the potatoes until well coated. Add the orange segments and cook for about 2 minutes or until heated through.

COOKING NOTE: **Canned small white potatoes can be substituted for yams.**

three 6- to 8-inch zucchini
⅓ cup Tarragon Dressing (see page 66)
¼ cup skim milk
1 tablespoon prepared mustard
1 tablespoon lemon or lime juice
½ teaspoon crushed crystallized ginger
8 ounces cooked ham, cut into matchsticks
4 ounces Edam or longhorn cheese, cut into matchsticks
2 cups finely chopped mustard greens
⅔ cup cooked orzo macaroni
¼ cup minced green onion
salt and pepper

1 Scoop the pulp from the zucchini, leaving a ¼-inch-thick shell. Discard the pulp or reserve for another use. Set the shells on a microwave-safe dish, cover with a paper towel and microwave on high (100 percent) power for 2 or 3 minutes, or until the zucchini are fork-tender but still offering some resistance.

2 In a large bowl, combine the dressing, milk, mustard, lemon juice, ginger, ham, cheese, mustard greens, orzo and onion and season with salt and pepper and mix well.

3 Spoon into the shells, spread evenly, cover and chill for at least 1 hour. Serve cold.

COOKING NOTE: Cooked long-grain rice may be substituted for the orzo macaroni.

ZUCCHINI BOATS
MAKES: *6 servings*

1 zucchini, shredded
2 tablespoons finely chopped white onion
2 tablespoons all-purpose flour
¼ teaspoon dried oregano leaves
1 tablespoon chopped parsley
1 large egg, lightly beaten
salt and pepper
butter
parsley for garnish
Parsley Butter (recipe follows)

1 In a bowl, combine the zucchini and onion and toss. Sprinkle with flour, oregano, and parsley and toss again. Add the egg, season with salt and pepper and mix well.

2 Heat a large skillet over medium-high heat until very hot. Add enough butter to coat the pan. Drop 2 tablespoons of the mixture for each pancake onto the skillet and cook for 2 or 3 minutes on each side until lightly browned (you will have to fry the pancakes in batches). Serve garnished with parsley and with the Parsley Butter on the side.

ZUCCHINI PANCAKES
MAKES: *24 to 30 small-sized pancakes*

PARSLEY BUTTER
MAKES: *About ¼ cup*

¼ cup unsalted butter
2 tablespoons chopped parsley

In a small bowl or cup, mash the butter until soft and creamy. Fold in the parsley until well blended.

ZUCCHINI-TOMATO MOLDED SALAD

MAKES: *4 servings*

1 can (14½ ounces) stewed tomatoes, drained, juice reserved
1 packet unflavored gelatin
1 teaspoon sugar
1 teaspoon chopped fresh parsley
1 small clove garlic, minced
1 tablespoon finely chopped fresh oregano
dash of hot pepper sauce
1 small zucchini, shredded
shredded mustard greens for garnish
Herb Mayonnaise (see page 104)

1 In a saucepan, combine the reserved tomato juice and gelatin and set aside for about 5 minutes until the gelatin softens. Cook over low heat, stirring, until the gelatin dissolves. Remove from the heat. Add the sugar, parsley, garlic, oregano and pepper sauce and mix well.

2 Chop the tomatoes coarsely. Add the tomatoes and zucchini to the gelatin mixture and pour into 4 ramekins or custard cups, filling each only halfway. Cover and chill for at least 2 hours or until firm.

3 Spread the greens on plates and unmold the salads on top of the greens. Serve with mayonnaise.

ARTICHOKE NIBBLES

MAKES: *About 40 servings*

1 tablespoon canola oil
1 white onion, chopped
1 clove garlic, minced
1 jar (7 ounces) water-packed artichoke hearts, drained and chopped, liquid reserved
3 large eggs
1 cup grated Cheddar cheese
¼ teaspoon dried crushed oregano
salt and pepper
2 tablespoons dry bread crumbs

1 Position the rack in the center of the oven and preheat to 325 degrees F. Lightly grease a 9-inch-square baking pan.

2 In a large skillet, heat the oil over medium heat and sauté the onions and garlic for about 5 minutes until translucent. Add the artichokes and stir.

3 In a large bowl, whisk the eggs until foamy and add the onion mixture. Add the cheese, reserved liquid from the artichokes and oregano and stir well. Season with salt and pepper and transfer to the baking pan. Sprinkle with the bread crumbs and bake for 25 to 30 minutes or until firm. Cool for about 10 minutes before cutting into small squares. Serve warm or cold.

ASPARAGUS HAM BUNDLES

MAKES: *24 servings*

24 thin asparagus tips
2½ ounces Montrachet cheese, at room temperature
2 tablespoons chopped fresh basil
1 tablespoon chopped toasted pine nuts
1 tablespoon water
1 teaspoon grated orange zest
salt and pepper
2 ounces thinly sliced ham, cut into 24 thin strips about 4 inches long

1 In a saucepan, combine the asparagus tips with enough water to cover. Salt lightly, bring to a boil over medium-high heat and cook for about 1 minute or until fork-tender. Drain.

2 In a bowl, combine the cheese, basil, pine nuts, water and orange zest and stir until blended. Season with salt and pepper. Spread on the ham strips and lay an asparagus tip at the end of each strip. Roll up, pressing the ends to seal. Transfer to a platter, cover and chill for at least 1 hour.

ASPARAGUS MOLD

MAKES: *8 to 10 servings*

1 can (10½ ounces) condensed cream of asparagus soup
1 package (3 ounces) lime-flavored Jell-O®
1 package (8 ounces) cream cheese, at room temperature
1 cup cold water
½ cup Kraft® Real Mayonnaise
½ cup finely chopped celery
¼ cup finely chopped green bell pepper
1 tablespoon grated white onions

1 In a saucepan, heat the soup over medium-high heat to the boiling point. Add the gelatin and stir until dissolved. Remove from the heat, add the cream cheese and stir until the cheese melts. Add the water, mayonnaise, celery, pepper and onion and stir to blend.

2 Transfer to a mold, cover and chill for at least 4 hours or until set.

AVOCADO-AND-EGG ROLLS

MAKES: *30 to 36 servings*

2 large hard-cooked eggs, chopped
2 teaspoons lemon juice
2 tablespoons mayonnaise or Kraft® Salad Dressing
2 tablespoons minced avocado
pinch of dry mustard
seasoned salt to taste
10 to 12 slices white bread, crusts trimmed

1 In a bowl, using an electric mixer on medium speed, blend together the eggs, lemon juice, mayonnaise, avocado, dry mustard and seasoned salt. Cover and chill for at least 1 hour.

2 Spread the filling over the bread and roll each slice into a tight roll. Cut each roll into thirds and secure with toothpicks. Serve immediately.

AVOCADO MOUSSE

MAKES: *6 to 8 servings*

1 package (3 ounces) lime-flavored Jell-O®
2 cups hot water
1 packet unflavored gelatin
2 tablespoons cold water
1 cup mashed ripe avocado
½ cup Kraft® Real Mayonnaise
½ cup heavy cream, whipped

1 In a bowl, combine the Jell-O and hot water and stir until the Jell-O dissolves.

2 In a cup, combine the gelatin and cold water and set aside for about 5 minutes to soften. Stir until gelatin dissolves. Add to the Jell-O, stir, cover and chill for about 1 hour or until nearly set.

3 Add the avocado, mayonnaise and whipped cream and stir until incorporated throughout the jelled mixture. Pour into a mold and chill for at least 4 hours.

4 To unmold, wrap the mold with a warm, damp towel and invert onto a plate. Chill until ready to serve.

BAKED ARTICHOKE SQUARES

MAKES: *About 24 servings*

½ cup plus 3 tablespoons canola oil
1 cup chopped mushrooms
¼ cup thinly sliced celery
1 clove garlic, minced
1 can (13 ounces) water-packed artichoke hearts, drained and finely chopped
1 cup shredded Monterey Jack or Wisconsin brick cheese
2 large eggs, lightly beaten
⅓ cup chopped green onion
½ teaspoon crushed dried marjoram
¼ teaspoon crushed dried oregano
¼ teaspoon cayenne
1½ cups all-purpose flour
¼ cup milk

1 Position the rack in the center of the oven and preheat to 350 degrees F.

2 In a skillet, heat 3 tablespoons of oil over medium heat and sauté the mushrooms, celery and garlic for 8 to 10 minutes or until the celery is tender. Remove from the heat and add the artichokes, cheese, eggs, onion, marjoram, oregano and red pepper and mix well.

3 In a bowl, combine the flour, remaining ½ cup of oil and milk and mix with a fork until cohesive and forms a ball. Press into a 13-by-9-inch baking pan, smoothing the dough over the bottom and about 1½ inches up the sides of the pan. Bake for about 10 minutes until firm.

4 Spread the artichoke mixture on the crust and bake for about 20 minutes longer or until the center of the filling is set. Cool on a wire rack for about 10 minutes and cut into squares. Serve warm.

BIG HAT TEXAS CAVIAR

MAKES: *24 to 30 servings*

1 package (less than 1 ounce) dry Italian salad dressing mix
2 tablespoons cider vinegar
4 cans (15 ounce) black-eye peas, rinsed and drained
1 red bell pepper, seeded and diced
1 green bell pepper, seeded diced
4 green onions, diced
⅛ teaspoon garlic powder
salt and pepper
saltine or wheat crackers

1 Prepare the dressing according to the package directions and stir in the vinegar.

2 In a bowl, combine the peas, peppers and onions. Add the dressing and garlic powder and stir well. Season with salt and pepper. Cover and chill for at least 8 hours. Serve on crackers.

2 packets unflavored gelatin
6 tablespoons cold water
2 packages (3 ounces each) cream cheese, at room temperature
2 cans (16 ounces each) black-eye peas, drained
1 shallot, quartered
2 cloves garlic
½ cup mild picante sauce
3 tablespoons Worcestershire sauce
¼ teaspoon hot-pepper sauce
½ cup chopped parsley

1 Lightly oil a 9-inch round pan.

2 In a saucepan, sprinkle the gelatin over the water and set aside for about 5 minutes to soften. Cook over how heat and stir until the gelatin dissolves.

3 In the container of a blender, combine the cream cheese, peas, shallot, garlic, picante sauce, Worcestershire sauce and hot pepper sauce and process for about 1 minute or until smooth. Add the gelatin and process for 30 seconds to incorporate.

4 Pour into the pan, cover and chill for at least 2 hours or until firm. Unmold and serve sprinkled with parsley.

BLACK-EYE PEA PÂTÉ

MAKES: *12 to 16 servings*

---

one 1-pound pumpkin
¼ cup canola oil
½ leek, chopped
¼ teaspoon sugar
½ cup water

1 Using a sharp knife, peel and seed the pumpkin. Cut the pumpkin pulp into 2-inch squares.

2 In a large skillet, heat the oil over medium heat and cook the pumpkin for 10 to 12 minutes or until just soft. Add the leeks, sugar and water and simmer, partially covered, for about 15 minutes. Serve hot.

BRAISED PUMPKIN

MAKES: *4 to 6 servings*

---

4 large eggs
½ cup butter or margarine, melted
1 cup grated Cheddar or Wisconsin brick cheese
1 box (11 ounces) corn muffin mix
1 package (10 ounces) frozen chopped broccoli, thawed and cooked
½ cup chopped white onion

1 Position the rack in the center of the oven and preheat to 425 degrees F. Grease a 9-by-5-inch loaf pan.

2 In a bowl, and using an electric mixer on medium speed, beat the eggs until light colored. Add the butter and cheese and mix well. Add the muffin mix, broccoli and onion, mix well and spread into the pan. Bake for 18 to 20 minutes or until a knife inserted in the center comes out clean. Cool on a wire rack and cut into squares to serve.

BROCCOLI BREAD

MAKES: *8 to 10 servings*

CABBAGE BALLS

MAKES: *About 44 servings*

2 tablespoons butter or margarine, at room temperature
1 packages (3 ounce) cream cheese, at room temperature
⅓ cup Philadelphia® Crumbled Blue Cheese
1 tablespoon red wine vinegar
2 tablespoons minced green bell pepper
2 tablespoons minced celery
¼ cup chopped pecans
¼ cup finely chopped red cabbage
finely chopped pecans

1 In a bowl, combine the butter, cream cheese, blue cheese, vinegar, pepper, celery, chopped pecans and red cabbage. Mix well and shape into balls about the size of walnuts.

2 Spread the finely chopped pecans in a shallow dish and roll the balls in the nuts until coated. Transfer to a plate, cover and chill for at least 1 hour.

COOKING NOTE: Substitute peanuts for the pecans.

CARCIFFE FRITTA

MAKES: *6 to 8 servings*

¼ cup plus 2 tablespoons olive oil
salt and pepper
1 can (14 ounces) water-packed artichoke hearts, drained
salt and pepper
2 large eggs
1 cup Italian bread crumbs

1 In a deep skillet, heat the oil over high heat until hot.

2 In a bowl, sprinkle salt and pepper over the artichoke hearts.

3 In a small bowl, whisk the eggs until foamy. Spread the bread crumbs in a shallow dish. Dip the artichoke hearts in the egg and then roll in the bread crumbs. Fry for about 3 minutes on each side until golden brown. Drain on paper towels. color.

CARROT FRITTERS

MAKES: *About 40 servings*

2¾ cups all-purpose flour
1½ cups milk
¼ cup plus 2 tablespoons chopped shallot
2 tablespoons minced parsley
2 tablespoons baking powder
1½ teaspoons crumbled dried thyme
salt and pepper
6 cups finely grated carrots
vegetable oil

1 In a large bowl, combine the flour, milk, shallot, parsley, baking powder and thyme and season with salt and pepper. Add the carrots and fold just until coated. Cover and set aside at room temperature for at least 3 hours.

2 In a deep skillet or deep-fat fryer, pour the oil to a depth of about 2 inches and heat until hot (375 degrees F. in a deep-fat fryer).

3 Drop the carrot mixture by heaping tablespoonfuls into the oil, taking care not to crowd the pan. Cook for 10 to 12 minutes or until golden brown, turning occasionally. Drain on paper towels and cook the remaining batter. Serve immediately.

1 cup small-curd cottage cheese
¼ cup crumbled blue cheese
1 teaspoon celery seeds
1 teaspoon prepared mustard
¼ teaspoon onion powder
30 cherry tomatoes, tops removed
   and seeded

In a bowl, combine the cottage cheese, blue cheese, celery seed, mustard and onion powder. Spoon into the tomatoes, cover and chill until ready to serve.

CHEESE-STUFFED TOMATOES

MAKES: *About 30 servings*

¼ cup mayonnaise
2 tablespoons plus 1½ teaspoons
   lemon or lime juice
1 tablespoon prepared mustard
1½ teaspoons dry mustard
⅛ teaspoon salt
⅛ teaspoon hot-pepper sauce
½ cup shredded cooked crabmeat
1 cup grated celery root
1 tablespoon finely chopped parsley
two 7-inch-long cucumbers,
   trimmed and scored with a fork

1 In a bowl, combine the mayonnaise, lemon juice, mustards, salt and hot-pepper sauce and stir

until smooth. Add the crabmeat, celery root and parsley and fold until incorporated. Cover and chill for 24 hours.

2 Cut the cucumbers into ⅓-inch-thick slices and arrange in a single layer on a plate or tray. Spoon rounded teaspoonfuls of the crab mixture in the center of each slice.

CUCUMBER CROWNS

MAKES: *About 36 servings*

2 cucumbers, trimmed and scored
   with a fork
1 tablespoon lime or lemon juice
1 teaspoon coarse salt
½ teaspoon chili powder

Cut the cucumbers lengthwise into quarters and cut the quarters into 2-inch-thick slices. Arrange

in a layer on a plate and drizzle with the lime juice. Sprinkle with salt and chili powder.

CUCUMBER WEDGES

MAKES: *About 30 servings*

DINOSAURUS BITES

MAKES: *About 16 servings*

1 unsliced loaf rye bread
1 package (10 ounces) frozen green peas
½ teaspoon baking soda
1 package (8 ounces) cream cheese, at room temperature
1 small shallot, minced
1 tablespoon onion powder
6 to 8 pitted green olives, halved
6 to 8 pitted ripe olives, halved

1 Cut the bread in half lengthwise.

2 Prepare the peas according to the package directions and remove from the heat. Immediately add the baking soda and stir (the mixture will foam).

3 In a bowl, using an electric mixer on medium speed, beat together the cream cheese, shallot and onion powder. Add the peas and beat until smooth.

4 Spread over the bread halves and garnish with olive halves, rounded sides up. Cut the bread into 1½-inch-thick slices.

EGGPLANT SALSA

MAKES: *About 6 to 8 servings*

2 eggplants
salt
1 can (8 ounces) tomato sauce
2 tablespoons canola oil
1 large Bermuda onion, finely chopped
2 stalks celery, finely chopped
1 large clove garlic, minced
10 pitted green olives, quartered
1 teaspoon cider vinegar
sugar to taste
1 jalapeño, finely chopped
white pepper
crackers

1 Peel and dice the eggplant into 1-inch pieces and transfer to a saucepan. Add water to cover, salt lightly and set aside to soak for about 30 minutes. Drain and add fresh water to cover. Set over medium heat and cook for about 15 minutes until tender. Drain again. Add the tomato sauce and stir to mix.

2 In a skillet, heat the oil over medium heat and sauté the onion, celery, garlic and olives for about 10 minutes until tender. Add the vinegar, sugar and jalapeño, season with salt and pepper and stir well.

3 Add the onion mixture to the pan with the eggplant and simmer, stirring occasionally, over medium heat for about 20 minutes until the flavors are blended and the vegetables are very soft. Serve with crackers on the side.

FRESH VEGETABLE PIZZA

MAKES: *60 servings*

2 packages (8 ounces each) refrigerated crescent dinner rolls
1 cup sour cream
1 tablespoon prepared horseradish
salt and pepper
2 cups chopped fresh mushrooms
1 cup chopped tomatoes
1 cup small broccoli florets
½ cup chopped green peppers
½ cup chopped green onions

1 Position the rack in the center of the oven and preheat to 375 degrees F.

2 Separate the rolls into 4 long rectangles and lay in an ungreased jelly-roll pan. Press the dough into the bottom of the pan and about 1 inch up the sides. Smooth along the perforations. Bake for 14 to 16 minutes or until golden brown. Transfer to a wire rack to cool.

3 In a bowl, combine the sour cream and horseradish, season with salt and pepper and blend until smooth. Spread over the cooled crust and top with mushrooms, tomatoes, broccoli, peppers and onions. Cut into small pieces to serve.

1 cup canola oil
½ cup apple cider vinegar
1 small clove garlic, minced
1 teaspoon crushed fresh oregano
   leaves
¼ teaspoon white pepper
1 pound fresh mushrooms
2 cups broccoli florets
2 cups cauliflower florets
3 large red bell peppers, cut into 1-
   inch pieces
2 cups diagonally-sliced carrots

In a large glass or ceramic bowl, combine the oil, vinegar, garlic, oregano and pepper and whisk until blended. Add the mushrooms, broccoli, cauliflower, peppers and carrots and toss to coat. Cover and chill for at least 2 hours. Drain and serve with toothpicks.

Fresh Vegetables in Marinade

MAKES: *12 to 16 servings*

---

1 pound firm tofu
salt
peanut oil
3 large eggs, lightly beaten
¼ cup all-purpose flour
2 tablespoons water
¼ teaspoon crushed fresh ginger
1 green onion, finely chopped
1 tablespoon soy sauce

1 Slice the tofu in half horizontally, put in a bowl and sprinkle with salt. Set aside for about 10 minutes. Pat dry with paper towels and cut into 1-by-2-inch pieces.

2 In a wok or heavy skillet, heat 1 tablespoon of peanut oil over high heat until very hot.

3 In a bowl, combine the eggs, flour and water and whisk until blended. Dip the tofu in the egg mixture and cook in batches for 3 or 4 minutes or until lightly browned. Add more oil to the wok as necessary. Lift the tofu from the wok and set aside in a bowl, covered, to keep warm.

4 Add more oil to the wok and heat until hot. Stir-fry the ginger and onion for about 10 seconds. Return the tofu to the wok and add the soy sauce. Cook for about 1 minute, partially covered, until heated through. Serve immediately.

Fried Tofu with Ginger

MAKES: *4 servings*

GREEK POTATO SKINS

MAKES: *About 24 servings*

3 medium-sized baking potatoes, scrubbed
4 ounces feta cheese, crumbled
1½ teaspoons crushed dried oregano
½ teaspoon crushed dried basil
¼ teaspoon crushed dried rosemary
½ teaspoon garlic salt
olive oil

1 Position the rack in the center of the oven and preheat to 400 degrees F.

2 Pierce the potatoes in several places with the tines of a fork and bake for 55 to 60 minutes, or until cooked through. Set aside to cool slightly. Raise the oven temperature to 450 degrees F.

2 Cut the potatoes lengthwise into quarters and scoop out the potato pulp, leaving a ¼-inch-thick shell. Discard the pulp or reserve it for another use. Cut each quarter into halves and put the skins on an ungreased baking sheet. Bake for about 5 minutes until the skins begin to crisp.

3 In a bowl, combine the cheese, oregano, basil, rosemary and garlic salt. Spoon on the skins and drizzle with olive oil. Bake for 2 or 3 minutes longer until the cheese is bubbly.

COOKING NOTE: **The potatoes can be baked several hours ahead of time.**

GREEN PEA NESTS

MAKES: *8 serving*

1 package (10 ounces) frozen green peas
½ teaspoon baking soda
8 melba toasts
2 tablespoons butter or margarine, at room temperature
3 tablespoons heavy cream
24 small white cocktail onions

1 Prepare the peas according to the package directions and remove from the heat. Immediately add the baking soda and stir (the mixture will foam).

2 Spread each melba toast with the butter.

3 In a bowl, using an electric mixer on high speed, beat the peas and 1 tablespoon of cream until mixed. Add the remaining cream a tablespoon at a time until the mixture forms a thick paste. Spread a thin layer over the buttered rounds and spoon the remaining paste into a pastry bag fitted with a medium star tip. Pipe a ring of paste around the edges of the rounds. Pipe a second ring on top of the first to create a nest and put 3 onions inside each one. Serve at once.

2 quarts water
1 pound fresh spinach, cooked and
  drained
¾ cup ricotta cheese
2 slices prosciutto, finely chopped
2 large egg yolks
2 tablespoons all-purpose flour
1 teaspoon chopped pine nuts
1 teaspoon chopped raisins
⅛ teaspoon ground nutmeg
¼ cup grated Parmesan cheese
¼ cup butter or margarine, melted

1 In a saucepan, heat the water
until simmering.

2 Press the spinach against the
sides of a sieve to extract the
moisture and coarsely chop.

Transfer to a bowl and add the
ricotta, proscuitto, egg yolks,
flour, pine nuts, raisins and nutmeg and 2 tablespoons of cheese
and mix well.

3 Form into balls about the size
of walnuts and dust lightly with
flour. Drop into the simmering
water, a few at a time, and when
the balls rise to surface, simmer
for about 4 minutes until cooked
through. Lift from the water and
transfer to a plate. Drizzle with
butter and the remaining cheese
and set aside to keep warm while
cooking the remaining balls.
Serve as soon as all the balls are
cooked.

ITALIAN SPINACH BALLS

MAKES: *10 to 12 servings*

---

6 sweet potatoes, cooked
¼ cup butter or margarine
½ cup maple syrup or maple-
  flavored syrup
½ teaspoon grated orange zest

1 Position the rack in the center
of the oven and preheat to 375
degrees F. Lightly grease a 13-by-
9-inch baking pan.

2 Cut the sweet potatoes lengthwise in half and arrange in the
dish.

3 In a small saucepan, melt the
butter over medium heat until it
turns light brown. Add the syrup
and orange zest and simmer for 4
or 5 minutes, stirring frequently,
until just slightly thickened. Pour
over the potatoes and bake for 18
to 20 minutes, basting frequently,
until well glazed. Serve
immediately.

MAPLE-FLAVORED SWEET POTATOES

MAKES: *6 servings*

MARINATED JICAMA

MAKES: *4 to 6 servings*

**1 pound jicama, peeled and very
  thinly sliced**
¼ teaspoon hosin sauce
2 tablespoons canola oil
**2 tablespoons plus 1½ teaspoons
  cider vinegar**
**2 tablespoons plus 1½ teaspoons
  soy sauce**
**1 tablespoon plus 1½ teaspoons
  sugar**
**1 tablespoon sesame oil or peanut
  oil**

1 In a small bowl, combine the jicama with enough cold water to cover and set aside to soak for about 10 minutes.

2 In a saucepan, bring about 2 cups of water to a boil over high heat. Drain the jicama and, using a slotted spoon or sieve, dip the slices in the boiling water for 10 to 20 seconds. Immediately plunge into a bowl of cold water.

3 In a skillet, heat the oil over medium heat, add the hoisin sauce and stir for 1 or 2 minutes until well mixed. Remove from the heat and add the vinegar, soy sauce, sugar and sesame oil and stir to blend.

4 Drain the jicama and immerse in the sauce. Cover and set aside for at least 2 hours. Serve with the marinade on the side.

MASHED POTATO-AND-BACON SCONES

MAKES: *5 to 7 servings*

6 strips bacon
1 cup unflavored mashed potatoes
1 large egg
salt and pepper
¼ cup all-purpose flour

1 In a skillet, cook the bacon over medium heat until crispy. Drain on paper towels and reserve the bacon drippings. Chop the bacon coarsely.

2 In a bowl, combine the potatoes and egg, season with salt and pepper and mix well. Add 2 tablespoons of the reserved bacon drippings and stir until well blended. Add the flour and bacon pieces and stir well.

3 In the same skillet, heat 1 tablespoon of the reserved bacon drippings over medium heat and drop the potato mixture by ¼ cupfuls into the pan. Cook for 3 or 4 minutes on each side, or until golden brown. Add more drippings or vegetable oil if necessary to prevent sticking. Drain on paper towels and serve.

3 cups cooked jasmine rice
1½ cups shredded Swiss cheese
4 large eggs
8 strips crisp bacon, crumbled
1 can (4 ounces) diced green chiles
¼ cup diced pimientos
¼ cup chopped parsley
1 cup milk
¾ teaspoon ground cumin
⅛ teaspoon hot-pepper sauce

1 Position the rack in the center of the oven and preheat to 400 degrees F. Lightly grease eight miniature 6-cup muffin pans.

2 In a bowl, combine the rice, 1 cup of cheese and 2 eggs and mix well. Drop the mixture by table-spoonfuls into the muffin cups and press to compact. Bake for 12 to 15 minutes, or until lightly browned.

3 In a bowl, combine the bacon, chiles, pimientos, parsley and remaining ½ cup of cheese and mix well. Spoon into the muffin cups over the rice.

4 In another bowl, combine the milk, cumin, pepper sauce and remaining 2 eggs and whisk well. Spoon into the muffin cups and bake for about 15 minutes or until set. Cool slightly and then lift the rice cups from the muffin pans and serve immediately.

MINI RICE CUPS

MAKES: *48 servings*

---

1 package (8 ounces) refrigerated crescent dinner rolls
2 cups sliced fresh or canned mushrooms
¼ cup butter or margarine, melted
grated romano cheese
¼ teaspoon marjoram
¼ teaspoon ground oregano

1 Position the rack in the center of the oven and preheat to 375 degrees F.

2 Separate the rolls into triangles and arrange on a 12-inch pizza pan, pressing along the edges to fit and smoothing together.

3 In a small bowl, combine the mushrooms and butter, stir gently and spread over the dough. Sprinkle with cheese. Combine the marjoram and oregano and sprinkle over the cheese. Bake for 20 to 25 minutes or until the crust is golden brown. Serve cut into wedges.

MUSHROOM BREAD PIZZA

MAKES: *8 to 10 servings*

---

1 tablespoon butter or margarine
1 can (4 ounces) sliced mushrooms, drained, liquid reserved
1 cup all-purpose flour
¼ cup sugar
1 tablespoon baking powder
1 teaspoon salt
1 large egg
¾ cup milk
½ cup grated Swiss cheese
¼ cup canola oil

1 Position the rack in the center of the oven and preheat to 400 degrees F. Lightly grease a 12-cup muffin pan.

2 In a skillet, heat the butter over medium heat and sauté the mushrooms for 3 or 4 minutes until very hot. Add the flour, sugar, baking powder and salt and stir until blended. Add the egg, ¼ cup of the reserved liquid from the mushroom can, milk, cheese and oil, stirring gently until barely mixed. Do not over-mix. Remove from the heat.

3 Drop the mixture by spoonfuls into the muffin cups, filling each about two-thirds full, and bake for 20 to 25 minutes or until golden brown. Serve hot.

MUSHROOM MUFFINS

MAKES: *12 muffins*

PINWHEEL ONION ROLLS

MAKES: *8 servings*

2 tablespoons butter or margarine
4 onions, thinly sliced
1¼ teaspoons salt
dash of cayenne
2 cups all-purpose flour
1 tablespoon baking powder
¼ cup vegetable shortening
⅔ cup milk
1 large egg, lightly beaten
⅓ cup evaporated milk

1 Position the rack in the center of the oven and preheat to 400 degrees F. Lightly grease a 13-by-9-inch baking pan.

2 In a skillet, melt the butter over medium heat and cook the onions for 8 to 10 minutes until golden brown. Remove from the heat, add ¼ teaspoon of the salt and the cayenne and stir well.

3 In a large bowl, combine the flour, baking powder and the remaining 1 teaspoon of salt and whisk well. Using a pastry blender or two knives, cut in the shortening until the mixture resembles coarse crumbs. Add the milk and blend to form a dough.

4 On a lightly floured work surface, roll the dough into a rectangle about 12-by-8 inches. Spread the onion mixture over the rectangle, leaving a ½-inch border, and starting from a short end, roll into a cylinder. Cut into 8 slices, each about 1 inch thick, and arrange on the baking pan.

5 In a cup, combine the egg and evaporated milk and whisk well. Pour over the rolls and bake for 20 to 25 minutes until golden brown.

POTATO BAKE

MAKES: *6 servings*

1 large egg
1 tablespoon evaporated milk
1 envelope (about 2.5 ounces) seasoned coating mix for chicken
1 tablespoon grated romano cheese
2 cans (16 ounces each) whole new potatoes, drained

1 Position the rack in the center of the oven and preheat to 350 degrees F. Lightly grease a 13-by-9-inch baking pan.

2 In a small bowl, whisk the egg until light colored. Add the milk and whisk well.

3 In a shallow bowl, combine the coating mix and cheese and stir until blended. Roll the potatoes first in the egg mixture and then in the coating mixture to coat and put in the pan. Bake for 25 to 30 minutes, or until golden brown. Serve immediately.

vegetable oil
3 large potatoes, peeled and halved
   horizontally
coarse salt

1 In a deep skillet or deep-fat
fryer, pour the oil to a depth of
about 2 inches and heat until hot
(390 degrees F. in a deep-fat
fryer).

2 Using a small melon baller,
scoop our as many balls as possible from the potatoes. Cook 6 to 8
balls at a time for 5 or 6 minutes
until golden brown. Drain on
paper towels and sprinkle with
salt. Serve hot.

POTATO BALLS
MAKES: *About 12 to 15 balls*

Betty Crocker Potato Buds®
2 tablespoons all-purpose flour
1½ cups shredded sharp Cheddar
   cheese
8 strips crisp cooked bacon,
   crumbled
sour cream or plain yogurt

1 Position the rack in the center
of the oven and preheat to 425
degrees F. Lightly grease a baking sheet.

2 In a bowl, prepare the potato
buds according to the package
directions for 4 servings, using 1
cup less of water. Add the flour

and stir until blended. Cover and
freeze for about 10 minutes or
until cold enough to handle
easily.

3 Divide the dough into 16 parts
and form each into a ball. Flatten
each ball to a thickness of ¼ inch
and transfer to the baking sheet.
Prick each patty with a fork and
bake for 20 to 25 minutes, or until
the bottom is a dark brown.
Sprinkle with cheese and bacon
and continue baking until the
cheese melts. Serve with sour
cream or yogurt.

POTATO SKINS
MAKES: *4 servings*

¼ cup packed light-brown sugar
2 tablespoons butter or margarine
2 tablespoons orange marmalade
½ teaspoon salt
1 can (18 ounces) packed sweet
   potatoes, drained,
1 can (11 ounces) mandarin orange
   segments, drained

In a skillet, combine the brown
sugar, butter, marmalade and salt
and cook over medium heat, stir-

ring constantly, until boiling.
Add the potatoes and cook, stirring gently, until the potatoes are
coated with the sugar mixture
and are very hot. Reduce the
heat, add the orange segments
and cook for about 1 minute
longer until heated through.
Serve hot.

POTATO SWEETS
MAKES: *4 servings*

POTATO WRAPS

MAKES: *About 16 servings*

½ teaspoon coarse salt
½ teaspoon seasoned pepper
¼ teaspoon crushed bay leaf
4 small new potatoes, quartered
8 strips bacon, halved
sour cream
snipped chives

1 Position the rack in the center of the oven and preheat to 400 degrees F.

2 In a cup, combine the salt, pepper and bay leaf and stir to mix. Sprinkle about half over the potatoes. Wrap the potatoes with the bacon and secure with toothpicks. Sprinkle with the remaining seasoning and transfer to a baking pan. Bake for 18 to 20 minutes, or until the bacon is crisp and the potatoes are cooked through. Drain on paper towels and serve with sour cream and chives.

COOKING NOTE: This works best if the potatoes are no more than 1½ inches in diameter.

PUMPKIN DOUGHNUTS

MAKES: *20 to 24 servings*

vegetable oil
4½ cups all-purpose flour
1 tablespoon plus 1 teaspoon baking
   powder
1 cup granulated sugar
1 teaspoon ground nutmeg
¾ teaspoon salt
1 large egg
1¼ cups milk
2 tablespoons butter or margarine,
   melted
½ teaspoon vanilla extract
¾ cup canned unsweetened
   pumpkin
powdered sugar

1 In a deep skillet or deep-fat fryer, pour the oil to a depth of about 2 inches and heat until hot (375 degrees F. in a deep-fat fryer).

2 In a bowl, combine the flour, baking powder, sugar, nutmeg and salt and whisk well.

3 In another bowl, combine the egg, milk, butter, vanilla and pumpkin and stir to blend. Add to the dry ingredients and stir until well blended.

4 On a lightly floured work surface, roll the dough to a thickness of ¼ inch. Using a 2½-inch doughnut cutter or cookie cutter, cut out as many doughnuts as possible.

5 Fry for 2 or 3 minutes on each side until golden brown. Drain on paper towels. When cool, dust with powdered sugar.

1 cup sauerkraut, drained, rinsed and chopped
1 package (3 ounces) sliced corned beef, chopped
1 cup dry rye bread crumbs
1 large eggs, lightly beaten
1 small white onion, minced
¼ cup water
2 tablespoons chopped parsley
1 teaspoon prepared horseradish
1 large clove garlic, minced
salt and pepper

COATING
2 large eggs, lightly beaten
¼ cup dry whole-wheat bread crumbs
prepared mustard

1 In a bowl, combine the sauerkraut, corned beef, bread crumbs, egg, onion, water, parsley, horse-radish and garlic and season with salt and pepper. Mix well. Cover and chill for at least 1 hour.

2 Position the rack in the center of the oven and preheat to 400 degrees F.

3 Put the eggs in a bowl and spread the bread crumbs in another.

4 Form the sauerkraut mixture into small bowls about the size of walnuts. Roll each in egg and then in crumbs to coat. Transfer to an ungreased baking sheet and bake for 18 to 20 minutes, or until a lightly browned. Serve hot with mustard.

REUBEN BALLS
MAKES: *24 to 36 servings*

---

3 baking potatoes, peeled and cubed
½ cup all-purpose flour
¼ cup yellow cornmeal
¼ cup olive oil
½ teaspoon garlic salt
½ teaspoon pepper
1 jar (8 ounces) mild picante sauce
1 cup shredded cooked chicken
1 cup (4 ounces) shredded Monterey Jack cheese with jalapeño peppers
1 tablespoon chopped parsley
sour cream or guacamole for garnish

1 In a large saucepan, combine the potatoes with enough water to cover by about 1 inch and bring to a boil over high heat. Reduce the heat and simmer for about 20 minutes until tender. Drain and return to the pan. Using a potato masher or fork, mash the potatoes until smooth.

2 Position the rack in the center of the oven and preheat to 350 degrees F.

3 In a large bowl, combine the potatoes, flour, cornmeal, 3 table-spoons of the olive oil, garlic salt and pepper and mix to form a smooth dough. Press the dough into the bottom and up the sides of a 10-inch tart or flan pan with a removable bottom. Spread the picante sauce over the dough and top with the chicken and cheese. Sprinkle with parsley and drizzle with the remaining tablespoon of olive oil.

4 Bake for 20 to 25 minutes, or until heated through. Release the sides of the pan, cut the flan into wedges and serve with the sour cream or guacamole on the side.

SOUTHWESTERN POTATO FLAN
MAKES: *8 to 10 servings*

SPANAKOPITA

MAKES: *About 70 servings*

12 sheets phyllo dough
½ cup butter or margarine, melted
2 packages (12 ounces each) Stouffer's® Spinach Soufflé, thawed
6 ounces feta cheese, crumbled
½ cup chopped parsley
½ cup crushed dried dill

1 Position the rack in the center of the oven and preheat to 400 degrees F. Lightly grease a 15-by-10-inch baking pan.

2 Brush 6 sheets of the phyllo with butter and fit into the pan, overlapping as necessary. Spread the soufflé over the dough and sprinkle with cheese, parsley and dill.

3 Brush the remaining 6 sheet of phyllo with butter and lay over the cheese, overlapping as necessary. Score the top into small rectangles and bake for 25 to 30 minutes, or until lightly browned. Cool slightly and cut along the scored lines to serve.

COOKING NOTE: When working with phyllo dough, keep the sheets covered with a damp, well-wrung dishtowel until you are ready to use them to prevent them from drying out.

SPINACH BALLS

MAKES: *72 servings*

6 large eggs
2 cups chopped cooked spinach, drained and squeezed dry
2 cups herb stuffing mix
1 large Bermuda onion, grated
1 cup freshly grated Parmesan or romano cheese
¾ cup butter or margarine, at room temperature
1 teaspoon poultry seasoning
salt and pepper

1 Position the rack in the center of the oven and preheat to 350 degrees F. Lightly grease 2 baking sheets.

2 In a large bowl, whisk the eggs until foamy. Add the spinach, stuffing mix, onion, cheese, but-

ter and poultry seasoning, season with salt and pepper and mix until the stuffing mix is well moistened. If a little stiff, add a teaspoon or two of water.

3 Pinch off pieces and form into balls the size of walnuts. Transfer to the baking sheets and bake for 18 to 20 minutes or until golden brown. Serve hot.

COOKING NOTE: These are particularly good with a creamy herb or cheese dip.

SPINACH SQUARES

MAKES: *About 24 servings*

3 large eggs, lightly beaten
1 cup all-purpose flour
1 cup milk
1 teaspoon baking powder
1 pound grated Monterey Jack or Wisconsin brick cheese
2 cups chopped fresh spinach
2 tablespoons butter or margarine

1 Position the rack in the center of the oven, and preheat to 350 degrees F. Lightly grease a 13-by-9-inch baking pan.

2 In a large bowl, combine the eggs, flour, milk, baking powder, cheese and spinach and stir until well mixed. Pour into the pan, dot with butter and bake for 30 to 35 minutes, or until cooked through. Cool on a wire rack for 5 minutes before cutting into small squares for serving.

1½ cups all-purpose flour
½ cup whole-wheat flour
¼ cup packed light-brown sugar
1 tablespoon baking powder
½ teaspoon ground cinnamon
¼ teaspoon ground nutmeg
¼ teaspoon ground cloves
2 large eggs, lightly beaten
¼ cup canola oil
¾ cup milk
½ cup cooked summer squash

1 Position a rack in the center of the oven and preheat to 400 degrees F. Lightly grease a 12-cup muffin pan.

2 In a bowl, combine the flours, sugar, baking powder, cinnamon, nutmeg and cloves and whisk well.

3 In a large bowl using an electric mixer on high speed, beat the eggs until light colored. Add the oil, milk and squash and beat until smooth. Add the dry ingredients all at once and blend until just moistened. Do not overmix. Spoon into the muffin cups, filling each about two-thirds full, and bake for 30 to 35 minutes, or until a toothpick inserted in the center of a muffin comes out clean. Cool on a wire rack.

SQUASH MUFFINS

MAKES: *12 servings*

1½ to 2 pounds Brussels sprouts
1 cup Kraft® Italian Dressing
½ cup small-curd cottage cheese
½ teaspoon grated shallot
1 package (2 ounces) Kraft®
   Crumbled Bleu Cheese
salt and pepper

1 In a steaming basket set over boiling water, cook the Brussels sprouts for about 15 minutes or until tender. Cool slightly and using a melon baller, scoop out the center of each sprout. Drain turned upside down on paper towels.

2 In a bowl, using an electric mixer on low speed, beat together the dressing, cottage cheese, shallot and cheese. Season with salt and pepper and stir well. Fill the sprouts, cover and chill for at least 1 hour. Serve cold.

STUFFED BRUSSELS SPROUTS

MAKES: *36 to 40 servings*

STUFFED CHERRY TOMATOES

MAKES: *18 to 20 servings*

1 pint cherry tomatoes
1 can (4½ ounces) deviled ham
2 teaspoons sour cream
2 teaspoons prepared horseradish

1 Cut a slice from the top of the tomatoes. Using a spoon or a melon baller, remove the pulp form the tomatoes. Drain turned upside down on paper towels.

2 In a small bowl, combine the deviled ham, sour cream and horseradish and mix well. Fill each tomato, cover and chill for at least 2 hours. Serve cold.

SWEET-AND-SOUR BEETS

MAKES: *6 servings*

2 cans (16 ounces each) sliced beets, drained
1 small Bermuda onion, thinly sliced and separated into rings
⅓ cup cider vinegar
¼ cup canola oil
½ cup sugar
salt

1 In a bowl, combine the beets and onions and toss to mix.

2 In a small bowl, whisk together the vinegar, oil and sugar until the sugar dissolves. Season with salt and pour over the beets and onions. Toss gently, cover and chill for at least 4 hours.

1½ cups shredded Swiss cheese, at room temperature
½ cup finely chopped red bell pepper
1 cup chopped fresh spinach
¼ cup mayonnaise
8 bagels or English muffins, halved

1 In a bowl, combine the cheese, pepper, spinach and mayonnaise and mix well.

2 Spread over the bagel halves. Set 2 halves on a double thickness of paper towels and microwave on high (100 percent) power for 30 to 40 seconds or until hot. Repeat with the remaining halves and serve immediately.

SWISS CHEESE-SPINACH SANDWICHES

MAKES: *8 servings*

1 cup all-purpose flour
1 cup whole-wheat flour
1 tablespoon baking powder
½ teaspoon crushed dried oregano
¼ cup grated Parmesan cheese
¼ teaspoon salt
⅔ cup tomato juice
¼ cup plus 2 tablespoons butter or margarine, melted, plus more for brushing

1 Position the rack in the center of the oven and preheat to 450 degrees F.

2 In a bowl, combine the flours, baking powder, oregano, cheese and salt and whisk well. Stir in the tomato juice and butter and stir to form a soft dough.

3 On a lightly floured surface, knead the dough for about 30 seconds and roll out to a thickness of ½ inch. Using a 2-inch cookie cutter, cut into rounds and transfer to an ungreased baking sheet. Brush with melted butter and bake for 10 to 12 minutes, or until golden brown. Cool on wire racks.

TOMATO BISCUITS

MAKES: *About 16 biscuits*

VEGETABLE BROCHETTES

MAKES: *About 8 servings*

12 cloves garlic, minced
½ cup water
2 teaspoons chopped fresh mint
½ teaspoon salt
½ cup olive oil
3 tablespoons lemon juice
3 tablespoons lime juice
16 small white onions
16 fresh mushrooms, trimmed
1 fennel bulb, cut into 1-inch cubes
1 red bell pepper, cut into 1-inch
    squares
16 cherry tomatoes

1 In the container of a blender, combine the garlic, water, mint, salt, oil and lemon and lime juices and process for 2 to 4 minutes until smooth.

2 In a saucepan, combine the onions and enough water to cover, bring to a boil over medium-high heat and cook for about 2 minutes or until tender. Remove from the heat and drain under cold running water.

3 Thread the onions, mushrooms, fennel, pepper and tomatoes on skewers, ending with fennel, and lay in a shallow baking pan. Pour the marinade over the brochettes and set aside at room temperature for 30 to 40 minutes, brushing occasionally with the marinade.

4 Preheat the broiler.

5 Broil the brochettes for 10 to 12 minutes, turning occasionally and brushing with the marinade, until the vegetables are tender. Serve immediately.

COOKING NOTE: **These can be prepared a day head and kept in the refrigerator. They can also be cooked over a charcoal or gas grill.**

VEGETABLE CHEESECAKE

MAKES: *12 to 16 servings*

2¼ cups crushed Hi Ho® crackers
½ cup butter or margarine, melted
1 package (8 ounces) cream cheese
1 carton (8 ounces) plain yogurt
½ cup pimiento-stuffed olives
1 green bell pepper, cut into 1-inch
    pieces
1 shallot, quartered
1 stalk celery, sliced
1 teaspoon Worcestershire sauce
¼ teaspoon paprika
salt and pepper
assorted raw vegetables for serving

1 In a bowl, combine the crackers and butter and stir until the crackers are well coated. Press half of the crumbs into the bottom of an ungreased 9-inch springform pan. Set the remaining crumb mixture aside.

2 In the container of a blender, combine the cheese and yogurt and process until smooth. Add the olives, pepper, shallot, celery, Worcestershire sauce and paprika and season with salt and pepper. Process until the vegetables are just chopped.

3 Pour over the crumb crust in the pan and sprinkle with the remaining crumbs. Press lightly to compress, cover and chill for at least 8 hours.

4 Release the sides of the pan and serve with raw vegetables on the side.

VEGETABLE CUT-OUTS

MAKES: *About 24 servings*

CUT-OUTS
prepared pastry dough for two 9-inch crusts
1 package (8 ounces) cream cheese, at room temperature
1 tablespoon milk
½ teaspoon onion salt
½ teaspoon Worcestershire sauce

GARNISHES
cucumber slices
chopped olives
fresh dill
green onion slices
radish slices
carrots curls or shreds
pimiento slices
small cooked shrimp

1 Position the rack in the center of the oven and preheat to 425 degrees F.

2 On a lightly floured surface, lay the pastry and using a 2½-inch fancy cookie cutter, cut out as may shapes as possible. Transfer to an ungreased baking sheet and prick each with the tines of a fork. Bake for 8 to 10 minutes or until golden brown. Cool on wire racks.

3 In a bowl, combine the cheese, milk, onion salt and Worcestershire sauce and mash until smooth. Spread over the cut-outs and top with the garnishes.

VEGETABLES SQUARES

MAKES: *About 32 servings*

2 packages (8 ounce each) refrigerated crescent dinner rolls
11 ounces cream cheese (one 3-ounce package and one 8-ounce package), at room temperature
⅓ cup mayonnaise or Kraft® Salad Dressing
1 teaspoon crushed dried dill
1 teaspoon buttermilk salad dressing mix
1 cup shredded Monterey Jack cheese or Cheddar cheese
finely chopped fresh vegetables, such as peppers, broccoli, tomatoes and green onions

1 Position the rack in the center of the oven and preheat to 350 degrees F.

2 Separate the dough into rectangles and press into a 15-by-10-by-2-inch pan, smoothing along the perforations. Bake for 12 to 15 minutes or until lightly browned. Cool to room temperature.

3 In a small bowl, combine the cream cheese, mayonnaise, dill and salad dressing mix and mix until smooth. Spread over the cooled crust, sprinkle with the cheese and vegetables. Cut into squares to serve.

WATERCRESS ROUNDS

MAKES: *60 servings*

½ cup butter or margarine, at room temperature
¼ cup Wish-Bone® Creamy Cucumber Dressing
1 cup chopped watercress
30 slices thin-sliced white bread
chopped ripe olives or pickles for garnish

1 In a bowl, combine the butter and dressing and whisk until smooth. Add the watercress and stir gently to blend.

2 Using 1½-inch biscuit cutter, cut out 4 rounds from each slice of bread. Using a ½-inch round cutter, cut the centers from half of the rounds.

3 Spread the dressing mixture over the solid rounds and top with the cut-out rounds. Stack the sandwiched rounds, wrap in plastic wrap and chill for at least 2 hours.

4 Serve sprinkled with chopped olives or pickles.

ZUCCHINI-AND-BASIL MUFFINS

MAKES: *10 to 18 muffins*

2 cups all-purpose flour
¼ cup sugar
1 tablespoon baking powder
2 tablespoons minced fresh basil
2 large eggs
¾ cup milk
⅔ cup canola oil
2 cups shredded zucchini
¼ cup grated romano cheese

1 Position the rack in the center of the oven and preheat to 425 degrees F. Lightly grease a 12-cup muffin pan.

2 In a bowl, combine the flour, sugar, baking powder and basil and whisk well.

3 In a large bowl, using an electric mixer on high speed, beat the eggs until light colored. Add the milk and oil and beat until mixed. Add the dry ingredients, all at once, and blend until the dry ingredients are just moistened. Add the zucchini and fold to blend. Spoon into the muffin cups, filling each about two-thirds full. Sprinkle with cheese and bake for 20 to 25 minutes, or until a toothpick inserted in the center of a muffin comes out clean. Cool on wire racks.

ZUCCHINI APPETIZERS

MAKES: *48 servings*

3 cups thinly sliced zucchini
1 cup Bisquick® Baking Mix
½ cup finely chopped white onion
½ cup grated Parmesan or romano cheese
2 teaspoons chopped parsley
¼ teaspoon crushed dried oregano
¼ teaspoon crushed dried chervil
1 clove garlic, chopped
pinch of red pepper flakes
½ cup canola oil
4 large eggs, lightly beaten
salt and pepper

1 Position the rack in the center of the oven and preheat to 350 degrees F. Lightly grease a 13-by-9-inch baking pan.

2 In a large bowl, combine the zucchini, baking mix, onion, cheese, parsley, oregano, chervil, garlic, red pepper flakes, oil and eggs. Season with salt and pepper and stir until blended. Spread into the pan and bake for 20 to 25 minutes or until lightly browned. Cut into rectangles and serve immediately.

ZUCCHINI-CHEESE PANCAKES

MAKES: *6 pancakes*

⅔ cup Bisquick® Baking Mix
¼ cup wheat germ
2 large eggs
½ cup milk
¼ teaspoon pepper
1 zucchini, grated
½ cup Parmesan cheese
1 cup grated Cheddar or Colby cheese

1 Heat a lightly greased griddle or skillet until hot.

2 In a bowl, combine the baking mix, wheat germ, eggs, milk and pepper and stir until well mixed. Add the zucchini, Parmesan cheese and Cheddar cheese and stir until mixed.

3 Drop the batter onto the hot griddle and cook for 2 or 3 minutes until lightly browned. Serve immediately.

Chapter 10

QUICK BREADS

Quick breads are those warm and comforting baked goods we all love: muffins, biscuits, fruit and nut loaves, corn breads and scones. They are made without yeast, relying instead on baking powder and baking soda for leavening. They are easy to make—requiring no resting or rising times and no kneading—and are meant to spend as little time as possible in the bowl after the batter is mixed. It behooves the home cook to get these breads into the oven quickly. This chapter also includes a smattering of recipes calling for store-bought bread—who can argue that these are anything but quick?

APRICOT BREAD

MAKES: *1 loaf*

¼ cup apricot-flavored brandy or liqueur
1 cup diced dried apricots
1 cup all-purpose flour
1 cup whole-wheat flour
1 cup oat bran
1 teaspoon baking soda
1 cup chopped almonds
¼ cup vegetable shortening
½ cup sugar
1 large egg
1 cup buttermilk

1 In a small bowl, combine the brandy and apricots. Stir gently and set aside in a warm place for about 30 minutes for the apricots to plump.

2 Position the rack in the center of the oven and preheat to 350 degrees F. Lightly grease and flour a large loaf pan.

3 In a bowl, combine the flours, oat bran, baking soda and almonds and whisk well.

4 Drain the apricots and reserve the brandy and apricots separately.

5 In a large bowl, using an electric mixer on high speed, cream the vegetable shortening and sugar. Add the egg and reserved brandy and beat until mixed. Stir in the apricots. Add the buttermilk and dry ingredients, alternating additions and beginning and ending with the dry ingredients, and mix just until blended. Do not overmix.

6 Spread in the loaf pan and bake for 60 to 70 minutes, or until a toothpick inserted in the center comes out clean. Cool in the pan on a wire rack for about 10 minutes before turning out to cool completely on the rack.

APRICOT TEA MUFFINS

MAKES: *12 muffins*

12 dried apricot halves
¼ cup packed brown sugar
2 tablespoons butter or margarine
2 cups all-purpose flour
1 tablespoon plus 1 teaspoon baking powder
½ teaspoon salt
¼ cup vegetable shortening
2 large eggs
⅔ cup milk
¼ cup granulated sugar

1 In a small bowl, combine the apricots with enough water to cover, stir gently and set aside in a warm place for about 2 hours for the apricots to plump.

2 Position the rack in the center of the oven and preheat to 400 degrees F. Lightly grease a 12-cup muffin pan.

3 Drain the apricots, discard the water and put an apricot half, hollow side up, in each muffin cup. Fill each apricot half with 1 teaspoon of brown sugar and ½ teaspoon of butter.

4 In a bowl, combine the flour, baking powder and salt and whisk well. Using a pastry blender or two knives, cut the vegetable shortening into the dry ingredients until the mixture resembles coarse crumbs.

5 In a bowl, using an electric mixer on medium speed, beat together the eggs, milk, and granulated sugar until smooth. Add to the dry ingredients and mix just until blended. Do not overmix. Spoon into the muffin cups, filling each about two-thirds full, and bake for 15 to 20 minutes, or until a toothpick inserted in the center of a muffin comes out clean. Cool slightly on wire racks and serve warm.

⅓ cup butter or margarine, at room temperature
¾ cup sugar
2 large eggs
1 cup mashed bananas
½ cup chopped walnuts or pecans
1¾ cups all-purpose flour
1¼ teaspoons baking powder
½ teaspoon baking soda
½ teaspoon salt
¼ cup flat beer, at room temperature

1 Position the rack in the center of the oven and preheat to 350 degrees F. Grease a 9-by-5-inch loaf pan.

2 In a bowl, using an electric mixer on medium speed, cream the sugar and butter together until fluffy. Add the eggs, 1 at a time, beating until smooth. Add the bananas and walnuts and stir until incorporated.

3 In a bowl, combine the flour, baking powder, baking soda and salt and whisk well. Add the beer and dry ingredients, alternating additions and beginning and ending with the dry ingredients and mix just until blended. Do not overmix.

4 Spread in the loaf pan and bake for 55 to 60 minutes, or until a toothpick inserted in the center comes out clean. Cool in the pan on a wire rack for about 10 minutes before turning out to cool completely on the rack.

BANANA BEER BREAD
MAKES: *1 loaf*

1¾ cups all-purpose flour
2 teaspoons baking powder
¼ teaspoon baking soda
½ teaspoon salt
⅔ cup sugar
⅓ cup vegetable shortening, at room temperature
2 large eggs
1 cup mashed bananas

1 Position the rack in the center of the oven and preheat to 350 degrees F. Grease a 9-by-5-inch loaf pan.

2 In a bowl, combine the flour, baking powder, baking soda and salt and whisk well.

3 In another bowl, using an electric mixer set on high, cream the sugar and shortening until fluffy. Beat in the eggs, 1 at a time. Add the bananas and beat until blended. Add the dry ingredients and stir just until blended. Do not overmix.

4 Spread in the pan and bake for 50 to 55 minutes, or until a toothpick inserted in the center comes out clean. Cool in the pan on a wire rack for about 10 minutes before turning out to cool completely on the rack. Wrap in plastic and chill for at least 24 hours before slicing.

BANANA TEA BREAD
MAKES: *1 loaf*

BANANA TEA MUFFINS

MAKES: *32 muffins*

1¾ cups all-purpose flour
2 teaspoons baking powder
¼ teaspoon baking soda
¾ teaspoon salt
1 large egg
⅓ cup canola oil
½ cup sugar
2 bananas, mashed

1 Position the rack in the center of the oven and preheat to 400 degrees F. Lightly grease four 8-cup muffin pans.

2 In a bowl, combine the flour, baking powder, baking soda and salt and whisk well.

3 In another bowl, using an electric mixer on medium speed, beat the egg, oil, sugar, and bananas until smooth and blended. Add the dry ingredients and stir just until blended. Do not overmix.

4 Spoon into the muffin cups, filling each about two-thirds full, and bake for 15 to 20 minutes, or until a toothpick inserted in the center of a muffin comes out clean. Cool slightly on wire racks and serve warm.

BEER BISCUITS

MAKES: *12 to 14 biscuits*

4 cups Bisquick® Baking Mix
3 tablespoons sugar
¾ cup flat beer, at room temperature

1 Position the rack in the center of the oven and preheat to 375 degrees F.

2 In a bowl, combine the baking mix, sugar and beer and stir until just blended. Do not overmix.

3 On a lightly floured work surface, roll out the dough to a thickness of ½ inch and using a 2-inch cookie or biscuit cutter, cut into rounds. Transfer to an ungreased baking sheet, leaving about ½ inch between the biscuits. Bake for 12 to 15 minutes, or until the biscuits are a golden brown. Cool on wire racks.

BEER MUFFINS

MAKES: *16 medium muffins*

4 cups Bisquick® Baking Mix
3 tablespoons sugar
¾ cup flat beer, at room temperature

1 Position the rack in the center of the oven and preheat to 350 degrees F. Lightly grease two 8-cup muffin pans.

2 In a bowl, combine the baking mix, sugar and beer and stir until just blended. Spoon into the muffin cups, filling each about two-thirds full. Bake for 15 to 20 minutes, or until a toothpick inserted in the center of a muffin comes out clean. Cool slightly on wire racks and serve warm.

2 cups all-purpose flour
1 cup sugar
1 tablespoon baking powder
1 teaspoon salt
⅓ cup vegetable shortening
1 large egg
1 tablespoon grated orange zest
1½ cups orange juice
3 tablespoons canola oil
½ cup wheat germ
6 ounces semisweet chocolate, grated
¼ cup golden raisins
¼ cup candied cherry halves
¼ cup walnuts, chopped

1 Position a rack in the center of the oven and preheat the oven to 350 degrees F. Lightly grease a 9-by-5-inch loaf pan.

2 In a bowl, combine the flour, sugar, baking powder and salt and whisk well. Using a pastry blender or two knives, cut the vegetable shortening into the dry ingredients until the mixture resembles coarse crumbs.

3 In another bowl, combine the egg, orange zest, orange juice and oil and whisk until blended. Add the dry ingredients and stir just until mixed. Add the wheat germ, chocolate, raisins, cherries and nuts and stir until incorporated. Do not overmix.

4 Spread in the pan and bake for 55 to 60 minutes, or until a toothpick inserted in the center comes out clean. Cool in the pan for about 10 minutes before turning out onto a wire rack to cool completely.

BISHOP'S BREAD
MAKES: *1 loaf*

1 package (10 count) Pillsbury® Refrigerator Biscuits
¼ cup butter or margarine
3 tablespoons crumbled blue cheese

1 Position the rack in the center of the oven and preheat to 400 degrees F. Lightly grease two 8-inch round baking pans.

2 Separate the biscuits and cut each into quarters. Arrange in the pans so that they fill the pans and barely touch each other.

3 In a small saucepan, combine the butter and cheese and heat over low heat, stirring, until the cheese melts and the mixture is blended. Pour over the biscuits and bake for 12 to 15 minutes, or until golden brown.

BLUE CHEESE BISCUITS
MAKES: *40 servings*

BOSTON BROWN BREAD

MAKES: *4 small loaves*

1 cup all-purpose flour
1 cup graham flour
1 cup cornmeal
1½ teaspoons baking soda
1 teaspoon salt
¾ cup molasses
2 cup sour milk or buttermilk

1 Position the rack in center of oven and preheat to 350 degrees F. Lightly grease four 6-by-3-inch loaf pans.

2 In a large bowl, combine the flours, cornmeal, baking soda and salt and whisk well.

3 In a bowl, using an electric mixer on high speed, beat the molasses and sour milk until blended. Add the dry ingredients and stir just until mixed. Do not overmix.

4 Spoon into the pans and bake for 55 to 60 minutes, or until a toothpick inserted in the center of a loaf comes out clean. Cool in the pans for about 5 minutes before turning out onto wire racks to cool completely.

BOSTON-STYLE POPOVERS

MAKES: *10 to 12 popovers*

1 cup all-purpose flour
¼ teaspoon salt
1 cup milk
1 large egg, separated, yolk lightly beaten
maple syrup or honey

1 Position the rack in the center of the oven and preheat to 425 degrees F. Lightly grease 12 ovenproof custard cups and set on a baking sheet. Put the baking sheet in the oven to heat the cups.

2 In a bowl, combine the flour and salt and whisk well. Add ½ cup of milk and stir gently until blended. Add the remaining ½ cup of milk and the egg yolk and stir until well mixed.

3 In a clean, dry bowl, using an electric mixer on high speed, beat the egg white until stiff, but not dry, peaks form. Add to the batter and fold just until incorporated. Scrape into the custard cups and bake for 15 to 18 minutes, or until puffed and golden brown. Remove from the oven, prick all over with the tines of a fork, and bake for 5 minutes longer until set. Serve immediately with syrup or honey.

COOKING NOTE: **While it's important that the custard cups are hot when filled with batter, take care not to leave them in the oven any longer than necessary to avoid the possibility of cracking. While the popovers are baking, do not open the oven door.**

BROWN RICE MUFFINS

MAKES: *12 muffins*

1¼ cups whole-wheat flour
2 tablespoons packed light-brown sugar
2 teaspoons baking powder
2 large eggs
⅔ cup skim milk
¼ cup canola oil
¼ teaspoon almond extract
1 cup cooked brown rice

1 Position the rack in the center of the oven and preheat to 400 degrees F. Lightly grease a 12-cup muffin pan.

2 In a bowl, combine the flour, brown sugar and baking powder and whisk well.

3 In another bowl, using an electric mixer on high speed, beat the eggs, milk, oil and extract until smooth. Add the rice and mix well. Add the dry ingredients and stir just until mixed. Do not overmix. Spoon into the muffin cups, filling each about two-thirds full and bake for 15 to 20 minutes, or until a toothpick inserted in the center of a muffin comes out clean. Cool slightly on wire racks and serve warm.

¾ cup sliced orange zest
3 cups all-purpose flour
1 cup sugar
1 tablespoon plus 2 teaspoons
  baking powder
1 teaspoon salt
1 cup sliced Brazil nuts
2 large eggs
1½ cups milk
2 tablespoons butter or margarine,
  melted

1 Position the rack in the center of the oven and preheat to 350 degrees F. Grease a 9-by-5-inch loaf pan.

2 In a saucepan, combine the zest with enough water to cover and bring to a boil over high heat. Reduce the heat and simmer for about 10 minutes or until the zest is tender. Drain and dry between paper towels.

3 In a large bowl, combine the flour, sugar, baking powder and salt and whisk well. Add the orange zest and nuts and toss to coat.

4 In a bowl, using an electric mixer on medium speed, beat the eggs until light colored. Add the milk and butter and beat until blended. Add the dry ingredients and stir just until mixed. Do not overmix. Spread in the pan and bake for 55 to 60 minutes, or until a toothpick inserted in the center comes out clean. Cool in the pan for about 10 minutes before turning out onto a wire rack to cool completely.

BRAZIL NUT-ORANGE BREAD

MAKES: *1 loaf*

⅔ cup all-purpose flour
2 cups whole-wheat flour
⅔ cup packed brown sugar
2 teaspoons baking soda
1 teaspoon pumpkin pie spice
2 cups buttermilk
¾ cup raisins

1 Position the rack in the center of the oven and preheat to 350 degrees F. Lightly grease a 6-cup jumbo muffin pan.

2 In a bowl, combine the flours, sugar, baking soda, and pumpkin pie spice and whisk well. Add the buttermilk and stir just until mixed. Do not overmix. Add the raisins and fold until incorporated. Spoon into the muffin cups, filling each about two-thirds full and bake for 35 to 40 minutes or until a toothpick inserted in the center of a muffin comes out clean. Cool slightly on wire racks and serve warm.

BROWN BREAD MUFFINS

MAKES: *6 large muffins*

BUTTER STICKS

MAKES: *24 servings*

⅓ cup butter or margarine
2 cups Bisquick® Baking Mix
½ cup cold water

1 Position the rack in the center of the oven and preheat to 425 degrees F.

2 Put the butter in a 13-by-9-inch baking pan and put it in the oven for about 5 minutes to melt. Tilt the pan so that the butter covers the bottom and set aside.

3 In a bowl, combine the baking mix and water and stir with a fork until it forms a soft dough.

Gather the dough into a ball and knead several times on a lightly floured surface. Roll into a 16-by-6-inch rectangle and cut in half lengthwise. Cut each half into twelve 3-inch-long strips.

4 Lay the strips in the pan and turn several times to coat with butter. Arrange the strips in rows in the pan and bake for 12 to 15 minutes, or until golden brown. Cool on wire racks and serve warm or at room temperature.

BUTTERNUT SQUASH MUFFINS

MAKES: *8 muffins*

2 cups all-purpose flour
2 tablespoons sugar
2½ teaspoons baking powder
1 teaspoon salt
1 large egg, beaten
1 cup milk
⅔ cup cooked butternut squash pulp
¼ cup butter, melted

1 Position the rack in the center of the oven and preheat to 400 degrees F. Lightly grease an 8-cup muffin pan.

2 In a bowl, combine the flour, sugar, baking powder and salt and whisk well.

3 In another bowl, combine the egg, milk, squash pulp and butter and mix well. Add the dry

ingredients and stir just until mixed. Do not overmix. Spoon into the muffin cups, filling each about two-thirds full and bake for 15 to 20 minutes, or until a toothpick inserted in the center of a muffin comes out clean. Cool slightly on wire racks and serve warm.

COOKING NOTE: For cooked squash pulp, prick a squash in several places with a sharp knife and bake in a 400 degree F. oven for about 45 minutes or until soft. Cool and peel, remove the seeds and fiber and push the pulp through a sieve. One squash will yield at least 1½ to 2 cups pulp.

3½ cups all-purpose flour
2 teaspoons baking soda
1½ teaspoons salt
4 large eggs
2 cups sugar
1 cup canola oil
1½ cups cooked butternut squash
  pulp
1 cup water
½ cup honey
1½ teaspoons ground nutmeg
1½ teaspoons ground cinnamon
1 teaspoon ground mace
1 cup seedless raisins

1 Position the rack in the center of the oven and preheat to 350 degrees F. Lightly grease three 9-by-5-inch loaf pans.

2 In a bowl, combine the flour, baking soda and salt and whisk well.

3 In another bowl, using an electric mixer on high speed, beat the eggs, sugar and oil until smooth. Add the squash, water, honey, nutmeg, cinnamon and mace and stir until mixed. Add the raisins and fold until incorporated. Add the dry ingredients and stir just until mixed. Do not overmix. Spread in the pans and bake for 55 to 60 minutes, or until a toothpick inserted in the center of 1 loaf comes out clean. Cool in the pans for about 10 minutes before turning out onto a wire rack to cool completely.

BUTTERNUT SQUASH-RAISIN BREAD

MAKES: *3 loaves*

1½ cups cornmeal
1½ cups all-purpose flour
3 tablespoons sugar
1 tablespoon plus 1½ teaspoons
  baking powder
1½ teaspoons salt
1½ teaspoons pepper
1 teaspoon cayenne
½ cup diced red bell pepper
¼ cup diced green bell pepper
¼ cup minced onion
2 large eggs
1½ cups butter or margarine
¼ cup canola oil

1 Position the rack in the center of the oven and preheat to 400 degrees F. Lightly grease a 12-cup muffin pan.

2 In a bowl, combine the cornmeal, flour, sugar, baking powder, salt, pepper and cayenne and whisk well. Add the peppers and onions and toss until coated.

3 In another bowl, using an electric mixer on high speed, beat the eggs, butter and oil until smooth. Add the dry ingredients and stir just until mixed. Do not overmix. Spoon into the muffin cups, filling each one about two-thirds full and bake for 18 to 20 minutes, or until a toothpick inserted in the center of a muffin comes out clean. Cool slightly on wire racks and serve warm.

CAJUN CORN MUFFINS

MAKES: *12 muffins*

CALIFORNIA FRUIT BREAD

MAKES: *1 loaf*

1½ cups all-purpose flour
1½ teaspoons baking powder
½ teaspoon baking soda
½ teaspoon salt
⅓ cup packed brown sugar
¼ cup butter, at room temperature
2 teaspoons grated orange zest
2 teaspoons grated lemon zest
1 large egg
1 cup small-curd cottage cheese
½ cup chopped dried prunes
½ cup chopped dried apricots
¼ cup chopped walnuts or pecans

1 Position the rack in the center of the oven and preheat to 350 degrees F. Lightly grease an 8-by-5-inch loaf pan.

2 In a small bowl, combine the flour, baking powder, baking soda and salt and whisk well.

3 In a bowl, combine the sugar, butter, orange zest and lemon zest and mash with a fork. Add the egg and cottage cheese and mix until blended. Add the prunes, apricots and pecans and mix well. Add the dry ingredients and stir just until mixed. Do not overmix. The dough will be stiff. Spread in the pan and bake for 55 to 60 minutes, or until a toothpick inserted in the center comes out clean. Cool in the pan for about 10 minutes before turning out onto a wire rack to cool completely. Wrap in plastic and chill for at least 4 hours before serving.

CARAWAY-ONION BISCUITS

MAKES: *12 biscuits*

2½ cups whole-wheat flour
2 teaspoons baking powder
½ cup canola oil
2 large eggs
1⅓ cups grated white onions
2 tablespoons caraway seeds

1 Position the rack in the center of the oven and preheat to 425 degrees F. Lightly grease a baking sheet.

2 In a bowl, combine the flour and baking powder and whisk well.

3 In another bowl, combine the oil, eggs and onions and mix well. Add the dry ingredients and stir until well blended.

4 On a lightly floured surface, roll the dough to a thickness of 1½ inches. Using a 2- to 2½-inch biscuit cutter, cut out rounds and transfer them to the baking sheet. Bake for about 10 minutes or until golden brown. Serve hot.

1½ cups all-purpose flour
¼ cup wheat germ
2 teaspoons baking powder
½ teaspoon baking soda
½ cup packed light-brown sugar
¼ teaspoon salt
⅛ teaspoon ground cinnamon
dash of ground mace
¼ cup chilled butter or margarine,
   cut into pieces
1 large egg
¼ cup plain yogurt or sour cream
1 teaspoon vanilla extract
1 cup grated carrots
⅔ cup golden raisins
½ cup chopped pecans or hazelnuts

1 Position the rack in the center of the oven and preheat to 400 degrees F. Lightly grease a baking sheet.

2 In a bowl, combine the flour, wheat germ, baking powder, baking soda, brown sugar, salt, cinnamon and mace. Using a pastry blender or two knives, cut the butter into the dry ingredients until the mixture resembles coarse crumbs.

3 In a bowl, using an electric mixer on medium speed, beat the egg until foamy. Add the yogurt and vanilla and beat until smooth. Add the dry ingredients and stir just until mixed. Add the carrots, raisins and pecans and fold until incorporated. The dough will be sticky.

4 With floured hands, spread the dough on the baking sheet and pat into an 8-inch circle. Cut the dough into 8 wedges and bake for about 18 to 20 minutes, or until golden brown. Cool on wire racks.

CARROT SCONES WITH PECANS

MAKES: *8 scones*

---

3 cups all-purpose flour
2 teaspoons baking powder
1 teaspoon baking soda
½ teaspoon salt
2 cups sugar
1¼ cups canola oil
4 large eggs, lightly beaten
2 cups grated carrots
½ cup chopped walnuts or pecans
½ cup raisins

1 Position the rack in the center of the oven and preheat to 350 degrees F. Lightly grease two 12-cup muffin pans.

2 In a bowl, combine the flour, baking powder, baking soda and salt and whisk well.

3 In another bowl, combine the sugar and oil and whisk until smooth. Add the eggs, 1 at a time, beating well after each addition. Add the dry ingredients and mix just until mixed. Add the carrots, walnuts and raisins and fold until incorporated.

4 Spoon into the muffin cups, filling each about two-thirds full, and bake for 35 to 40 minutes, or until a toothpick inserted in the center comes out clean. Cool slightly on wire racks and serve warm.

CARROT MUFFINS

MAKES: *24 muffins*

CHEDDAR CHEESE POPOVERS

MAKES: *12 popovers*

1 cup all-purpose flour
½ teaspoon baking powder
¼ teaspoon salt
1 large egg
1 cup milk
½ cup grated Cheddar cheese

1 Position the rack in the center of the oven and preheat to 450 degrees F. Lightly grease 12 ovenproof custard cups and set on a baking sheet. Put the baking sheet in the oven to heat the cups.

2 In a bowl, combine the flour, baking powder and salt and whisk well.

3 In another bowl, using an electric mixer on medium speed, beat the egg until light colored. Add the milk and stir to mix. Add the dry ingredients and stir just until mixed.

4 Spoon into the custard cups, filling each three-quarters full. Top evenly with the cheese and bake for about 25 minutes, or until the popovers begin to rise. Reduce the heat to 350 degrees and bake for about 5 minutes longer until the tops are set. Turn off the oven and let the popovers sit undisturbed for about 5 minutes. Prick with the tines of a fork and leave in the hot oven for about 5 more minutes. Serve immediately.

COOKING NOTE: While it's important that the custard cups are hot when filled with batter, take care not to leave them in the oven any longer than necessary to avoid the possibility of cracking. While the popovers are baking, do not open the oven door.

CHEDDAR CHEESE SCONES WITH HERBS

MAKES: *8 scones*

4 cups all-purpose flour
1 tablespoon plus 1 teaspoon baking powder
½ teaspoon crushed dried basil
¼ teaspoon crushed dried thyme
¼ teaspoon ground red pepper
1 teaspoon salt
⅔ cup vegetable shortening
1 cup Cheddar cheese
1 teaspoon Dijon mustard
1⅓ cups milk

1 Position the rack in the center of the oven and preheat to 425 degrees F. Lightly grease a baking sheet.

2 In a bowl, combine the flour, baking powder, basil, thyme, red pepper and salt. Using a pastry blender or two knives, cut the vegetable shortening into the dry ingredients until the mixture resembles coarse crumbs. Add ¾ cup of the cheese, the mustard and the milk and mix with a fork to form a soft dough.

3 On a lightly floured surface, knead the dough 6 or 7 times or until smooth and cohesive. Divide the dough in half and transfer to the baking sheet. Pat each piece into a 7-inch circle. Cut each circle into 4 wedges and prick with the tines of a fork. Brush lightly with water and sprinkle with the remaining cheese. Bake for 15 to 20 minutes, or until golden brown. Serve warm.

5 cups Bisquick® Baking Mix
4 cups shredded Cheddar cheese
½ cup finely chopped green onions, including the tops
1½ cups flat beer, at room temperature
¼ cup all-purpose flour

1 Position the rack in the center of the oven and preheat to 425 degrees F.

2 In a bowl, combine the baking mix, cheese and onions and mix well. Make a well in the center of the dry ingredients and add the beer. Stir with a fork just until moistened.

3 Sprinkle the flour on a work surface and knead the dough 8 or 9 times or until no longer sticky. Pat out to a thickness of about 1 inch and using a 3-inch biscuit cutter, cut out 12 to 14 buns. Transfer to an ungreased baking sheet and bake for 10 to 12 minutes or until golden brown. Serve warm.

CHEDDAR CHEESE BEER BUNS

MAKES: *12 to 14 buns*

---

1 cup all-purpose flour
½ teaspoon crushed dried dill
2 large eggs, lightly beaten
1 cup milk
pinch of salt
⅓ cup shredded Colby or Wisconsin brick cheese

1 Position the rack in the center of the oven and preheat to 450 degrees F. Lightly grease a 12-cup muffin pan.

2 In a bowl, combine the flour, dill, eggs, milk, salt and cheese and beat until smooth. Spoon into the muffin cups, filling each about two-thirds full, and bake for about 20 minutes. Reduce the heat to 350 degrees F and bake for about 25 minutes longer without opening the oven door. Poke the tops of the buns with the tines of a fork and bake for about 5 minutes longer to let the buns dry out. Serve hot.

COLBY CHEESE BUNS

MAKES: *12 buns*

---

2 cups all-purpose flour
2 teaspoons baking powder
¼ teaspoon baking soda
1 teaspoon salt
2 tablespoons vegetable shortening
1 large egg
⅔ cup sour milk or buttermilk
¼ cup snipped chives

1 Position the rack in the center of the oven and preheat to 400 degrees F. Lightly grease a 12-cup muffin pan.

2 In a bowl, combine the flour, baking powder, baking soda and salt and whisk well.

3 In another bowl, using an electric mixer on medium speed, beat the shortening until creamy. Add the egg and milk and beat until smooth. Add the dry ingredients and stir just until mixed. Do not overmix. Add the chives and fold to incorporate.

4 Spoon into the muffin cups, filling each about two-thirds full, and bake for 12 to 15 minutes or until a toothpick inserted in the center of a muffin comes out clean. Cool on wire racks.

CHIVE DINNER MUFFINS

MAKES: *10 to 12 muffins*

COCONUT TEA SQUARES

MAKES: *24 servings*

½ cup sweetened condensed milk
6 slices white bread, crusts trimmed, quartered
½ cup shredded coconut

1 Position the rack in the center of the oven, and preheat to 350 degrees F.

2 In a saucepan, heat the milk for about 5 minutes until tepid. Using a pastry brush or small spoon, spread the bread squares with milk and then sprinkle with coconut. Transfer to a baking sheet and bake for 8 to 10 minutes, or until the coconut starts to color. Serve hot or warm.

QUICK CORN BREAD

MAKES: *10 to 12 servings*

4 cups Corn Bread Mix (see page 82)
1⅓ cups water
⅓ cup sugar
1 egg

1 Position the rack in the center of the oven and preheat to 425 degrees F. Lightly grease a 9-inch-square baking pan.

2 In a bowl, combine the mix, water, sugar and egg and stir vigorously until well mixed. Pour into the pan and bake for 20 to 25 minutes or until golden brown Cool in the pan set on a wire rack.

CORN CRISPS

MAKES: *40 to 60 crisps*

1 cup water
1 cup less 2 tablespoons white cornmeal
¼ teaspoon salt
3 tablespoons vegetable shortening

1 Position the rack in the center of oven and preheat to 350 degrees F. Lightly grease a jelly-roll pan.

2 In a saucepan, bring the water to a boil over high heat and slowly add the cornmeal, stirring until smooth. Reduce the heat to medium, add the salt and shortening and continue to stir until incorporated.

3 Pour into the pan and spread evenly (this is most easily done using a metal spatula that has been dipped in cold water). Bake for 18 to 20 minutes, or until golden brown. Cool in the pan set on a wire rack and then cut or break into crisps.

½ cup all-purpose flour
1 cup yellow cornmeal
¼ teaspoon baking soda
½ cup milk
3 tablespoons canola oil
¼ teaspoon Worcestershire sauce
dash of hot-pepper sauce
butter or margarine, melted
caraway seeds or poppy seeds

1 Position the rack in the center of the oven and preheat to 350 degrees F. Lightly grease 2 baking sheets.

2 In a bowl, combine the flour, cornmeal and baking soda and whisk well.

3 In another bowl, combine the milk, oil, Worcestershire sauce and pepper sauce and whisk until blended. Add the dry ingredients and stir to form a soft dough.

4 On a lightly floured work surface, knead the dough 8 to 10 times or until smooth. Place by spoonfuls on the baking sheets and flatten into oblongs about 4 inches long and ¼ inch thick. Bake for 6 or 7 minutes, or until golden brown. While still warm, brush with melted butter and sprinkle with caraway seeds. Cool completely on wire racks.

CORNMEAL THINS
MAKES: *48 servings*

1 cup fresh cranberries, coarsely
   chopped
½ cup butter or margarine, melted
½ cup packed light-brown sugar
2 cups all-purpose flour
2 tablespoons granulated sugar
1 tablespoon baking powder
½ teaspoon salt
¼ cup raisins
1 large egg
1 cup milk

1 Position the rack in the center of the oven and preheat to 400 degrees F. Lightly grease a 12-cup muffin pan.

2 Divide the cranberries among the muffin cups and spoon about a teaspoon of butter into each

cup. Sprinkle about 2 teaspoons of brown sugar in each cup and set aside.

3 In a bowl, combine the flour, granulated sugar, baking powder, salt and raisins and mix well.

4 In another bowl, using an electric mixer on medium-high speed, beat the egg, milk and remaining butter. Add to the dry ingredients and stir just until moistened. Spoon into the muffin cups, filling each about two-thirds full, and bake for 25 to 30 minutes, or until a toothpick inserted in the center of a muffin comes out clean. Invert the muffins onto a platter and serve upside-down and warm.

CRANBERRY UPSIDE-DOWN MUFFINS
MAKES: *12 muffins*

DILL-AND-THYME MUFFINS

MAKES: *10 to 12 muffins*

⅔ cup oat bran
⅔ cup all-purpose flour
⅔ cup whole-wheat flour
1 tablespoon baking powder
1 teaspoon nonfat dry milk
1½ teaspoons crushed dried dill
½ teaspoon crushed dried thyme
½ teaspoon salt
¼ teaspoon garlic powder
1 cup milk
½ cup cottage cheese or ricotta cheese
¼ cup butter or margarine, at room temperature
2 large egg whites
1 teaspoon canola oil

1 Position the rack in the center of the oven and preheat to 400 degrees F. Lightly grease a 12-cup muffin pan.

2 In a bowl, combine the oat bran, flours, baking powder, dry milk, dill, thyme, salt and garlic powder.

3 In a bowl, using an electric mixer on high speed, beat together the milk, cheese, butter, egg whites and oil until smooth. Add the dry ingredients and stir just until mixed. Do not overmix. Spoon into the muffin cups, filling each about two-thirds full, and bake for 20 to 25 minutes, or until a toothpick inserted in the center of a muffin comes out clean. Cool slightly on a wire rack and serve warm.

ENGLISH MUFFIN SPECIALS

MAKES: *12 servings*

1½ cups shredded American cheese
1 cup chopped pitted ripe olives
½ cup thinly sliced green onions
½ cup Kraft® Real Mayonnaise
½ teaspoon curry powder
6 English muffins, halved and toasted

1 Position the broiler rack so that it is about 4 inches from the heat source and preheat the broiler.

2 In a bowl, combine the cheese, olives, onions, mayonnaise and curry powder and mix well. Spread on the muffin halves and broil for 2 or 3 minutes until the cheese melts.

GARLIC MUFFINS

MAKES: *8 servings*

4 English muffins, halved and toasted
6 tablespoons Garlic Butter (see page 109)
grated Parmesan cheese

1 Position the broiler rack so that it is about 4 inches from the heat source and preheat the broiler.

2 Spread the muffin halves with butter and sprinkle with cheese. Broil for 2 or 3 minutes or until the cheese melts and turns golden brown.

½ cup Garlic Butter (see page 109)
6 hot dog buns, sliced lengthwise into 4 sticks each
¼ cup grated romano or Parmesan cheese
toasted sesame seeds

1 Position the rack in the center of the oven and preheat to 450 degrees F. Lightly grease a baking sheet.

2 In a saucepan, melt the butter over low heat and brush on the buns. Sprinkle with cheese and sesame seeds and transfer to the baking sheet. Bake for 6 to 8 minutes or until lightly browned. Serve hot.

GARLIC STICKS

MAKES: *About 24 servings*

1½ cups graham flour
1 cup all-purpose flour
¼ cup sugar
1 teaspoon baking soda
1 teaspoon baking powder
½ teaspoon salt
2 large eggs
3 tablespoons butter or margarine, melted
1½ cups sour milk or buttermilk

1 Position the rack in the center of oven and preheat to 425 degrees F. Lightly grease a 12-cup muffin pan.

2 In a bowl, combine the flours, sugar, baking soda, baking powder and salt and whisk well.

3 In another bowl, using an electric mixer on high speed, beat the eggs until light colored. Add the butter and milk and stir to mix. Add the dry ingredients, stirring just until mixed. Do not overmix. Spoon into the muffin cups, filling each about two-thirds full, and bake for 15 to 20 minutes, or until a toothpick inserted in the center comes out clean. Cool slightly on wire racks and serve warm.

GRAHAM MUFFINS

MAKES: *15 to 20 muffins*

---

3 large hard-cooked eggs, chopped
2 tablespoons Kraft® Real Mayonnaise
1 tablespoon sliced green onion
1 tablespoon chopped pimiento
½ teaspoon seasoned salt
½ teaspoon Dijon mustard
1 can (5 ounces) Hungry Jack® Refrigerated Biscuits
½ cup shredded Cheddar or Wisconsin brick cheese

1 Position the rack in the center of oven and preheat to 375 degrees F.

2 In a bowl, combine the eggs, mayonnaise, onions, pimiento, salt and mustard and blend well.

3 Separate the dough into 5 biscuits and roll each one out to a 3½-inch circle. Transfer to an ungreased baking sheet and spread each with the egg mixture, leaving a ½-inch border. Sprinkle with cheese and bake for 12 to 18 minutes, or until the biscuits are a golden brown. Serve hot.

HUNGRY JACK EGG SALAD BISCUITS

MAKES: *5 servings*

HUSH PUPPIES

MAKES: *About 24 servings*

vegetable oil
1½ cups yellow cornmeal
½ cup all-purpose flour
1 teaspoon baking powder
½ teaspoon baking soda
1 teaspoon salt
1 large egg
1 small white onion, chopped
1 cup buttermilk
1 jalapeño pepper, finely chopped

1 In a heavy skillet or deep-fat fryer, pour the oil to a depth of about 2 inches and heat over medium-high heat until hot (370 degrees F. in a deep-fat fryer).

2 In a bowl, combine the cornmeal, flour, baking powder, baking soda and salt and whisk well.

3 In another bowl, combine the egg, onion and buttermilk and whisk well. Add the dry ingredients and stir until well mixed. Add the jalapeño and fold to incorporate. Drop by tablespoonfuls into the oil and fry for about 1 minute on each side, or until golden brown on both sides.

IRISH SODA SCONES

MAKES: *8 scones*

2 cups all-purpose flour
1½ teaspoons baking powder
½ teaspoon baking soda
3 tablespoons packed light-brown sugar
1½ teaspoons caraway seeds
½ teaspoon salt
⅓ cup chilled butter or margarine, diced
1 large egg
½ cup buttermilk or sour milk
¼ cup golden raisins
¼ cup seedless raisins
½ cup chopped walnuts or pecans

1 Position the rack in the center of the oven and preheat to 375 degrees F. Lightly grease a baking sheet.

2 In a bowl, combine the flour, baking powder, baking soda, sugar, caraway seeds and salt.

Using a pastry blender or two knives, cut the butter into the dry ingredients until the mixture resembles coarse crumbs.

3 In another bowl, using an electric mixer on low speed, beat the egg until foamy. Add the milk and stir until smooth. Add the dry ingredients and stir until moistened. The dough will be sticky. with floured hands, knead in the raisins and walnuts until incorporated. Transfer to the baking sheet and pat into a 9-inch circle. Cut the scone into 8 wedges and bake for 20 to 25 minutes, or until golden brown. Cool on a wire rack.

1 cup plus 2 tablespoons all-purpose
  flour
1½ teaspoons baking powder
½ teaspoon salt
½ cup finely grated Wisconsin brick
  or Tillamook cheese
2 tablespoons chopped tomato
1 teaspoon minced seeded jalapeño
½ cup milk

1 Position the rack in the center
of the oven and preheat to 450
degrees F. Lightly grease a baking sheet.

2 In a bowl, combine the flour,
baking powder and salt and
whisk to blend. Add the cheese,
tomato and jalapeño and stir.
Slowly add the milk, stirring
until the mixture forms a soft
dough.

3 Shape into 6 balls and place on
the baking sheet. Flatten each
ball into a 3-inch round and bake
for 12 to 15 minutes, or until
golden brown. Serve warm.

JALAPEÑO-AND-
CHEESE BISCUITS

MAKES: *6 biscuits*

2½ cups all-purpose flour
1 tablespoon plus 1 teaspoon baking
  powder
1 tablespoon sugar
1 teaspoon caraway seeds
½ teaspoon salt
¼ cup plus 1 tablespoon butter or
  margarine, at room temperature
1 large egg, beaten
¾ cup light cream
melted butter for topping

1 Position the rack in the center
of the oven and preheat to 400
degrees F. Lightly grease a baking sheet.

2 In a bowl, combine the flour,
baking powder, sugar, caraway
seeds and salt. Using a pastry

blender or two knives, cut the
butter into the dry ingredients
until the mixture resembles
coarse crumbs. Add the egg and
cream and mix until the dough
pulls away from the sides of the
bowl.

3 On a lightly floured surface,
roll out the dough to a thickness
of ¼ inch. Using a 2-inch biscuit
cutter, cut out 10 rounds and
transfer to the baking sheet.
Brush with butter and bake for 15
to 20 minutes, or until golden
brown. Serve hot.

LUNCHEON ROLLS

MAKES: *About 10 rolls*

MAYONNAISE POPOVERS

MAKES: *About 12 popovers*

2 cups all-purpose flour
1 teaspoon sugar
3 tablespoons mayonnaise
1 cup milk

1 Position the rack in the center of the oven and preheat to 350 degrees F. Grease a 12-cup muffin pan.

2 In a bowl, combine the flour, sugar, mayonnaise and milk and whisk until smooth. Pour into the muffin cups, filling each about three-quarters full, and bake for 15 to 20 minutes, or until the tops are firm and golden brown. Serve hot.

NUT BREAD SURPRISE

MAKES: *6 to 8 servings*

2½ cups all-purpose flour
1 cup sugar
1 tablespoon plus ½ teaspoon baking powder
1 teaspoon salt
¼ cup chopped hazelnuts
¼ cup chopped pecans
¼ cup chopped peanuts
¼ cup chopped Brazil nuts
1 large egg
3 tablespoons canola oil
1¼ cups milk
Roquefort Cheese Spread (recipe follows) or cream cheese

1 Position the rack in the center of the oven and preheat to 350 degrees F. Lightly grease a 9-by-5-inch loaf pan.

2 In a large bowl, combine the flour, sugar, baking powder, salt and nuts and toss to mix.

3 In another bowl, using an electric mixer on medium speed, beat the egg until foamy. Add the oil and milk and beat until mixed. Add to the dry ingredients and stir until blended. Transfer to the pan, smooth the top and bake for 55 to 60 minutes, or until a toothpick inserted in the center comes out clean. Turn out onto a wire rack to cool completely before serving with cheese spread.

COOKING NOTE: **For more flavor, add ½ teaspoon of almond or hazelnut extract with the oil and milk.**

ROQUEFORT CHEESE SPREAD

MAKES: *About 3 cups*

2 packages (3 ounces each) cream cheese, softened
3 ounces Roquefort cheese
2 cups heavy cream
pinch of salt

1 In a bowl, using an electric mixer on medium speed, beat the cream cheese, Roquefort cheese, and 1 cup of cream until smooth. Add the salt and beat vigorously for 1 to 2 minutes.

2 In another bowl, using an electric mixer on medium-high speed, whip the remaining cream until soft peaks form. Add to the cheese mixture and fold gently. Cover and chill for at least 1 hour.

½ loaf (8 ounces) frozen bread
   dough, thawed
¼ teaspoon crushed dried oregano
¼ teaspoon crushed dried basil
¼ teaspoon crushed dried dill
¼ teaspoon garlic powder
½ cup shredded Colby or Wisconsin
   brick cheese
¼ cup finely chopped cooked ham

1 Position the rack in the center
of the oven and preheat to 400
degrees F. Lightly grease a baking sheet.

2 On a lightly floured work surface, roll the dough into a rectangle about ¼-inch thick.

3 In a small bowl or cup, combine the oregano, basil, dill and
garlic powder and mix well.
Sprinkle over the dough. Sprinkle with cheese and then ham
and, starting at a long side, roll
into a log, tucking in the edges as
you roll. Seal the dough, transfer
to the baking sheet and bake for
55 to 60 minutes, or until lightly
browned. Cut into slices for
serving.

NORTHERN STROMBOLI

MAKES: *About 16 servings*

---

2 cups all-purpose flour
2 tablespoons sugar
1 tablespoon baking powder
½ teaspoon salt
¼ cup vegetable shortening
1 cup drained chopped canned
   peaches
¾ cup milk
1 teaspoon chopped orange zest
Orange Butter (recipe follows)

1 Position the rack in the center
of the oven and preheat to 425
degrees F. Lightly grease a baking sheet.

2 In a bowl, combine the flour,
sugar, baking powder and salt.
Using a pastry blender or two

knives, cut the vegetable shortening into the dry ingredients until
the mixture resembles coarse
crumbs. Add the peaches, milk
and zest and stir to make a soft
dough.

3 On a lightly floured work surface, knead the dough 6 to 8
times and then roll to a thickness
of ½ inch. Using a 1½- to 2-inch
cookie cutter, cut out rounds and
transfer to the baking sheet. Bake
for 10 to 12 minutes, or until
golden brown. Transfer to a wire
rack to cool.

PEACH BISCUITS

MAKES: *About 14 biscuits*

ORANGE BUTTER

MAKES: *About ½ cup*

½ cup unsalted butter, at room
   temperature
1 tablespoon finely grated orange
   zest

In a small bowl, combine the
butter and zest and blend well.
Cover and set aside at room
temperature for at least 2 hours.
Stir, cover and chill until ready
to use.

PRUNE SCONES WITH BRANDY

MAKES: *6 to 8 scones*

1 cup pitted and chopped prunes
⅓ cup Christian Brother's® brandy
2 cups all-purpose flour
2 teaspoons baking powder
⅓ cup packed light-brown sugar
⅓ cup chilled butter, diced
1 large egg
⅓ cup milk
1 teaspoon vanilla extract
½ cup chopped pecans or hazelnuts
3 ounces bittersweet chocolate, finely chopped

1 Position the rack in the center of the oven and preheat to 400 degrees F. Lightly grease a baking sheet.

2 In a saucepan, combine the prunes and brandy and bring to a boil over medium heat. Remove from the heat.

3 In a bowl, combine the flour, baking powder and sugar. Using a pastry blender or two knives, cut the butter into the dry ingredients until the mixture resembles coarse crumbs.

4 In a bowl, combine the prunes, egg, milk and vanilla and mix well. Add to the dry ingredients and stir just until mixed. Add the pecans and chocolate and stir well.

5 Using a ⅓-cup measure, drop the dough onto the baking sheet, leaving about 2 inches between each scone. Bake for 18 to 20 minutes, or until golden brown. Cool on wire racks or serve warm.

POPOVERS

MAKES: *6 popovers*

2 large eggs
1 cup milk
2 tablespoons all-purpose flour
3 tablespoons butter or margarine, melted
2 tablespoons finely chopped parsley

1 Position the rack in the center of the oven and preheat to 425 degrees F. Lightly grease a 6-cup muffin pan.

2 In a bowl, using an electric mixer on high speed, beat the eggs until thick and light. Add the milk and flour and beat well. Add the butter and parsley and beat until mixed. Pour into the muffin cups, filling each about half full. Bake for 35 to 40 minutes, or until puffed and browned. Do not open the oven door during baking. Serve hot.

RANCH CRACKERS

MAKES: *6 to 8 servings*

¾ cup canola oil
1 envelope Hidden Valley Ranch® Salad Dressing Mix
½ teaspoon crushed dill
¼ teaspoon lemon pepper
¼ teaspoon garlic powder
1 package (16 ounces) oyster crackers

1 Position the rack in the center of the oven and preheat to 275 degrees.

2 In a bowl, combine the oil, dressing mix, dill, lemon pepper and garlic powder and whisk well.

3 Put the crackers in a bowl, pour the dressing mixture over them and toss well. Spread on baking sheets and bake for 15 to 20 minutes or until heated through. Serve warm.

COOKING NOTES: For variety and a drier mixture, add 1 cup of pretzel sticks and ½ cup of chopped walnuts or almonds or 1 cup of Cherrios®.

RHUBARB MUFFINS

MAKES: *16 muffins*

2 cups chopped fresh rhubarb
½ cup sugar
1 teaspoon grated lemon zest
2½ cups all-purpose flour
1½ teaspoons baking powder
1 teaspoon baking soda
2 large eggs
3 tablespoons butter or margarine, melted
¾ cup buttermilk or sour milk

1 Position the rack in the center of the oven and preheat to 375 degrees F. Lightly grease a 16-cup muffin pan.

2 In a bowl, toss the rhubarb with ¼ cup of sugar and the lemon zest.

3 In another bowl, combine the flour, baking powder, baking soda and remaining ¼ cup of sugar and whisk well.

4 In a bowl, using an electric mixer on high speed, beat the eggs, butter and milk until smooth. Add to the dry ingredients and mix just until moistened. Add the rhubarb mixture and fold gently. Spoon into the muffin cups, filling each about two-thirds full. Bake for 20 to 25 minutes or until a toothpick inserted in the center comes out clean. Cool slightly on wire racks and serve warm.

PUMPERNICKEL LOAF

MAKES: *6 servings*

1 cup chopped fresh broccoli florets
1 loaf unsliced pumpernickel bread, halved lengthwise
3 tablespoons Dijon mustard
8 ounces thinly sliced cooked turkey
¼ cup sliced green onion
1 can (8.5 ounces) cream-style corn
6 ounces sliced mozzarella or provolone cheese

1 Position the rack in the center of the oven and preheat to 375 degrees F.

2 In a bowl, combine the broccoli and enough boiling water to cover and set aside for about 10 minutes. Drain.

3 Spread the bread halves with mustard and lay the turkey on the bottom half.

4 In a bowl, combine the broccoli, onion and corn and mix well. Spread over the turkey and top with cheese. Set the top half of the bread on the bottom half, wrap in aluminum foil and transfer to a baking sheet. Bake for 30 to 35 minutes, or until the cheese melts. Cut the loaf on the diagonal into 1½- to 2-inch slices.

RYE-AND-CURRANT SCONES

MAKES: *8 to 10 scones*

1 cup all-purpose flour
¾ cup rye flour
2½ teaspoons baking powder
½ teaspoon baking soda
2 tablespoons sugar
2 teaspoons caraway seeds
⅓ cup chilled butter or margarine, diced
⅔ cup buttermilk or sour milk
½ cup black currants

1 Position the rack in the center of the oven and preheat to 400 degrees F. Lightly grease a baking sheet.

2 In a bowl, combine the flours, baking powder, baking soda, sugar and caraway seeds and whisk well. Using a pastry blender or two knives, cut the butter into the dry ingredients until the mixture resembles coarse crumbs. Stir in the buttermilk and mix until blended. Add the currants and knead until incorporated.

3 On a lightly floured surface, pat the dough to a thickness of ½ inch. Using a 2-inch cutter, cut out rounds and transfer them to the baking sheet. Bake for 15 to 18 minutes, or until golden brown. Cool on a wire rack and serve warm.

RYE BISCUITS

MAKES: *About 8 biscuits*

½ cup all-purpose flour
½ cup rye flour
1 teaspoon baking powder
¼ teaspoon baking soda
1 teaspoon unsweetened cocoa powder
⅛ teaspoon salt
3 tablespoons chilled butter or margarine
⅓ cup buttermilk
2 teaspoons molasses
½ teaspoon ground aniseed

1 Position the rack in the center of the oven and preheat to 450 degrees F.

2 In a bowl, combine the flours, baking powder, baking soda, cocoa and salt. Using a pastry blender or two knives, cut the butter into the dry ingredients until the mixture resembles coarse crumbs.

3 In a small bowl or cup, combine the buttermilk and molasses and mix well. Add the aniseed and stir. Add to the dry ingredients and stir until mixed. Do not overmix.

4 On a lightly floured surface, knead the dough 5 or 6 times and pat to a thickness of about ½ inch. Using a ½- to 2-inch cookie cutter, cut out rounds and transfer to an ungreased baking sheet. Bake for 12 to 15 minutes, or until golden brown. Serve warm.

1 package (16 ounces) frozen bread dough, thawed
1 pound sliced boiled ham
½ pound sliced Italian salami
½ pound sliced pepperoni
3 cups grated mozzarella cheese
1 can (12 ounces) pizza sauce

1 Position the rack in the center of the oven and preheat to 350 degrees F. Lightly grease a baking sheet.

2 Divide the dough in half and roll each into a rectangle about ¼-inch thick. Lay the ham on the rectangles and top with salami and pepperoni.

3 In a bowl, combine the cheese and pizza sauce and drizzle over the meat. Starting at the long sides, roll each into a log, tucking in the edges as you roll. Seal the dough, transfer the logs to the baking sheet and bake for 55 to 60 minutes, or until lightly browned. Cut into slices for serving.

COOKING NOTE: **To reduce the oiliness of the salami and pepperoni, dip the slices in boiling water for 2 or 3 seconds, drain on paper towels and then proceed with the recipe.**

SOUTHERN STROMBOLI

MAKES: *32 servings*

1 cup chopped pitted dates
½ cup raisins
½ cup chopped pitted prunes
1 cup water
½ cup butter or margarine, at room temperature
1 cup all-purpose flour
½ cup chopped walnuts or pecans
1 teaspoon baking soda
2 large eggs, slightly beaten
1 teaspoon vanilla or almond extract

1 Position the rack in the center of the oven and preheat to 350 degrees F. Lightly grease three 10-cup miniature muffin pans.

2 In a saucepan, combine the dates, raisins, prunes and water and bring to a boil over high heat. Cook for about 5 minutes or until the liquid reduces slightly. Add the butter, stir gently, remove from the heat and set aside.

3 In a bowl, combine the flour, nuts and baking soda and whisk well.

4 In a bowl, combine the eggs and vanilla and whisk well. Add to the dry ingredients, alternating with the fruit mixture and stirring just until moistened. Spoon into the muffin cups, filling each about two-thirds full. Bake for 12 to 15 minutes, or until lightly browned. Cool slightly on wire racks and serve warm.

SUGARLESS MUFFINS

MAKES: *About 30 servings*

WHOLE-WHEAT DIGESTIVE BISCUITS

MAKES: *About 55 biscuits*

1½ cups bread or all-purpose flour
9 cups whole-wheat flour
1 tablespoon baking powder
1 tablespoon baking soda
1¾ cups packed brown sugar
1 large egg
1½ cups butter or margarine
2 cups water

1 In a bowl, combine the flours, baking powder, baking soda and sugar and whisk well.

2 In a bowl, using an electric mixer on low speed, beat the egg, butter and water until smooth. Add the dry ingredients and mix until the mixture forms a dough. Cover and chill for at least 4 hours.

3 Position the rack in the center of the oven and preheat to 325 degrees F.

4 On a lightly floured surface, roll the dough to a thickness of ¼ to ⅛ inch. Divide the dough in half and lay each half on an ungreased baking sheet, stretching it to fit, if necessary. Score the dough into 1½-inch squares and bake for 10 to 13 minutes, or until golden brown. Cool on the sheet set on a wire rack and then separate into biscuits.

COOKING NOTE: **The biscuits will feel soft when removed from the oven, but will become crisp as they cool.**

Chapter 11

FUN WITH FRUIT

Perfectly ripe, juicy fruit eaten out of hand is nature's most perfect snack. But we could not have a chapter without recipes! You will find fruit used throughout the book in other chapters, but here are those preparations that rely most heavily on fruit. It may be fresh, canned or frozen, depending on the recipe. When buying fresh fruit, buy it in season whenever possible and from local growers. It will taste of the sun and the earth and never disappoint.

APPLE BARS

MAKES: *2 to 4 dozen bars*

2 cups all-purpose flour
2 teaspoons baking powder
½ teaspoon ground nutmeg
½ teaspoon salt
2 teaspoons grated lemon zest
4 large eggs
2 cups sugar
1½ cups peeled, diced apples
1 cup chopped walnuts
powdered sugar for sprinkling

1 Preheat the oven to 350 degrees F. Lightly grease a 13-by-9-inch baking pan.

2 In a bowl, combine the flour, baking powder, nutmeg and salt and whisk well. Stir in the lemon zest.

3 In a bowl, using an electric mixer set on medium-high speed, beat the eggs and sugar until thick and light colored. Gradually blend in the dry ingredients and then fold in the apples and nuts.

4 Spread the dough in the pan and bake for 15 to 20 minutes, or until firm. Cool in the pan set on a wire rack. Cut into small or large bars and sprinkle with powdered sugar.

APPLE-CHEESE CUSTARD

MAKES: *About 6 servings*

5 large apples, peeled, cored and sliced
1 cup cottage cheese
¾ cup sugar
½ cup half-and-half
2 large eggs
1 teaspoon vanilla extract
½ teaspoon cinnamon
¼ teaspoon ground cardamom
whipped cream for garnish

1 Position the rack in the center of the oven and preheat to 350 degrees F. Lightly grease a 2½-quart baking dish.

2 Spread the apple slices in an even layer in the baking dish.

3 In the container of a blender, combine the cottage cheese, sugar, half-and-half, eggs, vanilla and cinnamon and process until smooth. Pour over the apples and sprinkle with cardamom. Bake for 55 to 60 minutes, or until the apples are tender and the top is golden brown. Serve warm with the whipped cream on the side.

2 packages (16 ounces each) frozen
   puff pastry
2 large egg whites
1 tablespoon milk
1 cup raisins
1 cup sugar
¼ cup plus 2 tablespoons fresh
   bread crumbs
1 tablespoon cinnamon
4 to 6 small apples, peeled, cored
   and halved

1 Position the rack in the center
of the oven and preheat to 400
degrees F. Lightly grease a baking sheet.

2 Roll the dough into large rectangles and cut each into 4-inch
squares.

3 In a small bowl, whisk the egg
whites with the milk and brush
over the dough squares.

4 In a bowl, combine the the
raisins, sugar, bread crumbs and
cinnamon and toss well. Place
about a tablespoon of the crumb
mixture in the center of each
square and lay an apple half on
top. Sprinkle with more crumb
mixture and fold the dough
around the apple to enclose it
completely. Brush with the egg
mixture. Repeat with the remaining ingredients.

5 Transfer to the baking sheet
and bake for about 15 minutes or
until the pastry begins to brown.
Reduce the oven temperature to
350 degrees F. and bake for 25 to
30 minutes longer, or until the
apple is baked through. Cool on
wire racks.

APPLE WRAPS

MAKES: *8 to 12 servings*

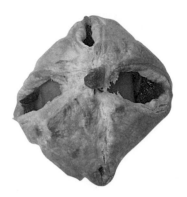

---

1 cup dried apricots, diced
½ cup bran cereal
½ cup orange juice
1½ cups all-purpose flour
1 teaspoon baking powder
¾ teaspoon cinnamon
½ teaspoon salt
½ cup vegetable shortening
½ cup granulated sugar
½ cup packed light-brown sugar
1 large egg
1 teaspoon vanilla extract
⅓ cup chopped walnuts

1 Preheat the oven to 375
degrees F. Lightly grease 2 baking sheets.

2 In a small bowl, combine the
apricots with enough boiling
water to cover. Set aside to soak
for 15 to 20 minutes.

3 In a bowl, combine the bran
cereal and orange juice and stir
well.

4 In a bowl, combine the flour,
baking powder, cinnamon and
salt and whisk well.

5 In a bowl, using an electric
mixer set on medium-high speed,
beat the vegetable shortening
and sugars until smooth. Add the
egg and vanilla and beat until
mixed. Gradually blend in the
dry ingredients. Fold in the cereal and orange juice and the walnuts. Drain the apricots and add
to the dough, folding until
mixed.

6 Drop by spoonfuls onto the
baking sheets, leaving 1½ inches
between the cookies, and bake
for 8 to 10 minutes until golden
brown. Cool on wire racks.

APRICOT-BRAN
COOKIES

MAKES: *2 to 3 dozen cookies*

BAKED FRUIT COMPOTE

MAKES: *4 to 6 serveings*

1 jar (10 ounces) black currant jelly
1 can (16 ounces) pear halves,
    drained, liquid reserved
1 can (16 ounces) peach halves,
    drained, liquid reserved
6 fresh plums, halved and pitted
ice cream for garnish

1 Position the rack in the center of the oven and preheat to 350 degrees F.

2 In a saucepan, combine the jelly and 2 tablespoons of the reserved pear liquid and 2 tablespoons of the reserved peach liquid and cook over medium heat, stirring, until boiling. Remove from the heat.

3 Arrange the fruit, cut side down, in a a 13-by-9-inch baking pan. Pour the liquid over the fruit and bake for 18 to 20 minutes, basting frequently, until most of the liquid evaporates. Serve warm with scoops of ice cream.

COOKING NOTE: **A flavored whipped cream can be used in place of the ice cream.**

BANANA ROYALE

MAKES: *4 servings*

⅓ cup butter or margarine
⅓ cup packed dark-brown sugar
¼ teaspoon cinnamon
¼ teaspoon ground nutmeg
4 bananas, halved lengthwise
¼ cup half-and-half
⅓ cup brandy
1 quart vanilla ice cream

1 In a deep skillet, melt the butter over medium heat. Add the sugar, cinnamon and nutmeg and stir until the sugar dissolves. Add the bananas and cook for 3 to 4 minutes until the fruit begins to soften.

2 Add the half-and-half, stir gently, and cook for 2 or 3 minutes, or until slightly thickened.

3 Divide the ice cream among 4 plates and top each serving with 2 banana halves.

4 In a small saucepan, heat the brandy over low heat. Remove the pan from the heat and carefully ignite the brandy. Pour the flaming brandy over the bananas.

COOKING NOTE: **This can be made in a chafing dish.**

1 cup all-purpose flour
½ cup butter or margarine, at room
  temperature
3 tablespoons powdered sugar
1 can (21 ounces) berry pie filling
1 small container (4 ounces)
  whipped topping
chopped pecans or almonds for
  garnish

1 In a bowl, combine the flour, butter and sugar and mix until smooth. Add the pie filling and mix well. Divide the dough into

sixths and shape each into a flattened 3-inch round. Transfer to an ungreased baking sheet, cover with wax paper and chill for at least 1 hour.

2 Position the rack in the center of the oven and preheat to 350 degrees F.

3 Bake for 15 to 20 minutes, or until golden brown. Top with the whipped topping and sprinkle with nuts.

BERRY BUTTERCAKE

MAKES: *6 servings*

⅔ cup butter or margarine, at room
  temperature
¼ cup rice flour
½ teaspoon Amaretto
1 tablespoon plus 1 teaspoon
  orange-flavored liqueur
10 ounces cream cheese, at room
  temperature
2 cups all-purpose flour
approximately 1 cup glacé cherries,
  halved
1 cup warm water

1 In a bowl, using an electric mixer set on medium speed, beat the butter and rice flour until smooth. Add the Amaretto and 1 teaspoon of liqueur and beat to mix. Beat in the cream cheese. Gradually blend in the all-purpose flour. Cover and chill for at least 4 hours.

2 In a small bowl, combine the cherries, water and remaining 1 tablespoon of liqueur and set aside at room temperature to plump for at least 1 hour.

3 Preheat the oven to 350 degrees F.

4 Drain the cherries and discard the soaking liquid.

5 On a lightly floured surface, roll the dough out to a thickness of ¼ inch. Using a 2- to 2½-inch cookie cutter, cut into rounds and place on ungreased baking sheets, leaving about 1 inch between the cookies. Press a cherry half into the center of each cookie. Bake for 10 to 15 minutes until the edges are lightly colored. Cool on wire racks.

CHERRY-ALMOND KOLACKY

MAKES: *3 to 4 dozen cookies*

CHOCOLATE BERRY COOLER

MAKES: *2 to 4 servings*

¼ cup fresh raspberries, sliced strawberries or blackberries
1 tablespoon Dutch-processed cocoa powder
1 tablespoon plus 1½ teaspoons sugar
1½ cups milk
½ cup chilled seltzer water
1 cup whipped topping
fresh berries for garnish

In the container of a blender, combine the raspberries, cocoa and sugar and process for about 10 seconds until mixed. Add the milk and seltzer and blend on low speed for about 10 seconds longer until smooth. Pour into tall glasses and garnish with whipped topping and fresh berries.

DELUXE PEAR SALAD

MAKES: *8 servings*

1 cup (8 ounces) small-curd cottage cheese
¼ cup thinly sliced celery
¼ cup coarsely chopped hazelnuts or walnuts
8 canned pear halves
lettuce leaves
¼ cup Wish-Bone® Deluxe French Dressing

1 In a bowl, stir the cottage cheese with a fork until creamy. Add the celery and nuts and mix well.

2 Set the pear halves on lettuce leaves and spoon the cottage cream filling in the cavity of each. Drizzle the dressing over the filling, letting it drip down the sides of the pear.

FRIED FIGS

MAKES: *8 servings*

8 firm black figs
½ cup dark rum
½ cup water
⅓ cup all-purpose flour
½ teaspoon vanilla extract
¼ cup chopped pecans or walnuts
canola oil
powdered sugar for sprinkling

1 In a bowl, combine the figs and rum, cover and set aside to soak at room temperature for at least 2 hours.

2 In another bowl, combine the water, flour and vanilla and whisk until smooth. Gently fold in the nuts.

3 In a skillet, pour the oil to a depth of 2 inches and heat over medium-high heat until hot.

4 Lift the figs from the rum and roll in the batter until well coated. Fry for about 3 minutes until browned on all sides. Drain on paper towels and sprinkle with powdered sugar. Serve hot.

4 cups all-purpose flour
1 teaspoon baking powder
1 teaspoon baking soda
1½ cups vegetable shortening
1 cup packed light-brown sugar
2 large eggs
1 cup raisins
1 cup chopped walnuts
1 cup chopped candied citron
1 cup chopped pitted prunes
½ cup flaked coconut
sugar for sprinkling
finely ground almonds for
    sprinkling

1 Preheat the oven for 350 degrees F. Lightly grease 2 baking sheets.

2 In a bowl, combine the flour, baking powder and baking soda and whisk well.

3 In another bowl, using an electric mixer set on medium-high speed, beat the vegetable shortening and brown sugar until smooth. Beat in the eggs, 1 at a time. Gradually blend in the dry ingredients. Fold in the raisins, walnuts, candied citron, prunes and coconut.

4 On a lightly floured work surface, roll out the dough until very thin. Using cookie cutters, cut the dough into shapes. Place on the baking sheets, leaving about 1 inch between the cookies. Bake for 12 to 15 minutes, until lightly colored. Sprinkle with sugar and almonds while still warm and cool on wire racks.

FRUIT COOKIES

MAKES: *5 to 6 dozen cookies*

---

1 honeydew melon
1 cup chilled white port wine or
    sherry
¼ cup Kirsch liqueur
1 cup sliced strawberries
powdered sugar
whole fresh strawberries for garnish
fresh mint for garnish

1 Using a sharp knife, cut a 3- to 3½-inch circle in the top of the melon. Scoop out the seeds and using a melon baller, scoop out as much flesh as possible. Take care not to pierce the rind. Slice the bottom of the melon so that it stands upright.

2 In a bowl, combine any juice from the melon, wine and Kirsch and mix well.

3 Fill the melon with alternating layers of melon balls and strawberries. Sprinkle each layer with sugar. When filled, carefully pour the liquid over the fruit, cover and chill for at least 3 hours.

4 Garnish the melon with strawberries and mint and serve cold.

COOKING NOTE: The filled melon can marinate in the refrigerator for up to 24 hours.

STRAWBERRY-
FILLED MELON

MAKES: *4 servings*

FRUITED CHEESE LOG

MAKES: *8 to 10 servings*

1 package (8 ounces) cream cheese, at room temperature
1 can (8.25 ounces) crushed pineapple, drained
2 cups shredded Cheddar cheese
½ cup chopped pecans
½ cup chopped dried cranberries
1½ teaspoons chopped crystallized ginger
coarsely chopped pecans
crackers

1 In a bowl, using an electric mixer on low speed, beat the cream cheese and pineapple until smooth. Add the Cheddar cheese, pecans, cranberries and ginger and stir until blended. Cover and chill for at least 4 hours.

2 Spread the nuts in a shallow dish. Form the cream cheese mixture into a log, roll in the chopped nuts and transfer to a platter. Cover and chill for at least 1 hour until firm. Serve with crackers.

COOKING NOTE: **Press pecan halves into the sides of the log to make it more attractive.**

FRUIT PIZZA

MAKES: *8 servings*

2 bananas, sliced lengthwise
1 can (11 ounces) mandarin orange seegments, drained, liquid reserved
2 kiwi fruit, peeled and thinly sliced
1 cup thinly sliced fresh strawberries
1 can (11 ounces) pineapple tidbits, drained, liquid reserved
1 cup fresh blueberries
1 package (17 ounces) refrigerated sugar cookies
1 package (8 ounces) cream cheese, at room temperature
⅓ cup sugar
1 teaspoon vanilla extract
½ cup apricot preserves
2 tablespoons water

1 Position the rack in the center of the oven and preheat to 375 degrees F. Lightly grease a 12-inch pizza pan or a small baking sheet.

2 Spread the bananas, orange segments, kiwi, strawberries, pineapple and blueberries in a shallow pan. Whisk the reserved orange and pineapple liquid together and use it to brush the fruit.

3 Form the cookie dough into a ball and then press it into the pizza pan, patting gently to fill the pan. Bake for 12 to 15 minutes or until lightly browned. Cool on a wire rack.

4 In a bowl, using an electric mixer on medium speed, beat the cream cheese, sugar and vanilla until smooth. Spread over the crust and arrange the fruit over the cheese.

5 In a cup, combine the preserves and water and spoon over the fruit. Cover lightly with wax paper and chill for at least 1 hour or until ready to serve.

2 cups coarsely chopped seedless
   green grapes
½ cup chopped green onion
½ cup chopped Anaheim chiles
2 tablespoons chopped cilantro
   (Chinese parsley)
2 tablespoons red wine vinegar
1 large clove garlic, minced
⅛ teaspoon hot red-pepper sauce

In a bowl, combine the grapes, onion, chiles, cilantro, vinegar, garlic and pepper sauce and toss well. Cover and set aside at room temperature for at least 1 hour. Drain excess liquid and serve.

GRAPE SALSA

MAKES: *About 6 servings*

---

1 can (8 ounces) pineapple chunks,
   drained and chopped
1 can (11 ounces) mandarin orange
   segments, drained and chopped
¼ cup flaked unsweetened coconut
1 cup miniature marshmallows
1 large banana, diced
1¼ cups whipped topping
6 flat-bottomed ice cream cones
red or green maraschino cherries, for
   garnish

1 In a bowl, combine the pineapple, orange segments, coconut, marshmallows and banana and stir to mix. Add the topping and fold until the fruit and marshmallows are coated. Cover and chill for at least 2 hours

2 Spoon into the ice cream cones or chilled parfait glasses, garnish with cherries and serve.

INDIVIDUAL
FRUIT SALADS

MAKES: *6 servings*

1½ cups pizza sauce
1 loaf French bread, halved
   lengthwise
6 strips crisp bacon, crumbled
1 small green bell pepper, sliced
1 can (20 ounces) pineapple tidbits,
   drained
2 cups shredded mozzarella or
   provolone cheese

1 Position the broiler rack about 4 inches from the heat source and preheat the broiler.

2 Spread the pizza sauce over the bread halves and sprinkle with bacon, pepper slices and pineapple. Spread the cheese over the top and broil for about 5 minutes, or until the cheese melts.

PINEAPPLE PIZZA

MAKES: *8 servings*

STRAWBERRIES WITH CHOCOLATE WHIPPED CREAM

MAKES: *4 to 6 servings*

½ cup heavy cream
1 tablespoon plus 1½ teaspoons Dutch-processed cocoa
3 tablespoons plus 1½ teaspoons powdered sugar
1 quart fresh strawberries, hulled and sliced

1 In a bowl, using an electric mixer on high speed, beat the cream until foamy.

2 In another bowl, combine the cocoa and sugar and whisk well. with the mixer on low speed, add to the cream and mix well. Increase the speed to high and beat just until stiff peaks form. Cover and chill for at least 1 hour.

3 Serve cream with the strawberries.

STRAWBERRY PUFFS

MAKES: *4 servings*

SAUCE
2 cups fresh strawberries
¼ cup sugar
¼ cup heavy cream

PUFFS
6 large eggs, separated
2 cups small-curd cottage cheese
½ cup all-purpose flour
1 tablespoon sugar
½ teaspoon grated orange zest
½ teaspoon cream of tartar
sliced strawberries for garnish

1 To make the sauce, combine the strawberries and sugar in a saucepan and heat over medium heat, mashing the berries until the sugar dissolves and the mixture begins to simmer. Remove the sauce from the heat and set aside to cool for about 15 minutes.

2 In a bowl, using an electric mixer on high speed, beat the cream until stiff peaks form. Add the whipped cream to the berries and stir gently to mix. Set aside.

3 Preheat a griddle or nonstick skillet until very hot.

4 To make the puffs, in a bowl, using an electric mixer on low speed, beat together the egg yolks, cottage cheese, flour, sugar and orange zest until mixed.

5 In another bowl, using an electric mixer with clean beaters, beat the egg whites until foamy. Add the cream of tartar and beat until stiff peaks form. Add to the cottage cheese mixture and fold gently. Drop by large spoonfuls onto the hot griddle and cook for 2 or 3 minutes on each side or until golden brown on both sides. Serve with sliced strawberries and sauce.

1 prepared angel food loaf cake (10 ounces)
⅓ cup strawberry jam or jelly
⅓ cup cream sherry
3 cups sliced fresh strawberries
Custard Sauce (recipe follows)
¾ cup heavy cream
2 tablespoons powdered sugar
1 teaspoon vanilla extract
2 tablespoons toasted sliced almonds for garnish

1 Using a serrated knife, cut the cake lengthwise into 3 equal layers. Spread jam between the layers and reassemble the cake. Cut into 2-inch cubes.

2 In a bowl, arrange the cubes in even layers to fill the bowl. Sprinkle with sherry and top with the berries. Pour the custard sauce over the berries and cake, cover and chill for at least 1 hour, or until the custard sets.

3 In a bowl, using an electric mixer on high speed, beat the cream until soft peaks form. Add the powdered sugar and vanilla and continue to whip until stiff peaks form. Spread over the trifle and garnish with almonds. Cover and chill for at least 2 hours.

COOKING NOTE: You can substitute 2 packages of ladyfingers for the cake.

STRAWBERRY TRIFLE

MAKES: *About 8 servings*

CUSTARD SAUCE

MAKES: *About 1½ cups*

1¼ cups milk
1 tablespoon plus 1½ teaspoons cornstarch
¼ cup sugar
1 teaspoon vanilla extract
3 large egg yolks, lightly beaten

1 In a small bowl, combine ½ cup of milk and the cornstarch and whisk to mix.

2 In a saucepan, combine the remaining ¾ cup of milk and the sugar and heat until boiling. Immediately remove from the heat, add the cornstarch and stir until smooth. Return to the heat and cook, stirring constantly, until simmering and thickened. Simmer for about 3 minutes longer and remove from the heat. Add the vanilla and egg yolks, whisking well. Cover and chill until ready to use.

PRUNE SURPRISES

MAKES: *24 servings*

½ cup finely chopped walnuts or
  pecans
½ cup finely chopped mixed
  candied fruits
1 tablespoon sherry or white port
  wine
1 tablespoon honey
24 large pitted prunes

In a bowl, combine the walnuts,
fruits, sherry and honey and mix
well. Spoon the filling into the

prunes, pressing to compact.
Transfer to a platter, cover and
chill for at least 1 hour.

COOKING NOTE: **The prunes
should be soft before filling. To
soften them, microwave them
for 5 to 10 seconds on medium
(50 percent) power, if necessary.**

TOASTED BREAD WITH CHERRIES

MAKES: *8 to 10 servings*

½ cup butter or margarine
4 slices honey whole-wheat bread,
  toasted
4 slices white bread, toasted
¼ cup packed light-brown sugar
1 can (21 ounces) cherry pie filling
2 tablespoons ground almonds
1 cup whipped topping

1 Position the rack in the center
of the oven and preheat to 425
degrees F.

2 In a large skillet, melt the butter over medium heat. Dip 1 side
of 4 slices of toast in the butter

and transfer to an ungreased 9-
inch-square baking pan, buttered
side down. Sprinkle with about 2
tablespoons of the brown sugar
and spread with the pie filling.
Sprinkle with the almonds.

3 Dip 1 side of the remaining 4
slices of toast in the butter and
place, buttered side up, on top of
the pie filling and almonds.
Sprinkle with the remaining
brown sugar and bake for 12 to
15 minutes, or until lightly gold-
en. Cut into squares and top with
whipped topping.

1 cup orange juice
¼ cup plus 2 tablespoons guava
  paste
¼ cup prepared brown mustard
1 teaspoon curry powder
1 teaspoon lemon juice
1 teaspoon lime juice
20 ½-inch squares carambola (star
  fruit)
20 ½-inch squares mango
20 ½-inch squares papaya
20 ½-inch squares loquat

1 In a saucepan, combine the
orange juice, guava paste, mustard and curry powder and cook
over medium heat, whisking
until smooth. Bring to a boil,
reduce the heat and simmer for
about 20 minutes until slightly
thickened. Remove from the heat
and stir in the lemon and lime
juices.

2 Position the broiler rack about
4 inches from the heat source and
preheat the broiler.

3 Thread 4 squares of fruit onto a
wooden skewer, alternating the
kinds of fruit, and brush with the
sauce. Transfer the skewer to a
broiling pan. Repeat until all the
fruit is used and there are 20
skewers. Broil for 2 to 4 minutes
on each side until lightly
browned. Serve warm, with any
remaining sauce on the side.

COOKING NOTE: **Guava paste is
available at specialty food
stores. Loquats are Chinese
fruits grown in much of Asia,
Central and South America and
the warmer regions of the Unit-
ed States. If you cannot find
fresh loquats, substitute canned.**

TROPICAL FRUIT BROCHETTES

MAKES: *20 servings*

1¼ cups all-purpose flour
⅔ cup butter or margarine, at room
  temperature
⅓ cup packed light-brown sugar
3 tablespoons powdered sugar
4 packages (3 ounces each) cream
  cheese, at room temperature
½ cup granulated sugar
1 teaspoon vanilla or almond extract
1½ cups sliced bananas
1 cup sliced fresh strawberries
3 kiwi fruit, thinly sliced
1 can (8 ounces) crushed pineapple
1 carambola (star fruit), thinly sliced

1 Position the rack in the center
of the oven and preheat to 350
degrees F. Lightly grease a 12-
inch pizza pan.

2 In a bowl, combine the flour,
butter, brown sugar and powdered sugar and stir with a fork
until crumbly. Press into the pan
and bake for 8 to 10 minutes, or
until lightly browned. Cool on a
wire rack.

3 In a bowl, using an electric
mixer on high speed, beat the
cream cheese, granulated sugar
and vanilla until smooth. Spread
over the crust and arrange the
sliced fruit over the cheese mixture. Save the carambola for the
top of the pizza. Slice into
wedges to serve.

WORLD'S BEST PIZZA

MAKES: *About 8 servings*

Chapter 12

BREAKFAST AT DAWN

No one will argue that breakfast is a meal—not a snack. But because the recipes in this chapter fall so neatly into the parameters of the other recipes in the book, happily they are included. Breakfast fare is quick and easy to prepare, welcome just about any time of day or night. But too many of us grab breakfast on the run, gobbling it as we stand at the kitchen counter or drive down the highway. This is a contradiction of what snacking should be all about. All food should be eaten slowly and with appreciation—and perhaps this credo applies nowhere more than it does to breakfast, the meal that fuels us for the rest of the day.

BEER PANCAKES

MAKES: *4 to 6 pancakes*

1½ cups all-purpose flour
1½ teaspoons sugar
1½ teaspoons baking powder
½ teaspoon salt
1 large egg, separated
¾ cup milk
½ cup flat beer, at room temperature
2 tablespoons butter or margarine, melted

1 Preheat a lightly greased griddle or skillet.

2 In a bowl, combine the flour, sugar, baking powder and salt and whisk well.

2 In another bowl, using an electric mixer set on high speed, beat the egg yolk until thick. Add the milk, beer and butter and beat until smooth. Add the dry ingredients and stir until smooth.

4 In a clean, dry bowl, using an electric mixer on high speed, beat the egg white until stiff, but not dry, peaks form. Fold into the batter just until mixed. Drop by generous tablespoonfuls onto the griddle and cook for 2 or 3 minutes on each side, or until a golden brown. Serve warm or at room temperature.

COOKING NOTE: **These can also be larger or smaller, using more or less batter.**

BREAKFAST FRITTERS

MAKES: *10 to 12 servings*

vegetable oil for frying
2 cups Bisquick® baking mix
1 cup cooked medium-grain rice
1¼ cups sugar
2 tablespoons plus 2 teaspoons grated orange zest
½ teaspoon ground nutmeg
½ teaspoon cinnamon
½ cup water
1 large egg
1 teaspoon vanilla or almond extract
raspberry or strawberry preserves for serving

1 In a heavy skillet or saucepan, pour the oil to a depth of 2 inches and heat until hot.

2 In a medium bowl, combine the baking mix, rice, ⅓ cup of sugar, 2 teaspoons of orange zest, the nutmeg and cinnamon.

3 In a cup, whisk the water, egg and vanilla together and add to the baking mix mixture. Using a fork, stir until the batter is moist and thick.

4 Drop by teaspoonfuls into the hot oil and fry for 2 to 2½ minutes on each side until lightly browned. Drain on paper towels.

5 Combine the remaining sugar and orange zest in a shallow bowl and stir to mix. While the fritters are still very warm, roll them in the sugar mixture to coat. Serve immediately with the preserves on the side.

1 package (10 ounces) frozen broccoli florets
¼ cup shredded carrots
¼ cup uncooked rotelle pasta
6 large eggs, lightly beaten
2 tablespoons butter or margarine
½ green bell pepper, chopped
3 sliced green onions (white portions only)
½ teaspoon crushed dried basil leaves
salt and pepper
2 tablespoons grated romano or Parmesan cheese

1 In a saucepan, combine the broccoli, carrots and pasta and enough water to cover and bring to a boil over high heat. Reduce the heat, cover and simmer for 6 to 8 minutes or until the noodles are soft. Remove from the heat, cool until tepid and add the eggs, stirring briskly until mixed. Take care the eggs do not scramble.

2 In a large skillet, melt the butter over medium heat and sauté the pepper and onions for about 5 minutes until the vegetables begin to soften. Pour the egg mixture in the skillet, season with basil, salt and pepper, cover and cook for 2 or 3 minutes, lifting the edges to allow the egg to run underneath. Cook until firm. Sprinkle with cheese and cut into wedges to serve.

MIXED VEGETABLE OMELET
MAKES: *4 servings*

---

2 large potatoes, diced
¼ cup canola oil
½ cup sliced fresh mushrooms
½ cup sliced white onion
8 large eggs
½ cup heavy cream
salt and pepper
½ cup shredded Swiss or Port Salut cheese

1 Position the rack in the center of the oven and preheat to 350 degrees F. Lightly grease a 9-inch-square baking pan.

2 In a saucepan, combine the potatoes with enough water to cover by about 1 inch and bring to a boil over high heat. Reduce the heat and simmer for about 15 minutes or until the potatoes are fork tender but still offer resistance. Drain.

3 In a large skillet, heat the oil and sauté the potatoes over medium heat for about 3 minutes. Add the mushrooms and onion and cook for about 3 minutes longer or until the potatoes are tender. Transfer to the prepared pan.

4 In a bowl, using an electric mixer set on medium speed, beat the eggs until thick and light colored. Add the cream, season with salt and pepper and beat until well mixed. Pour over the potatoes, shake the pan to distribute evenly and bake for about 20 minutes, or until the eggs are puffy. Sprinkle the cheese over the top and bake for about 5 minutes, or until the cheese melts. Cut into squares and serve.

POTATO-MUSHROOM OMELET
MAKES: *4 servings*

BACON DROP BISCUITS

MAKES: *9 to 12 biscuits*

2 cups all-purpose flour
1 tablespoon baking powder
1 teaspoon salt
¼ cup vegetable shortening
6 strips crisp bacon, crumbled
1 cup milk

1 Position the rack in the center of the oven and preheat to 450 degrees F. Lightly grease a baking sheet.

2 In a bowl, combine the flour, baking powder and salt and whisk well. Using a pastry blender or two knives, cut the vegetable shortening into the dry ingredients until the mixture resembles coarse crumbs. Add the bacon and enough milk to form a soft dough. Do not overmix. Drop by spoonfuls onto the baking sheet and bake for 10 to 12 minutes or until golden brown. Serve hot.

BACON MUFFINS

MAKES: *12 to 16 muffins*

8 strips crisp bacon, chopped
1⅓ cups all-purpose flour
1 tablespoon sugar
1 tablespoon baking powder
1 teaspoon salt
1 large egg
¾ cup milk
1 tablespoon bacon drippings

1 Position the rack in the center of the oven and preheat to 425 degrees F. Lightly grease and flour a 12-cup muffin pan.

2 In a bowl, combine the bacon, flour, sugar, baking powder and salt and whisk well.

3 In another bowl, using an electric mixer set on medium-high speed, beat the egg until thick and light colored. Add the milk and drippings and beat until smooth. Add to the dry ingredients and stir just until mixed. Spoon into the muffin cups, filling each about halfway, and bake for 15 to 20 minutes, or until a toothpick inserted in the center of a muffin comes out clean. Cool slightly on wire racks and serve warm.

COOKING NOTE: For more flavor, sprinkle with grated cheese when the muffins are nearly baked, after 13 or 14 minutes.

FLAKY BISCUITS WITH HONEY BUTTER

MAKES: *10 to 12 biscuits*

BISCUITS
1 cup all-purpose flour
1½ teaspoons baking powder
¼ teaspoon salt
½ cup heavy cream
2 tablespoons milk
3 tablespoons butter or margarine, melted

BUTTER
½ cup butter or margarine, at room temperature
3 tablespoons honey

1 Position the rack in the center of the oven and preheat to 425 degrees F.

2 In a bowl, combine the flour, baking powder and salt. Add the cream and stir with a fork until the mixture is crumbly. Add the milk very slowly, until the dough clings together.

3 On a lightly floured work surface, knead the dough about 10 times. Roll out to a thickness of about ½ inch. Using a 2-inch cookie cutter, cut out rounds and transfer to the baking sheet. Brush with the butter and bake for 12 to 15 minutes or until golden brown.

4 Meanwhile, make the honey butter by mashing the butter and honey together until smooth.

5 Serve the biscuits hot with the honey butter on the side.

2¼ cups all-purpose flour
½ cup packed dark-brown sugar
2 teaspoons baking powder
½ teaspoon salt
½ cup chilled butter or margarine,
  diced
2 large eggs
½ cup milk
1 teaspoon vanilla extract
½ cup chopped almonds
½ cup chopped pecans
¼ cup chopped walnuts
¼ cup chopped cashews
½ cup chopped dried apricots
½ cup shredded coconut

1 Position the rack in the center of the oven and preheat to 425 degrees F. Lightly grease a baking sheet.

2 In a bowl, combine the flour, sugar, baking powder and salt. Using a pastry blender or two knives, cut the butter into the dry ingredients until the mixture resembles coarse crumbs.

3 In a bowl, using an electric mixer set on low speed, beat the eggs until foamy. Add the milk and vanilla and mix well. Add the dry ingredients and mix just until combined. The dough will be sticky.

4 With floured hands, knead in the almonds, pecans, walnuts, cashews, apricots and coconut. Transfer the dough to the baking sheet and pat into a 9-inch circle. Score the circle into 8 wedges and bake for 20 to 25 minutes, or until golden brown. Cool on a wire rack and break into wedges to serve.

FULL-OF-NUTS SCONES

MAKES: *8 scones*

---

4 cups all-purpose flour, sifted
1 tablespoon plus 1 teaspoon baking
  powder
¼ teaspoon ground nutmeg
¼ teaspoon salt
2 large eggs
1⅓ cups sugar
2 tablespoons butter, melted
1 cup milk
¼ teaspoon lemon juice
powdered sugar for dusting
  (optional)

1 In a bowl, combine the flour, baking powder, nutmeg and salt and whisk well.

2 In another bowl, using an electric mixer set on medium speed, beat the eggs until thick and light colored. Beat in the sugar and the butter. Add the dry ingredients, alternating them with the milk, starting and ending with the dry ingredients, and mix until smooth. Stir in the lemon juice, cover and chill for at least 2 hours.

3 In a deep skillet of deep-fat fryer, pour oil to a depth of 2 or 3 inches and heat until hot (365 degrees F. in a deep-fat fryer). Bring a saucepan of water to a boil over high heat, reduce the heat slightly and keep the water at a low boil.

4 On a lightly floured work surface, roll out the dough to a thickness of ½ inch. Using a 2- or 3-inch doughnut cutter, cut out as many doughnuts as possible and drop them in the oil. Cook for 2 or 3 minutes on each side until golden brown. Lift from the oil and immediately plunge the doughnuts into the gently boiling water. Drain on paper towels and serve plain or dusted with powdered sugar.

GREASELESS DOUGHNUTS

MAKES: *1 to 2 dozen doughnuts*

MEXICAN EGG BAKE

MAKES: *8 to 10 servings*

6 corn tortillas
12 large eggs
½ cup milk
1 cup shredded Cheddar cheese
1 cup shredded Monterey Jack
    cheese
¼ cup chopped red bell pepper
1 can (4 ounces) green chiles,
    drained and chopped
1 tablespoon vegetable oil
1¼ cups sliced fresh mushrooms
½ green bell pepper, cut into 1-inch
    long strips
1 can (10 ounces) mild enchilada
    sauce

1 Position the rack in the center of the oven and preheat to 350 degrees F. Lightly grease a 13-by-9-inch baking pan.

2 Warm the tortillas according to the package directions and arrange them in the bottom of the pan, overlapping the edges.

3 In a bowl, using an electric mixer set on high speed, beat the eggs until foamy. Beat in the milk. Add the Cheddar and Jack cheeses, red pepper and chiles and mix well with a fork. Pour over the tortillas and bake for 25 to 35 minutes, or until a knife inserted in the center comes out clean.

4 In a saucepan, heat the oil over medium heat. Add the mushrooms and green peppers and cook, stirring, for about 5 minutes until tender. Add the enchilada sauce, stir and heat through. Spoon over the baked egg mixture and serve.

APPLE-PUFF OMELET

MAKES: *About 2 servings*

1 cup chopped apples
1 tablespoon firmly packed brown
    sugar
¼ cup plus 1 tablespoon water
4 strips crisp bacon, crumbled
    (optional)
4 large eggs, separated
½ teaspoon cream of tartar
½ teaspoon salt
1 tablespoon bacon drippings
½ cup shredded Cheddar cheese
1 apple, cored and cut into wedges

1 Position the rack in the center of the oven and preheat to 350 degrees F.

2 In a small saucepan, combine the chopped apples, brown sugar and 1 tablespoon of water and bring to a boil over medium-high heat. Cover and simmer for 4 or 5 minutes, or until the apple is crisp-tender. Stir in the bacon and set aside.

3 In a bowl, using an electric mixer set on high speed, beat the egg whites with the remaining ¼ cup of water and the cream of tartar until stiff but not dry.

4 In another bowl, using an electric mixer set on medium-high speed, beat egg yolks and salt until thick and light colored. Add to the egg whites, folding until well blended.

5 In an ovenproof skillet, heat the bacon drippings over medium-high heat for about 30 seconds until hot. Pour in the egg mixture, reduce the heat to medium-low and cook for about 5 minutes until puffed and browned on the bottom.

6 Transfer to the oven and bake for 10 to 12 minutes, or until a toothpick inserted in the center comes out clean. Transfer to a platter and spread the apple-bacon mixture and cheese over the omelet. Fold it in half, garnish with apple wedges and cut into wedges to serve.

3 large eggs
½ cup melted butter
1½ cups milk
½ cup Bisquick mix
½ cup minced cooked sausage
choice of cheese for sprinkling

1 Position the rack to the center of the oven and preheat to 350 degrees F.

2 In a blender, place the eggs, butter and milk. Blend for about 15 seconds. Add the baking mix and blend until smooth. Adjust the seasoning. Pour the mix into a quiche pan, top with sausage, sprinkle with the cheese and bake for 40 to 45 minutes, or until set. Remove from the oven and cool in the pan on a wire rack for 5 minutes before cutting and serving.

BREAKFAST QUICHE
MAKES: *About 6 servings*

---

1 pound bulk country-style sausage
1 onion, chopped
3 cups Bisquick® baking mix
1 pound grated mild Cheddar cheese
¾ cup milk

1 Position the rack in the center of the oven and preheat to 425 degrees F. Lightly grease a baking sheet.

2 In a bowl, combine the sausage and onion and mix well. Add the baking mix, cheese and milk and mix well. Drop by teaspoonfuls onto the baking sheet and bake for 10 to 15 minutes, or until browned. Serve warm.

CHEESE-AND-SAUSAGE SNACKS
MAKES: *About 6 servings*

½ pound bulk fresh pork sausage
2½ tablespoons dry bread crumbs
1 small egg, lightly beaten
4 large hard-cooked eggs
½ can (4 ounces) refrigerated
  crescent dinner rolls

1 Position the rack in the center of the oven and preheat to 450 degrees F.

2 In a bowl, combine the sausage, bread crumbs and beaten egg and mix well. Divide into eighths and shape into patties.

3 Wrap the patties around each hard-cooked egg, encasing it completely. Place on a ungreased jelly-roll pan and bake for 12 to 15 minutes, or until the meat is

cooked. Drain on paper towels and cool for at least for 10 minutes.

4 Reduce the oven temperature to 375 degrees F.

5 Separate the dough into 4 triangles and press each triangle to enlarge it slightly. Lay a sausage-wrapped egg on the shortest side of the triangle and roll up until the dough is wrapped around the egg. Repeat with the remaining eggs. Pinch the edges of the dough to seal and completely cover the egg. Place on an ungreased jelly roll pan and bake for 12 to 15 minutes, or until golden brown. Cut each egg into wedges and serve warm.

SCOTTISH EGG WEDGES
MAKES: *16 servings*

CHINESE-STYLE SCOTCH EGGS

MAKES: *About 8 servings*

8 large hard-cooked eggs, shells on
3 tablespoons soy sauce
3 whole star anise
2 black tea bags
2 large eggs
1 tablespoon sesame-flavored prepared mustard
2 cups dried bread crumbs
2 tablespoons sesame seeds
1 pound bulk country-style sausage
2 teaspoons chopped fresh ginger
2 cloves garlic, mined
canola oil

1 Gently crack the hard-cooked eggs all over but leave the shells on them. Put them in a saucepan with the soy sauce, anise, tea bags and enough water to cover and bring to a simmer over medium-low heat. Simmer for about 25 minutes and set aside at room temperature for at least 24 hours.

2 In a shallow bowl, combine the eggs and mustard and mix well.

3 In another bowl, combine the bread crumbs and sesame seeds and mix.

4 In another bowl, combine the sausage, ginger and garlic and mix well.

5 Peel the eggs. Pinch off pieces of the sausage and mold the meat around the eggs to encase them completely. Dip in the egg-mustard mixture and then in the bread crumbs. Cover and chill for at least 4 hours.

6 In a deep skillet or deep-fat fryer, pour the oil to a depth of 2 or 3 inches and heat over high heat until hot. Fry the eggs, 2 or 3 at a time, turning occasionally, for 10 to 15 minutes until browned on both sides. Drain on paper towels and cut into quarters for serving, with additional sesame mustard, if desired.

HONEYED CHEESE-AND-FRUIT BREAKFAST SANDWICHES

MAKES: *4 servings*

½ cup cream cheese, at room temperature
¼ cup honey
¼ cup hulled sunflower seeds
8 slices honey whole-grain bread
1 peach, pitted and thinly sliced
1 Bartlett pear, cored and thinly sliced
2 small apricots, pitted and thinly sliced

In a bowl, combine the cream cheese, honey and sunflower seeds and mash until mixed. Spread on 4 slices of bread, top with the fruit and the remaining bread. Cut in half on the diagonal and serve.

4 red potatoes, cut into ½-inch cubes
4 Italian sausages, cut into ¼-inch cubes
1 Bermuda onion, diced
1 green bell pepper, cubed
1 red bell pepper, cubed

In a saucepan, combine the potatoes and sausages with enough water to cover and bring to a simmer over medium heat and cook, covered, for about 20 minutes or until the sausage is cooked through and the potatoes are tender. Drain, add the onions and peppers and simmer, covered, for about 10 minutes longer, stirring occasionally, until the peppers are tender. Serve immediately.

HOT-POT SAUSAGE
MAKES: *About 4 servings*

1½ cups Bisquick® baking mix
5 ounces grated extra-sharp Cracker Barrel® Cheese
½ pound bulk hot sausage

1 Position the rack in the center of the oven and preheat to 300 degrees F. Lightly grease a jelly-roll pan.

2 In a bowl, combine the baking mix and cheese and mix well. Add the sausage and mix by hand.

3 Break off pieces of the meat mixture and form into balls about the size of walnuts. Put the balls in the pan and bake for 40 to 45 minutes, or until a golden brown. Drain on paper towels and serve hot.

HOT SAUSAGE BALLS
MAKES: *About 24 servings*

¼ cup butter or margarine, melted
¼ pound smoked salmon, coarsely chopped
2 tablespoons minced Bermuda onion
pinch of black pepper
6 large eggs, lightly beaten
10 sprigs parsley, minced

1 Position the rack in the center of the oven and preheat to 325 degrees F. Put the butter in an 8-inch-square baking pan and put the pan in the oven to melt the butter.

2 Add the salmon, onions and pepper to the pan and stir to mix with the butter.

3 In a bowl, whisk the eggs until foamy and pour over the salmon, stirring gently to blend. Bake for 20 to 25 minutes or until the eggs are set. Sprinkle with parsley and cut into 1-inch squares for serving.

SALMON-EGG SQUARES
MAKES: *About 24 servings*

SOUR CREAM BISCUITS WITH PEACH BUTTER

MAKES: *About 8 biscuits*

BISCUITS
2 cups all-purpose flour
2 tablespoons sugar
1 tablespoon baking powder
¼ teaspoon baking soda
1 teaspoon chopped fresh rosemary
pinch of salt
⅓ cup butter or margarine, diced
1 cup sour cream or plain yogurt
1 tablespoon half-and-half
2 teaspoons milk

BUTTER
½ cup butter or margarine, at room temperature
3 tablespoons peach preserves

1 Position the rack in the center of the oven and preheat 425 degrees F.

2 In a bowl, combine the flour, sugar, baking powder, baking soda, rosemary and salt and whisk well. Using a pastry blender or two knives, cut the butter into the dry ingredients until the mixture resembles fine crumbs. Add the sour cream and half-and-half, stirring just until blended and moist. Add a teaspoon more of half-and-half, if necessary.

3 On a lightly floured work surface, knead the dough several times and roll out to a thickness of ½ inch. Using a 2½-inch biscuit or cookie cutter, cut out the biscuits and put them on an ungreased baking sheet, leaving about 1 inch between them. Brush with the milk and bake for 8 to 12 minutes, or until a golden brown. Cool on wire racks.

4 In a bowl, combine the butter and preserves and mash with a fork until mixed. Serve with the hot biscuits.

CHERRY RED SCONES

MAKES: *About 8 servings*

1 jar (10 ounces) maraschino cherries, drained, quartered and juice reserved
2 cups all-purpose flour
½ cup flaked coconut
¼ cup sugar
2 teaspoons baking powder
¼ teaspoon salt
⅓ cup butter or margarine, cubed
1 large egg
½ cup buttermilk or sour milk
1 cup powdered sugar

1 Position the rack in the center of the oven and preheat to 400 degrees F.

2 In a bowl, combine the cherries, flour, coconut, sugar, baking powder and salt. Using a pastry cutter or two knives, cut the butter into the dry ingredients until the mixture resembles coarse crumbs.

3 In a bowl, whisk the egg until thick and light colored. Beat in the buttermilk. Add the dry ingredients and stir just until mixed.

4 On a lightly floured work surface, knead the dough several times and then roll out to a thickness of ½ inch. Using a 4-inch-round cutter, cut out 8 scones and transfer them to an ungreased baking sheet. Score each into 4 wedges and bake for 10 to 12 minutes, or until a golden brown. Cool for about 5 minutes on wire racks.

5 In a bowl, combine the powdered sugar and about 2 tablespoons of cherry juice and stir until smooth. Drizzle over the scones and serve.

1 cup cream cheese, at room temperature
½ cup sugar
2 large egg yolks
2 (1 pound each) loaves thin-sliced white bread, crusts trimmed
1 cup butter or margarine, melted
cinnamon sugar
sour cream, whisked until light
grape or strawberry jelly

1 Position the rack in the center of the oven and preheat to 400 degrees F. Lightly grease a baking sheet.

2 In a bowl, combine the cream cheese and sugar and mash until smooth. Add the egg yolks and beat until well mixed.

3 On a work surface, roll each slice of bread until thin. Spread the cream cheese mixture on each slice and roll into cylinders. Dip in the melted butter and sprinkle with cinnamon sugar. Place on the baking sheet and bake for 8 to 10 minutes, or until golden brown. Serve with sour cream and jelly.

MINI BLINIS
MAKES: *12 to 16 servings*

SAUSAGE MUFFINS
MAKES: *12 muffins*

½ pound bulk sausage
½ cup shredded Cheddar cheese
melted butter
2 cups all-purpose flour
2 tablespoons sugar
1 tablespoon baking powder
¼ teaspoon salt
1 large egg
1 cup milk

1 Position the rack in the center of the oven and preheat to 375 degrees F. Lightly grease a 12-cup muffin pan.

2 In a saucepan, cook the sausage over medium heat, stirring, until browned and crumbled. Drain, reserving the drippings. Add the cheese to the sausage and mix well. Pour the drippings into a measuring cup and add enough butter to measure ¼ cup. Set both the drippings and sausage aside.

3 In a bowl, combine the flour, sugar, baking powder and salt and whisk well.

4 In another bowl, using an electric mixer set on high speed, beat the egg, milk and reserved drippings until smooth. Add to the dry ingredients, stirring until just moistened. Add the cheese and sausage and mix well. Spoon into the muffin cups, filling each about halfway, and bake for 15 to 18 minutes, or until a toothpick inserted in the center of a muffin comes out clean. Cool slightly on wire racks and serve warm.

CHEESE-AND-BACON SQUARES

MAKES: *About 20 servings*

½ cup Kraft® Real Mayonnaise
1 teaspoon Worcestershire sauce
⅛ teaspoon sweet Hungarian paprika
1 cup shredded Cheddar or Colby cheese
4 strips crisp bacon, crumbled
2½ tablespoons chopped unsalted peanuts
2 tablespoons chopped green onions (green portions only)
7 slices white bread

1 Position the rack in the center of the oven and preheat to 400 degrees F.

2 In a bowl, combine the mayonnaise, Worcestershire sauce and paprika and stir well. Add the cheese, bacon, peanuts and onions and mix well.

3 Spread the mayonnaise mixture on each slice of bread, put the bread on an ungreased baking sheet and bake for 8 to 10 minutes or until the cheese melts and the topping is hot. Cut into quarters and serve.

COTTAGE CHEESE-PECAN ROLLS

MAKES: *12 rolls*

½ cup packed dark-brown sugar
¼ cup butter or margarine, at room temperature, diced
¼ cup chopped pecans
1¾ cups all-purpose flour
½ cup granulated sugar
1½ teaspoons baking powder
⅛ teaspoon baking soda
⅛ teaspoon salt
1 teaspoon cinnamon
1 large egg
1 cup cottage cheese
¼ cup butter or margarine, melted

1 Position the rack in the center of the oven and preheat to 375 degrees F. Lightly grease a baking sheet.

2 In a bowl, combine the brown sugar and butter and stir with a fork, mashing the butter into the sugar until the mixture is crumbly. Add the pecans and mix well. Spread on a plate or shallow dish.

3 In a bowl, combine the flour, ¼ cup of granulated sugar, baking powder, baking soda and salt and whisk well.

4 In a small bowl, combine the remaining ¼ cup of sugar and the cinnamon and stir well.

5 In another bowl, combine the egg and cottage cheese and mix well. Add the dry ingredients and stir until a dough forms. Form into a ball and turn out onto a lightly floured work surface. Brush with melted butter and sprinkle with the cinnamon sugar. Cut the ball into 12 pieces, shape the pieces into rolls and roll them in the pecan-sugar mixture, pressing it to adhere to the rolls. Arrange the rolls on the baking sheet and bake for 20 to 25 minutes or until lightly browned. Serve warm.

8 cups lightly packed torn spinach leaves (approximately 2 large bunches)
¼ cup butter or margarine
3 tablespoons all-purpose flour
salt and pepper
1¾ cups half-and-half
½ cup shredded Swiss cheese
1 package (6 ounces) sliced Canadian bacon
½ teaspoon prepared mustard
pinch of ground nutmeg
4 large hard-cooked eggs, coarsely chopped
2 tablespoons grated Parmesan or romano cheese

1 Position the rack in the center of the oven and preheat to 450 degrees F. Lightly grease four 1½-cup custard cups.

2 In a steaming basket set over boiling water, steam the spinach over medium-high heat for about 5 minutes until wilted. Shake dry, chop coarsely and transfer to a bowl.

3 In a large skillet, melt 3 tablespoons of the butter over medium heat.

4 In a bowl, combine the flour and salt and pepper and whisk well. Add to the butter and cook over medium heat, stirring, until bubbling. Remove from the heat and stir in the half-and-half. Return to the heat and cook, stirring, for 3 or 4 minutes or until thickened.

5 Add ½ cup of the half-and-half mixture to the spinach and stir to mix.

6 Add the Swiss cheese, mustard and nutmeg to the remaining half-and-half mixture and cook for 4 or 5 minutes, stirring, until the cheese melts and the mixture is smooth. Remove from the heat and add the eggs, stirring until incorporated.

7 In a small skillet, melt the remaining tablespoon of butter over medium-high heat and add the bacon, sautéing until lightly browned. Drape the bacon in the custard cups, spoon the spinach mixture into the cups and pour the eggs over the spinach. Fold any overhanging bacon over the top. Set the custard cups in a larger roasting pan and add enough hot water to come about a third of the way up the sides of the cups and sprinkle with Parmesan cheese. Bake for about 8 to 10 minutes, or until the egg mixture is set and firm.

EGG-AND-CANADIAN BACON FLORENTINE

MAKES: *About 4 servings*

---

2 cups all-purpose flour
¼ cup sugar
2 teaspoons baking powder
¼ teaspoon salt
5 tablespoons butter or margarine, chilled, diced
1 large egg
½ cup light cream
1½ teaspoons vanilla extract
½ cup chopped dried papaya
½ cup chopped dried pineapple
½ cup chopped macadamia nuts
½ cup shredded coconut
3 ounces white chocolate, finely chopped

1 Position the rack in the center of the oven and preheat to 375 degrees F. Lightly grease a baking sheet.

2 In a bowl, combine the flour, sugar, baking powder and salt and whisk well. Using a pastry blender or two knives, cut the butter into the dry ingredients until the mixture resembles coarse crumbs.

3 In a bowl, and using an electric mixer set on low speed, beat the egg until foamy. Beat in the cream and vanilla. Add the dry ingredients and mix until just blended. Fold in the papaya, pineapple, macadamia nuts, coconut and chocolate.

4 With floured hands, transfer the dough to the baking sheet and pat it into an 8-inch circle. Score into 8 wedges and bake for 18 to 20 minutes, or until golden brown. Cool on a wire rack and break into the wedges to serve.

ALOHA SCONES

MAKES: *8 scones*

APPLE-PECAN SCONES

MAKES: *8 scones*

1¾ cups all-purpose flour
¼ cup plus 1 tablespoon sugar
1 teaspoon grated lemon zest
½ teaspoon baking powder
¼ teaspoon baking soda
¼ cup butter or margarine, diced
¾ cup chopped apples
¼ cup lemon-flavored yogurt
¼ cup chopped pecans
⅛ teaspoon cinnamon

1 Position the rack in the center of the oven and preheat to 375 degrees F. Lightly grease a baking sheet.

2 In a bowl, combine the flour, ¼ cup of the sugar, lemon zest, baking powder and baking soda.

Using a pastry blender or two knives, cut the butter into the dry ingredients until the mixture forms coarse crumbs. Fold in the apples, yogurt and pecans until just mixed.

3 With floured hands, transfer the dough to the baking sheet and pat the dough into an 8-inch circle. Score into 8 wedges.

4 In a small bowl, combine the remaining tablespoon of sugar and the cinnamon and sprinkle over the wedges. Bake for 15 to 20 minutes, or until golden brown. Cool on a wire rack and break into wedges to serve.

APRICOT OMELET

MAKES: *About 4 servings*

8 large eggs, separated
¼ cup sugar
¼ cup butter or margarine
1 can (8 ounces) apricot halves, drained
½ cup apricot jam
¼ cup finely chopped almonds
powdered sugar for garnish

1 Position the rack in the center of the oven and preheat to 350 degrees F.

2 In a bowl, using an electric mixer set on high speed, beat the egg whites until frothy. Continue to beat, adding the sugar gradually until stiff peaks form.

3 In another bowl, beat the egg yolks until thick and light colored. Fold into the whites.

4 In a 10-inch ovenproof omelet pan or skillet, heat 2 tablespoons of the butter over medium heat until frothy. Add half of the egg mixture and cook just until puffy and golden on 1 side. Transfer to the oven and bake for 8 minutes. Remove from the oven and top with half of the apricots, half of the jam and half of the almonds. Slide onto a serving dish and fold in half. Cut in half to serve. Repeat with the remaining ingredients to make a second omelet.

one 9-inch prepared pastry shell
2 large eggs
1½ cups half-and-half
2 to 3 tablespoons sugar
1 tablespoon cornstarch
¼ teaspoon grated nutmeg
½ teaspoon almond extract
¼ cup sliced almonds
1 can (16 ounce) apricot halves,
    drained

1 Position the rack in the center of the oven and preheat to 375 degrees F.

2 Prick the bottom of the pastry and bake for 9 or 10 minutes until lightly browned.

3 In a bowl, combine the eggs and half-and-half and whisk well.

4 In a small bowl, combine the sugar, cornstarch and nutmeg and whisk well. Add to the egg mixture with the almond extract and almonds. Pour into the pastry shell and bake for about 15 minutes until partially set. Arrange the apricots over the outer edge of the filling and bake for 15 to 20 minutes longer, or until firm and golden brown. Cool on a wire rack.

APRICOT QUICHE

MAKES: *About 8 servings*

2 cups all-purpose flour
2½ tablespoons baking powder
2 tablespoons sugar
⅛ teaspoon salt
2 large eggs, lightly beaten
¾ cup butter or margarine, melted
¼ cup milk
⅔ cup fresh blueberries

1 Position the rack in the center of the oven and preheat to 350 degrees F. Lightly grease a baking sheet.

2 In a bowl, combine the flour, baking powder, sugar and salt and whisk well.

3 In another bowl, using an electric mixer set on low speed, beat the eggs until foamy. Beat in the butter and milk and add the dry ingredients, stirring just until mixed. Fold in the blueberries.

4 With floured hands, transfer the dough to the baking sheet and pat into a 9-inch-round circle. Score into 8 wedges and bake for 15 to 20 minutes, or until golden brown. Cool on a wire rack and break into wedges for serving.

BLUEBERRY SCONES

MAKES: *8 scones*

Chapter 13

SWEET INDULGENCES

Few of us turn down a freshly baked cookie or a spoonful of chocolate pudding. And we are not shy about indulging in sweets any time of day, not just after a meal. The recipes in this chapter may be served for dessert but are even better as snacks. Regardless of what the clock says, they are deliciously seductive treats that satisfy the craving for sweets familiar to so many of us, morning, noon or night. Don't feel guilty. You deserve these every now and then.

BAKED PEARS

MAKES: *About 6 servings*

3 large pears
2 teaspoons lemon juice
⅔ cups packed light-brown sugar
2 tablespoons unsalted butter
mint sprigs for garnish

1 Position the rack in the center of the oven and preheat to 300 degrees F. Lightly grease a 9-inch-square baking dish.

2 Peel, core and slice the pears into ¼- to ½-inch-thick slices. Brush with lemon juice and arrange decoratively in the pan.

Sprinkle with about 2 tablespoons of the sugar, dot with 1 tablespoon of butter and cover with aluminum foil. Bake for 25 to 30 minutes or until the pears are tender. Sprinkle with remaining sugar and butter.

3 Increase the oven temperature to 550 degrees F and bake uncovered for 1 or 2 minutes, or until the edges of the pears are golden brown. Serve garnished with mint sprigs.

CHOCOLATE-PEANUT BUTTER SNACKS

MAKES: *11 to 12 cups*

1 cup creamy peanut butter
1 package (12 ounces) butterscotch chips
8 cups Wheat Chex® cereal
1 package (12 ounces) chocolate chips

1 In a large saucepan, combine the peanut butter and butterscotch chips and cook over low heat until melted. Add the cereal and stir to mix.

2 Spread onto an ungreased baking sheet, using a spatula to spread into an even layer. Sprinkle evenly with chocolate chips. Cover and freeze for at least 4 hours or until firm. Using a sharp knife, slice into bite-sized pieces and serve frozen.

CHOCOLATE CRISPIX SNACKS

MAKES: *8 to 12 servings*

1 box (14 ounces) Crispix® cereal
2 cups chopped peanuts
¼ cup butter or margarine
2 bars (8 ounces each) Hershey® Milk Chocolate Candy, broken into pieces
2 cups creamy peanut butter
4 cups powdered sugar, sifted

1 In a large bowl, combine the cereal and peanuts and toss well.

2 In a saucepan, melt the butter over low heat. Stir in the chocolate and peanut butter and cook, stirring, until smooth. Remove from the heat and immediately pour over the cereal and nuts, tossing to coat. Cool slightly, transfer to a large plastic bag and add 2 cups of the sugar. Shake vigorously to mix. Add the remaining sugar and continue to shake until well coated. Serve at once or keep tightly sealed.

½ cup butter or margarine, melted
1 cup crunchy peanut butter
2 cups powdered sugar
1 box (12 ounces) Rice Chex® cereal
1 package (6 ounces) semisweet
    chocolate chips
1 package (6 ounces) milk chocolate
    chips

1 In a bowl, using an electric mixer on medium speed, blend together the butter, peanut butter and sugar until smooth.

2 In a large bowl, combine the cereal and chocolate chips and toss well. Add the butter mixture and stir until blended. Transfer to a plastic container with a tight-fitting lid and store in a cool place for up to 1 week.

CHOCOLATE-CHIP CHOW

MAKES: *6 to 7 cups*

---

1 package (11 ounces) pie crust mix
¼ cup cornmeal
3 large egg yolks
¼ cup sugar
1 tablespoon rice flour
¼ teaspoon salt
1¼ cups heavy cream
1 teaspoon vanilla extract
1 cup pitted, chopped dates
1 cup chopped pecans
whipped cream, whipped topping or
    frozen vanilla yogurt
16 pecan halves for garnish

1 Position the rack in the center of the oven and preheat to 350 degrees F. Lightly grease two 8-cup muffin pans.

2 In a large bowl, prepare the pie crust following the package instructions for 2 crusts. Add the cornmeal and stir to mix. Divide into 16 equal parts, rolling each into a ball. On a lightly floured work surface, roll each ball into a 4-inch circle. Fit each into a muffin cup.

3 In a bowl, using an electric mixer on medium speed, beat the egg yolks until thick and light. Beat in the sugar, rice flour and salt. Add the cream, vanilla, dates and chopped pecans and fold until mixed.

4 Divide evenly among the muffin cups and bake for 45 to 50 minutes, or until the tops are golden brown. Top with whipped cream and serve garnished with pecan halves.

PECAN-DATE TARTS

MAKES: *About 16 servings*

PEANUT BUTTER TWISTS

MAKES: *8 to 10 servings*

1 cup all-purpose flour
½ teaspoon salt
⅔ cup vegetable shortening
2 packages (3 ounces each) cream cheese
½ cup creamy peanut butter

1 Position the rack in the center of the oven and preheat to 375 degrees F. Lightly grease a baking sheet.

2 In a bowl, combine the flour and salt. Using a pastry blender, cut in the shortening and cream cheese to make a soft dough. On a lighlty floured work surface, roll out half of the dough to a thickness of ¼ inch and spread with the peanut butter.

3 Roll out the remaining dough and lay over the peanut butter. Roll the 2 layers of dough out to a thickness of ¼ inch. Cut into strips 4 to 6 inches long. Lay the strips on the baking sheet and twist each one. Bake for 4 to 6 minutes or until lighlty browned. Cool slightly on a wire rack.

QUICK ENERGY BANANA BOATS

MAKES: *About 6 servings*

6 bananas, unpeeled
½ cup semisweet chocolate chips
½ cup miniature marshmallows

1 Cut a 3- to 4-inch slit along one side of each banana skin, pressing on the ends to open the cut and expose the fruit.

2 Spoon the chocolate chips into the openings and place the bananas on a microwave-safe tray. Microwave on medium (50 percent) power for 30 to 45 seconds until the chocolate begins to soften.

3 Cool slightly and sprinkle with marshmallows. Eat directly from the banana skin, spooning the fruit, chocolate and marshmallows together.

COOKING NOTE: Depending on the size of the microwave, you may have to cook the bananas in batches.

SUGAR-COATED WALNUTS

MAKES: *About 2 cups*

1 cup sugar
½ cup water
1 teaspoon ground cinnamon
½ teaspoon ground nutmeg
½ teaspoon ground cloves
2 cups walnut halves

1 In a saucepan, combine the sugar, water, cinnamon, nutmeg and cloves and bring to a boil over medium-high heat; stirring. Insert a candy thermometer and cook until the mixture reaches 236 degrees F. Remove from the heat, add the walnuts and stir until well coated.

2 Lay a piece of wax paper on a work surface and spread the walnuts on the paper to cool. Serve immediately or store in an airtight container for up to a week.

1 cup wheat germ
½ cup all-purpose flour
2 teaspoons baking powder
½ teaspoon baking soda
¼ teaspoon sea salt
1 cup packed light-brown sugar
½ cup vegetable shortening
1 large egg, lightly beaten
½ teaspoon vanilla extract
1½ cups Kellogg's® Cornflakes
½ cup shredded sweetened coconut
½ cup old-fashioned rolled oats

1 Position the racks in the center of the oven and preheat to 350 degrees F. Lightly grease 2 baking sheets.

2 In a bowl, combine the wheat germ, flour, baking powder, baking soda and salt and toss well.

3 In another bowl, using an electric mixer on high speed, beat the sugar and shortening until light and fluffy. Add the egg and vanilla and beat until mixed. Stir in the wheat germ and flour mixture. Add the cornflakes, coconut and rolled oats and fold until well incorporated.

4 Drop by teaspoonfuls onto the baking sheets, leaving about 1 inch between each, and bake for 12 to 15 minutes or until golden. Cool on wire racks.

WHEAT GERM CRUNCHIES

MAKES: *About 36 servings*

1 cup heavy cream or half-and-half
¼ cup sugar
1 ounce unsweetened chocolate, grated or finely chopped
3 cups cold strong brewed coffee
ice

1 In a saucepan, combine the cream, sugar and chocolate and bring to a boil over medium heat,

stirring constantly. Remove from the heat and plunge the saucepan in a larger bowl filled with ice and water.

2 When cool, combine the chocolate mixture with the coffee in a pitcher. Add ice and serve.

CHILLED EUROPEAN COFFEE

MAKES: *2 to 4 servings*

CHOCOLATE DRINK

MAKES: *4 servings*

2 cups milk
¼ cup sugar
¼ cup Dutch-processed cocoa
  powder
1 package (3.4 ounces) chocolate
  instant pudding mix
1 teaspoon chocolate extract
8 ice cubes
mint sprigs for garnish

In the container of a blender, combine the milk, sugar, cocoa powder and pudding mix and process for 15 to 20 seconds until smooth. Add the chocolate extract and ice cubes and process until the ice is crushed. Immediately pour into chilled glasses and garnish with the mint sprigs.

CHOCOLATE MILK SHAKE

MAKES: *2 servings*

1 pint chocolate ice cream
¾ cup milk
3 tablespoons Chocolate Syrup
  (recipe follows)
sliced fresh strawberries or kiwi for
  garnish

In the container of a blender, combine the ice cream, milk and syrup and blend until smooth. Pour into glasses and garnish with fruit.

COOKING NOTE: **Vary the flavor of ice cream for different flavored milk shakes. Add a few drops of almond or peppermint extracts for extra flavor.**

CHOCOLATE SYRUP

MAKES: *1½ to 2 cups*

5 ounces unsweetened chocolate,
  grated or finely chopped
1⅓ cups boiling water
1 cup sugar
1 teaspoon chocolate extract

In a saucepan set over hot, almost simmering water, combine the chocolate and water and cook over medium heat, stirring, until the chocolate melts and the mixture is smooth. Add the sugar and cook for 3 to 5 minutes, stirring, until the sugar dissolves. Remove from the heat and stir in the extract.

1 pint chocolate ice cream
2 cups milk
¼ cup Grand Marnier or another orange-flavored liqueur
Chocolate Whipped Cream for garnish (recipe follows)
grated chocolate or chocolate curls for garnish

In the container of a blender, combine the ice cream, milk and Grand Marnier and process on low speed for 30 to 40 seconds until smooth. Pour into 4 large chilled glasses, garnish with dollops of chocolate whipped cream and grated chocolate.

COOKING NOTE: **More ice cream can be added to make the mixture thicker.**

ULTRA CHOCOLATE MILK SHAKE

MAKES: *4 servings*

CHOCOLATE WHIPPED CREAM

MAKES: *2 to 2½ cups*

3 tablespoons powdered sugar
2 tablespoons Dutch-processed cocoa powder
1 cup heavy cream

1 In a cup, combine the sugar and cocoa powder and mix well.

2 In a bowl, using an electric mixer on high speed, whip the cream until soft peaks form. Fold in the dry ingredients, cover and chill for 30 minutes.

¼ cup Chocolate Syrup (see page 396)
1 tablespoon milk
2 large scoops chocolate ice cream
¾ to 1 cup chilled seltzer water
whipped cream for garnish
ground hazelnuts or walnuts for garnish
1 maraschino cherry for garnish

1 In a tall soda glass, combine the syrup and milk and stir vigorously. Gently drop the ice cream into the glass and pour enough seltzer water into the glass to fill it.

2 Top with whipped cream, a sprinkling of nuts and a cherry.

CHOCOLATE SODA

MAKES: *1 serving*

CHOCOLATE SPIKE

MAKES: *1 serving*

¾ cup milk
1 large scoop chocolate or vanilla ice cream
1½ teaspoons Sweet Chocolate Syrup (recipe follows)
⅛ teaspoon ground nutmeg
⅛ teaspoon ground cloves
⅛ teaspoon cinnamon

In the container of a blender, combine the milk, ice cream, syrup, nutmeg, cloves and cinnamon and process for 30 to 40 seconds until smooth and blended. Pour into a tall glass and serve.

SWEET CHOCOLATE SYRUP

MAKES: *1¼ to 1½ cups*

3 ounces unsweetened chocolate, grated or finely chopped
⅔ cup water
½ cup sugar
½ cup light or dark corn syrup
½ teaspoon chocolate or vanilla extract

1 In a saucepan, combine the chocolate and water and heat over low heat, stirring, until smooth and thick. Stir in the sugar. Raise the heat and bring to a boil. Lower the heat and simmer for about 2 minutes.

2 Add the corn syrup and bring the mixture to a boil. Remove from the heat and cool slighlty. Add the extract and stir to mix. Cool completely.

CINNAMON COCOA

MAKES: *4 to 6 servings*

¼ cup Dutch-processed cocoa powder
¼ cup sugar
¼ teaspoon cinnamon
⅛ teaspoon salt
1 cup water
3 cups milk
1 teaspoon chocolate extract

1 In a saucepan, combine the cocoa powder, sugar, cinnamon, salt and water and cook over medium heat, whisking, until thick and hot. Do not boil. Add the milk and chocolate extract and mix well. Remove from the heat.

2 Using an electric mixer set on medium speed, beat until foamy. Pour into warmed cups and serve immediately.

COOKING NOTE: For richer cocoa, use half-and-half instead of milk. Ground nutmeg or all-spice can be substituted for the cinnamon, or omit the spice and serve with a stick of cinnamon in each cup.

1 cup milk
1 tablespoon Dutch-processed cocoa
   powder
1 tablespoon sugar
miniature marshmallows for garnish

In a saucepan, heat the milk over medium heat until bubbles form around the edges. Do not boil. Add the cocoa powder and sugar and stir until the sugar dissolves. Pour into a mug and serve with marshmallows on top.

COCOA IN A MUG

MAKES: *1 serving*

2 cups milk
⅔ cups instant cocoa mix
1 teaspoon instant coffee powder
2 cups chocolate ice cream, softened

In the container of a blender, combine all of the ingredients and process on low speed for 10 to 15 seconds until smooth. Pour into chilled glasses and serve.

MOCHA MILK SHAKE

MAKES: *2 to 4 servings*

BANANA SPLIT CAKE

MAKES: *12 to 15 servings*

CRUST
1⅔ cups graham cracker crumbs
¼ cup sugar
⅓ cup vegetable shortening

FILLING
4 bananas, sliced
1 cup (6 ounces) semisweet
  chocolate chips
1 pint fudge ripple or chocolate ice
  cream, softened

TOPPING
1⅓ cups evaporated milk
1 cup (6 ounces) semisweet
  chocolate chips
½ cup butter or margarine
½ teaspoon vanilla or chocolate
  extract
1 cup heavy cream

1 Position a rack in the center of the oven and preheat the oven to 375 degrees. Lightly grease a 13-by-9-inch baking pan.

2 In a bowl, combine the crumbs and sugar. Using a pastry blender or two knives, cut the vegetable shortening into the dry ingredients until the mixture resembles coarse crumbs. Press onto the bottom of the prepared pan and bake for about 5 minutes, or until golden brown. Cool on a wire rack.

3 Lay the bananas on the crust in a single layer. Sprinkle with 1 cup of chocolate chips and spread the ice cream over the top. Chill in the freezer for at least 1 hour or until the ice cream is firm.

4 In a saucepan, combine the milk, 1 cup of chocolate chips and butter and bring to a boil over medium heat. Reduce the heat and simmer for about 5 minutes, or until slightly thickened. Remove from the heat and stir in the vanilla extract. Cool completely. Spread over the ice cream layer and freeze for at least 1 hour until firm.

5 In a bowl, using an electric mixer on medium-high speed, beat the cream until soft peaks form. Spread the whipped cream over the top of the cake.

COOKING NOTE: Chocolate Whipped Cream (see page 397) can be used in place of the plain whipped cream.

CHOCOLATE BUTTERMILK CUPCAKES

MAKES: *24 servings*

2 ounces semisweet chocolate,
  grated or finely chopped
2 ounces unsweetened chocolate,
  grated or finely chopped
2 cups all-purpose flour
1½ teaspoons baking soda
pinch of salt
1 cup butter or margarine, at room
  temperature
1¾ cups granulated sugar
4 large eggs
1½ cups buttermilk
1½ teaspoons cherry extract or
  brandy
24 large maraschino cherries,
  stemmed

1 Position a rack in the center of the oven and preheat the oven to 325 degrees. Lightly grease three 8-cup muffin pans.

2 In a saucepan set over hot, barely simmering water, melt the chocolates over low heat, stirring until smooth. Do not let the chocolate scorch. Set aside.

3 In a bowl, combine the flour, baking soda and salt and whisk well.

4 In another bowl, using an electric mixer on high speed, beat the butter and sugar until fluffy. Beat in the eggs, 1 at a time, beating well after each addition. Add the dry ingredients, alternating with the buttermilk, and beating until smooth. Stir in the cherry extract and melted chocolate and spoon into the muffin cups, filling each about two-thirds full. Press a cherry deep into the center of each cupcake.

5 Bake for 15 to 20 minutes, or until a cake tester inserted into the center comes out clean. Cool in the pan on wire racks for about 5 minutes. Turn out onto the racks to cool completely.

½ cup butter or margarine

2 ounces unsweetened chocolate, grated or finely chopped

2 large egg whites

3 cups powdered sugar

2½ cups flaked coconut

1 teaspoon almond extract

1 cup All-Bran cereal

1 Line a 9-by-5-inch loaf pan with wax paper.

2 In a saucepan set over hot, barely simmering water, combine the butter and chocolate and melt over medium-low heat, stirring until smooth. Remove from the heat.

3 In a small bowl, whisk the egg whites until foamy.

4 In a bowl, combine the sugar, coconut, egg whites, almond extract and melted chocolate, mixing until smooth. Press half of the mixture onto the bottom of the pan.

5 Add the cereal to the bowl, stirring it into the remaining chocolate mixture. Smooth over the top of the mixture in the pan. Lay a piece of wax paper on top and weight with dried beans or uncooked rice. Chill for at least 1 hour, or until firm. Remove the paper and weights and cut into pieces for serving.

BLACK-AND-WHITE SQUARES

MAKES: *About 35 servings*

---

1 cup sugar

3 ounces unsweetened chocolate, grated or finely chopped

1 teaspoon chocolate or vanilla extract

1 cup slivered almonds

1 Line a baking sheet with wax paper.

2 In a saucepan set over hot, barely simmering water, melt the sugar over low heat until lique-

fied. Add the chocolate and chocolate extract and cook, stirring, until smooth and blended. Remove from heat and stir in the almonds. Immediately scrape onto the baking sheet and spread evenly. Cool at room temperature until set. Break into pieces for serving.

CHOCOLATE ALMOND BARK

MAKES: *About ¾ pound*

---

1 cup (6 ounces) semisweet chocolate chips

1 cup (6 ounces) butterscotch chips

1 can (7 ounces) unsalted peanuts, finely chopped

1 cup puffed rice cereal

1 Line 2 baking sheets with wax paper.

2 In a saucepan set over hot, barely simmering water, combine the chocolate and butterscotch

chips and melt over medium-low heat, stirring until smooth. Add the peanuts and cereal and stir until coated.

3 Drop by rounded teaspoonfuls onto the baking sheets. Chill for at least 1 hour or until firm. Store in an airtight container.

CHOCOLATE BUTTERSCOTCH DROPS

MAKES: *About 1½ pounds*

CHOCOLATE-COVERED STRAWBERRIES

MAKES: *36 servings*

4 ounces semisweet chocolate, grated or finely chopped
¼ cup plus 1 tablespoon butter or margarine
1 tablespoon light corn syrup
36 fresh strawberries, cleaned, long stems intact

1 Line a baking sheet with wax paper.

2 In a saucepan set over hot, barely simmering water, combine the chocolate and butter and melt over medium-low heat, stirring until smooth. Remove from the heat and place the saucepan in a larger pan of warm water.

3 Holding the strawberries by the tops, dip each at an angle into the chocolate mixture and transfer to the baking sheet. Let stand at room temperature until hard.

COOKING NOTE: A bamboo skewer can be used to dip the strawberries. Do not dip the strawberries straight down into the chocolate, but at an angle.

CHOCOLATE FUDGE WITH MARSHMALLOWS AND NUTS

MAKES: *4 to 4½ pounds*

4 cups sugar
1 can (14 ounces) evaporated milk
1 cup butter
1½ cups (9 ounces) semisweet chocolate chips
2 jars (7 ounces each) marshmallow creme
1 teaspoon chocolate or vanilla extract
1 cup chopped walnuts

1 Lightly grease a 13-by-9-inch pan.

2 In a saucepan, combine the sugar, milk and butter, insert a candy thermometer and cook over medium heat, stirring gently and frequently, until the temperature reaches 236 degrees F. Remove from the heat and add the chocolate chips, marshmallow creme and chocolate extract and stir until blended. Add the walnuts and fold gently. Pour into the pan and cool until slightly set. Score the top into triangles and cool completely. Cut into triangles.

1 package (3.4 ounces) Jell-O®
   Chocolate Instant Pudding Mix
12 to 15 chocolate wafer cookies
3 bananas, sliced
1 cup heavy cream

1 Make the pudding according to the package directions and set aside to thicken slightly.

2 Line the bottom of a serving bowl with cookies and top with a layer of bananas. Spoon a layer of pudding over the bananas. Place another layer of cookies over the pudding and top with more bananas and pudding. Continue layering until the cookies, pudding and bananas are used. Cover and chill for at least 30 minutes.

3 In a bowl, using an electric mixer on high speed, whip the cream until soft peaks form. Serve the pudding with the whipped cream on the side.

BANANA CHOCOLATE PUDDING

MAKES: *4 servings*

---

1 large egg
1 envelope unflavored gelatin
1 tablespoon cornstarch or arrowroot
1 tablespoon water
1 cup boiling water
2 tablespoons mocha-flavored
   instant coffee powder
½ cup ricotta cheese
½ cup skim milk, chilled
2 tablespoons Dutch-processed
   cocoa powder
½ cup sugar
⅛ teaspoon salt

1 In the container of a blender, combine the egg, gelatin, cornstarch and tablespoon of water and process for about 20 seconds until smooth. Add the boiling water and blend for 30 seconds longer. Add the coffee powder, ricotta cheese, skim milk, cocoa powder, sugar and salt and process for about 1 minute or until smooth.

2 Pour into four chilled custard cups and chill for at least 8 hours or until set.

COOKING NOTE: **Owing to the raw egg in this recipe, it should be kept refrigerated at all times, and for no longer than 3 days.**

BLENDER CHOCOLATE MOUSSE

MAKES: *4 servings*

CHOCOLATE DREAM PUDDING

MAKES: *6 to 8 servings*

4 ounces unsweetened chocolate, grated or finely chopped
4 large eggs, separated
½ cup sugar
½ cup heavy cream
2 tablespoons crème de cacao
¼ cup coffee liqueur
whipped cream for serving

1 In a saucepan set over hot, barely simmering water, melt the chocolate over low heat, stirring until smooth. Do not let the chocolate scorch. Remove from the heat and cool to room temperature.

2 In the top of a double boiler over simmering water, using an electric mixer on medium speed, beat the egg yolks and ¼ cup of the sugar until smooth and light. On low speed, mix in the melted chocolate. Add the cream and stir until the mixture thickens. Remove from the heat and stir in the crème de cacao and liqueur.

3 In a bowl, using an electric mixer with clean beaters on high speed, beat the egg whites until they form peaks. Continue beating on low speed and blend in the remaining ¼ cup sugar. Add to the chocolate mixture and fold gently until mixed. Cover and chill for at least 30 minutes or until set.

4 Spoon the mixture into chilled custard cups or parfait glasses. Serve with whipped cream on the side.

COOKING NOTE: **Owing to the raw egg in this recipe, it should be kept refrigerated at all times, and for no longer than 3 days.**

CHOCOLATE PARFAIT

MAKES: *8 servings*

2 cups skim milk
⅔ cup sugar
¼ cup Dutch-processed cocoa powder
2 tablespoons cornstarch
1 tablespoon butter-flavored vegetable shortening
1 teaspoon chocolate extract
1 tablespoon grated orange zest
½ cup heavy cream
1 teaspoon crème de cacao
1 orange, thinly sliced, for garnish

1 In a saucepan, combine the milk, sugar, cocoa powder and cornstarch and cook over medium heat, stirring constantly, until the mixture starts to boil. Remove from the heat. Add the shortening and chocolate extract and stir until smooth. Fold in the zest. Pour into a bowl and cover with wax paper or plastic wrap, pressing it onto the surface of the mixture. Chill for at least 3 hours.

2 In a bowl, using an electric mixer on high speed, whip the cream until soft peaks form. Fold in the crème de cacao. Fold half of this mixture into the chilled pudding.

3 Spoon the pudding, alternating with the remaining whipped cream, into 8 chilled parfait glasses and chill until ready to serve. Garnish with orange slices.

¼ cup sugar

2 tablespoons cornstarch or arrowroot

¼ teaspoon salt

2 ounces unsweetened chocolate, grated or finely chopped

2 cups milk

½ teaspoon vanilla or chocolate extract

⅓ cup miniature chocolate chips

½ cup Chocolate Syrup (see page 396)

1 Combine the sugar, cornstarch and salt and whisk well.

2 In a saucepan set over hot, barely simmering water, combine the chocolate and milk and cook, stirring, until the chocolate melts. Add the dry ingredients and cook for about 10 minutes longer, stirring once or twice. Add the vanilla and cook, stirring constantly, until the mixture thickens. Remove from the heat, cool slightly, and quickly stir in the chocolate chips. Spoon into 4 chilled custard cups and chill for at least 30 minutes.

3 Drizzle chocolate syrup over four small plates. Invert a pudding onto the center of each plate.

CHUNKY CHOCOLATE PUDDING

MAKES: *4 servings*

---

1 package (3.4 ounces) Jell-O® Chocolate Instant Pudding Mix

1 package (3.4 ounces) Jell-O® Banana-Flavored Instant Pudding Mix

1 box (16 ounces) chocolate graham crackers

1 Prepare each of the pudding mixes according to the package directions.

2 Line the bottom of a 13-by-9-inch baking pan with a layer of graham crackers. Add enough chocolate pudding to the pan, smoothing it over the crackers, just to cover the crackers. Top with another layer of graham crackers and just enough banana-flavored pudding to cover the crackers. Repeat the layers, ending with a layer of pudding.

3 Crush the few remaining graham crackers and sprinkle the crumbs over the top. Cover and chill for at least 3 hours.

ICE BOX PUDDING CAKE

MAKES: *12 to 15 servings*

SKILLET SOUFFLÉ

MAKES: *8 to 10 servings*

4 ounces semisweet chocolate, grated or finely chopped
2 tablespoons water
4 large eggs, separated, plus 2 large egg whites
⅓ cup sugar plus a little more for coating the skillet
1 teaspoon mocha-flavored instant coffee powder
1 teaspoon coffee liqueur
pinch of salt
1 tablespoon butter or margarine
whipped topping for serving

1 Preheat the oven to 375 degrees.

2 In a saucepan set over hot, barely simmering water, melt the chocolate over low heat, stirring until smooth. Do not let the chocolate scorch. Add the water, stir and remove from the heat.

3 In a large bowl, using an electric mixer on high speed, beat the 6 egg whites until stiff but not dry.

4 In a large bowl, using an electric mixer on medium speed, beat the 4 egg yolks until thick and light. Beat in the ⅓ cup of sugar, melted chocolate, coffee powder, liqueur and salt. Gently fold in the egg whites, a little at a time, blending until no white streaks remain.

5 In an 8 or 9-inch ovenproof skillet, melt the butter over medium heat, swirling it to grease the bottom and sides. Sprinkle with sugar and pour in the egg mixture.

6 Bake for 12 to 15 minutes, or until a toothpick inserted in the center comes out clean. Cool in the pan set on a wire rack for about 10 minutes. Serve with the whipped topping on the side.

COOKING NOTE: Sprinkle finely ground nuts, flaked coconut, chocolate sprinkles or a sprinkle of freshly ground nutmeg over the soufflé as soon as it comes from the oven, if desired.

UPSIDE-DOWN CHOCOLATE PUDDING

MAKES: *8 to 10 servings*

¼ cup butter or margarine
½ cup Dutch-processed cocoa powder
1 cup all-purpose flour
¾ cup sugar
3 tablespoons mocha-flavored instant coffee powder
1½ teaspoons baking powder
1 large egg
½ cup milk
1¼ cups boiling water
Whipped cream for garnish

1 Position a rack in the center of the oven and preheat to 350 degrees. Lightly grease a 1½-quart casserole dish.

2 In a small saucepan, melt the butter over low heat, stirring until smooth. Remove from the heat, add the cocoa and stir until smooth.

3 Combine the flour, ½ cup of the sugar, the coffee powder and baking powder.

4 In a small bowl, using an electric mixer on high speed, beat the egg until foamy. Beat in the milk. On low speed, beat in the cocoa mixture. Gradually add the dry ingredients, a little at a time, blending well after each addition. Transfer to the casserole.

5 Sprinkle the remaining ¼ cup of sugar over the batter and gently pour the boiling water over it. Place the casserole in a larger pan and set it on the oven rack. Pour more boiling water into the pan so that it comes halfway up the side of the dish. Bake for 30 to 35 minutes, or until the center springs back when touched. Cool for 15 to 30 minutes. Invert onto a serving plate and serve with whipped cream for garnish.

6 bananas, halved horizontally
1 cup semisweet chocolate chips
2 tablespoons butter or margarine
½ cup finely chopped pecans

1 Insert a wooden popsicle stick into the uncut, tapered end of each banana half and put on a wax paper-lined baking sheet. Freeze for at least 2 hours, or until hard.

2 In a saucepan set over hot, barely simmering water, combine the chocolate chips and butter and cook over medium heat, stirring until smooth.

3 Spread the nuts in a shallow bowl. Dip the bananas in the chocolate and roll in the pecans. Freeze until the chocolate hardens.

COOKING NOTE: These will keep for a few days wrapped in plastic and stored in the freezer.

CHOCOLATE-COVERED BANANAS

MAKES: *12 servings*

---

2 slices 1-inch-thick French bread
1½ ounces semisweet chocolate, grated of finely chopped
1 large egg
¼ cup milk
1 tablespoon powdered sugar
½ teaspoon chocolate extract
⅛ teaspoon ground cinnamon
1½ tablespoons butter or margarine
powdered sugar for garnish
Chocolate Syrup (page 396) or ice cream

1 Using a serrated knife, cut the slices of bread in half horizontally, but do not cut all the way through. Lay each slice flat, hold one half of the slice open and sprinkle the grated chocolate inside. Put in a dish just large enough to hold both slices next to each other.

2 In a bowl, using an electric mixer on medium speed, beat the egg, milk, sugar, chocolate extract and cinnamon until the sugar dissolves. Pour over the bread and set aside to soak, turning once, until most of the egg mixture is absorbed into the bread.

3 In a skillet, melt the butter over medium-low heat. Add the bread and cook, turning occasionally, for about 10 minutes, or until golden brown on both sides. Transfer to warm plates and dust with powdered sugar. Serve with syrup or ice cream.

CHOCOLATE-FILLED FRENCH TOAST

MAKES: *2 servings*

CHOCOLATE FONDUE

MAKES: *8 to 10 servings*

6 ounces unsweetened chocolate, grated or finely chopped
1½ cups sugar
1 cup heavy cream
½ cup butter or margarine
3 tablespoons crème de cacao
bread or cake cubes or fresh fruit

1 In a saucepan set over hot, barely simmering water, combine the chocolate, the sugar, cream and butter and cook over medium heat for 10 to 12 minutes, stirring constantly, until the chocolate melts and the sugar dissolves. Remove from the heat and stir in the crème de cacao.

2 Transfer to a fondue pot. Serve warm with bread, cake or fresh fruit for dipping.

COOKING NOTE: If the chocolate mixture becomes too thick, stir in 1 tablespoon of milk.

PEANUT BUTTER-CHOCOLATE DIP

MAKES: *3½ cups*

½ cup creamy peanut butter
2½ cups evaporated milk
1 package (3.4 ounces) Jell-O® Chocolate Instant Pudding Mix
plain unsalted crackers or cookies

In a bowl, using an electric mixer on low to medium speed, beat the peanut butter until smooth. Beat in the milk and then the pudding mix. Serve immediately with crackers or cookies on the side.

½ cup packed light-brown sugar
⅓ cup vegetable shortening
1 cup almonds, ground
1 cup rice flour

1 Preheat the oven to 350 degrees F.

2 In a bowl, using an electric mixer set on medium-high speed, cream the sugar and vegetable shortening until smooth. Beat in ¾ cup of the almonds. Gradually blend in the rice flour.

3 Pinch off balls of dough about the size of walnuts. Roll the balls in the remaining ¼ cup almonds and place 1 inch apart on ungreased baking sheets. Flatten each cookie with the bottom of a glass dipped in flour. Bake for 10 to 12 minutes, until the edges of the cookies just start to brown. Cool on wire racks.

COOKING NOTE: If the cookies are too grainy for your taste, substitute half the rice flour with all-purpose flour.

ALMOND COOKIES

MAKES: *4 to 5 dozen cookies*

1¼ cups all-purpose flour
½ teaspoon baking powder
½ teaspoon baking soda
½ teaspoon salt
1 cup vegetable shortening
1 cup packed light-brown sugar
¼ cup granulated sugar
2 large eggs
¼ cup milk
1 teaspoon almond extract
3 cups old-fashioned rolled oats
1 cup (6 ounces) semisweet
   chocolate chips (see note)

1 Preheat the oven to 350 degrees F.

2 In a bowl, combine the flour, baking powder, baking soda and salt and whisk well.

3 In a large bowl, using an electric mixer set on medium speed, cream the vegetable shortening and sugars until smooth. Beat in the eggs. Add the milk and almond extract and beat until smooth. Gradually blend in the dry ingredients and then fold in the oats and chocolate chips.

4 Drop the dough by teaspoonfuls, about 1½ inches apart, onto ungreased baking sheets. Bake for 10 to 12 minutes, or until golden brown. Cool on wire racks.

COOKING NOTE: Substitute milk chocolate, white chocolate, peanut butter or butterscotch chips for the semisweet chocolate chips. Or omit the chips and press 4 or 5 M & M's into the top of each cookie.

OATMEAL CRISPS

MAKES: *2 to 3 dozen cookies*

APRICOT BARS

MAKES: *2 to 4 dozen bars*

2 cups all-purpose flour
2 teaspoons baking powder
½ teaspoon ground nutmeg
½ teaspoon salt
2 teaspoons grated orange zest
4 large eggs
2 cups sugar
1½ cups dried apricots, diced
1 cup walnuts, chopped
powdered sugar for garnish

1 Preheat the oven to 350 degrees F. Grease a 13-by-9-inch baking pan.

2 In a bowl, combine the flour, baking powder, nutmeg and salt and whisk well. Stir in the orange zest.

3 In a bowl, using an electric mixer set on medium-high speed, beat the eggs and sugar until thick and light. Gradually blend in the dry ingredients. Fold in the apricots and walnuts.

4 Spread the batter in the pan and bake for 15 to 20 minutes, until the top is golden and a toothpick inserted in the center comes out clean. Cool in the pan on a rack before cutting into large or small bars. Sprinkle with powdered sugar.

BANANA DROPS

MAKES: *3 to 4 dozen cookies*

1½ cups all-purpose flour
1 cup sugar
½ teaspoon baking soda
¾ teaspoon ground cinnamon
¼ teaspoon ground nutmeg
1 teaspoon salt
¾ cup vegetable shortening
1 large egg
2 to 3 bananas, mashed
1¾ cups old-fashioned rolled oats
2 cups (12 ounces) semisweet
  chocolate chips

1 Preheat the oven to 400 degrees F.

2 Sift the flour, sugar, baking soda, cinnamon, nutmeg and salt into a large bowl. Cut in the veg-etable shortening. Stir in the egg and bananas until smooth. Fold in the oats and chocolate chips.

3 Drop the dough by spoonfuls 1½ inches apart onto ungreased baking sheets.

4 Bake for 12 to 15 minutes, until lightly colored. Transfer to wire racks to cool.

COOKING NOTE: **Raisins may be added to the dough at the same time as the chips. Substitute milk chocolate, white chocolate, peanut butter or butterscotch chips for the semisweet chocolate chips.**

1½ cups all-purpose flour
1½ teaspoons baking powder
¼ teaspoon salt
¾ cup sugar
¼ cup plus 2 tablespoons vegetable shortening
1 large egg
2 tablespoons milk
½ teaspoon vanilla extract

1 Preheat the oven to 375 degrees F. Lightly grease 2 baking sheets

2 In a bowl, combine the flour, baking powder and salt and whisk well.

3 In another bowl, using an electric mixer set on medium-high speed, cream the sugar and vegetable shortening until fluffy. Beat in the egg and then the milk and vanilla extract. Gradually blend in the dry ingredients.

4 Drop the dough by spoonfuls 1½ inches apart onto the baking sheets. Bake for 10 to 12 minutes, until the edges start to color. Cool on wire racks.

COOKING NOTE: **This basic recipe is the starting point for endless variations. Add nuts, raisins, coconut, chocolate chips, peanut butter, peanut butter chips, and/or candied citrus peel. Add cinnamon and/or nutmeg, or other spices, as you like.**

BASIC DROP COOKIES

MAKES: *3 to 4 dozen cookies*

1½ cups all-purpose flour
¼ teaspoon baking powder
¼ teaspoon salt
1½ cups packed light-brown sugar
¾ cup butter or margarine, at room temperature
2 large eggs
1 teaspoon vanilla extract
½ cup sesame seeds, toasted

1 Preheat the oven to 350 degrees F. Grease 2 baking sheets.

2 In a bowl, combine the flour, baking powder and salt and whisk well.

3 In another bowl, using an electric mixer set on medium speed, cream the sugar and butter until smooth. Beat in the eggs and vanilla extract. Gradually blend in the dry ingredients. Fold in the sesame seeds.

4 Drop the dough by spoonfuls 1½ inches apart onto the baking sheets and bake for 10 to 12 minutes, until lightly colored. Cool on wire racks.

COOKING NOTE: **Sesame seeds are called "benne seeds" in the South. To toast them, spread them in a dry skillet and toss them over high heat for a minute or so until fragrant and lightly colored. Immediately transfer the seeds to a plate to cool.**

SESAME SEED COOKIES

MAKES: *3 to 4 dozen cookies*

BUTTER-ALMOND STRIPS

MAKES: *5 to 6 dozen cookies*

COOKIES
2 cups all-purpose flour
¼ teaspoon salt
¾ cup butter, at room temperature
¼ cup sugar
½ teaspoon almond extract

TOPPING
2 tablespoons sugar
¼ teaspoon ground cinnamon
½ cup almonds, finely ground
1 large egg white, lightly beaten

1 In a bowl, combine the flour and salt and whisk well.

2 In bowl, using an electric mixer set on medium-high speed, cream the butter and sugar until smooth. Beat in the almond extract and gradually blend in the dry ingredients. Cover and chill for at least 1 hour.

3 Preheat the oven to 350 degrees F. Lightly grease 2 baking sheets.

4 In a small bowl, combine the sugar, cinnamon and almonds and mix well.

5 On a lightly floured work surface, roll out the dough to a thickness of ⅛ inch. Cut into 2-by-1-inch strips and place 1 inch apart on the baking sheets. Brush the cookies with beaten egg white and sprinkle lightly with the topping. Bake for 8 to 10 minutes, or until lightly colored. Cool on wire racks.

BUTTERSCOTCH BROWNIES

MAKES: *1 to 1½ dozen brownies*

⅔ cup all-purpose flour
½ cup walnut halves, finely ground
1 teaspoon baking powder
¼ teaspoon salt
1 cup packed light-brown sugar
¼ cup vegetable shortening
1 large egg
1 teaspoon vanilla extract

1 Preheat the oven to 350 degrees F. Lightly grease an 8-inch-square baking pan.

2 In a bowl, combine the flour, walnuts, baking powder, and salt and whisk well.

3 In another bowl, using an electric mixer set on medium-high speed, cream the sugar and vegetable shortening until smooth. Beat in the egg and vanilla. Gradually blend in the dry ingredients. Spread the dough in the baking pan. Bake for 20 to 25 minutes, or until a toothpick inserted in the center comes out clean. Cut into large or small bars and cool in the pan on a wire rack.

2¼-cups all-purpose flour
1 teaspoon baking soda
1 package (3.4 ounces) vanilla-flavored instant pudding mix
1 cup vegetable shortening
¼ cup granulated sugar
¾ cup packed light-brown sugar
2 large eggs
1 teaspoon vanilla extract
1½ cups (9 ounces) semisweet chocolate chips
1 cup walnut halves, finely chopped

1 Preheat the oven to 375 degrees F.

2 In a bowl, combine the flour, baking soda and vanilla pudding mix and whisk well.

3 In another bowl, using an electric mixer set on medium-high speed, cream the vegetable shortening and the sugars. Beat in the eggs and vanilla. Gradually blend in the dry ingredients. Fold in the chocolate chips and walnuts.

4 Drop the dough by spoonfuls 1½ inches apart onto ungreased baking sheets. Bake for 8 to 10 minutes, or until lightly browned. Cool on wire racks.

COOKING NOTE: For chocolate-chocolate chip cookies, use chocolate instant pudding in place of vanilla pudding.

CHOCOLATE-CHIP COOKIES

MAKES: *6 to 7 dozen cookies*

---

2 cups all-purpose flour
½ cup unsweetened cocoa powder
½ teaspoon baking soda
¼ teaspoon salt
½ cup sugar
¼ cup vegetable shortening
1 large egg
½ cup buttermilk
½ cup molasses
1 teaspoon vanilla extract
¾ cup chopped walnuts

1 Preheat the oven to 350 degrees F. Lightly grease 2 baking sheets.

2 In a bowl, combine the flour, cocoa powder, baking soda and salt and whisk well.

3 In a bowl, using an electric mixer set on medium-high speed, cream the sugar and vegetable shortening until smooth. Beat in the egg. Beat in the buttermilk, molasses and vanilla. Gradually blend in the dry ingredients. Fold in the walnuts.

4 Drop the dough by spoonfuls 1½ inches apart onto the baking sheets. Bake for 12 to 15 minutes, until firm to the touch. Cool on wire racks.

COOKING NOTE: Substitute sour milk for buttermilk.

FUDGIES

MAKES: *4 to 6 dozen*

GINGERSNAPS

MAKES: *3 to 4 dozen cookies*

2¼ cups all-purpose flour
1 teaspoon ground ginger
1 teaspoon cinnamon
1 teaspoon ground cloves
1 teaspoon salt
1 cup packed light-brown sugar
¾ cup vegetable shortening
1 large egg
¼ cup molasses
granulated sugar for rolling

1 Preheat the oven to 375 degrees F. Lightly grease 2 baking sheets.

2 In a bowl, combine the flour, spices and salt and whisk well.

3 In another bowl, using an electric mixer set on medium-high speed, cream the brown sugar and vegetable shortening until smooth. Add the egg and beat until mixed. Add the molasses and beat until mixed. Gradually blend in the dry ingredients.

4 Pinch off pieces of dough and roll into balls about the size of walnuts. Roll in granulated sugar and place on the baking sheets, leaving about 2 inches between them. Bake for 10 to 12 minutes or until lightly colored. Cool on wire racks.

LEMON BARS

MAKES: *1 to 3 dozen bars*

2 cups all-purpose flour
1 teaspoon baking soda
1 teaspoon cinnamon
½ teaspoon ground nutmeg
½ teaspoon salt
1½ cups packed light-brown sugar
¾ cup vegetable shortening
2 large eggs
3 tablespoons lemon juice
3 tablespoons grated lemon zest
1 cup raisins

1 Preheat the oven to 350 degrees F. Lightly grease a 9-inch-square baking pan.

2 In a bowl, combine the flour, baking soda, spices and salt and whisk well.

3 In another bowl, using an electric mixer set on medium-high speed, cream the brown sugar and vegetable shortening until smooth. Beat in the eggs, 1 at a time. Add the lemon juice and zest and beat to mix. Stir in the raisins and spread the dough evenly in the prepared baking pan. Bake for 25 to 30 minutes, until lightly colored on top. Cool in the pan on a wire rack before cutting into large or small bars.

MACAROONS

MAKES: *3 to 4 dozen cookies*

4 large egg whites
¼ teaspoon salt
1½ cups sugar
1 teaspoon almond extract
1 cup shredded coconut
½ cup almonds, ground fine
3 cups cornflakes

1 Preheat the oven to 350 degrees F. Line 2 baking sheets with parchment paper.

2 In a bowl, using an electric mixer set on high speed, beat the egg whites and salt until they hold stiff peaks. Fold in the sugar and almond extract. Fold in the coconut and almonds and then fold in the cornflakes.

3 Drop the dough by spoonfuls onto the baking sheets, leaving about 1½ inches between them. Bake for 12 to 15 minutes, until lightly colored. Cool slightly on the pans set on wire racks before removing from the paper.

2¼ cups all-purpose flour
2 teaspoons baking powder
1 teaspoon salt
1 cup sugar
¾ cup vegetable shortening
2 large eggs
1 tablespoon lemon extract
1 tablespoon grated lemon zest
sugar for sprinkling

1 In a bowl, combine the flour, baking powder and salt and whisk well.

2 In a bowl, using an electric mixer set on medium-high speed, cream the sugar and vegetable shortening until smooth. Beat in the eggs, 1 at a time. Add the lemon extract and zest and beat to mix. Gradually blend in the dry ingredients.

3 Divide the dough in half. Form each into a log about 2 inches in diameter, wrap in wax paper and chill for at least 4 hours.

4 Preheat the oven to 400 degrees F. Lightly grease 2 baking sheets.

5 On a lightly floured work surface, roll out the dough to a thickness of ¼ inch. Using a 3-inch round cookie cutter, cut into rounds and place on the baking sheets, leaving about 1 inch between them. Sprinkle with sugar. Bake for 6 to 8 minutes, until lightly colored. Cool on wire racks.

COOKING NOTE: You may substitute orange extract and orange zest for the lemon extract and zest for Orange Sugar Rounds.

LEMON SUGAR ROUNDS

MAKES: *1 to 2 dozen cookies*

⅔ cup all-purpose flour
¼ teaspoon baking powder
¼ teaspoon salt
1 cup (6 ounces) semisweet
    chocolate chips
¼ cup vegetable shortening
¾ cup sugar
2 large eggs
½ teaspoon vanilla extract
½ cup walnuts, chopped

1 Lightly grease an 8-inch-square microwave-safe baking pan.

2 In a bowl, combine the flour, baking powder and salt and whisk well.

3 In the top of a double boiler set over medium-low heat, melt the chocolate chips and vegetable shortening, stirring until smooth. Remove from the heat and beat in the sugar. Beat in the eggs, 1 at a time. Beat in the vanilla extract. Gradually blend in the dry ingredients and then stir in the walnuts. Spread in the baking pan.

4 Microwave on high (100 percent) power for 7 minutes until the center is set. (If the microwave does not have a turntable, turn the pan a quarter turn every 2 minutes.) Cool in the pan on a wire rack before cutting into large or small bars.

MICROWAVE FUDGE BROWNIES

MAKES: *1 to 2 dozen brownies*

MOLASSES SNAPS

MAKES: *5 to 6 dozen cookies*

2¼ cups all-purpose flour
2 teaspoons baking soda
1 teaspoon ground cinnamon
1 teaspoon ground ginger
½ teaspoon ground cloves
½ teaspoon salt
1 cup packed dark-brown sugar
¾ cup vegetable shortening
1 large egg
¼ cup molasses
1 cup golden raisins
sugar for sprinkling

1 Preheat the oven to 350 degrees F.

2 In a bowl, combine the flour, baking soda, cinnamon, ginger, cloves and salt and whisk well.

3 In a bowl, using an electric mixer set on medium-high speed, cream the brown sugar and vegetable shortening until smooth. Beat in the egg and then the molasses. Gradually blend in the dry ingredients and fold in the raisins.

4 Pinch off pieces of dough and roll into balls about the size of walnuts. Roll in sugar and place on ungreased baking sheets, leaving about 1½ inches between each. Flatten each ball with the bottom of a glass that has been dipped in water and then sprinkle with sugar. Bake for 10 to 12 minutes, until lightly colored. Cool on wire racks.

OATMEAL COOKIES

MAKES: *3 to 4 dozen cookies*

1 cup butter
2 cups quick-cooking oatmeal
1 cup packed light-brown sugar
2 large egg whites

1 Preheat the oven to 375 degrees F. Lightly grease 2 baking sheets.

2 In a saucepan, melt the butter over medium heat. Add the oatmeal and brown sugar and cook, stirring, for about 2 minutes until well mixed. Transfer to a bowl to cool slightly.

3 In a bowl, using an electric mixer set on high speed, beat the egg whites until stiff but not dry. Fold the beaten egg whites into the oatmeal mixture.

4 Drop the mixture by spoonfuls onto the baking sheets, leaving about 2 inches between them. Flatten the cookies with the back of a spoon dipped in flour. Bake for 7 to 10 minutes, or until the edges are lightly browned. Cool on wire racks.

COOKING NOTE: **For fruity cookies, add chopped dried mango or papaya to the dough.**

2 cups all-purpose flour
1 teaspoon baking soda
1 teaspoon ground cinnamon
1 teaspoon salt
1 cup sugar
¾ cup vegetable shortening
2 large eggs
1 cup old-fashioned rolled oats
1 cup raisins

1 Preheat the oven to 350 degrees F.

2 In a bowl, combine the flour, baking soda, cinnamon and salt and whisk well.

3 In another bowl, using an electric mixer set on medium-high speed, cream the sugar and veg-etable shortening until smooth. Beat in the eggs, 1 at a time. Gradually blend in the dry ingredients. Fold in the oats and raisins.

4 Drop the dough by spoonfuls onto ungreased baking sheets, leaving about 1½ inches between them. Bake for 10 to 12 minutes, until lightly colored. Cool on wire racks.

COOKING NOTES: Add vanilla extract or almond extract to the dough to enhance the flavor of these cookies.

OATMEAL-RAISIN COOKIES

MAKES: *3 to 4 dozen cookies*

1½-cups all-purpose flour
½ cup whole-wheat flour
½ teaspoon baking powder
½ cup canola oil
4 large eggs
½ cup frozen orange juice
  concentrate, thawed
¼ cup orange-flavored brandy
1 tablespoon grated orange zest

1 Preheat the oven to 375 degrees F. Lightly grease 2 baking sheets.

2 In a bowl, combine the flours and the baking powder and whisk well.

3 In another bowl, using an electric mixer set on medium-high speed, beat the oil and the eggs until thick and light colored. Beat in the orange juice concentrate and brandy and then add the orange zest, beating well. Gradually blend in the dry ingredients.

4 Drop by spoonfuls onto the baking sheets, leaving 1½ inches between them. Bake for 6 to 8 minutes, until lightly colored. Cool on wire racks.

ORANGE DROPS

MAKES: *3 to 4 dozen cookies*

---

1 cup raisin bran
½ cup sugar
1 apple, peeled, cored and grated
½ cup milk
1 teaspoon vanilla extract

1 Preheat the oven to 350 degrees F. Lightly grease 2 baking sheets.

2 In a bowl, combine the raisin bran, sugar and apple. Stir in the milk and vanilla and mix well.

3 Drop by spoonfuls onto the baking sheets, leaving 2 inches between them. Bake for 12 to 15 minutes, until lightly colored. Cool on wire racks.

RAISIN BRAN COOKIES

MAKES: *3 to 5 dozen cookies*

SUGAR COOKIES

MAKES: *3 to 4 dozen cookies*

3 cups all-purpose flour
2 teaspoons baking powder
½ teaspoon baking soda
½ teaspoon salt
1 cup sugar
⅔ cup butter, at room temperature
2 large eggs
¼ cup buttermilk
½ teaspoon brandy
milk for glazing
sugar for sprinkling

1 Preheat the oven to 375 degrees F. Lightly grease 2 baking sheets.

2 In a bowl, combine the flour, baking powder, baking soda and salt and whisk well.

3 In another bowl, using an electric mixer set on medium-high speed, cream the sugar and butter until smooth. Beat in the eggs, 1 at a time. Beat in the buttermilk and brandy. Gradually blend in the dry ingredients.

4 On a lightly floured work surface, roll out the dough to a thickness of ¼ inch. Using a 2-inch round or shaped cookie cutter, cut out cookies and place on the baking sheets, leaving 1½ inches between them. Brush with milk and sprinkle liberally with sugar. Bake for 10 to 12 minutes, until lightly colored. Cool on wire racks.

WALNUT SHORTBREAD

MAKES: *4 to 5 dozen cookies*

4½ cups all-purpose flour
1 cup walnut halves, finely ground
2½ cups packed light-brown sugar
2 cups vegetable shortening
2 teaspoons vanilla extract

1 Preheat the oven to 350 degrees F.

2 In a bowl, combine the flour and walnuts and whisk well.

3 In another bowl, using an electric mixer set on medium-high speed, cream the sugar and vegetable shortening until smooth. Add the vanilla extract and beat to mix. Gradually blend in the dry ingredients.

4 Pinch off pieces of dough and roll into balls about the size of walnuts. Place on ungreased baking sheets, leaving about 1 inch between them. Flatten with the back of a spoon dipped in flour. Bake for 10 to 15 minutes, until lightly colored. Cool on wire racks.

INGREDIENTS EQUIVALENCY CHARTS

Bread Crumbs (includes cookie and cracker crumbs)

1 cup fresh bread crumbs	equals 2 ounces or 60 grams
1 slice bread with crust	equals ½ cup breadcrumbs,
1 cup dried or toasted bread crumbs	equals 4 ounces or 110 grams
1 pound of bread	equals 14 to 20 slices, or 454 grams
1 cup saltine soda crackers crushed	equals 28 crackers
1 cup graham cracker crumbs	equals 7 to 10 crumbled crackers, 4 ounces or 110 grams
1⅓ cups graham cracker crumbs	equals 16 crumbled crackers,
1 cup vanilla wafer crumbs	equals 30 wafers, 4 ounces, or 110 grams
2 cups vanilla wafer crumbs	equals 8 ounces
1⅔ cups chocolate wafer crumbs	equals 22 wafers
1½ cups gingersnap crumbs	equals 20 snaps
2 cups zwieback crumbs	equals 24 slices, 6 ounces, or

Dairy Products (includes cream, milk, sour cream, yogurt, and buttermilk)

CHEESE

8 ounce package cream cheese	equals 1 cup or 16 tablespoons
3 ounce package cream cheese	equals 6 tablespoons
1 pound cheese	equals 4 cups grated cheese

CREAM

½ pint heavy cream	equals 1 cup or 2 cups whipped cream
1 cup whipping cream	equals 2 to 2½ cups whipped cream

MILK

1 cup dry skim milk	equals 1 quart skim milk when mixed.
1 cup whole milk	equals 8 ounces weight
1 cup heavy cream	equals 8⅜ ounces weight
1 6 ounce can evaporated milk	equals ⅔ cup evaporated milk
1 14½ ounce can evaporated milk	equals 1⅔ cups evaporated milk
1 cup sweetened condensed milk	equals 10½ ounces weight
1 14 ounce can sweetened condensed milk	equals 1½ cups sweetened condensed milk
⅓ cup evaporated milk	equals ⅓ cup dry milk plus 6 tablespoons water

SOUR CREAM

1 8 ounces package sour cream	equals 1 cup sour cream

Eggs

1 large whole egg	equals 3 tablespoons, 2 ounces, or 60 grams
1 cup large whole eggs	equals approx. 5 eggs
1 large egg yolk	equals 1 generous tablespoon
1 cup large egg yolks	equals approx. 12 egg yolks
1 large egg white	equals 2 tablespoons, ⅛ cup or
2 large eggs	equals scant ½ cup, 3 medium ages, or 180 grams
1 cup large eggs	equals 4 to 5 large eggs
1 cup eggs	equals 5 to 6 medium eggs
1 cup egg yolks	equals 12 to 14 large egg yolks
1 cup egg whites	equals 7 to 10 large egg whites
1 large egg	equals 2 egg yolks in the recipe
1 large fresh egg	equals ½ tablespoon dry plus 2½ tablespoons water
3 large egg whites stiffly beaten	equals 3 cups meringue

Fats (includes butter, margarine and vegetable shortening)

½ ounce butter	equals 1 tablespoons or ⅛ stick
1 ounce butter	equals 2 tablespoons or ¼ stick
2 ounces butter	equals 4 tablespoons or ½ stick
1 pound butter	equals 2 cups, 4 sticks, 32 tablespoons, or 454 grams
½ pound	equals 1 cup, 1 stick, 8 tablespoons, or 227 grams
¼ pound	equals ½ cup, 1 stick, 4 tablespoons, or 113 grams
1 cup butter or margarine	equals ⅞ cup of large
1 cup hydrogenated fat	equals 6⅔ ounces
2 tablespoons	equals ¼ stick, 2 tablespoons, or 1 ounce

Dry Ingredients (includes arrowroot, baking powder, baking soda, cornmeal, cornstarch, cream of tartar, flour and salt)

ARROWROOT

1 teaspoon arrowroot	equals 1 teaspoon all-purpose flour or 1 teaspoon cornstarch
1 tablespoon arrowroot	equals 3 tablespoons all-purpose flour or 2 tablespoons cornstarch
1 tablespoon arrowroot	equals 1 tablespoon all-purpose flour plus 1 teaspoon cornstarch

BAKING POWDER & BAKING SODA

2 tablespoons baking powder or soda	equals 1 ounce
1½ teaspoons	equals ¼ ounce
1 tablespoon	equals 0.5 ounce
1 teaspoon	equals 0.17 ounce

CORNMEAL

1 cup cornmeal	equals 3 to 4 ounces cornmeal
1 cup uncooked cornmeal	equals 4 cups cooked cornmeal

Dry Ingredients (continued)

CORNSTARCH

1 pound sifted cornstarch	equals 4 cups
1 cup sifted cornstarch	equals 4 ounces
1 ounce sifted cornstarch	equals 4 tablespoons, ¼ cup
1 tablespoon sifted cornstarch	equals 0.29 ounce
1 pound unsifted cornstarch	equals 3½ cups
1 cup unsifted cornstarch	equals 4.5 ounces
1 ounce unsifted cornstarch	equals 3½ tablespoons
1 tablespoon unsifted cornstarch	equals 0.2 ounce

CREAM OF TARTAR

4 tablespoons	equals 1 ounce or 30 grams
1 tablespoon	equals ¼ ounces or 7 grams
1 teaspoon	equals 0.08 ounce

FLOUR

3 tablespoons all-purpose flour	equals ¼ cup
6 tablespoons all-purpose flour	equals ⅓ cup
9 tablespoons all-purpose flour	equals ½ cup
12 tablespoons all-purpose flour	equals ⅔ cup
15 tablespoons all-purpose flour	equals ¾ cup
18 tablespoons all-purpose flour	equals 1 cup
1 pound all-purpose flour	equals 4 cups
1 cup bleached white all-purpose flour	equals 1 cup unbleached white all-purpose flour
1 cup bleached all-purpose flour	equals 1 cup whole wheat flour
1 cup bleached all-purpose flour	equals ⅞ cup stone ground whole wheat flour
1 pound of sifted bread flour	equals 4 cups
1 cup sifted bread flour	equals 4 ounces
1 pound unsifted bread flour	equals 3½ cups
1 cup unsifted bread flour	equals 4.75 ounces
1 pound sifted cake flour	equals 4¼ cups
1 cup sifted cake flour	equals 3.75 ounces
1 pound unsifted cake flour	equals 3½ cups
1 cup unsifted cake flour	equals 4.5 ounces

SALT

5 teaspoons salt	equals 1 ounce or 30 grams
1¼ teaspoons	equals ¼ ounce or 7 grams
1 teaspoon	equals 0.2 ounce

Fruits and Vegetables

APPLES

4 medium sized apples	equals 4 cups peeled and sliced
1 pound medium apples	equals 2 whole apples or 3 cups sliced apples

APRICOTS

1 pound dried apricots	equals 3 cups dried apricots

BANANA

1 pound banana	equals 3 medium or 1⅓ to 2 cups mashed

BERRIES

1 pint fresh berries	equals 1¾ cups of fresh berries

CARROTS

1 cup sliced	equals 2 medium size carrots
1 cup shredded	equals 1½ medium size carrots

COCONUT

1⅓ cups dissicated flaked coconut	equals 3½ ounces
1⅓ cups dissicated shredded coconut	equals 4 ounces or 115 grams

CHERRIES

1 pound candied cherries	equals 3 cups candied cherries

DATES

1 pound pitted dates	equals 2 to 2½ cups chopped dates

FIGS

1 pound whole figs	equals 2⅔ cups chopped figs

LEMON

1 medium sized lemon	equals 2 tablespoons lemon juice
1 medium sized lemon	equals 2 teaspoons lemon zest
1 teaspoon lemon juice	equals ½ teaspoon lemon extact

LIME

1 large sized lime	equals 2 tablespoons lime juice

ORANGE

1 medium sized orange	equals ⅓ cup orange juice
1 medium sized orange	equals 2 tablespoons orange zest

POTATOES

1 pound potatoes	equals 3 medium potatoes
1 pound new potatoes	equals 10 small new potatoes

PRUNES

1 pound unpitted prunes	equals 2¼ cups pitted prunes

Fruits and Vegetables (continued)

RAISINS

1 pound seedless raisins	equals 2¾ cups raisins
1 pound seeded raisins	equals 3¼ cups raisins

STRAWBERRIES

1 quart fresh strawberries	equals 4 cups sliced

Gelatin

1 envelope unflavored gelatin	equals 1 scant tablespoon, enough to hard set 2 cups liquid
3 tablespoons	equals 1 ounce or 30 grams
2¼ teaspoons	equals ¼ ounce or 7 grams
1 tablespoon	equals 0.33 ounce
1 teaspoon	equals 0.11 ounce

Grains

OATS

5 ounces rolled oats	equals 1 cup
1 cup uncooked oats	equals 1¾ cups cooked

RICE

1 cup uncooked rice	equals 7½ ounces
1 cup uncooked rice	equals 2 cups cooked rice

Nuts

ALMONDS

1 pound almonds in shell	equals 1¼ cups nutmeat
1 pound almonds shelled	equals 3 cups nutmeat or 454 grams
¼ pound almonds shelled	equals 1 cup nutmeat
1 pound slivered almonds	equals 5⅔ cups nutmeat or 454 grams

BRAZIL NUTS

1 pound Brazil nuts in shell	equals 1½ cups nutmeat
1 pound Brazil nuts shelled	equals 3¼ cups nutmeat or 454 grams

CASHEWS

4½ ounces cashews, shelled	equals 1 cup nutmeat or 130 grams

CHESTNUTS

1 pound chestnuts, unshelled	equals 1½ cups nutmeat

HAZELNUTS

1 pound hazelnuts, unshelled	equals 1½ cups nutmeat
1 pound hazelnuts, shelled	equals 3½ cups nutmeat
4½ ounces hazelnuts, shelled	equals 1 cup nutmeat or 130 grams

Nuts (continued)

MACADAMIA NUTS

4 ounces macadamia nuts, shelled   equals 1 cup nutmeat or 110 grams

PEANUTS

1 pound peanuts, unshelled   equals 2 to 2½ cups nutmeat
1 pound peanuts, shelled   equals 3 cups nutmeat or 454 grams

PECANS

1 pound pecans, unshelled   equals 2¼ cups nutmeat
1 pound pecans, shelled   equals 4 cups nutmeat or 454 grams

PISTACHIO NUTS

5 ounces pistachio nuts, shelled   equals 1 cup nutmeat or 150 grams

WALNUTS

1 pound walnuts, unshelled   equals 2 cups nutmeat
1 pound walnuts, shelled   equals 4 cups nutmeat or 454 grams

Sugar (to included granulated, brown, powdered sugar, and molasses)

BROWN SUGAR

1 pound firmly packed brown sugar   equals 2½ cups

GRANULATED

1 pound granulated sugar   equals 2¼ cups
1 cup granulated sugar   equals 7 ounces
1 cup granulated sugar   equals 1 cup packed brown sugar
1 cup granulated sugar   equals 1¾ cups confectioners sugar
1 tablespoon granulated sugar   equals 1 tablespoon maple sugar

HONEY

1 cup honey   equals 12 ounces

MOLASSES

11 ounces of molasses   equals 1 cups

POWDERED

1 pound sifted powdered sugar   equals 4 cups
1 cup sifted powdered sugar   equals 4 ounces
1 pound unsifted powdered sugar   equals 3½ cups
1 cup unsifted powdered sugar   equals 4.5 ounces

SUBSTITUTE

2 teaspoons sugar   equals 1 packet or ¼ teaspoon aspartame
1 tablespoon sugar   equals 1½ packets or ½ teaspoon aspartame
¼ cup sugar   equals 6 packets or 1¾ teaspoons aspartame
⅓ cup sugar   equals 8 packets or 2½ teaspoons aspartame
½ cup sugar   equals 12 packets or 3½ teaspoons aspartame
1 cup sugar   equals 24 packets or 7¼ teaspoons aspartame

Equivalency Chart

WEIGHT

¼ oz.	07 g
½ oz.	17 g
1 oz.	28 g
2 oz.	57 g
5 oz.	142 g
8 oz.	227 g
12 oz.	340 g
16 oz.	454 g
32 oz.	907 g
64 oz.	1.8 kg

VOLUME

¼ tsp.	1.25 ml
½ tsp.	2.5 ml
1 tsp.	5 ml
1 tbl.	15 ml
¼ cup	59 ml
⅓ cup	79 ml
½ cup	119 ml
¾ cup	177 ml
1 cup	237 ml
1 pint (2 cups)	473 ml
1 quart (4 cups)	946 ml
1 gallon (4 quarts)	3.78 litres

LENGTH

¼ in.	5 mm
½ in.	1 cm
¾ in.	2 cm
1 in.	2.5 cm
2 in.	5 cm
4 in.	10 cm
1 foot (12 in.)	30 cm

HEAT

very cool	250–275 F.	130–140 C.
cool	300 F.	150 C.
warm	325 F.	170 C.
moderate	350 F.	180 C.
moderate hot	375–400 F.	190–200 C.
hot	425 F.	220 C.
very hot	450–475 F.	230–250 C.

INDEX